WHAT ON EARTH

IS GOING ON?

Patricia Diane Cota-Robles

New Age Study of Humanity's Purpose, Inc.
PO BOX 41883
Tucson, AZ 85717
FAX 520-751-3835

Cover by Sharon Maia Nichols
Printed in the United States of America

ISBN: 0-9615287-5-3
LIMITED FIRST EDITION April 4, 1997

DEDICATION

This book is lovingly dedicated to *every* man, woman and child evolving on Earth.

Precious Ones, we have always known, in the recesses of our hearts, that this glorious moment would one day come. We just never dared to dream that we would be here to witness it.

We are on the dawn of the Permanent Golden Age, and we are now working through the labor pains of the most miraculous rebirth ever known. We have each volunteered to assist in this birthing process by weaving the multifaceted, multidimensional aspects of our God Selves into the tapestry of this unfolding Divine Plan.

It is time for each of us to remember who we are and why we are here.

We are Sons and Daughters of God, standing on the threshold of the greatest leap in consciousness ever experienced in the history of the Universe.

The Cosmic Moment is NOW, and our time is at hand.

Thank you for all you *are* and all you have come to Earth to *do*.

ACKNOWLEDGMENT

In deepest gratitude and love, I would like to acknowledge...

Dickie, my precious husband of thirty-three years who, at this moment in our lives together, continually lifts me into higher octaves of bliss, ecstasy, joy, wonder and awe. I love you!

My son, Joao, and my daughter, Victoria, who have allowed me the incredible experience of expressing a Mother's love. I love you!

My two grandsons, Dylan and Hayden, who teach me about God and elation. I love you!

Kay Meyer, my dear friend and co-worker, who works endlessly to keep our Light expanding logistically in the world of form. I love you!

The myriad selfless volunteers who give of the very substance of their Beings to propel our work into the hands and use of anyone who might benefit from it. I love you!

And, all of the rest of my Earthly family and Heavenly family who fill the cup of my consciousness with love and the glory of Divinity in all Its forms. I love you!

INTRODUCTION

For decades profound Spiritual Truths have been presented to Humanity in the guise of fairy tales, myths, science fiction and fanciful novels. Because Truth has always been stranger than fiction, it was easier and less threatening for us to read about mystical, supernatural, metaphysical, miraculous things if we thought of them as figments of someone's imagination rather than reality. However, at this moment, we are experiencing a unique phenomenon on Earth, and there is an awakening taking place within us. Something is stirring in the very core of our Beings, and we are invoking greater levels of understanding and Truth. Deep inside our hearts we are beginning to remember who we are and why we are here. As this inner knowing surfaces into our conscious minds, it often challenges our present belief systems causing confusion and, sometimes, even fear. The natural tendency is for us to close down and try to suppress that surfacing knowledge, like pushing the snooze button on our alarm clock. But the Divinity within our hearts is not giving us the luxury of going back to sleep anymore, and it is persistently prodding and prompting us to awaken.

This phenomenon is not happening by chance. It is being orchestrated by God and the entire Company of Heaven. It is the fulfillment of a glorious Divine Plan that has been in the works for millenia, and each and everyone of us on Earth has volunteered to play a very special role in bringing God's Plan to fruition.

Every world religion has taught that there will be a time when the negativity manifesting on Earth in the form of poverty, disease, war, crime, pain and suffering will be purged and cease to exist. This sweet Earth and all life evolving upon Her will then be transformed into Heaven on Earth. Each world religion has its own interpretation of how that scenario will take place, but the end result is always the same...the physical, tangible transformation of our Planet and all Her maladies into the glory of Heaven on Earth.

It was easy for us to believe this prophecy as long as we thought of it happening in the far distant future. With all of the negativity occurring at this time, it seems as though the concept of Heaven manifesting on Earth anytime soon must be nothing more than wishful thinking. From outer appearances, it certainly seems that anyone who believes that we are on the dawn of a Permanent Golden Age must be suffering from flights of fancy or self-delusion. After all, look at the mess we are in!

In Truth, we *are* on the threshold of planetary transformation, and God's Light is flowing into Earth in ever-increasing frequencies.

The reason it *seems* as though things are getting worse is because the Light of God pushes the negativity to the surface to be healed. It is like putting a pot on the stove to boil causing all of the scum to bubble up to the surface. That is why this time was referred to in the Bible and other religious books as *"the time of screaming and the gnashing of teeth."* I think that is a pretty accurate description, don't you?

In order to assist us through this very confusing and difficult phase of the Divine Plan, unprecedented Ageless Wisdom and Knowledge is pouring forth from the Realms of Illumined Truth. This information is being given to Humanity at this time to enhance our understanding and to expand our awareness.

Because of the urgency of the hour, this sacred Truth can no longer be cloaked in the label of myth nor be spoon-fed to us as fantasy. It is time for each of us to *see with new eyes and hear with new ears.* It is time for us to lift above the numbing drone of mass consciousness and pierce through the veil of illusion into the Divine Mind of God.

At the same time, it is imperative for us to know that we are each in our right and perfect place. Our God Selves have guided us through precisely the experiences we needed in order to prepare us for this moment.

Our beliefs are sacred and vital for the fulfillment of our individual Divine Plans. This information is *not* intended to dispute those beliefs, but rather to *enhance* what we already know. As we read this information, it is critical that we invoke the full-gathered momentum of Divine Discerning Intelligence, Reason and Common Sense. Then, let us take each word into our hearts and see if it resonates as Truth for us. If it does not, just let it go. If it *does* resonate as Truth, let us ask our God Selves to integrate this Ageless Wisdom into our Earthly experiences so that we will absorb effectively the Truth that will set us FREE.

I would like very much for you to read this book with an open mind and an open heart. ***The information is not new. It is merely reminding us of what we have forgotten.***

I only share information that I have proven to myself beyond a shadow of a doubt to be true, but I don't want you to ever accept anything as Truth just because someone told you it is Truth.

Read this book through the eyes of discernment as food for thought. Ask the Presence of God blazing in your heart to reveal to you every facet of this information that will, in any way, shape or form, enhance your ability to fulfill your Divine Plan. Accept only that which will transform your personal life experience into the bliss, ecstasy, wonder and awe of Heaven on Earth.

These are wondrous times, and the Divine Intent of this book is to awaken within you a renewed sense of HOPE, LOVE, ABOUNDING JOY and EXPECTANCY.

As you read this book, feel the elation pouring forth from the Heart of God in deep gratitude that, at long last, we are coming Home.

I wish you a glorious God-Victorious FOREVER,

Patricia Diane Cota-Robles

vii

TABLE OF CONTENTS

CHAPTER
ONE

IT IS TIME FOR US TO SOAR!

I want to begin this glorious adventure by sharing with you the wonder of this precise moment on Earth. There may be aspects of this initial information that you don't understand just yet, but all of it will be explained in detail later in the book.

Beloved Lightworker...and that means YOU...if your God Presence has magnetized this information to you, through whatever means, *know* that it specifically applies to you. Throughout the book, I use the term "WE". *Know* that each time that reference is used it ***INCLUDES YOU***. Ask your God Presence to reveal to you the magnitude of this moment and the Truth of this information. Then, through the full-gathered momentum of Divine Discerning Intelligence, respond according to your inner Heart Call.

WE HAVE DONE IT!
NOW IS OUR TIME TO SOAR!

For aeons of time we have been struggling to get our heads above the sea of human miscreation so that we could see the Light of our Father-Mother God. Through trials and tribulations that would have boggled the minds of the most courageous souls, we endured. Through pain and suffering that took us to the brink of our level of tolerance, we survived. Through grief and despair that engulfed every fiber of our Beings, we persevered. And now, *it is time to reap the fruits of our labor. It is time to Ascend into the Octaves of Eternal Peace and Joy. It is time to live the reality of "All that my Father-Mother God has is mine." It is time to accept our Divine Birthright of Heaven on Earth. And it is time to experience tangibly in our everyday lives all of the Joy, Love, Abundance, Success, Peace, Illumination, Wisdom, Truth, Happiness, Ecstasy and Bliss that our Father-Mother God have to offer.*

Knowing as much as we do about the Universal Laws of Cause and Effect, it is perplexing that no matter what we do to improve our lot in life, we still find ourselves dealing with poverty, lack, limitation, low self-esteem, dysfunctional relationships, disease, compulsive/addictive behaviors, failure consciousness and every other human malady. From outer appearances it seems as though our efforts to change the course of our lives have been ineffectual, but I assure you our efforts have not been in vain. We have been fulfilling the vows we took in the very Heart of our Father-Mother God to love this Earth and all Her life FREE. We volunteered to be part of the most unique experiment that has ever been attempted in the history of our Universe, and *we have succeeded God Victoriously!*

If this does not appear to be true in your personal life, it is because you haven't realized or accepted that you can now Ascend out of your old reality of lack and limitation into your new reality of Heaven on Earth.

During this unique moment on Earth, the entire Company of Heaven is waiting to assist us the maximum that Cosmic Law will allow to move into the new reality of Heaven on Earth. I know that "Heaven on Earth" may seem like a lofty platitude, but as expressed here, it means that because enough of Humanity has now awakened Spiritually, we can move into the reality of Limitless Abundance, Limitless Physical Perfection, Fulfilling Jobs and Careers, Loving Relationships, Inner Peace, Reverence for all Life, Spiritual Fulfillment, Harmony, Happiness and every other state of Divine Consciousness that we perceive to be Heaven on Earth.

As you read these words, open your heart and REMEM-BER.

We have been in training for thousands of years preparing for this Cosmic Moment on Earth. Prior to this embodiment each of us was drawn into the Heart of our Father-Mother God, and as They embraced us in Their essence of pure Divine Love, we reviewed our lives. Due to the urgency of the hour, it was clear that this lifetime would be unpredecented, and we would be asked to reach into the very depths of our souls and draw on every electron of strength, courage, skill, talent and knowledge we have. Further, this lifetime was going to be the culmination of everything we had been working toward...a unique opportunity to save this fallen Planet and lift this sweet Earth and all Her life into the Octaves of Heaven on Earth.

Standing before our Father-Mother God, we understood that never before has a Planet this contaminated with nega-tivity been given the opportunity to Ascend into the Light in such a short period of time. Truly, this would be an experi-ment of mercy and compassion unparalleled in the annals of history. With this understanding, we volunteered to be the Hands of God in the physical plane. We promised to bring this extraordinary Divine Plan to fruition.

Our Father-Mother God, in cooperation with our God Selves, designed a plan for each and every one of us that would take full advantage of our aeons of preparation and stretch us to the very limits of our capacities. Our God Parents revealed to each of us a panorama of our upcoming life, and we clearly saw the opportunities and challenges that would be presented to us. From that level of God Con-sciousness, we understood that we had been prepared to face every adversity that would be presented to us, and we KNEW that we had all the skill, talent, strength, courage and knowl-edge we needed to succeed God Victoriously.

We clearly understood the Universal Law, *"As 'I Am' lifted up, all life is lifted up with me,"* and we recognized that in order for the depths of human degradation, pain and suffering to be healed and lifted up, we had to connect with those discordant frequencies of energy. We volunteered to descend into the "dens of iniquity" on Earth in order to heal Humanity's suffering and lift every painful experience into the Light. This was an act of incredible selfless service.

The Divine Plan was set into motion, and we—the Lightworkers—embodied into every conceivable situation on Earth. It was not enough for us to intellectually know about Humanity's suffering; we actually had to FEEL the pain to effectively connect with it. Feeling the pain of the experience was important so that those energies would be woven into our Etheric Bodies, thus connecting us to the collective mass consciousness of every other person who had ever experienced a similar situation.

As we came into embodiment, the **Band of Forgetfulness** was placed about our brows by our Father-Mother God so that we would feel the separation, despair and hopelessness on Earth. We didn't agree to this because we were masochistic, but because, from our God Conscious Selves, we knew that this was the *only* way we would experience the pain and suffering on Earth to the degree that was necessary in order to have these energies woven into our Etheric Bodies. This was imperative so that we could heal and lift up these miscreated energies.

If we had come into frivolous, superficial lives, when we eventually awakened and lifted into the Light, we would only lift frivolous, superficial energies up with us. We knew, however, that if we reached into the very depths of human suffering, we would one day awaken and draw all manner of depravity on Earth into the Light as we Ascended into our next Spiral of Evolution.

With this understanding and inner knowing, we took our vows, and as Lightworkers, we began our descent into the most difficult challenges we had ever known. We were born into lives of abuse, neglect, abandonment, rejection, ridicule, poverty, disease, corruption, crime, war, pollution, addiction, pain, suffering, fear, hate, low self-esteem and unworthiness. We descended into every corner of the World and took on the woes of every race, culture, nationality, religion, creed, country, state, city, town and hamlet. We became one with the suffering on Earth, connecting with it through every fiber of our Beings, all the time knowing, at a level beyond the comprehension of our finite minds in the stillness of the Divinity blazing in our hearts, that **our suffering would be temporary.** We KNEW there would be a Cosmic Moment when everything would change *"in the twinkling of an eye."*

When we volunteered to participate in this inconceivable experiment, we were also shown by our Father-Mother God what would occur once we connected completely enough with the human miscreations on Earth. We were shown that through a process of Divine Intervention, the Light on Earth would be increased to the point where It would begin to activate the Spark of Divinity within our hearts and AWAKEN us to our Divine Missions. Through our God Selves, we watched in breathless wonder as we witnessed our individual transformation and the transformation of this blessed Planet into Her Divine Birthright—Freedom's Holy Star—Heaven on Earth.

We saw the assistance that would be given to us from On High. We saw the Earth receive the greatest influx of Divine Love any Planet has ever experienced. This love came from Galaxies beyond Galaxies and Suns beyond Suns. We saw the Band of Forgetfulness being removed from our brows, and we observed the joy and elation we felt as we began to remember who we are and why we had come to Earth. All of a sudden our lives made sense. We were not just the victims of circumstances floundering in lives that were beyond our control. We were Divine Sons and Daughters of God who had volunteered to come to Earth to fulfill our greatest Mission ever.

As we witnessed the overwhelming opportunity we were being given to take this sweet Earth from the depths of human degradation into the Octaves of Heaven on Earth, we KNEW that no matter how much human suffering we volunteered to endure, THE END RESULT WOULD BE INFINITELY WORTH IT.

We saw this precious Planet in all Her resplendent glory. We saw every man, woman and child in his/her Light Body of Limitless Physical Perfection living lives of Limitless Abundance; Blissful Relationships; Creative, Fulfilling Jobs and Abounding Joy and Happiness. We witnessed the manifestation of *true* Eternal Peace with every government working toward the highest good for all concerned, expressing reverence and mutual respect for every part of life. We saw the Elemental Kingdom working in harmony with Humanity as Humanity loved and honored every facet of Beloved Mother Earth. We saw Humanity living Her highest potential as She interrelated with the Angels and the entire Company of Heaven, perpetually expanding the borders of Divinity.

This was the fulfillment of the Divine Blueprint for Planet Earth, the Immaculate Concept being held in the Heart of our Father-Mother God. This was what we had been preparing for thousands of years to accomplish on Earth, and finally **our time was at hand**.

As we witnessed the vision of the rebirth of Mother Earth in humble, blissful awe and elation, we consecrated our very Beings to bring this Divine Plan to fruition God Victoriously. Then, with full conviction, courage and knowing, we entered our present embodiments.

Our lives have been difficult. We have been through the gamut of human dysfunction. We have experienced grieving, weeping and wailing as we stumbled through our Valley of Tears.

But, I want you to read the following words with the full

magnitude of your consciousness.

WE HAVE DONE IT!!!

We have been as miserable as we needed to be; we have been in as much pain as we needed to experience; we have suffered as much as was necessary in order to weave the pain of Humanity into our Etheric Bodies. So now...

WE ARE THROUGH
WITH THAT PHASE OF THE PLAN!

DONE, FINISHED, COMPLETE, FINAL, OVER, CONCLUDED, FULFILLED, ENDED, ACHIEVED!!!

Understand? *We don't have to be miserable anymore.* We have the Free Will choice to stay stuck in our negative life experiences, but if we do, **WE ARE IN CONFLICT WITH OUR DIVINE PLANS.**

This Cosmic Moment on Earth is being dedicated by the entire Company of Heaven to specifically assist all Humanity in letting go of the negative baggage from our pasts and all of the negative life experiences we have manifested as a result of that baggage. This includes lack, limitation, abusive or dysfunctional relationships, poor health, disease, unfulfilling jobs, poverty, low self-esteem, failure consciousness, fear, hate, greed, corruption, selfishness, violence, death as we know it, addictive/compulsive behavior, prejudice, lack of integrity, dishonesty, abuse of power, the tendency to lie and on and on ad infinitum.

Any area of our lives that is not reaching its highest potential and reflecting the joy of Heaven on Earth can now be healed and transformed into its original Divine Intent.

I know there is not a single person who *wants* to stay in the pain of human suffering, but our human egos have controlled us through our fear and pain for so long that we don't believe things can ever be different. This attitude is exactly what our lower human egos want us to believe.

We have accepted the negativity in our lives so completely that we've created a sense of identity around it. "If I'm not this miserable speciman of Humanity, then who am I?" Remember, we needed to connect with the pain and experience separation, desperation and grief at one time in order to heal it, *but not any longer.* What we need to do now is remember who we are and why we are here. Then, we need to lift up in consciousness and Ascend into the Light, bringing all life evolving on Earth with us.

There is nothing more self-empowering than recognizing the Truth of our own God Reality. Once we begin to remember who we are, precious Sons and Daughters of God, then we will also remember that Heaven on Earth is our Divine Birthright and that we have the ability to co-create it with our Father-Mother God. The assistance we are being given at this time to accomplish just that is unprecedented. We have never been so close.

Because of the wonderful life-transforming activities that have taken place over the past several years, we are now in a position to receive more Light from the Heart of our Father-Mother God than we have been able to withstand since the "fall" of Humanity, which occurred aeons ago.

Daily and hourly our God Presences are assisting us, with the help of the entire Company of Heaven, to let go of any baggage from our pasts or the present that is preventing us from reaching our highest potential. Any experience that we have ever had in any time frame or dimension that is preventing us from experiencing Heaven on Earth can now be loved FREE and transmuted into the Light.

It seems like it would be very easy to just let go of anything that causes us pain but, in fact, it is extremely difficult. You see, we have been living in these painful conditions for a long time, and even though we are suffering, it's all we remember. Our fear-based lower human egos keep telling us, *"Even though I'm miserable, at least it's familiar."* The fear of the unknown is so great that our egos think, *"It's better to face the devil I know than to find out what I don't know."* What we have forgotten is that we are *not* just victims being buffeted about by the whims of the Universe. We are very scientifically and specifically creating our own realities. Every single thing that is occurring in our lives involving any person, place, condition or thing is a direct result of the thoughts, words, actions and feelings we have expressed since we were first breathed forth from the Heart of our Father-Mother God. Not *one* event is accidental, therefore, we are in a position to co-create, with our Beloved God Parents, exactly what we perceive to be Heaven on Earth. We don't have to fear the unknown. When we are creating Heaven on Earth, there is no unknown—only **unmanifest potential** which, when creating Heaven on Earth, is always glorious.

So, what does all of this mean. It means that moment-by-moment, we are receiving unprecedented assistance from On High to transmute the negativity from our pasts and love it FREE. Our God Selves direct us through our heart's desire. If you are feeling the heart desire to transform your life, then respond to your Inner Calling. Invoke the Company of Heaven for assistance, and any blocks or resistance will be swept aside.

During each of the incredible activities of Light you will read about in this book, there were, at the very least, hundreds, sometimes thousands, sometimes hundreds of thousands and, a few times, millions of people in embodiment on Earth consciously and actively participating in the events. I'm sharing that information as a word of encouragement to let you know that the number of awakened Lightworkers on the Planet is legion and growing daily.   Our Victory is assured, and there is no turning back!

The Spiritual Hierarchy has promised us that anyone accepting this Divine Opportunity will receive an *Anointing* from his/her God Self and our Father-Mother God to show the deep gratitude and appreciation these Beings have for our selfless service to the Light. **This is our moment!**

This is the opportunity that we have been waiting for, when we would, at long last, let go of the negative experiences of our lives and joyfully move into the energy, vibration and consciousness of Heaven on Earth.

Ask your God Self for clarity. Listen to your heart, and respond according to your inner promptings and longings.

We are truly blessed to be able to consciously participate in the glorious rebirth of this sweet Earth and all Her life.

We have all come to save the Earth, and OUR TIME IS AT HAND!

CHAPTER
TWO

WHERE DOES THIS INFORMATION COME FROM?

I would like to address this question now so that as you continue reading this book you will have a clearer understanding about where this information is coming from.

That is a very reasonable and important question, but it is a subject I have not formally addressed up until this time. The reason for that is because I know the most important thing I can do is to *empower everyone* who comes in contact with the information I am sharing, ***to KNOW that there is not a single thing that I can communicate to you that you cannot access for yourself in the Realms of Truth.***

It seems we are always looking outside of ourselves for someone who is more Illumined or Enlightened to give us the answers we are seeking, but the most *anyone* can do at this point in our evolution is to remind us of the Truth we already have blazing within our own Heart Flames. That is why it is far more important for each of us to take the information that is being presented to us and regardless of where the source of the information claims it is coming from, ask our God Selves to blaze the Flame of Illumined Truth through every word. Then we must ask our God Selves to allow only that which is in alignment with our Divine Plans to resonate as Truth in our hearts.

If an Angel of God appears before you and gives you a "Pearl of Wisdom," but your heart tells you something else, LISTEN TO YOUR HEART! If it is *truly* an Angel of God bringing you a gift of knowledge that will awaken a remembrance within you and enhance your Spiritual Growth, then the Angel will continue to present the "Pearl of Wisdom" in various gentle and loving ways until you can hear the Truth and allow it to resonate in your heart. God and the Company of Heaven are infinitely patient, and They would much rather we be overly cautious than gullible and careless.

The only reason we believe that other people know more than we do is because we have forgotten who we are. We look at our limited fear-based human egos, and we think that distorted fragment of our outer personality is our total Being. *In reality, we are ALL magnificent, multifaceted, multidimensional reflections of our Father-Mother God who have been preparing for thousands of years to accomplish what we have volunteered to do in this lifetime. We already have within us all of the knowledge, skill, talent, courage and strength to succeed God Victoriously. Each one of us is a radiant Sun expressing ALL of the various frequencies of Divinity that are pulsating in the Causal Body of God. We are Gods and Goddesses standing on the threshold of the greatest leap in consciousness ever experienced in ANY System of Worlds. We are on the brink of co-creating a new Octave of Godhood, expanding, without measure, the infinite Body of God, thus lifting every particle of life ever breathed forth from the Core of Creation into the Dawn of a New Cosmic Day.*

Okay, so why don't we remember that? Well, the reasons are complex, but it's imperative at this juncture of our Ascension Process that we remember who we are and reconnect with the multidimensional, radiant Sun of our God Selves, so that *each of us* can reach into the Realms of Illumined Truth and tap the Divine Mind of God. This will allow us direct access to the Truth of our Beings; then we will not have to depend on *any* outside source to remind us of our true God Reality or our purpose and reason for being ever again.

Finally, after aeons of floundering in the cesspool of human miscreation and struggling to get our heads above the oppressive sea of negativity that surrounds the Planet, *every man, woman and child is in a position to permanently heal his/her self-inflicted separation from the Realms of Illumined Truth and the Divine Mind of God.* That is why this information can now be discussed openly. In the past, only

Adepts, High Initiates and Avatars could manage to reach up in consciousness effectively enough to tap the Realms of Truth and Divine Knowledge. To discuss this process at that time would only have increased the sense of separation and made people feel more unworthy, which would have exacerbated our tendency to seek answers outside of ourselves. However, that is no longer the case. Now *all of us* have the ability to reach into the Realms of Truth. As is always the case, there will be those who recognize this fact first and test the waters. Gradually, little by little, others will see that this process is available to them as well. Then, one by one, they will take advantage of the opportunity at hand and lift up in consciousness into the multidimensional Sun of their True God Reality and experience first hand the Realms of Illumined Truth.

It was never the intent of God that we separate ourselves from the Truth and sink into our humanly created quagmire of chaos and confusion. In fact, in the beginning everything was provided to keep us in constant communication with all of the multifaceted, multidimensional aspects of our own Divinity. In the beginning our God Presence, which is a tremendous radiant Sun that pulsates in the Realms of Perfection, projected a minuscule aspect of Itself (the equivilent of one Ray of that Sun) into the physical plane of Earth to experience this school of learning. The purpose of this physical embodiment on Earth was for us to learn how to use our creative faculties of thought and feeling to co-create greater expressions of Divinity in physical form. The original Divine Intent was for us to keep totally connected to the Heavenly Realms of Perfection so that we could fulfill the Universal Law of *"As above, so below."* In order to do this, we had Twelve Solar Strands of DNA which functioned as a very elaborate communication system between our God Selves and our physical Presences. In addition to our Twelve-fold Helix of DNA, our right and left brain hemispheres were perfectly balanced. This allowed for the perfect function of our brain centers: the pituitary, pineal, hypothalamus glands and the ganglionic centers at the base of our brains. These activated brain centers opened the Centers of Enlightenment within our heads, our Crown Chakras. When a Crown Chakra is open, it is the portal that connects one directly to the Divine Mind of God.

At that time in our human evolution, we had total awareness of the Realms of Illumined Truth. We could easily pass in consciousness from one dimension into another. We could **be** with Beings of Light in the Realms of Perfection and openly communicate with Them through our open heart and mind telepathic communication. We walked and talked with the entire Company of Heaven, Angels and Elementals. As we consciously shifted between dimensions at will, we were able to bring all of the knowledge and wisdom from the Realms of Truth into the physical plane and project those perfection patterns into our physical reality through our thoughts, words, actions and feelings. There was no "veil of maya" to distort our perception. The psychic-astral realm of human miscreation didn't exist.

At that time, we could effortlessly shift our consciousness into the Higher Realms and directly communicate with our Father-Mother God and all of the members of the Spiritual Hierarchy. Together we would create plans that would expand the borders of the Kingdom of Heaven on Earth.

It was only after we began experimenting with our gift of life and began *"partaking of the tree of knowledge of good and evil"* that we created thought patterns that conflicted with God's Will, thus manifesting as the "veil of maya" that eventually resulted in our "fall" and separation from the Realms of Truth. The "veil of maya" or the "veil of illusion" is the accumulation of every electron of precious life energy Humanity has ever misqualified. This "veil" is called the psychic-astral plane. It is comprised of the negative patterns of Humanity's thoughts, words, actions and feelings that have not been transmuted back into their original perfection through the power of Divine Love and Forgiveness. This literally means the electrons and subatomic particles of energy in every thought, word, action or feeling Humanity has ever released that are not expressing the purity they were pulsating with when they first entered our Beings as our gift of life from God.

As the heavy frequencies of our distorted thoughts and feelings began accumulating in, through and around our physical bodies and the body of Mother Earth, we "fell" into such denseness that our Twelve-fold Helix of DNA short-circuited into the Double Helix DNA our scientists have now "discovered." Even though this Double Helix of DNA contains several billion genetic codes, it is still *barely enough to sustain brain consciousness.* When this happened, we closed down our Heart Centers so that we wouldn't feel so much pain. This blocked the flow of the Feminine Polarity of God that activated our right brain hemispheres and our feeling natures. Consequently, our right brains became almost dormant, which caused the centers within our brains to atrophy. This resulted in the closing of our Crown Chakras of Enlightenment.

This tragic scenario cut us off from the Realms of Truth and our God Selves so completely that we began developing another aspect of our personality, our human ego. This fragmented part of our consciousness is fear-based and functions strictly to gratify the physical senses. Our human egos perceive the physical plane to be the only reality and our physical bodies to be the totality of who we are. Needless to say, this distortion of the Truth has manipulated us for millenia, and century after century we have been struggling to reconnect with our God Selves and the Realms of Truth. Instead, our human egos have manipulated us into denser and denser frequencies of human miscreation, thus separating us even more from the Realms of Perfection and creating greater problems for us to deal with in the psychic-astral plane.

The psychic-astral plane contains not only destructive thoughtforms, clouds of our depraved and dysfunctional behavior patterns and the energy associated with all of our tumultuous emotions, it also contains trapped discarnate souls and earthbound spirits as well.

When we leave the Earth through the process we call "death," we are magnetized to our like vibration. If we have experienced an exceptionally negative life, sometimes we won't make it through the "tunnel" in the psychic-astral plane into the Light. Sometimes we are pulled into the psychic-astral plane of human miscreation and temporarily trapped there. This is *never* our Divine Plan, and when this occurs, there are always messengers from God that enter that realm to try and convince us to move into the higher schools of learning where we are supposed to go between our Earthly experiences.

Unfortunately, some of these trapped souls choose to remain in the psychic-astral plane. They roam the Earth, wreaking havoc in the lives of the people still abiding in the physical plane. Some of these discarnate souls have been trapped for so long that they have degenerated into what we have labeled demonic entities. They have truly separated from God and are "lost" in every sense of the word.

It is very important for us to really comprehend at this time that this realm has nothing whatsoever to do with God. It was created solely by Humanity through the misuse of our free will and the abuse of our gift of life. Even though the world religions have misinterpreted what this realm is and have said it is *hell* and was created by God to punish us, that is a misunderstanding. The psychic-astral realm is certainly what we would call hell, but it is a human creation and has nothing to do with the Divine Plan for this Planet. It is in the process of being transmuted back into Light through the infinite Mercy and Compassion of our Father-Mother God and the constant invocations of Forgiveness and Divine Love by the Lightworkers on Earth.

The problem is that this dimension has fallen so far into the frequencies of discord and pandemonium that it doesn't understand the opportunity it is being given to return to its original Divine Intent. Consequently, it is doing everything it can to prevent the rest of us from moving into the Light, hence, the exteme confusion and deception taking place on Earth. This realm knows that we aren't stupid, so it does not say, *"I'm the sinister force, and I've come to ruin your life."* It says, *"I'm god, follow me."* Therefore, if a person is trying to get information from a source in another dimension and s/he has **not taken the precautions or the time to reach through the psychic-astral plane into the Realms of Illumined Truth** *before* opening up his/her mind and heart, s/he will end up smack dab in the middle of that realm of deception. Once a person has connected with an entity in that dimension, the entity can say it's anybody. It can say it is Jesus, Mother Mary, Buddha, Saint Germain, an Angel, a loved one who has passed away or anyone else under the Sun. The entity of deception will always give us enough Truth according to our own belief systems to make us believe it is trustworthy, but then it will cunningly weave its plan of deception, which is ALWAYS designed to keep us trapped in negativity and prevent us from moving into the Light.

Beloved Jesus told us that in these latter days we will hear, *"Lo, 'I Am' here, and lo, 'I Am' there, but by their works alone shall they be known."*

At the beginning of this century (*1900*), a Cosmic Dispensation was granted by our Father-Mother God to allow the Beings of Light in the Heavenly Realms to *come through the veil to meet us halfway.* This greatly enhanced our ability to reconnect with the Realms of Truth, but we still had to struggle to reach up through the dense veil of human miscreation in order to connect with the Beings of Light who were patiently waiting to remind us of who we are and why we are here.

Various modalities began appearing on the screen of life to assist us in reaching through the "veil." We developed **conscious channeling, trance channeling, automatic writing, psychic readings, tarot cards, ouija boards, pendulums, dousing, crystals and various other means of accessing information.** The problem with *all* of those techniques, of course, is that unless we are able to raise our vibrations and lift up in consciousness effectively enough to pierce through the "veil of maya" to meet the Beings of Light halfway, we are vulnerable to being tricked and deceived by the souls trapped in the lower psychic-astral plane of human miscreation.   These wayward entities are committed to keeping us stuck in the grip of human effluvia.

God will not give one electron of precious life energy to sustain the psychic-astral plane of human miscreation. Consequently, the only way that dimension of chaos can survive is by living parasitically off of our negative energy. Every time we are angry, fearful, depressed, hateful, sad, mean, negative, critical or any other discordant expression of life, we energize the psychic-astral plane around the Earth. That is why this dimension is committed to keeping us stuck in pain and suffering. It is desperately trying to prevent us from reconnecting with the Realms of Truth and Ascending into the Harmony and Balance of our God Selves.

During this unparalleled time of awakening, Humanity, en masse, is beginning to perceive the Light and remember our Divinity. This is causing the souls trapped in the psychic-astral plane to redouble their efforts to block our Ascension in the Light. That realm is in panic, and pandemonium is ensuing. The prophets of old perceived this moment and proclaimed that, *"In the latter days Satan will be loosed on the Earth."* As a result of our awakening and the resistance of the psychic-astral plane, there is a tremendous amount of confusion and interference.

There is not only a great deal of misinformation and disinformation, there is also a new level of deception beyond anything we have ever experienced. This confusion is not by chance. It is the deliberate interference of the forces of imbalance who are fighting tooth and nail to hold the Earth in Her present state of discord so that She won't accomplish the next phase of Her Divine Plan, which is Her glorious Ascension into the Fourth/Fifth Dimensional Octaves of Perfection.

In order to bypass this realm of deception and reach into the Realms of Illumined Truth, *we don't need to be involved in conscious channelings, trance channelings, automatic writing, psychic readings, tarot cards, ouija boards, pendulums, dousing, crystals or any other means of accessing information that* **can be manipulated and distorted without our knowledge by the forces of imbalance in the psychic-astral plane.** Once we heal our separation from our God Selves, we can Ascend in consciousness into the Realms of Truth and telepathically communicate with our Father-Mother God and the Company of Heaven through an open mind and heart without the obstruction of the "veil of illusion" that surrounds the Earth.

The most common example we have of this process is what people describe when they go through the near-death experience. These experiences vary a great deal, but what people most consistently report is that they have the sensation of traveling through a dark tunnel toward a brilliant Light. The "dark tunnel" is their passage through the psychic-astral plane into the Realms of Illumined Truth. Once they enter the Light, they have the experience of remembering, and they awaken to a wealth of knowledge that they realize has always been within them. They understand that even though the knowledge has been there, in the dense Earth plane they couldn't access it. They usually experience an open heart and mind telepathic communication with the tangible Presence of a Divine Being, and they fully grasp the incredible Love, Peace and Truth of the Realms of Light.

The people that return to share their experience either

choose or are told they must come back and finish their mission on Earth. As they re-enter the atmosphere of Earth and pass through the "tunnel" into their physical bodies, they sometimes forget the specifics of what they remembered in the Realms of Light, but they know that they have a wealth of knowledge pulsating within that they will one day access. Their connection with that Realm of Eternal Peace and Light is life transforming, and they never experience this physical plane in the same way again.

We are now entering a wondrous, glorious time when, as Revelations states, *"the mystery of God will be fulfilled."* The "veil of illusion" is gradually being transmuted into Light, and we no longer have to "die" in order to reach into the Realms of Illumined Truth. Our Twelve Solar Strands of DNA are being rewoven, reconnecting us to the Realms of Perfection, and our right brains and brain centers are being activated. This is allowing our Crown Chakras of Enlighten- ment to open once again to the Divine Mind of God, and at last we are able to Ascend in consciousness and walk and talk with the Angels, Ascended and Cosmic Beings and the Elementals. Throughout the World, many awakening souls are reaching into the Octaves of Light where the Sacred Wisdom of the Ages is accessible to everyone and is, in fact, common knowledge. These souls are bringing the Truth back to Earth for the benefit of all Humanity. Unfortunately, this is causing the psychic-astral realm to strive even harder to confuse the issue by contaminating the Truth. Therefore, it is also a time when we must invoke the full-gathered mo- mentum of Divine Discerning Intelligence, Reason and Common Sense as never before.

The Sacred Knowledge that is being shared in this book is being revealed to us from the Realms of Illumined Truth through open heart and mind telepathic communication as we Ascend in consciousness into the Octaves of Truth and walk and talk with the Beings of Light in the Realms of Perfection. The information is being given to enhance what we already know and to give us greater clarity and new levels of understanding and awareness. It is correcting previous misperceptions and expanding us into new Octaves of Wisdom and Knowledge. This information will assist us through our Earthly challenges by letting us clearly see the Divine Intervention and assistance we are being given from On High, and it is being unveiled now for the sole purpose of giving us the courage, strength, confidence and commitment to persevere unto our God Victorious Accomplishment in the Light.

Even having said that, **I want to clearly state that I don't ever want you to accept anything as TRUTH just because someone told you it's true. Take every word that you read in this book and blaze the Flame of Illumined Truth through it. Ask the Presence of God in your heart to filter out every trace of human consciousness and accept ONLY the words that resonate in your heart as "the Truth that will set you FREE!!!"**

As far as the psychic-astral plane is concerned, it has ABSOLUTELY NO POWER OVER THE LIGHT. Even the darkest night cannot prevail over a single candle flame.

All we have to do to reconnect with the Realms of Illumined Truth is invoke the Light of God which is always Victorious and envelop ourselves in an invincible **Forcefield of Protection.** Then, we must command that only the purest Truth from the highest Realms of Perfection enter our consciousness as we Ascend into the Octaves of Light. *As long as our sincere INTENT is to be the greatest source of Light and Comfort on the Planet we're capable of being, without the slightest thought of ego or self-aggrandizement, the floodgates of Heaven will open to us, and we will become an open door of Divine Light and Wisdom that no one can shut.* We will be lifted into the Realms of Illumined Truth where we will tangibly communicate with the Beings of Light and tap the Divine Mind of God, awakening within us the Wisdom of the Ages. We will then be able to bring back clearly the wisdom and knowledge pulsating there for the benefit of all life evolving on Earth.

In order for something to manifest in the physical plane of Earth, the unformed primal Light of God for that particular creation must flow through the Heart Flame of Divinity of someone abiding on Earth. We truly are the Hands of God in the world of form, and we're here now to reclaim this Earth and restore Her to Her original Divine Intent, which is Heaven on Earth. We have been preparing for thousands of years for the Divine Mission we have volunteered to fulfill IN THIS LIFETIME. The Cosmic Moment is NOW!

CHAPTER THREE

WHAT IS THE NEW AGE...REALLY?

In order for us to truly grasp the significance of this moment on Earth, it is important for us to clear away all of the confusion and misinformation that is being spewed forth regarding the concept of the New Age.

My friend, Kay Meyer, and I founded and named our non-profit organization The New Age Study of Humanity's Purpose, Inc. many years ago, long before the term New Age became a bad word. During the *1980s* when so much misinformation, confusion and fear began to be associated with the words "New Age," I asked the Beings of Light in the Heavenly Realms if it would be better for us to change the name of our organization. They said *"absolutely not."* Instead, we must educate and inform people about the Truth of the New Age.

The reality is that we actually *are* on the dawn of a New Age, and for us to avoid that Truth just because of Humanity's lack of understanding would be inappropriate, and it would be reneging on the very reason we founded our educational organization in the first place.

So, just for a moment, please put aside any preconceived notions you have about the New Age, and read these words with an open mind and heart from a place of neutrality.

Contrary to all of the clamor and fear being projected onto the term New Age, the New Age is NOT a religion; it is NOT a movement; it is NOT a particular philosophy; it is NOT the forum for psychic-astral glamour, UFO phenomenon, witchcraft, the occult, crystals, tarot cards, pendulums, ghosts or goblins, and it is certainly NOT the work of the devil.

THE NEW AGE IS NOTHING MORE THAN A SPAN OF TIME!

It is no more the "work of the devil" than is a new day or a new month, year, century or millenium.

As our Earth revolves on Her axis once in every twenty-four hour period, we experience a new day. As She revolves around the Sun once every 365 and 1/4 days, we experience a new year.   During the Earth's orbit around the Sun, She passes very quickly through the forcefields of the twelve constellations that surround our Solar System. We call the time She spends in the embrace of each constellation (approximately 28-31 days) a Sun Cycle, and the Sun Cycles correspond fairly closely to our months, beginning with Capricorn (December 21-January 19) and ending with Sagittarius (November 23-December 20).

In addition to these two movements of the Earth which we are very familiar with, our entire Solar System is revolving in a much larger orbit around a distant Sun called Alcyon. In this orbit, the Earth moves very slowly through the Universe in a counterclockwise movement that is called the Precession of the Equinox. The entire orbit takes approximately 24,000 years.

Each Vernal Equinox the Sun passes the equator at a slightly different point. The movement is measured at about 50.2 seconds a year, so in this orbit it takes approximately 70 years for the Earth to move one degree. As She slowly moves through the Universe, the Earth once again passes through the forcefields of the twelve constellations. This time She is held in the forcefield of each constellation for approximately 30 degrees, which averages out to a time span of a little more than 2000 years.

The 2000-year period that the Earth is held in the embrace of a particular constellation is called an AGE. As the Earth moves from the forcefield of one constellation into the forcefield of the next constellation in Her counterclockwise journey, it is called a NEW AGE.

At the present time, we're ending one 2000-year cycle, and the Earth is moving from the forcefield of Pisces into the forcefield of Aquarius to begin Her next 2000-year cycle.

In the *1960s* when the singing group, known as the "5th Dimension", recorded their hit song "This is the Dawning of the Age of Aquarius," they were telling us the Truth.

So why is there so much confusion? Why is there so much misinformation, disinformation and fear surfacing about this New Age?

Well, there are several reasons for that, but the information now pouring forth from the Realms of Illumined Truth will help us to dissipate the confusion and greatly enhance our clarity on this subject.

Everything is comprised of energy, vibration and consciousness. Each of the twelve constellations that surround our Solar System pulsates with its own unique forcefield of God's Light. Each constellation reflects one of the Twelve Solar Aspects of Deity that resonate in the Causal Body of God. As the Earth slowly moves through the forcefield of a particular constellation, She is bathed with the Solar Aspect of Deity that flows through that constellation for the entire 2000-year cycle. The God Qualities associated with that specific Aspect of Deity flow into the Planet, and as they build in momentum throughout the 2000-year cycle, they assist all life evolving here on Earth.

A New Age is a very significant event. When we move from a particular forcefield that has been building in momentum for 2000 years into an entirely different frequency of God's Light, it creates a major shift of energy, vibration and consciousness on Earth. To get a minuscule glimpse of this phenomenon, all we have to do is observe the shifts of energy that occur when we have a Full Moon or a New Moon. Look at the vibrational changes we experience during Solar and Lunar Eclipses. Even passing comets and solar flares wreak havoc with our electro-magnetic fields. Just imagine the magnitude of change we endure when we shift out of an energy field that has been building for 2000 years into a brand new forcefield. The effects are awesome!

As we come to the close of a 2000-year cycle and begin moving out of the forcefield of a constellation, the energies begin to recede. This shift of vibration can occur anywhere from 300 to 150 years prior to the time we begin experiencing the forcefield of the next constellation. During this lull in vibration, a window of opportunity is opened, and Humanity is more susceptible to the rarified frequencies of the Realms of Perfection. God and the entire Company of Heaven take full advantage of that fact.

As the window of opportunity opens, the Beings of Light in the Realms of Illumined Truth very carefully evaluate what is occurring on Earth. They monitor Humanity's progress, and They devise a plan that They feel will provide the maximum assistance for Humanity and the Earth in our evolutionary process during the new 2000-year cycle. This is done in cooperation with the God Selves of all life evolving on Earth at the time.

Prior to the "fall" of Humanity, this window of opportunity was used by the Spiritual Hierarchy to bathe the consciousness of Humanity with the knowledge and wisdom of our next level of Spiritual development. This gently assisted us into the next octave of our self-mastery. After the "fall," however, everything changed. Instead of this opportunity being used to enhance our Spiritual growth, it had to be used to devise plans to rescue us from our own human miscreation and self-destruction.

I will discuss the "fall" and how it occurred in detail in another chapter, but for clarity here, I'll describe the plans that have been implemented through the "window of opportunity" during the past several New Age experiences.

Several Ages ago the Earth was writhing in the depths of ignorance and suffering when the window of opportunity for the dawning New Age began to open. At that time it was very rare for anyone to get their head above the mud puddle of human miscreation effectively enough to actually attain Spiritual Enlightenment, but occasionally some tenacious, courageous soul did. This enabled that soul to attain his/her Ascension into the higher schools of learning and thus complete his/her Earthly experience.

As the window of opportunity for that dawning New Age opened, the Spiritual Hierarchy evaluated the need of the hour on Earth and devised an experiment that had never been tried before. Our Father-Mother God granted a special dispensation, which allowed the Spiritually developed souls who had attained their Ascension from the Earth to lower their frequency of vibration so that their physical forms could still be seen by the rest of Humanity.

When a soul attains his/her Ascension, s/he Ascends into the frequency of the Light Body, which usually vibrates beyond what we can perceive with our physical sight. A simple demonstration of that is what we experience when we observe a fan. If the fan is rotating in slow motion, we can clearly see the individual blades, but as the revolutions increase, the blades become invisible to our physical sight. If, however, the vibration of the cones and rods of our eyes increased to the same frequency as the revolutions of the fan, we would still be able to see the individual blades.

The Spiritual Hierarchy thought that if fallen Humanity could only see what it was like to be Ascended and free, we would be movitated to aspire to greater levels of self-mastery. They knew that if we would imitate the examples of our more highly evolved sisters and brothers, we would eventually regain our direction and attain our Ascension in the Light.

The plan was set into motion, and the Ascended Beings from the evolutions of Earth lowered their frequency of vibration to the range of physical sight. As the Age progressed, Humanity became very aware of the advanced abilities of these highly evolved souls. But, unfortunately, instead of recognizing that these Beings were merely our sisters and brothers who had evolved to a higher level of self-mastery, Humanity began to Deify these Beings and worship them. We implored the Ascended Beings to do for us the very things we were supposed to be learning to do for ourselves. This caused Humanity to sink even deeper into the consciousness of separation and worthlessness, thus complicating the problems on Earth instead of helping.

This was the time historically referred to in Greek Mythology as the time when the so-called Gods and Goddesses walked the Earth.

On the dawn of the next New Age, when the window of opportunity opened, the Spiritual Hierarchy realized that the plan had failed and that Humanity had actually allowed the Ascended Beings to be a distraction and a hindrance instead of motivating ourselves to emulate their example. At that point, our Father-Mother God withdrew Their dispensation, and once again the Ascended Beings were accelerated in vibration beyond our physical sight.

This terrified Humanity, and we began to build huge statues to try and replace the Gods and Goddesses. We began to worship the stone idols, and we developed the belief that they had the power to bless or damn the Earth. This created even more chaos and perpetuated our downward spiral.

Since the Gods and Goddesses, for all intents and purposes, just disappeared from the face of the Earth without a trace, the future historians could not believe that such advanced Beings ever really existed, so they classified the accounts of them as myths.

It is important for us to understand that the ebb and flow of these New Age cycles may not coincide precisely with our historical documentation. Remember that the influx of these energies and Divine Momentums can bathe the Planet and subtly influence us for centuries before someone actually integrates them effectively enough to draw the attention of the outer world for historical documentation.

After the evolved Beings Ascended beyond our physical sight, the Spiritual Hierarchy came up with a contingency plan. It was obvious that the "veil" of human miscreation surrounding the Planet had become so dense that the Light on Earth was practically non-existent. I'm referring, of course, to God's Light, not physical Sunlight. The Spiritual Hierarchy determined that the greatest need of the hour was for the Earth to once again be bathed with God's Light.

In order for something to manifest in this physical world of form, it must be drawn through the Divinity blazing in the heart of someone abiding in this physical dimension. In other words, God needs a body. God won't just wave a wand and transform the Planet. God gave us the gift of Free Will, and we are responsible for invoking the assistance we need to clean up the mess we have created. *"Ask and you shall receive. Knock and the door will be open."*

The Spiritual Hierarchy knew that the only way God's Light could return to Earth was if Beings abiding on Earth would raise up in consciousness and pierce through the "veil of maya" into the Realms of Illumined Truth. It would then be necessary for them to hold those portals open while the Light of God flowed into their Heart Centers and was projected into the physical plane of Earth on the Holy Breath.

As the Sacred Knowedge and techniques to accomplish this plan began to flow into the consciousness of Humanity, through the open window of opportunity of the New Age that was dawning, the concepts of meditation and the utilization of the Prana in the air through breathing exercises began to appear on the screen of life.

Gradually, many souls learned how to pierce the veil and reach up into "nirvana." Then, as they magnetized the Light of God into their Heart Flames, they projected that Divine Light into the physical plane of Earth on the Holy Breath. This plan had a degree of success, but there were still many souls who were entrenched in the concept of idol worship and who continued to worship fragmented aspects of Deity through various Beings.

As the window of opportunity for the next New Age

opened, the Company of Heaven became acutely aware that the greatest need of the hour was for Humanity to remember the Oneness of God. This Divine Truth from the Heart of God began to flood into the consciousness of Humanity, and the realization of the all-encompassing Presence of God began to register in our hearts and minds. We realized the futility of idol worship, and we began to focus the power of our prayers and attention on the Universal Source of all life through the sacred Doctrine of Monotheism/Judaism. This sacred Truth greatly accelerated our progress, but due to the fragmented understanding of our fear-based human egos, it was impossible for us to perceive ourselves as being part of God. This caused us to distort the concept of the Oneness of God into a powerful Being outside of ourselves. Because of our *"worthless, worm in the dust"* consciousness, we felt we deserved to experience the full *"wrath and punishment"* of God. Therefore, as the Age progressed, God became a vengeful, wrathful God in our minds, and through our self-flagellation, we were continually riddled with guilt and shame. This perpetuated our separation from God and gave our human egos new fuel to manipulate and control us.

Next, we moved into the dawn of the Piscean Age. That is the Age that is now coming to a close. At the inception of the Piscean Age, once again as the window of opportunity began to open, God and the Company of Heaven evaluated the greatest need of the hour for Humanity.

At that point in our evolution, it was clear that we had so severely separated ourselves from the awareness of our own Divinity that only an act of unprecedented Divine Intervention could shock us out of our mesmerized state of consciousness and awaken us to the realization of our true God Reality. It was critical that Humanity now experience the Love of God in manifest, tangible form and experience the God within, the Christ, through the path of Divine Love.

An incredible plan was set into motion, and a magnificent Being of Light volunteered to come to Earth and demonstrate to Humanity the Truth of our own Divinity.

Pisces reflects the Sixth Solar Aspect of Deity to Earth, which contains within Its frequencies the God Qualities of Eternal Peace, Devotional Worship, Healing and Ministering Grace. Beloved Jesus absorbed the full momentum of these Divine Gifts to assist Him in his glorious mission. He was known as the Prince of Peace as He drew the God Qualities of the Sixth Solar Aspect of Deity into His Being, and His symbol was the fish, which is the symbol of Pisces.

Jesus came to Earth in His full capacity as a Son of God. He clearly demonstrated to us the Enlightened state of Christ Consciousness and the unmanifest potential lying dormant in every human heart. He reiterated to us time and again our innate value as Sons and Daughters of God and told us of our Divine Birthright as Children of God. Jesus proved that the path of love is the only way and demonstrated through His own crucifixion and resurrection that the Divinity within is immortal, and life is eternal.

His words still reverberate through the Ethers:

Jesus answered them, "Is it not written in your law, I said, 'YE ARE GODS'?"   *John 10:34*

"YE ARE GODS, and all of you are Children of the most High."   *Psalms 82:6*

"Verily, verily, I say unto you, he that believeth in me, the works that I do shall he do also, AND EVEN GREATER WORKS THAN THESE SHALL HE DO..."
John 14:12

"For as many as are led by the Spirit of God, they are the Sons of God - the Spirit itself beareth witness with our Spirit that we're the Children of God; and if Children, then heirs, Heirs of God, JOINT HEIRS WITH CHRIST..."
Romans 8:14-17

"When I consider Thy Heavens, the work of Thy fingers, the moon and the stars which Thou hast ordained, what is man, that Thou art mindful of him and the son of man, that Thou visitest him? For Thou hast made him a little lower than the angels and has crowned him with glory and honor. Thou madest him TO HAVE DOMINION OVER THE WORKS OF THY HANDS; THOU HAST PUT ALL THINGS UNDER HIS FEET."   *Psalms 8:3-6*

Even though Jesus continually expressed our worth and stated, *"It is not I, but the Father within Who does the work,"* we still couldn't accept His Truth. Alas...as has happened time after time, we misunderstood His message and, once again, we separated ourselves from Him, Deified Him and expected Him to do for us the very things He came to teach us to do for ourselves.

Jesus knew that He was paving the way for our return to Christ Consciousness and our Eternal Ascension into the Light (the Rapture), and He also knew that it would be a while before we would be ready.

He said not at that time but *at the time of the Second Coming of the Christ, things will change in the twinkling of an eye.* Then Heaven will manifest on Earth; *"Thy Kingdom come, Thy Will be done on Earth as it is in Heaven."* Not in His day, but "IN THE DAY OF THE SEVENTH ANGEL, WHEN HE BEGINS TO SOUND, THE MYSTERY OF GOD WILL BE FULFILLED."

The Age of Pisces is ending, and the new window of opportunity is opening. The Seventh Angel is beginning to sound, and we are experiencing the initial impulses of the forcefield of Aquarius. The Seventh Solar Aspect of Deity, which is pulsating with the God Qualities of Freedom, Forgiveness, Mercy, Compassion, Divine Justice, Liberty,

Victory and Limitless Physical Perfection, is now bathing the Earth. We are reaching into the Realms of Illumined Truth and tapping the Divine Mind of God. The mystery of God is being fulfilled, and all is in readiness for the Second Coming of the Christ.

We are on the dawn of what is being heralded as the Permanent Golden Age. As the Divine Plan for this New Age begins to flood the consciousness of Humanity, it is sweeping through our illusions and our distorted perceptions of the Truth and shattering the concepts that our lower human egos have used to manipulate us, keeping us trapped in fear and ignorance.

It is always scary to have our perception of the Truth challenged. When this happens, it is very normal for us to cling to our beliefs even more tenaciously, as we desperately try for a while to deny the new knowledge and wisdom pouring from the Realms of Truth. At least this time we are not going to be fed to the lions or burned at the stake. There is some fear and resistance, but the Love of God is incredibly powerful, and the new levels of understanding are comforting and clear. We need to just lighten up, and let go and let God.

We are being gently embraced in the arms of our Father-Mother God as we move through our glorious transformation into Heaven on Earth, and when all is said and done, the Christians, Jews, Buddists, Muslims, Hindus and other world religions are going to say, *"See, it happened just the way we thought it would, "* and the people awakening to the Divine Plan of the New Age are going to say, *"See, it happened just the way we thought it would."*

All is in Divine Order, and the Light of God is Eternally Victorious!

Now, let's go back to the beginning and briefly review what has happened on Earth to bring us to the unprecedented, wondrous **New Age** that is now dawning in all of its glory and splendor.

CHAPTER
FOUR

HOW DID WE GET HERE
FROM THERE?

From outer appearances, it looks as though Humanity is thrashing about in chaos and confusion as we spiral into oblivion nearing the brink of self-annihilation. In reality, however, we are just experiencing labor pains of the most glorious rebirth any Planet has ever known. Contrary to outer appearances, this birthing process is not a fragmented conglomeration of muddled attempts to salvage the Earth. This birthing process is the combined efforts of Heaven and Earth synchronized into a symphony of Divine Light within the embrace and assistance of our Father-Mother God. It is an event unparalleled in the annals of time, and when it is God Victoriously Accomplished, we will tangibly and physically be in the boundless splendor and infinite Light of the New Heaven and the New Earth.

The Permanent Golden Age of Enlightenment and Spiritual Freedom is now dawning, and it is time for us to clearly know about the assistance we are receiving from On High. Our awareness of the Divine Intervention taking place on Earth will give us the hope and courage we need to "keep on keeping on" as we lift this Earth and all Her life into the Octaves of Limitless Physical Perfection and Supreme Harmony.

The Company of Heaven has requested that this book be written to reveal what has taken place on Earth to bring us to this critical moment in the history of our evolution. Much of this information has never been revealed to the conscious minds of Humanity. It is only because of our incredible advancement in the Light over the past few years that it can be brought to our outer consciousness at this time. As you read this information, feel the Flame of Divinity blazing within your heart as it expands and expands. Know that **you** are an integral part of this unfolding Divine Plan. Know that **you** have been prepared for thousands of years to assist in the healing and salvation of this Blessed Planet. Know, too, that the reason this information is being revealed to **you** now is because **you** are ready to actively participate in the final stages of Mother Earth's birthing process, and know that the sacred Truth revealed in this book will assist **you** to RE-MEMBER WHO YOU ARE SO THAT YOU CAN ACCOMPLISH WHAT YOU HAVE COME TO EARTH TO DO!

HOW DID WE GET IN THIS MESS?

Obviously, God is not a sadistic masochist Who decided to create a school of learning just to see how incredibly miserable His/Her Sons and Daughters would be as they writhed in the depths of human suffering and agony. So, what in the world happened?

Well, in order to fully understand this unique moment on Earth, we need to go back to our inception and briefly look at how our original Divine Plan went awry.

There are Galaxies beyond Galaxies and Suns beyond Suns evolving throughout the Universe. There are other Systems of Worlds that are countless trillions of years older than our Solar System and new Systems that are even younger than ours. These Planets and Suns are all teaming with life evolving at different levels of consciousness. To keep us on purpose, however, I am going to focus on our particular Solar System.

For clarity, know that what we call "God" is the Omnipotent, Omniscient, Omnipresent and all-encompassing luminous Presence of Divinity that envelopes all life, including every electron of precious energy evolving in any time frame or dimension, known or unknown, throughout infinity. Everything that exists anywhere in the whole of Creation is a "cell" in the Body of God. Knowing that, we can then understand that there are myriad levels of Divinity that are evolving at different degrees of God Consciousness within that One Universal Source. *From the full All-Encompassing Presence of God to the most minute Elemental Intelligence pulsating as a subatomic particle...ALL of these Lifeforms are pulsating as ONE unified forcefield of Light*.

This is the reality of our Oneness, and every single expression of life affects the whole Body of God. Every thought, word, action or feeling we have changes the dynamics of the whole Universe. At any given moment we are either adding to the Light of the World or adding to the shadows. That is really an awesome responsibility, isn't it?

God created Solar Systems as schools of learning for the individualized expressions of Him/Her Self (the Sons and Daughters of God) to expand the borders of Divinity. By creating Sons and Daughters and investing them with the creative faculties of thought and feeling and the gift of Free Will, God knew that we would experience the whole of Creation and come up with brand new ideas that would "push the envelope" of Divinity into new, uncharted expressions of Godhood, thus eternally expanding the Body of God.

The Divine Intent of this plan, of course, was that we would use our Free Will for the sole purpose of deciding how to co-create, with our Father-Mother God, greater and greater Octaves of Perfection. It was *never* the intent of our God Parents that we use our Free Will to distort the unformed primal Light substance pouring forth from the Core of Creation into the gross mutations of disease, aging, death, poverty, lack, limitation, hate, war, corruption, crime, plagues, pestilence, famines, earthquakes, adverse weather conditions, inhumanity to each other, abuse of the animal and nature kingdoms and all of the other maladies that are classified under the one label that represents the inversion of "LIVE"...which is "EVIL" or "LIVED"...which is "DEVIL."

Unfortunately, long before our Solar System was created, in far distant Universes, some of the evolving Sons and

Daughters of God used their creative faculties of thought and feeling to create fragmented thought patterns and feelings that did not reflect the Will of God. Gradually, as these patterns of imperfection reflected onto primal Light substance, mutations of life began to form that adversely affected the whole of Creation. The lifewaves evolving at that time included not only the individualized expressions of God, the Sons and Daughters of God from the Human Kingdom, but Beings from the Angelic Kingdom and the Elemental Kingdom, as well.

The Angelic Kingdom is responsible for projecting the Divine Feeling Nature of God into the atmosphere of every evolving Being and every school of learning. This Divine Feeling Nature includes the Harmony of God as expressed through Divine Love, Protection, Healing, Illumination, Grace, Purity, Adoration, Devotion and every other Quality of God.

The Elemental Kingdom is responsible for drawing the primal Light that forms the school of learning itself and the sustenance that sustains the evolving lifestreams in that particular school, such as the earth, air, water, fire, plants, animals, four lower bodies of Humanity (physical, etheric, mental and emotional) and the bodies of the very Planets and Suns themselves.

When some of the Sons and Daughters of God began creating discord in the Universe, some of the Angels and Elementals got caught up in the negativity. The allegory in the Bible about Lucifer and the "fallen angels" tells us that God cast these lifestreams out of Heaven. *In the past, we could only grasp, from our limited consciousness, the concept that these souls were bad and needed to be punished.* However, God is only Divine Love and Perfection and never punishes us; we merely create our own experiences by our behavior. Since these souls were creating discord, they fell in energy, vibration and consciousness below the frequencies of Heaven. God would not project

Divine Life Force into frequencies of discord, so God would not give one electron of precious life energy to sustain this dimension of chaos. Therefore, the only way these fallen Humans, Elementals and Angels could survive was by parasitically living off of other negative energy. Consequently, these fallen lifestreams roamed the Universe, striving to entice other evolving civilizations into releasing negative energy that would feed and nourish them.

This collective force of negativity came to be known throughout the Universe as "cosmic evil," and it is the force God was referring to when we were given our very first commandment, *"Do not partake of the Tree of Knowledge of good and evil."*

Now, having that little bit of background, let's focus on our Solar System. Although there were those lifestreams who "fell" in their learning experiences, there were many, many more who *soared* into incredible heights of Divinity. These illumined Sons and Daughters of God evolved into greater and greater levels of co-creation with our Father-Mother God until they reached the point where they were given the opportunity to create their own Solar Systems in the Body of God.

The course of evolution is such that souls who have evolved into extremely high levels of attainment will eventually be given the option of becoming *Planetary* Logos. The Planetary Logos is the enfolding Presence responsible for holding the Divine Blueprint for a *Planet* and all life evolving on that Planet. After their God Victorious Accomplishment at that level, the souls Ascend into the position of *Solar* Logos, which is the enfolding Presence responsible for holding the Divine Blueprint for a *Solar System*. Each system is comprised of a physical Sun and the Planets associated with that specific Sun. The next opportunity given to the evolving souls is to Ascend into the position of *Solar* Logos of a *Central Sun*, the enfolding Presence responsible for holding the Divine Blueprint for a *Galaxy*, which consists of a Central Sun, several physical Suns and the Planets associated with each of those Suns.

The next step in this evolutionary path is for the souls to Ascend into a *Solar* Logos of a *Great Central Sun*, the enfolding Presence responsible for holding the Divine Blueprint for a *Universe*, which includes the Great Central Sun, several Galaxies of Central Suns and all of the physical Suns and Planets associated with those Central Suns. And so our evolutionary progress continues, ever and ever expanding back to the Heart of our Father-Mother God.

In our particular Universe, the Divine Beings that radiate as our Great Central Sun are known as Elohae (masculine) and Eloha (feminine). They are the enfolding Presences that are responsible for holding the Divine Blueprint for the twelve Central Suns in our System of Worlds. Each of these Central Suns has twelve physical Suns that they are responsible for, and each physical Sun has twelve Planets.

Our Universe reverberates with the Sacred Geometry of the number TWELVE. Consequently, our learning experience in this Universe is to fully develop into the energy, vibration and consciousness of the Twelve Solar Aspects of Deity.

The Sacred Geometry in other Universes is often different. There are Universes with fewer Central Suns than twelve and Universes with many more Central Suns than twelve. In the overall scheme of things, all we need to focus on is what is happening in our Universe at this Cosmic Moment.

The Twelve Solar Aspects of Deity

The Twelve Solar Aspects of Deity that blaze forth from the Causal Body of our Great Central Sun, Elohae and Eloha are briefly described as follows:

1. THE FIRST SOLAR ASPECT OF DEITY IS GOD'S WILL. THE COLOR IS SAPPHIRE BLUE.

The Attributes of this Aspect of Deity are: God's Will, Illumined Faith, Power, Protection, Decision, The Will to Do, Divine Order, Obedience, Intuition, Unity and the Masculine Polarity of our Father God.

2. THE SECOND SOLAR ASPECT OF DEITY IS ENLIGHTENMENT. THE COLOR IS SUNSHINE YELLOW.

The Attributes of this Aspect of Deity are: Enlightenment, God Illumination, Wisdom, Understanding, Reason, Discernment, Perception, Constancy, Stimulation and Intensification of Spiritual Growth, a Momentum of Progress, Precipitation and Christ Consciousness—the Son and Daughter of God.

3. THE THIRD SOLAR ASPECT OF DEITY IS DIVINE LOVE. THE COLOR IS PINK.

The Attributes of this Aspect of Deity are: Divine Love, Adoration, Tolerance, Humanitarianism, Reverence for All Life, The Holy Breath, Comfort and the Feminine Polarity of our Mother God/Holy Spirit.

4. THE FOURTH SOLAR ASPECT OF DEITY IS PURITY. THE COLOR IS WHITE.

The Attributes of this Aspect of Deity are:
Purity, the Immaculate Concept, Hope,
Restoration, Resurrection and Ascension.

5. THE FIFTH SOLAR ASPECT OF DEITY IS TRUTH. THE COLOR IS EMERALD GREEN.

The Attributes of this Aspect of Deity are:
Illumined Truth, Inner Vision, Consecration,
Concentration, Healing, Dedication, The All-
Seeing Eye of God and the Empowerment of
All God Qualities on Earth.

6. THE SIXTH SOLAR ASPECT OF DEITY IS DIVINE GRACE. THE COLOR IS RUBY.

The Attributes of this Aspect of Deity are:
Divine Grace, Selfless Service, Healing,
Devotional Worship, Focus of Love, The
Christ Working Through the Human Person-
ality, Eternal Peace and the Divine Embodied
in Flesh.

7. THE SEVENTH SOLAR ASPECT OF DEITY IS FREEDOM. THE COLOR IS VIOLET.

The Attributes of this Aspect of Deity are:
Spiritual Freedom, Limitless Transmutation,
Forgiveness, Mercy, Compassion, Rhythm, the
Power of Invocation, Liberty, Divine Justice,
Victory and Limitless Physical Perfection.

8. THE EIGHTH SOLAR ASPECT OF DEITY IS CLARITY. THE COLOR IS AQUAMARINE.

The Attributes of this Aspect of Deity are: Clarity, Vivification, Divine Perception, Discernment, Lucidity and the Qualities of a Spiritually Free Being.

9. THE NINTH SOLAR ASPECT OF DEITY IS HARMONY. THE COLOR IS MAGENTA.

The Attributes of this Aspect of Deity are: Harmony, Balance, Solidity, Assurance and Confidence in Being in the World, but not of It.

10. THE TENTH SOLAR ASPECT OF DEITY IS ETERNAL PEACE. THE COLOR IS GOLD.

The Attributes of this Aspect of Deity are: Eternal Peace, The Great Silence, Inner Calm, Prosperity, Opulence, Abundance and Financial Freedom.

11. THE ELEVENTH SOLAR ASPECT OF DEITY IS DIVINE PURPOSE. THE COLOR IS PEACH.

The Attributes of this Aspect of Deity are: Divine Purpose, Fulfillment, Selfless Service, Loving Life Free, Happiness, Joy, Enthusiasm, the Cosmic Moment of Victorious Accomplishment and Comfort.

12. THE TWELFTH SOLAR ASPECT OF DEITY IS TRANSFORMATION. THE COLOR IS OPAL.

The Attributes of this Aspect of Deity are: Transformation, Transfiguration, Rejuvenation and Rebirth.

These Twelve Solar Aspects of Deity blaze from the Causal Body of Elohae and Eloha, our Great Central Sun, into the twelve Central Suns in our System. As this occurs, the Power of the Twelve times Twelve amplification (12 Solar Aspects of Deity into 12 Central Suns) is intensified into the Sacred Geometric number...144. Then the twelve Central Suns in our System blaze the Twelve Solar Aspects of Deity from their Causal Bodies into each of their twelve physical Suns. Each Central Sun is responsible again for the Power of the Twelve times Twelve amplification (12 Solar Aspects of Deity into 12 physical Suns). Finally, the twelve physical Suns under each Central Sun blaze the Twelve Solar Aspects of Deity from their Causal Bodies into each of their twelve Planets. Each physical Sun in responsible for the Power of the Twelve times Twelve amplification (12 Solar Aspects of Deity into 12 Planets).

This process was designed to amplify the Twelve Solar Aspects of Deity through our entire Universe in a way that would ensure that we would be embraced in the Divine Light of our Great Central Sun throughout our entire evolutionary process. That was to guarantee our Universe's God Victorious Accomplishment in the Light.

So what happened? Well, we volunteered to participate in a unique experiment that had never been tried before, and for the very first time in history, we descended into a frequency of vibration that prevented us from having access to the full spectrum of the Twelve Solar Aspects of Deity.

For greater clarity and understanding, I would like to

condense this information down once again to include just our Galaxy, so that we can truly focus on our immediate mission and not dissipate our energies with too many extraneous details.

Our Galaxy, under the radiance of the Great Central Sun Elohae and Eloha, is held in the Divine embrace of the Central Sun known as Alpha (masculine) and Omega (feminine). These magnificent Beings of Light drew into their Heart Flames, from the Heart Flames of Elohae and Eloha, the unformed primal Light substance that would be used to create every facet of life that would be given an opportunity to evolve in our Galaxy. This is the normal procedure in creating a Galaxy, and that is why the Divine Beings Whose radiant Light emanates as the Central Sun are referred to as God Parents or the Father-Mother God of their particular Galaxy.

Remember when Moses spoke to the burning bush and asked, "Who are you?" The response was, *"I Am that I Am. I Am Alpha; I Am Omega. I Am the beginning. I Am the ending."*

"I" comes from Alpha, meaning the One or the beginning. "Am" comes from Omega, meaning the ending. "I Am" that "I Am" is a sacred affirmation that unifies us with the beginning and the ending of the Father-Mother God of this Galaxy, and it lifts us into the Divine Intent of our purpose and reason for being in this Galaxy.

Alpha and Omega embrace twelve physical Suns. Seven of them originally experienced a dense, Third Dimensional physical reality, while five of them originally experienced a more rarified Fourth Dimensional reality. The seven dense physical Suns are the ones we're going to focus on because that is where the Earth and our Solar System are located.

Each of the seven dense physical Suns has twelve Planets. Seven of their Planets originally vibrated at a dense Third Dimensional frequency and the other five were originally in the Fourth Dimension. Again, I am going to condense this information down to the 49 dense Planets in the System of Alpha and Omega because these are the ones that got into trouble in our evolutionary process.

On the following page is a very simplified diagram that shows the seven dense physical Suns I will be referring to and the 49 dense Planets which are involved with what is happening on Earth at this moment.

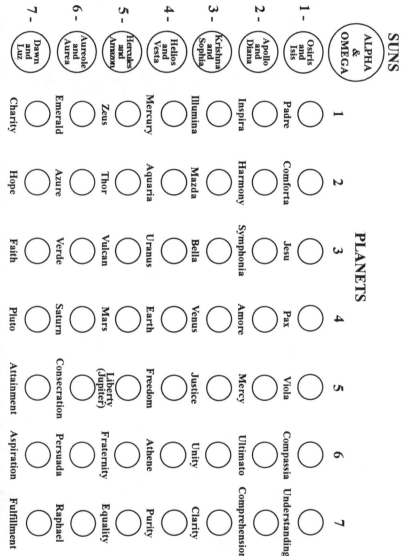

SUNS

- ALPHA & OMEGA
- 1 - Osiris and Isis
- 2 - Apollo and Diana
- 3 - Krishna and Sophia
- 4 - Helios and Vesta
- 5 - Hercules and Amazon
- 6 - Aureole and Aurea
- 7 - Dawn and Luz

PLANETS

	1	2	3	4	5	6	7
	Padre	Comforta	Jesu	Pax	Viola	Compassia	Understanding
	Inspira	Harmony	Symphonia	Amore	Mercy	Ultimato	Comprehension
	Illumina	Mazda	Bella	Venus	Justice	Unity	Clarity
	Mercury	Aquaria	Uranus	Earth	Freedom	Athene	Purity
	Zeus	Thor	Vulcan	Mars	Liberty (Jupiter)	Fraternity	Equality
	Emerald	Azure	Verde	Saturn	Consecration	Persuada	Raphael
	Charity	Hope	Faith	Pluto	Attainment	Aspiration	Fulfillment

Those with the names of qualities are English derivatives of Sanskrit, Pali, Latin, Greek and ancient languages.

As you can see from the chart, the Earth belongs to the Solar System of Helios (masculine) and Vesta (feminine). Their luminous Presence radiates as our physical Sun. These Divine Beings drew into their Heart Flames, from the Heart Flames of Alpha and Omega, the unformed primal Light substance that would be used to create every facet of life that would be given an opportunity to evolve in our Solar System. This Divine Light had been imprinted with the Divine Blueprint of our *Universe* (which is held in the Heart of Elohae and Eloha) and our *Galaxy* (which is held in the Heart of Alpha and Omega). When Helios and Vesta received It, the Divine Blueprint of our *Solar System* was imprinted on It and added to the overall Divine Plan.

Helios and Vesta are considered the God Parents of our *Solar System.* Alpha and Omega are considered the God Parents of our *Galaxy*, and Elohae and Eloha are considered the God Parents of our *Universe*.

On a "scientific level," we know so very little about the true composition of our Universe. Several of the Planets that our astronomers think are rotating around our physical Sun are, in fact, not associated with the physical Sun of Helios and Vesta at all. They are on the fourth spiral out from their Suns, so we can see them more clearly but, in fact, we are merely observing an optical illusion. None of that really matters at this point. When we complete our Ascension into our next Spiral of Evolution, things will be clearer. Right now, nothing is as it actually appears. (So what's new?) As you can also see, contrary to outer appearances, TV sitcoms and Country Western songs, we are not the "third rock from the Sun" either.

THE EXPERIMENT

Our Galaxy is a very young System. The reason that seven of our physical Suns and 49 of our Planets vibrate at a denser frequency than the other five Suns and 95 Planets of Alpha and Omega is because we volunteered to go through a very unique experiment that had never been attempted in any System of Worlds.

As stated previously, God created Sons and Daughters and invested us with the creative faculties of thought and feeling and the gift of Free Will so that we would learn, through the process of co-creation, to expand the borders of Divinity. Our Father-Mother God determined that we could experience the results of our thoughts, words, actions and feelings much more tangibly if we learned the process of co-creation within the constraints of a time and space continuum. Time and space do not exist in the higher Octaves of Perfection, so in order to create a time and space continuum, the frequency of vibration of unformed primal Light substance had to be stepped-down into the Fourth Dimension. Within a Fourth Dimensional frequency, we were able to experience time and space, but we were still vibrating at a high enough frequency to maintain contact with all of the Twelve Solar Aspects of Deity and the multifaceted aspects of our God Selves.

From the time we are first breathed forth from the Core of Creation as individualized Sons and Daughters of God, we go through many experiences to develop the vehicles our God Selves will use in our evolutionary process. Our God Selves consist of several Light Bodies.

The Light Bodies of our God Selves

Our first expression as an individualized Son/Daughter of God is known as the WHITE FIRE BEING. This resplendent Presence is the perfect balance of our Father-

Mother God. This is the Presence that is truly created in God's Image.

Pulsating as the Permanent Seed Atom of our White Fire Being is our Immortal Three-fold Flame, which reflects the Blue/Power/Father God; Pink/Love/Mother God; Yellow-Gold/Wisdom/Son and Daughter—Christ. Our WHITE FIRE BEING pulsates with the balanced polarities of both our FATHER GOD—the DIVINE MASCULINE/POWER and our MOTHER GOD—the DIVINE FEMININE/LOVE.

After myriad experiences in the Celestial Realms, our WHITE FIRE BEING eventually chose to continue its evolutionary process by volunteering to learn the lessons of co-creation.

This required that our WHITE FIRE BEING become part of an evolving Universe. Our Heart Call went forth and, if we were to become part of this *Universe*, our WHITE FIRE BEING was drawn into the Heart of the Great Central Sun of Elohae and Eloha to begin our preparation. The Divine Plan for this Universe was imprinted into every electron of our Beings, and the Divine Blueprint for our individual experience in this Universe was encoded through all levels of our consciousness. Once this preparation was complete, if we were to become part of this Galaxy, our WHITE FIRE BEING was drawn into the Heart of our Central Sun, Alpha and Omega. The Divine Plan for this Galaxy was imprinted into every electron of our Beings, and the Divine Blueprint for our individual experience in this Galaxy was encoded through all levels of our consciousness.

With that completed, our WHITE FIRE BEING was ready for the next step that would prepare It to enter a physical reality. In order to experience a physical reality to learn the lessons of co-creation by becoming masters of energy, vibration and consciousness, our WHITE FIRE BEING had to polarize Itself into a Divine Masculine and a Divine Feminine *"I AM" PRESENCE* with a Three-fold Flame blazing in each Heart Center. These two Beings are known as Twin Flames or Divine Complements. Once They are formed by our WHITE FIRE BEING, They evolve as two separate Beings through Their physical school of learning until They complete Their physical experience and eventually Ascend back into the unified Presence of one WHITE FIRE BEING.

There is a lot of confusion about Twin Flames at the present time. There are many people who believe that they must be united with their Twin Flame in a romantic relationship in the physical plane in order to fulfill their highest Spiritual potential on Earth. They spend tremendous energy searching for the "other half" of themselves, and they allow themselves to feel fragmented and incomplete without this physical, romantic relationship. This is a tragic disservice to themselves and their Twin Flames.

If it is your Divine Plan to be with your Twin Flame in a romantic relationship in a particular embodiment, it will happen very naturally. But, that is *very rare*. We are always working with our Twin Flames at Inner Levels, but usually we are going through separate experiences on Earth in order to experience the maximum lessons and opportunities for our growth. Often we don't even embody at the same time, so while one Twin Flame is working in the physical plane, the other can assist from "above."

If we *are* in embodiment at the same time, there is never any guarantee that our Twin Flames will be the right gender, age or even in the right location to be in a romantic relationship with us. Our Twin Flame could actually be our parent or our child. S/he might even be on the other side of the World in a situation where our paths will never cross in this lifetime.

For us to spend our life searching for our Twin Flame

instead of being in the moment and experiencing *every* relationship that is drawn to us to the fullest, we are missing the boat. Searching for our Twin Flame in the physical plane is actually a distraction that can deter us from our Divine Plan. ***Communing with our Twin Flame at Inner Levels through meditation and prayer, however, can enhance our growth and fill us with a sense of Joy and Oneness.***

Okay, now back to our story!

Once our Masculine and Feminine "I AM" PRESENCES were formed, They began to develop the other vehicles that would be necessary for Their sojourn into a physical reality. The next vehicle to be formed was the *SOLAR CAUSAL BODY.* This vehicle is comprised of the Twelve Solar Aspects of Deity.

In order to build this Forcefield of Light, our Masculine and Feminine "I AM" PRESENCES entered into the First Solar Aspect of Deity that is pulsating in the Causal Body of Alpha and Omega. There our "I AM" PRESENCES began Their journey as two separate Beings and absorbed the totality of God's First Cause of Perfection and all of the other Divine Qualities of the First Aspect of Deity. The first band of our Causal Body was formed from the Sapphire Blue Light, and it was anchored within the "I AM" PRESENCE along our Solar Spine through the Solar Chakra in the area of our throat. The first Solar Meridian expanded from this Chakra and flooded the body of our "I AM" PRESENCE with the Perfection of God's First Solar Aspect.

When that process was complete, our "I AM" PRES-ENCE progressed to the Second Solar Aspect of Deity where the identical procedure took place, creating the second band of our Causal Body, our second Solar Chakra and our second Solar Meridian. (See chart on page 58)

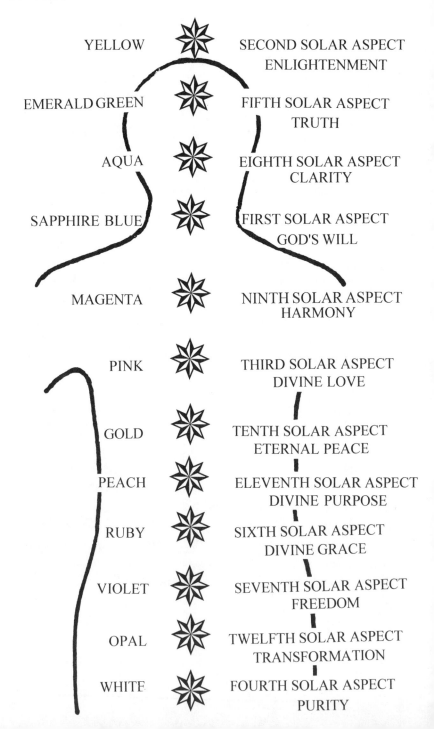

YELLOW — SECOND SOLAR ASPECT ENLIGHTENMENT

EMERALD GREEN — FIFTH SOLAR ASPECT TRUTH

AQUA — EIGHTH SOLAR ASPECT CLARITY

SAPPHIRE BLUE — FIRST SOLAR ASPECT GOD'S WILL

MAGENTA — NINTH SOLAR ASPECT HARMONY

PINK — THIRD SOLAR ASPECT DIVINE LOVE

GOLD — TENTH SOLAR ASPECT ETERNAL PEACE

PEACH — ELEVENTH SOLAR ASPECT DIVINE PURPOSE

RUBY — SIXTH SOLAR ASPECT DIVINE GRACE

VIOLET — SEVENTH SOLAR ASPECT FREEDOM

OPAL — TWELFTH SOLAR ASPECT TRANSFORMATION

WHITE — FOURTH SOLAR ASPECT PURITY

This procedure continued as our "I AM" PRESENCE gradually moved through all Twelve Solar Aspects of Deity in the Causal Body of Alpha and Omega. When our journey through the Causal Body of our Father-Mother God was complete, we had developed our *Twelve-fold Solar Causal Body*, our *Twelve-fold Solar Spine* with *Twelve Solar Chakras* pulsating along its axis and *Twelve Solar Meridians*. To secure the balance of all of these Systems, an Immortal *Twelve-fold Solar Heart Flame* was anchored around the Permanent Seed Atom of the Three-fold Flame in the heart of our "I AM" PRESENCE, which completed the formation of the Vehicles of our "I Am" Presences.

Our Twin Flame had proceeded through the same process at His/Her own pace and developed the same vehicles of expression.

Once this process was complete, our "I Am" Presence was ready for the next step of Its evolution. It was now time for our "I Am" Presence to project an aspect of Itself into the stepped-down frequencies of a physical experience. What normally happened at this point in the process of evolution is that an "I Am" Presence projected a reflection of Itself from the Fifth Dimensional Octaves of Perfection into the Fourth Dimensional physical plane of Its physical Sun. This Fourth Dimensional physical aspect of the "I Am" Presence is called the SOLAR CHRIST PRESENCE.

The SOLAR CHRIST PRESENCE vibrates at a denser frequency than an "I AM" Presence, but It is still rarified enough to remain connected to the Twelve-fold Causal Body, Solar Spine, Chakras, Meridians, Immortal Twelve-fold Solar Heart Flame and the "I Am" Presence. It maintains the ability to receive the full benefit of the Twelve Solar Aspects of Deity.

In the normal evolutionary process, the formation of the SOLAR CHRIST PRESENCE completed the creation of the vehicles of the God Self, which are, in summary:

1. WHITE FIRE BEING and THREE-FOLD

        FLAME
2. MASCULINE and FEMININE "I AM"
        PRESENCES with THREE-FOLD
        FLAMES
3. TWELVE-FOLD CAUSAL BODY,
        TWELVE-FOLD SOLAR SPINE with
        TWELVE SOLAR CHAKRAS,
        TWELVE SOLAR MERIDIANS and
        the IMMORTAL TWELVE-FOLD
        SOLAR HEART FLAME
4. SOLAR CHRIST PRESENCE

At a certain point in our evolutionary process, Alpha and Omega decided to "push the envelope" of creation. They began to wonder if we were learning to become co-creators effectively in a Fourth Dimensional time and space reality, would it accelerate our development into Godhood by collapsing down physical matter from a Fourth Dimensional frequency into an even more condensed time and space continuum of a Third Dimensional frequency?

This would mean that physical matter would be vibrating much slower and be much denser than evolving souls had ever experienced.

This was a little risky because it changed the dynamics of our entire evolutionary process, and since it had never been done before, no one knew exactly how it would affect us.

Nevertheless, Alpha and Omega were granted permission by Elohae and Eloha to try the experiment. Alpha and Omega asked for volunteers for this unique experiment, and many Suns and Planets responded.

Of all who volunteered to be part of this unprecedented experiment, Alpha and Omega chose the seven Suns and 49 Planets from Their Galaxy whom They felt were literally the "cream of the crop" and the most likely to succeed.

The Divine Plan for the experiment was imprinted into every electron of our Beings. Since no soul had ever evolved in a physical plane this dense, not even our Father-Mother God knew for sure what the outcome would be. Still, we voluntarily entered into the experiment with a tremendous sense of adventure and expectation.

When it was time for the experiment to begin, Alpha and Omega breathed the seven Suns into the densest frequency of vibration a physical Sun had ever experienced. Then the seven Suns breathed Their seven Planets into the densest frequency of vibration any Planet had ever experienced. Our entire Universe was aware of this unique experiment, and we drew the attention of Suns and Galaxies throughout infinity.

Our descent into the Third Dimension was a gradual two-step process. First, the "I Am" Presences of those who were chosen for the experiment projected the Solar Christ Presences into the Heart of the physical Sun. If we were chosen to evolve in the *Solar System*, we were projected into the Heart of Helios and Vesta. The Divine Plan for this Solar System was imprinted into every electron of our Beings, and the Divine Blueprint for our individual experience in this Solar System was encoded through all levels of our consciousness. Once this preparation was complete, our Solar Christ Presence was ready to create Its four Fourth Dimensional physical bodies. It drew, from the core of creation, the unformed Primal Light substance that would form Its physical, etheric, mental and emotional bodies. These were the vehicles It would use to navigate around in the Fourth Dimensional plane and the vehicles through which It would express Its creative faculties of thought and feeling as It learned to co-create with our God Parents by becoming the master of energy, vibration and consciousness. Even though these Fourth Dimensional vehicles are considered "physical," they are very etherial and are actually Light Bodies.

These Light Bodies continually reflect the perfection of our *Solar Christ Presence*, and they never descend into the discord of aging, degeneration or disease.

The Light Bodies of our Solar Christ Presence are in perfect alignment with our Fifth Dimensional "I Am" Presence and easily receive the Divine Light of the Solar Aspects of Deity through the Twelve-fold Solar Causal Body, Solar Spine, Chakras and Meridians.

After our Solar Christ Presence finished creating Its Fourth Dimensional vehicles, It was ready for the second step of the plan. This step was a little tricky. In order to step down the frequencies of the Fourth Dimensional Solar Christ Presence into a dense Third Dimensional reality, major changes had to take place.

The Twelve Solar Aspects of Deity had to be stepped down enough to reach into the Third Dimension. They had to be slowed down to the pigment octave of color and sound. In this frequency only the base colors could be accessed and utilized. Consequently, the Children of God did not have access to the full spectrum of the Twelve Solar Aspects of Divine Light to assist in their evolutionary process. Instead, the Twelve Solar Aspects of Deity were blended into what is known as the Circle of the Sacred Twelve and stepped down through the prism of the Fourth Dimension into the Third Dimension. This converted the full spectrum of the Twelve Solar Aspects of Deity into the seven-fold spectrum of color and sound we experience in the Third Dimension. We can witness this same process when we put the full spectrum of Light from the Sun through a prism and see the reflection of the Rainbow on the other side of the crystal.

Our Solar Christ Presence projected a stepped-down replica of Itself into the frequencies of the Third Dimension. This formed the Planetary Christ Presence that we call our **Holy Christ Self**. Our Holy Christ Self absorbed the stepped-down seven-fold spectrum of Light and sound and created a Seven-fold Causal Body and a Seven-fold Planetary Spine with seven major Chakras and seven major Meridians. For the first time, the evolving Children of God did not have access to the full spectrum of the Twelve Solar Aspects of Deity through their Causal Bodies and the electrical systems of their Planetary Spines, Chakras and Meridians.

As a safety measure, our God Selves came up with a plan to avert any problems our Holy Christ Selves might have in trying to communicate with the Higher Realms. Since our Holy Christ Selves didn't have the benefit of the full spectrum of a Twelve-fold Solar Spine, the God Self of each soul co-created, with our Father-Mother God, a very elaborate communication system that was specifically designed to keep the Holy Christ Self connected with all of the various Divine aspects of Itself. That system allowed the Holy Christ Self constant access to the Realms of Illumined Truth and the Divine Mind of God.

The communication system consisted of *Twelve Solar Strands of DNA* that pulsated into every cell of the Holy Christ Self. Each strand of DNA was programmed with the total God Consciousness, Wisdom and Love of one of the Twelve Solar Aspects of Deity. The Twelve Solar Strands of DNA not only functioned as a communication system through which our Holy Christ Selves could maintain constant contact with the Realms of Truth, they also provided an open portal through which the energy, vibration and consciousness of the Twelve Solar Aspects of Deity could flow into the physical plane, in spite of the fact that our Holy Christ Selves had Seven-fold Planetary Spines and Chakra Systems.

Our God Selves and our God Parents knew, as long as the Holy Christ Selves had the full benefit of the Twelve Solar Strands of DNA, our sojourn in the Third Dimension would be God Victorious, and our development into Godhood would be greatly accelerated.

DESCENT OF THE HOLY INNOCENTS

When the "Holy Innocents," the first Human Beings to inhabit the Earth, descended into the physical world of form, they were escorted by the resplendent Presence of Archangel Michael.

When all was prepared and Beloved Mother Earth had donned Her verdant garment of beauty, the Elemental substance that would sustain Humanity, the Planet was ready for the descent of the Holy Innocents. Before the eyes of the entire Company of Heaven and Silent Witnesses from Suns beyond Suns, the Gates of Heaven opened. There, in regal splendor, stood the luminous Presence of Archangel Michael, wearing the Crown of Immortality, clothed in the Light of the Central Sun, from Whose bosom He had come to protect and guide the children of Earth through the centuries of experience in the life yet to come. Mother Earth began to sing Her Cosmic Song. The Angelic Host poured forth Their praise to His Presence. The Devas and Builders of Form joined the Spiritual Anthem with Their Majestic Overtones, and the Sister Planets of our System added to the Symphony of Celestial Sound.

Archangel Michael, in the full-gathered momentum of His Divine Service to our Father-Mother God, *came to ensure the safe return of every Son and Daughter of God, every Angel and every Elemental at the closing of the Cosmic Day that was just beginning.* The Trumpet sounded, and Archangel Michael began His descent sweeping Earthward along the Blue Fire Ray, which was anchored into the Earth in the vicinity of the northern part of the powerful range of mountains we call the Rocky Mountains on the North American continent, the Grand Tetons in Wyoming. Following Him, in majestic grace, were the first Human Beings to be given the opportunity to embody on Earth and learn, through the lessons of co-creation, to develop into mature God Beings. This was to be done in the new Third Dimensional time and space continuum of Earth's physical realm.

Hand-in-hand they came, following Archangel Michael, until the entire number designed by our Father-Mother God for this first experiment of human life on Earth had descended. The Holy Innocents were accompanied by myriads of Guardian Angels, the Protective Aura of the Seraphim and the Light of the Cherubic Hosts Who carried within Their very essence the atmosphere of Heaven.

Thus, in great pageantry, beauty and limitless abundance, held in the visible, tangible embrace of Archangel Michael, the First Golden Age was entered into by the Sons and Daughters of God.

When the first Holy Christ Selves began to inhabit the Earth, everything that they could possibly need to assist us in this school of learning had been provided by the Elemental Kingdom and the Angelic Kingdom. The Earth was a veritable paradise, and all that was needed to maintain that level of perfection was readily available.

In an atmosphere of incredible joy and harmony, the Holy Christ Selves began drawing the primal Light substance from the Elemental Kingdom that would form the four Earthly bodies. These were the vehicles the Holy Christ Selves would need to experience the Third Dimension and learn the process of co-creating greater expressions of Divinity.

The Four Lower Bodies

Physical Body

The Physical Body is the vehicle that we are most aware of, and it is the vehicle that gave the Holy Christ Selves mobility on Earth. In the beginning the Holy Christ Self was the same size as the Physical Body, and It radiated through every cell and organ.

Once the Physical Body was formed, the Holy Christ Self anchored Its Three-fold Flame as the Permanent Seed Atom in the physical heart and It anchored the Twelve Solar Strands of DNA into every electron of elemental substance in the physical body. This secured the connection to the multifaceted, multidimensional aspects of the God Self, and it ensured the ability to communicate openly and clearly with all of the Octaves of Perfection.

The Holy Christ Self then anchored Its Seven-fold Planetary Spine through the spinal column of the Physical Body and activated the Seven-fold Chakra System and Meridians. This enabled the Solar Christ Presence in the Fourth Dimension to project a tremendous shaft of Divine Light through the body that would be the Life Force to sustain the Holy Christ Self in the Third Dimension, and it would also provide the Light the Holy Christ Self would use to co-create Its experience on Earth through Its thoughts, words, actions and feelings.

The Holy Christ Self then activated the physical brain structure. This was done by anchoring the Divine Masculine Polarity of our Father God, which reverberates with the Sapphire Blue First Aspect of Deity—Divine Power— into the left brain hemisphere and the Power Chakra in the throat. The Holy Christ Self then anchored the Divine Feminine Polarity of our Mother God, which reverberates with the Crystalline Pink Third Aspect of Deity—Divine Love—into the right brain hemisphere and Love Chakra in the heart. This created the perfect balance of the Father-Mother God within each soul and created an atmosphere that ensured the Masculine Power would always be balanced by Feminine Love.

When the radiance of the Father-Mother God is balanced in the right and left brain hemispheres, it creates a vibration that activates the Spiritual Centers within the brain. These centers are associated with the endocrine system and specifically reflect through the pituitary, pineal, hypothalamus glands and the ganglionic centers at the base of the brain. The activation of these Spiritual Centers opens the Crown Chakra of Enlightenment, which is located at the top of the head. This allows the consciousness of the Holy Christ Self to have access to the physical world of form, and it creates an open portal that directly connects each evolving soul with the Divine Mind of God. This is done through the Sunshine Yellow Second Solar Aspect of Deity—Enlightenment/Wisdom.

The term Holy Trinity has evolved into various meanings, but the true meaning of the Holy Trinity is expressed through the process I have just described. The Holy Trinity is the perfect balance of our Father God—Power and our Mother God—Love/Holy Spirit, which results in the birth of the Son/Daughter of God—the Christ—Enlightenment/Wisdom.

To ensure that this Holy Trinity would always be balanced within us, the Holy Christ Self expanded the Seed Atom of the Immortal Three-fold Flame *within* our hearts so that It would continually reflect the Divine Balance of the Father—Power—Blue...Mother—Love/Holy Spirit—Pink...Son/Daughter—Christ/Enlightenment/Wisdom—Yellow/Gold through all of our Earthly vehicles. In the beginning, our Three-fold Flame engulfed our four lower bodies.

Once this process was complete and the Physical Body was activated with Light and God Consciousness, the Holy Christ Self was ready to co-create, with our Father-Mother God, the remainder of Its Earthly Vehicles.

Etheric Body

The Etheric Body is composed of various chemical and Spiritual Ethers. It interpenetrates every cell and organ of the Physical Body, and it contains the Divine Blueprint of the Holy Christ Self. The original intent of the Etheric Body was to blaze the perfection of the Holy Christ Self into the atomic cellular consciousness of the Physical Body so that it would always maintain the Limitless Physical Perfection of Eternal Youth, Vibrant Health and Radiant Beauty even though it was vibrating in a dense Third Dimensional reality.

The Etheric Body also serves as the Record Keeper. Every thought, word, action or feeling we express in any time frame or dimension is recorded in the sensitive ethers of our Etheric Body. This vehicle contains within its essence the sum total of everything we have ever experienced since we first stepped forth into the physical plane. It is known as the seat of all memory, and it is what we now loosely call the subconscious mind.

The Etheric Body extends a little beyond the Physical Body, and it is the energy field we perceive as the aura. It is also the energy field that is caught on film through high frequency Kirlian Photography.

The frequency of the Etheric Body is deeply affected by our emotional, mental and physical states, and that is what causes the extreme changes in our auras.

Mental Body

The Mental Body is the mind, and it is the vehicle that transmits thoughts and words through the Physical Brain. There has always been a lot of debate as to whether the mind and the brain are two separate entities or one in the same. Actually, they are two separate entities. The Mental Body/ Mind is always whole and complete. It functions in the

Realms of Thought, and it is receptive to the Divine Mind of God.

The brain, on the other hand, is the computer of the Physical Body, and it is the instrument that the Mental Body uses to project thoughts into the physical plane. The physical brain can be damaged or chemically imbalanced, which prevents the mind from effectively transmitting thoughts into the physical plane. This affliction is called mental illness or mental retardation, but, in fact, only the physical brain is impaired, not the mind. In that situation, the Mental Body is still absorbing the total experience of the person, and the Etheric Body is recording every single event that takes place in the person's life. So, even if it seems, from outer appearances, that a person is so severely brain damaged that s/he can't think, that life is never in vain, and the soul still learns the lessons that it was supposed to in the Earthly experience.

The original intent of the Mental Body was to absorb thoughts and ideas from the Divine Mind of God and the Realms of Perfection and then project those patterns of perfection through the brain into the world of form, thus manifesting the perfection of the Heavenly Realms on Earth, fulfilling the Universal Law of *"As above, so below."*

Emotional Body

The Emotional Body contains the feelings and the emotional nature. This is the largest vehicle, and 80 percent of our energy is expressed through this body. That means that of all of the energy we expend every day of our lives, 80 percent is emotional, and the other 20 percent is expressed through our thoughts, words and actions. When we grasp this Truth, it becomes perfectly clear why our feelings are so important and why they have such a powerful effect on the health of the Physical Body and the mental state. Discordant feelings such as anger, hate, resentment, etc., cause genuine chemical changes in the Physical Body that actually suppress the natural immune system. Harmonious feelings such as joy, laughter, happiness and peace cause chemical changes that enhance the immune system.

The Emotional Body is predominantly water. That is why we are so very affected by the shifts of energy that take place on Earth when there is a change in the Heavenly Bodies surrounding the Planet. The emotional stratum of the Earth is associated with the water element as well, and when we have a Full Moon, the added gravitational pull creates a change in the tides of the ocean and in our Emotional Bodies. If we are centered and our four lower bodies are at peace, the Full Moon has a very positive effect on our energy field. There are always Global meditations that take place during the Full Moon to take advantage of this positive influx of energy.

If, however, we are out of balance and inharmonious, the Full Moon can wreak havoc on us. This can cause us to behave in unusual or bizarre ways. That is where the terms lunacy and lunatic came from. They are derivatives of the Latin word luna, which means moon.

The original intent of our Emotional Body was to absorb the Harmony of God and then flood the thought patterns of perfection from the Mind of God with the Divine Emotions of Enthusiasm, Joy, Bliss, Happiness, Love, etc. This empowered the thought patterns into physical manifestation and accelerated the process of co-creation, allowing us to rapidly expand the Borders of the Kingdom of Heaven on Earth.

The formation of the Emotional Body completed our Earthly Vehicles. Then, God gave us the gift of Free Will.

THE GIFT OF FREE WILL

In order to empower us with the unlimited opportunity to expand the Borders of Divinity in the Third Dimensional world of form, our Father-Mother God gave us the gift of Free Will. The Divine Intent of this sacred gift was to give us the limitless freedom to reach into the highest Octaves of Perfection and explore the various qualities, attributes, expressions and dimensions of Godhood, and then decide how we wanted to expand and reflect those patterns of perfection on Earth.

For example:

How today shall I express the essence of Divine Love?
How today shall I reveal the Realms of Illumined Truth?
How today shall I experience Eternal Peace?
How today shall I revel in the Harmony of God?
How today shall I become a reflection of Purity?
How today shall I project greater levels of Freedom?
and on and on ad infinitum.

It was *never* the Divine Intent of our Father-Mother God that we use our gift of Free Will to create patterns of discord and inharmony that would eventually manifest into the distorted patterns of poverty, disease, death, decay, war, hate, pain and suffering.

In order to prevent us from ever having to experience such gross mutations of our gift of life, God gave us *one* commandment, "DO NOT PARTAKE OF THE TREE OF KNOWLEDGE OF GOOD AND EVIL!"

God knew that what we allowed to enter our consciousness and what we energized with our creative faculties of thought and feeling would be brought into form. God also knew that if we didn't learn from an outside source of the fallen patterns of poverty, disease, death, war, pain etc., there would be no way for us to know about those maladies or energize them into our experience on Earth through our thoughts and feelings.

Upon receiving the gift of Free Will, the Holy Christ Self was ready to begin Its sojourn on Earth to learn the lessons of becoming a co-creator with our Father-Mother God.

THE ORIGINAL DIVINE PLAN

Since no System of Worlds had ever experienced evolving in the denseness of the time and space continuum of a Third Dimensional reality, and since this was the very first time evolving souls would not have access to the full spectrum of the Twelve Solar Aspects of Deity from their Great Central Sun through the usual Twelve-fold Solar Spine and Chakra System, a brand new plan was devised for the Children of God who were going to evolve on Earth and on the other 48 Planets included in the experiment.

The Seven-fold Planetary Spine and Chakra System of each person reflected the physical octave of color and frequency which we experience in the Rainbow.

> Root Chakra...................red
> Central Chakra...............orange
> Solar Plexus Chakra......yellow
> Heart Chakra..................green
> Throat Chakra.................blue
> Third Eye Chakra...........indigo
> Crown Chakra.................violet

The original plan was that we would come into embodiment two times in every 2000-year cycle, once as a male and once as a female. In each cycle we would absorb the full momentum of Light bathing the Planet and develop both the masculine (when we were in a male body) and the feminine (when we were in a female body) polarities of one of our Chakras. We began with the Root Chakra at the base of the spine and worked one by one up to the Crown Chakra of Enlightenment—at the top of the head.

In each embodiment we lived 800 to 900 years, and we retained conscious knowledge of all that we learned from lifetime to lifetime. By the time all seven Chakras were fully developed, we had attained full mastery over the physical plane and learned the lessons of co-creation and Enlightenment.

In the original plan our Earthly sojourn took approximately 14,000 years, and we had 14 embodiments, 7 as males and 7 as females.

When the masculine and feminine polarities of all seven of our Chakras were fully developed, we were ready for the next step of our evolutionary process. We were ready for our Ascension into the Fourth Dimension. Our Ascension into the more rarefied Fourth Dimensional Octaves of Light completed our cycles of rebirth on Earth and began a whole new experience. In the Fourth Dimension we began the development of our Twelve-fold Solar Spine and continued learning greater and greater ways to express our Divinity.

This Divine Plan proceeded without a flaw for many millenia. One Root Race after another, with its various subraces, came into embodiment, completed the development of its Seven-fold Planetary Spine and its lessons of co-creation and Enlightenment, then Ascended into its next school of learning. In the middle of the Fourth Root Race, however, something happened that profoundly and drastically changed the plan on Earth forever.

At that time, the force I spoke of earlier known as "cosmic evil" was desperately trying to find souls whom it could manipulate into releasing negative thought and feeling patterns that would feed it and keep it alive. Since the 49 Planets in our Galaxy that were participating in the experiment were vibrating at an unusually dense frequency, we were much more vulnerable, and it was much easier for the force of "cosmic evil" to access our consciousness.

This negative force, in its cunning and deceptive ways, projected thought patterns into the consciousness of souls evolving on all 49 Planets and tried to confuse and tempt us into experimenting with our gift of life by creating thought patterns and feelings that were not in alignment with God's Will and the Realms of Perfection.

Its efforts were relentless, and on some of the Planets, the force of "cosmic evil" broke through the safeguards and enticed some souls to buy into its plan of deception. Some souls began to create discordant patterns of thoughts and feelings and projected them into the physical planes of their Planets. This negativity began to spread like a plague throughout the land. Other evolving souls became involved and overwhelmed with the negativity, and the physical planes of some of the other Planets in our Galaxy began to spiral into the depths of human miscreation. This reflected as poverty, plagues, pestilence, war, hate, disease, adverse weather conditions, destructive earthquakes, death and all of the horror of "cosmic evil."

At that time, the Earth seemed invincible, and even though other Planets in the experiment were being overwhelmed with the influence of "cosmic evil," the Earth remained pristine and perfect and free from any trace of negativity.

All of the assistance that Cosmic Law would allow was given by the Heavenly Realms to try and free the afflicted Planets from the grip of "cosmic evil," but our sacred gift of Free Will which was intended to be a blessing became a curse, and the fallen souls were ensnared in the temptations of the flesh. "Cosmic evil" taught the entrapped souls to be black magicians, and they learned how to manipulate energy to control others and perpetuate evil for their personal gain.

As our Father-Mother God observed the plight of our Galaxy, They determined that the experiment was failing and issued a Divine Fiat to breathe the 7 Suns and 49 Planets back into the Fourth Dimension. Preparations were made for a Cosmic Inbreath that would magnetize the Suns and Planets in the Third Dimension into the next Spiral of Evolution...the Fourth Dimension.

The Sons and Daughters of God who had fallen to the ploy of "cosmic evil" would not be able to withstand the higher frequencies of the Fourth Dimension, so our God Parents decreed that they would be returned to the Great Central Sun. Nothing is ever completely lost, but if a soul refuses to do what is necessary to Ascend into the next octave of learning, s/he is returned to the Great Central Sun, and his/her substance is repolarized for future Systems of Worlds. This means that s/he looses his/her individuality as that particular soul. This is referred to as the *Second Death,* and it is the most tragic thing that can happen to an evolving "I Am" Presence.

EARTH'S ACT OF DIVINE LOVE

The Holy Christ Selves evolving on Earth and the Spiritual Hierarchy assigned to the Earth were very aware of what was about to happen to the six-billion souls from the other Planets in our Galaxy who had fallen into the grip of "cosmic evil." In an act of unprecedented Compassion and Divine Love, the Human Beings evolving on Earth pleaded with our Father-Mother God to allow the fallen souls to come here to be redeemed. Since the Earth had not been contaminated with the force of "cosmic evil" and the souls evolving here had only experienced the Realms of Light and Perfection, they believed that their Light would be strong enough to transcend the discord of the laggard souls while they were being taught to transmute their negative, miscreated patterns of energy and regain their direction on the path of Light.

No Planet had ever volunteered for such a selfless act of Divine Love. Consequently, even our Father-Mother God didn't know if we were going to be able to pull that off or not. But, whenever there is a powerful expression of Divine Love, Cosmic Dispensations can be granted to balance that love.

As the Cosmic Tone for the Galaxy of Alpha and Omega reverberated throughout the Universe, our Father-Mother God granted permission for the six-billion laggard souls to be transferred to Earth. On one Cosmic Inbreath, all 7 Suns and the remaining 48 Planets were breathed into the next Spiral of Evolution, permanently shattering the grip of "cosmic evil" and freeing them to continue their evolutionary process in the Fourth Dimension. *Only the Earth remained in the frequencies of the Third Dimension.*

In one mighty stroke, our Father-Mother God transferred six-billion laggard souls to the Inner Temples surrounding the Earth and began preparation for their physical embodiment on this Planet. The God Parents of our physical Sun, Helios and Vesta, volunteered to project a stepped-down frequency of Sunlight to sustain the Earth in the Third Dimension. They lovingly agreed to embrace us in Their Divine Essence until we could complete our merciful mission of redemption and regain our rightful place with the rest of our Solar System in the Fourth Dimension.

The Earth was originally designed to have four-billion souls evolving here at any one time, both in and out of embodiment. With the coming of the laggards, our numbers were increased to ten-billion evolving souls. This caused a tremendous strain on the Planet, but we were sure, if we persevered, we would be God Victorious.

For over 100 years, the physical bodies of the women on Earth were prepared to begin bringing in the incarnating laggards. Never, in the history of the Universe, has such a sacrifice been made as when the women of Earth volunteered to let the contaminated vehicles of the laggards be conceived into their radiant, pure bodies. Never has there been a more awesome demonstration of Divine Love.

When all was in readiness, the first wave of laggards were conceived by the men and women on Earth who had volunteered to be the parents of these incoming wayward souls. The parents created an atmosphere of Divine Love and awaited the arrival of their recalcitrant sons and daughters with great anticipation and joy.

Initially everything seemed to be working as planned. In the beginning, the Light of the parents was able to balance and transmute the frequencies of discord that emanated from the infants. But, when the laggard children were old enough to start receiving some of their misqualified energy, everything went awry. As the energy that they had misused in their previous lifetimes began returning to them to be transmuted back into Light, thought patterns that conflicted with God's Will began to reflect onto the physical plane of Earth for the very first time. The laggard souls began going through their Karmic lessons and experiencing difficult challenges that gave them an opportunity to experience the results of their previous actions. The people of Earth knew that with the coming of the laggards, challenges were going to occur, but since they had never experienced discord of any kind before, they became confused and even a little curious about the new fragmented energy.

Some of the laggard souls fell back into their old patterns, and instead of healing their pasts, they began enticing souls from Earth to experiment with their creative faculties of thought and feeling. In some instances, the Divine Plan was inverted, and instead of the people from Earth redeeming the laggards, the laggards led the people from Earth astray and tempted them to *"partake of the tree of knowledge of good and evil."*

This was the critical turning point on Earth that catapulted us into the depths of human miscreation. Today, after millions of years of writhing in excruciating pain and agony, we are finally at our moment of healing.

It is imperative for us to really understand what happened during the "fall" and the ramifications we experienced as a result of using our Free Will to create thoughts and feelings that conflicted with the Divine Plan on Earth. This will empower us to consciously participate in reversing the adverse effects of that tragic event. It will assist us in regaining our direction as we Ascend into our rightful place in the Universe and claim our Divine Birthright as Sons and Daughters of God.

THE FALL

The story of Adam and Eve is an allegory that *symbolically* describes what happened on Earth in the beginning. Even though many have erroneously tried to interpret the story literally, it is still filled with wonderful symbols of Truth.

In the beginning the Earth was a veritable Paradise of Splendor as represented by the "Garden of Eden." Everything that evolving Human Beings needed to sustain their Earthly vehicles and learn their lessons of co-creation was provided by the Elemental and Angelic Kingdoms who had volunteered to serve and sustain the Earth for the evolving Sons and Daughters of God.

Adam and Eve represented the duality of God...the Divine Masculine—Power...and the Divine Feminine—Love. The reason "Adam" came first is because the Divine Masculine is the First Aspect of Deity, and it reflects the First Cause of God, which is Perfection for all things through Divine Power and the *Sound Ray,* which is expressed through our Power Center in the throat. *"In the beginning was the **word** (sound), and the word was with God."* On the Sound Ray a Cosmic Tone is released from the Heart of our Father

God to form the vibrational matrix that draws unformed primal Light substance into form. Every person, place, condition or thing existing in any dimension has been drawn into a particular pattern by the Masculine Power of God's First Cause of Perfection—the Sound Ray.

"Eve" represents the Divine Feminine which is the Third Aspect of Deity. That aspect reflects Divine Love, the cohesive power of the Universe. It is the frequency of our Mother God, the Divine Feminine—Divine Love—that *holds* the primal Light in a particular pattern that has been drawn into form on the Divine Masculine Sound Ray. Without the cohesive power of Divine Love, the primal Light would dissipate into unmanifest potential again, and the form would cease to exist.

Adam and Eve symbolically represented the original parents of all souls evolving on Earth because the balance of the Divine Masculine and the Divine Feminine results in the birth of the Son/Daughter of God, the Christ, which reflects the Second Aspect of Deity...Enlightenment or Christ Consciousness.

In the Biblical allegory, Adam and Eve were given the gift of Free Will and commanded *"not to partake of the tree of knowledge of good and evil."*

The reason the serpent ("cosmic evil") tempted Eve to *"eat the apple"* is because ***Eve represents the Divine Feminine within us which is our emotional feeling nature***. It was that aspect of our Beings that felt the compassion that prompted us to volunteer to bring the laggard souls to Earth, and it was our feeling nature that caused us to open our hearts to the laggard souls in a way that ultimately caused our downfall.

Once Eve "ate the apple," symbolically representing our decision to take on the laggard souls who were being manipulated by the force of "cosmic evil," she and Adam were *banished* from the Garden of Eden and forced to experience pain and suffering and all of the maladies that were created when the laggards came to Earth.

During Jesus' Divine Mission on Earth, he continually warned his disciples not to *"cast pearls before swine."* Jesus was not calling people pigs; he was advising his followers not to give the masses information that they were incapable of understanding.

The story of Adam and Eve was given to Humanity as a simple allegory in language that we could understand in our fragmented state of mind at the time. Due to the urgency of the hour and the incredible assistance we are receiving from On High, we are now being lifted into greater Octaves of Illumined Truth, and our ability to comprehend and grasp greater Truths has opened the door to new levels of Sacred Knowledge. We are now able to perceive the details of what really occurred during the "fall." This Truth is being given to us so that we can actively participate in healing our self-inflicted separation from God and reverse our descent into oblivion. As our healing progresses, we will attain our God Victorious Ascension into incredible heights of Divinity.

OUR SEPARATION FROM GOD

Prior to the coming of the laggards, the Holy Christ Self was in full control of our four lower bodies and used these vehicles very effectively to create thoughts, feelings, words and actions that expressed the perfection patterns of the Heavenly Realms. The Holy Christ Self remained in constant communication with all of the higher aspects of the God Self through the Twelve Solar Strands of DNA, and It was able to project Its consciousness into the Realms of Truth and walk and talk with the Beings of Light abiding there.

The "I Am" Presence projected the gift of life from the Heart of God to the Solar Christ Presence who, in turn, projected that Divine Light to the Holy Christ Self through a tremendous shaft of Light that enveloped our four lower bodies. Then, the Holy Christ Self absorbed the Divine Light and qualified it with creative thoughts and feelings. As the gift of life passed through the Heart Center and was sent forth into the physical plane through our thoughts, words, actions and feelings, every electron of that precious life energy was stamped with our own *individual electronic pattern* which pulsates in the permanent seed atom in the heart.

We each have unique fingerprints, respiration patterns, voice patterns, DNA patterns and electronic Light patterns. Every electron of energy that passes through us is stamped with our unique electronic pattern and charged with the vibration of the thoughts and feelings we are experiencing at the time we receive it. This is how the Universe knows what energy belongs to whom, and it is how the Law of the Circle is scientifically applied and accurately enforced through all dimensions of existence.

When we receive our gift of life from God, that life force is neutral and vibrating at a frequency of harmony and perfection. As we send it forth with our thoughts, words, actions and feelings, it is stamped with our individual electronic pattern and charged with the energy, vibration and consciousness of our thoughts and feelings at the time. The energy then goes directly to the person, place, condition or thing we send it to, just like a radio wave or a television wave. The frequency of the energy we are sending forth reflects on everything it passes on the way to its destination. This is known as the process of *involution*—energy flowing from the Heart of God through our Heart Flames into the physical world of form.

Then, Cosmic Law dictates through the Law of the Circle that once the energy has reached its final destination in the physical plane, it must return to its Source. This involves the energy first being magnetized back to its identical electronic pattern blazing in the Heart Flame of the person who sent it forth and then, passing through the Heart Flame as it returns to the Father-Mother God, carrying with it all of the new frequencies of perfection from the Divine Ideas and experiments of the Holy Christ Self. That is the process of *evolution*. Prior to the coming of the laggard souls, this process worked flawlessly, and the Holy Christ Selves of evolving Humanity daily and hourly learned the lessons of co-creation and expanded the borders of the Kingdom of God on Earth through the Law of the Circle.

CREATING THE VEIL OF MAYA

When the Cosmic Dispensation was granted to allow the six-billion laggard souls from the other Planets participating in our unique Third Dimensional experiment to be transferred to Earth and gradually embody here, everything drastically changed.

When the incarnating laggards were old enough for the Karmic Board to start releasing some of their misqualified energy to be transmuted back into Light, the Earth began experiencing frequencies of discord for the very first time. More negativity flooded into Earth than the Children of Earth were equipped to handle, and instead of the people evolving on Earth lifting up the laggard souls, the laggards began pulling the souls evolving on Earth down into the quagmire of their human miscreations.

Misqualified thoughts, words, actions and feelings cannot return to the Source through the Divine Heart Flame, so the patterns of discord being created by the laggards began to accumulate around the Planet. The negative patterns began interpenetrating all physical form, and every electron of precious life energy evolving on Earth became contaminated and cloaked in frequencies of inharmony. The maladies of disease, poverty, aging, death, decay, etc., began manifesting in the physical plane. This created an atmosphere of fear and pain that was a totally new experience to the souls evolving on Earth. As the consciousness of fear increased, the sea of negative thought and feeling patterns accumulating around the Planet formed a "veil" that began to block the Light of God. This created even more fear and catapulted Humanity into even denser frequencies of existence. At this point, we began to close down our Heart Centers so that we wouldn't feel so much pain. This blocked the flow of Divine Love from our Mother God and caused our right brain hemispheres to become almost dormant. When this happened, the centers within our brain structures that open the Crown Chakras and allow us to remain connected to the Divine Mind of God began to atrophy. This caused our Crown Chakras to close, which blocked our contact with the Mind of God. The only centers that remained active were our left brain hemispheres and the Power Centers in our throats. Since our Masculine Power Centers were no longer balanced with our Feminine Heart Centers of Divine Love, we began to use our power, for the first time, in ways that did not reflect a reverence for all life. This abuse of power reflected all of our fear, and it accelerated our "fall" into the depths of human degradation.

As we fell into denser and denser frequencies of discord, our Twelve Solar Strands of DNA began to short circuit until we had just two remaining strands that formed a double helix of DNA. These are the visible strands of DNA that our scientists have now discovered. Even though our two strands of DNA contain billions of genetic codes, they are still barely enough to sustain brain consciousness. Our brain capacity deteriorated to just 10 percent of its former ability, and we lost contact with the multifaceted, multidimensional aspects of our God Presences.

When this occurred, we began to perceive the physical plane of Earth as the only reality, and we thought we were just our physical bodies. This incredibly distorted perception developed within us a sense of lack and limitation that perpetuated our abuse of power. We became fear-based and greedy. We felt we needed to dominate and control others in order to get what we needed to survive. The heinous patterns of war, crime, hate, prejudice, corruption, inhumanity, pollution, physical abuse, etc., became the order of the day.

As our consciousness began to reflect the full magnitude of the "fall," we developed a wayward personality that was based in fear and motivated strictly by the gratification of our physical senses. This compulsive, addictive personality is what we now refer to as the **human ego**. It is our extremely limited, corrupt, ignorant, fear-based, compulsive, dysfunctional human egos that we have identified with and considered to be who we truly are since the fall of Humanity. No wonder we are in such a mess!

Once the human ego gained control of our four lower bodies, it became clear to the Holy Christ Self that the shaft of Light flowing through our vehicles had to be reduced in order to prevent us from destroying ourselves. The Holy Christ Self decided to withdraw Itself until It was a mere fraction of an inch pulsating in the Heart Flame. It became what we now refer to as our *"Spark of Divinity."* As that occurred, the mighty shaft of Light that flowed through our vehicles was withdrawn and became what we now call our *"silver cord."* This was done as a merciful act of Divine Love, but it tragically allowed us to receive only a minuscule amount of our former God Light. Needless to say, this created even more fear and confusion on Earth and empowered our human egos to wreak even more havoc in our lives.

As the "veil" grew denser and the negativity on Earth increased, it became obvious to our Father-Mother God and the Company of Heaven that the Light sustaining the Body of Mother Earth through the Crystal Grid System was amplifying Humanity's pain and suffering. The Crystal Grid System of the Earth is the electrical system through which the Light of God pours to sustain life on Earth. It works in the same way the electrical system in our physical bodies works, through our Chakras and corresponding Meridians. The Light pouring through the Crystal Grid System is neutral and harmonious. It is specifically designed to amplify the life force on Earth, so it amplifies everything in its path. When the Earth became buried in human miscreation, the negativity as well as the good was being amplified by the Crystal Grid System. Our Father-Mother God decreed that the Light flowing into the crystals must be withdrawn. In one mighty stroke, the Light was withdrawn from Earth, and the crystals were allowed to receive just enough energy to keep the Body of Mother Earth alive. A Divine Fiat was issued by our God Parents commanding that we not use or empower the crystals until the Earth regained Her direction. For aeons of time the crystals have lain dormant except for when the dark forces on Earth misused the crystals for the black arts to manipulate and control others.

When the Light was withdrawn from the Crystal Grid System, the Earth became "the dark Star" in our System of Worlds. The weight of the negativity, inflicted on the Planet by the human egos of Humanity, caused the axis of the Earth to bend, and the Earth fell off the *Spiral of Evolution* onto the *Wheel of Karma.* When this occurred, it was truly our darkest hour. From that time on, we no longer came into embodiment just to learn the process of co-creation and self- mastery. Now we were coming into embodiment to try and clean up the messes we had created in our previous lifetimes. Our human egos were so recalcitrant and rebellious that in each succeeding lifetime we actually created more negativity and buried ourselves even deeper in human suffering. Our Father-Mother God decided to place a *"Band of Forgetfulness"* around our brows before each embodiment. The hope was that if we did not remember all of the hate and anger of the past, we could start each lifetime afresh and have a greater chance of healing our dysfunctional relationships and learn to love our enemies.

This helped to a degree, but it caused a great deal of confusion. Without knowing about our previous lifetimes and the negativity we had created in the past, we had no explanation as to why we were going through such horrendous challenges. We felt very victimized and abused. We felt unloved and worthless. Those who were able to believe in God said that the suffering on Earth must be God's Will, and God was perceived as being a punishing, wrathful God, a God to be feared.

Without any memory of our previous lifetimes, we tried to use "logic" to explain the maladies on Earth. We tried to justify human suffering by saying God wanted us to experience the negativity so that we would know the difference between good and evil. We began believing that **God** created the negativity on Earth as part of our learning experience. We understood that everything is comprised of energy, vibration and consciousness, so we were aware of duality and polarities.

Our lower human egos looked at the circumstances existing in the physical plane and tried, with their fragmented consciousness, to explain what they perceived to be polarity and duality.

They looked at the "opposites" of our misqualified thoughts, words, actions and feelings and came to the following erroneous and distorted conclusion. Our egos knew that all things originated with God, so they decided that God created everything. Therefore, our egos' *logical* deduction was that all conditions manifesting in the physical plan were "Divine"...

POSITIVE	"OPPOSITE"	**NEGATIVE**
HARMONY	"	DISCORD
LIVE	"	EVIL
LIVED	"	DEVIL
LIGHT	"	DARKNESS
LOVE	"	HATE
PEACE	"	WAR
ABUNDANCE	"	POVERTY
HEALTH	"	DISEASE
JOY	"	SADNESS

HAPPINESS	"	DEPRESSION
COMFORT	"	ANXIETY
SECURITY	"	FEAR
SILENCE	"	NOISE
WISDOM	"	IGNORANCE
TOLERANCE	"	PREJUDICE
FRIENDS	"	ENEMIES

...and on and on ad finitum.

The entire purpose and reason for being in the schoolroom of Earth is for us to learn how to use our creative faculties of thought and feeling to become co-creators with our Father-Mother God. When the human ego came to its incredibly distorted conclusion, it began to truly believe that we **had** to experience the "bad" in order to experience the "good." This belief, of course, caused our human egos to perpetuate the negativity on Earth. THIS WAS THE MOST DESTRUCTIVE BELIEF SYSTEM WE COULD HAVE POSSIBLY ENTERTAINED.

The polarity of God is NOT "good" and "evil"...

THE POLARITY OF GOD IS THE DUALITY
OF THE DIVINE MASCULINE AND
THE DIVINE FEMININE.

With the Band of Forgetfulness, we forgot that these opposite polarities of God reverberated through ALL of God's Creation and that GOD DOES NOT RELEASE ONE ELECTRON OF PRECIOUS LIFE ENERGY THAT IS VIBRATING AT A FREQUENCY THAT IS LESS THAN THE **TOTAL PERFECTION OF GOD!!!**
We forgot that ANYTHING that is vibrating at a frequency that is less than the Limitless Physical Perfection of HEAVEN ON EARTHis...A **HUMAN MISCREATION**...A

MUTATION OF OUR PRECIOUS GIFT OF LIFE THAT **WE** CREATED THROUGH THE **MISUSE** OF OUR CREATIVE FACULTIES OF THOUGHT AND FEELING...and it must, therefore, be transmuted back into its original Divine Intent in order for us to Ascend into the Fourth/Fifth Dimensional Octaves of Perfection.

With the Band of Forgetfulness, we no longer knew that the opposite polarity of Light is *not* the darkness that we had known as evil or discord or pain and suffering. Those manifestations are in OPPOSITION to the Light, which is a very different thing.

The dual polarities of Light are RADIANCE—ACTIV-ITY—CREATION and THE GREAT SILENCE—STILL-NESS—UNMANIFEST POTENTIAL.

This rule applies to every single Divine Quality or Attribute of God...every experience that we were destined to walk through in this Earthly schoolroom of learning before we fell into the abyss of human miscreation—opposite frequencies of vibrations, yes, but ALWAYS HARMONIOUS, CELESTIAL, PERFECT AND DIVINE.

In essence, the BAND OF FORGETFULNESS caused us to sink into even deeper frequencies of ignorance and chaos. We became pitiful and pathetic on one hand and enraged and contemptuous on the other. Each lifetime our progress was virtually non-existent, and we were forced to embody thousands of times, experiencing the depths of human depravity each time with very little hope of redemption, as we revolved on the Wheel of Karma lifetime after lifetime. This was the lowest ebb of human existence on Earth, and our extreme vulnerability drew the attention of "cosmic evil."

THE COMING OF "COSMIC EVIL"

When "cosmic evil" saw how the Earth was floundering in negativity and realized how easily our human egos were manipulated by the desire for physical gratification, it knew that this fallen Planet would be a lucrative source of discordant energy on which it could feed and sustain itself. At that point in our evolution, "cosmic evil" seized the Earth and literally took us hostage. This sinister force created a magnetic grid that reversed the frequency of Light flowing through the Crystal Grid System and trapped us on the Wheel of Karma.

Once the force of "cosmic evil" gained dominion on Earth, our plight worsened. We struggled to extricate ourselves from the grip of our human egos and the negative interference of "cosmic evil," but our greatest efforts were virtually futile. We felt as though we were walking through tar into 150-mile-an-hour winds, unable to make the slightest trace of progress. Every lifetime was spent struggling to survive, and the battle to sustain our physical bodies became paramount. All of our energy was expended to obtain food, clothing, shelter and physical gratification. We totally lost the awareness of why we had come to Earth in the first place. As our human egos became even more self-obsessed, our greed and selfishness multiplied. Money became the object of our "worship," and our sexuality deteriorated into a manipulative, obsessive activity of abuse and control. Each successive lifetime seemed to exacerbate these tendencies and bury us deeper in our miscreated human effluvia.

As if our predicament was not devastating enough, "cosmic evil" decided at that point to claim the Earth as a school of learning for the dark forces. Because we were oblivious to our true God Reality and since we had separated ourselves so effectively from our Holy Christ Selves, "cosmic evil" realized how very easy it was to manipulate our human egos to do its will. It opened highways into the psychic-astral plane of Earth that gave access to the Earth to depraved, degenerate souls from other Solar Systems outside of our Galaxy. Once these souls from other Systems entered the astral plane of Earth, they were taught how to manipulate Humanity to perpetuate evil. They learned how to amplify the dysfunctional behavior patterns of our human egos through projected thoughtforms, and they became very adept at keeping us stuck in feelings of worthlessness and low self-esteem. They used our fear to intensify our feelings of hate, prejudice, war, greed, selfishness, lack and limitation. They exacerbated our feelings of grief, sadness, loss and separation, and they created a perpetual atmosphere of despair and hopelessness.

There are legends and stories that have been passed down through time that describe bizarre scenarios of just how these entities from other Star Systems "invaded" the Earth and added to our plight. There is probably an element of Truth in all of them, and there is a reflection of Truth in the outrageous stories of extraterrestrials being bandied about today.

Many of the stories are indicating that the invasion of extraterrestrials *caused* the "fall." That is not true. The extraterrestrials were able to have access to the Earth only after "cosmic evil" took the Earth hostage and opened the highways into the psychic-astral plane.

In the midst of all of our struggles, the world religions grasped a fragment of what was actually going on and declared that *Satan ruled the Earth*. Unfortunately, this realization did not inspire them to change the situation, but rather caused them to profess that Humanity was innately evil and comprised of worthless *"sinners"* and *"worms in the dust."* This assessment kept us bound in guilt and a consciousness of hopelessness which enabled the force of "cosmic evil" to manipulate us even further into the frequencies of self-destruction. We became its pawns, and in a dulled consciousness that bordered on mass hypnosis, we became the unwilling victims of our human egos, and the Earth became a virtual den of iniquity. That is when Human Beings deteriorated into the dense Neanderthal caveman state of consciousness.

A CALL FOR ASSISTANCE

Normally a Planet that had fallen into such a state of wickedness would be deemed unsalvageable, in which case the Light of the physical Sun would be withdrawn and the Planet would be allowed to "die." The souls evolving on the Planet would return to the Central Sun to be repolarized for future Systems of Worlds, but they would lose their individuality as Children of God and experience the Second Death.

Since the Earth got into Her horrendous situation through an original act of *unprecedented, selfless Divine Love,* our Father-Mother God were not willing to give up on us. Our God Parents sent forth a Clarion Call throughout the Universe asking for assistance. The response came from Galaxies beyond Galaxies and Suns beyond Suns. Divine Ideas were placed before the throne of our Father-Mother God, and in unison, Beloved Elohae and Eloha, Alpha and Omega and Helios and Vesta chose a plan of Divine Intervention that had been offered by the Star System of Sirius.

The initial impetus of our "fall" began on the continent of Lemuria, a huge land mass that used to exist in the Pacific Ocean. At the time of the coming of the laggards, the Divine Mother energy was at Its most intense frequency on Lemuria, so it was decided by the Company of Heaven to allow the laggard souls to embody in that area first. The Divine Intent was to flood these incoming souls with such a momentum of the Divine Mother/Goddess essence of Divine Love that their negativity would be transformed into Light.

When the plan went awry and Humanity began closing down our Heart Centers to avoid feeling the pain manifesting on Earth, there was no place more adversely affected than Lemuria. This continent experienced an overwhelming shock that catapulted it into the depths of human depravity.

The Divine Intelligence in the Star System of Sirius had witnessed this tragedy and knew that the normal portals through which the Divine Love of our Mother God entered the Third Dimensional plane of Earth (our right brain hemispheres and our Heart Centers) had been closed by a fearful Humanity.

Sirius believed that the only hope for the Earth was for someone else to come to our rescue and establish an open portal through which the Divine Mother's Love could flow into Earth until Humanity could regain our direction and trust enough to open our hearts once again.

Recognizing the gravity of Earth's plight, Sirius, in deep humility and selfless love, volunteered to project a tremendous shaft of Light into the continent of Lemuria that would serve as an open portal for the Divine Love of our Mother God. As Sirius sustained this open portal of Divine Love, our Mother God bathed the Earth and all life evolving here in Her nurturing Light. This portal is known as the *Vortex of the Goddess.*

For a period of time the plan worked gloriously. The Divine Love pouring through the Vortex of the Goddess held the negativity on Earth in abeyance. This enabled the souls evolving on the continent of Lemuria to begin to heal their self-inflicted separation from God, and as they lifted up in consciousness and reclaimed their path of Light, they created a Golden Age. This occurred hundreds of thousands of years ago, and from outer appearances, it looked as though Sirius' plan had truly saved the Earth.

Cosmic Law dictates, however, that our evolution into Godhood must be self-sustained through our own self-mastery. Nobody else can do it for us *permanently.* The Vortex of the Goddess gave us a boost up out of the quagmire of human miscreation, but Cosmic Law would allow this Divine Intervention only temporarily, hoping that it would give us the strength to open our hearts and re-establish our own portals of Divine Love.

THE SINKING OF LEMURIA

In the midst of the Golden Age of Lemuria, a Cosmic Tone sounded, and Sirius was commanded by Divine Law to close the Vortex of the Goddess. There were a few illumined souls who had developed the self-mastery and trust to open the Stargates of their Hearts, but unfortunately, the masses on Lemuria had not. When the Divine Mother's Love receded from the Earth, Humanity began to falter and fell once again into the abyss of negativity, degradation and abuse of power.

Sirius realized that the Earth was not going to survive without further assistance. The Beings of Light from Sirius appealed to the Father-Mother God Presences of our Suns Elohae and Eloha, Alpha and Omega and Helios and Vesta. They asked for permission to continue bathing the Earth in the Love of our Mother God until Humanity could resume this activity on our own. A special dispensation was granted to allow Sirius to project a small amount of Divine Love into Earth, but the frequency allowed by Cosmic Law was a mere fraction of the Light that originally poured through the Vortex of the Goddess.

Elohae and Eloha, our God Parents from our Great Central Sun, told Sirius that in a distant future time there would be a Cosmic Moment on Earth when Humanity would regain our direction and reach into the embrace of our Solar Christ Presences. They said that during that moment, They would hold the Earth in the Solar frequencies of God's Perfection, and as a gift of love for the selfless service the Earth rendered to the laggards, and as a gift of gratitude to the Star System of Sirius for the selfless service It rendered to Earth, They would allow Sirius to *PERMANENTLY* OPEN THE VORTEX OF THE GODDESS/DIVINE MOTHER.

The few illumined souls who had reached great heights

of Enlightenment on Lemuria realized that the magnetic grid of "cosmic evil" was the main resistance preventing Humanity from being able to move off the Wheel of Karma. They devised a plan to try and activate the Crystal Grid System with the Divine Intent of shattering "cosmic evil's" magnetic grid and freeing the Earth from its oppressive grip. To the horror of all involved, their numbers were too few, and when "cosmic evil" realized what was happening, it increased the frequency of its magnetic grid and inverted the Light flowing into the Crystal Grid System. As the inverted Light imploded through the crystals into the Body of Mother Earth, it amplified the pain and suffering of Humanity. The results were excruciating, and as Humanity writhed in agony, our Father-Mother God, in an act of Mercy and Compassion, issued a Cosmic Fiat to the Mighty Elohim and decreed that the Builders of Form submerge Lemuria beneath the healing waters of the Pacific Ocean.

This cataclysmic event caused that tremendous continent to break apart as it sank into the water. A fragment of Lemuria was pushed into the western side of the North American continent. The area west of the San Andreas Fault is that portion of Lemuria. Los Angeles, California is the focus of the original anchorage point of the Vortex of the Goddess that was on the continent of Lemuria.

THE TEAR IN MOTHER EARTH'S ETHERIC BODY

The sinking of Lemuria was such a horrific event that the trauma of it tore the Etheric Body of Mother Earth. This Etheric tear created a vacuum that trapped hundreds of thousands of souls who left the physical plane through the process we call death when Lemuria sank into the Pacific Ocean. These souls were trapped in limbo, a virtual time warp. They were unable to move forward into the higher schools of learning and unable to return to Earth to transmute the effects of their Karmic liabilities. This tragedy created yet another problem for evolving Humanity.

Since it was our own misqualified energy that the crystals amplified and since we are responsible for transmuting the negativity we have created through the misuse of our precious gift of life, no outside force could intervene and heal the Etheric tear. Humanity alone was responsible for creating a powerful enough forcefield of Divine Healing to heal the Etheric Body of Mother Earth and free the trapped souls. Until that healing could occur, we would not move forward in our evolutionary process.

The problem was that the majority of the souls remaining on Earth had fallen so far into the depths of darkness and confusion that they didn't even realize the Etheric wound existed or that there were hundreds of thousands of souls trapped in the tear. We just went blindly about our business, struggling to survive and trying to move forward an inch at a time. Even with all of our efforts, we made very little progress. It was like pressing on the gas peddle of our car while our gears were in neutral. We would expend tremendous energy striving to change our Earthly experiences, but we saw very little, if any, results. We began to scoff at the idea that we are the creators of our own realities, and we began to really buy into the belief that we are victims. This attitude began to manifest in our consciousness as a feeling of hopelessness, which became a self-fulfilled prophecy. The more hopeless we felt, the more unable we were to affect change in our lives, and the more victimized we became. This vicious circle became such a prevalent part of our experience on Earth that we began to accept it as normal.

Not only did this flaw in the Etheric Garment of Mother Earth create a distorted perception of our ability to have influence over the circumstances of our lives, but it created a scar in our own Etheric Bodies as well. All life is interrelated, and as we interpenetrated the Etheric substance of Earth through physical embodiment, over and over again the Etheric tear in the body of Mother Earth began to reflect in the substance of our individual Etheric Bodies. This caused a weakness, sometimes even a hole in this vehicle, which has made us even more vulnerable and susceptible to the influence of the psychic-astral plane of confusion and chaos. Needless to say, this has wreaked all manner of havoc in our lives. This weakness in our auras has allowed the force of "cosmic evil" to have direct access to our lower human egos. Through this vulnerable spot in our energy field, the psychic-astral realm that is striving to maintain control of the Earth and trying to keep us bound to fear and limitation has been able to amplify our feelings of inadequacy and failure consciousness. It has been able to perpetuate our belief in lack and limitation, and it has been able to thoroughly convince us that our limited, struggling, oppressive lower human egos are who we actually are.

This hole in our aura has also complicated our situation on Earth because it allowed more negativity from the mass consciousness surrounding us to seep into our electromagnetic energy field. This *amplified* our difficult experiences. For instance, if we were grieving, as the vibration of grief built in our energy field through our thoughts and feelings, it magnetized to itself similar frequencies of grief from the atmosphere around us. If our Etheric Body is strong and whole, frequencies of grief may accumulate around us, but they will *not enter* our four lower bodies and cause us problems. If, however, we have a hole in our Etheric Body, the additional frequencies of grief will interpenetrate our four lower bodies and intensify greatly the grief we are experiencing. As a result of the Etheric tear, we have been going through much more pain and suffering than we would normally have experienced. With the flaw in our Etheric Bodies, everything we have gone through has been compounded by negative outside influences and greatly amplified.

Over aeons of time special dispensations were granted

by our Father-Mother God to allow Illumined Beings to embody on Earth with the specific goal of awakening sufficient numbers of people who would be able to invoke the Light powerfully enough and magnetize It effectively enough into the physical plane to heal the Etheric tear. Because of our recalcitrance, progress was painfully slow. The lifestreams who were evolving on the continent of Lemuria at the time of its submersion, and who made it through the transition of death without being caught up in the Etheric tear, volunteered to do whatever was necessary to help free the trapped souls. They agreed to embody in the vicinity of the lost continent of Lemuria and work according to their wisdom and understanding to free their loved ones. For thousands of years, these Lemurian souls embodied in the Southwestern United States of America. They embodied in the indigenous vehicles known as the American Indians, and through their Spiritual Enlightenment and reverence for Mother Earth, they worked ceaselessly to heal the Etheric Body of this Blessed Planet.

In the Southwestern United States of America, in the area of Tucson, Arizona, there is a sacred mountain named Picacho Peak. For centuries of time the Lemurian souls, embodied as American Indians, prepared this holy place for the time when the Etheric tear would be healed, and their sisters and brothers would be freed from their horrible plight and released to continue their evolutionary path. Century after century, with great patience, these selfless souls invoked the full-gathered momentum of the Violet Transmuting Flame of Freedom and the Crystalline White Ascension Flame. They amplified these Sacred Flames daily and hourly in preparation for a future time when Humanity would be able to consciously invoke the Light effectively enough to heal the Etheric tear and free the trapped souls.

DIVINE INTERVENTION

Even with all of our problems, our Father-Mother God and the Company of Heaven were not willing to let us self-destruct. They never gave up on us or stopped implementing various experiments to try to extricate us from the grip of our human egos and the force of "cosmic evil." Even after the attempted activation of the Crystal Grid System failed a second time and the continent of Atlantis sank beneath the healing waters of the Atlantic Ocean, the Spiritual Hierarchy of Earth still persevered relentlessly.

Age after Age various experiments were tried to heal our separation from God. With varying degrees of success we progressed at a painfully slow pace. Then, about 500 years ago, a Cosmic Tone rang forth from the Core of Creation proclaiming that the Universe of Elohae and Eloha was about to be breathed into our next Spiral of Evolution. That meant that the Suns and Planets in the Galaxy of Alpha and Omega were going to be breathed into the Fifth Dimension. All the Suns and Planets evolving in the Universe of Elohae and Eloha were ready for this vibrational Ascension EXCEPT THE EARTH. This was because during the last Cosmic Inbreath, we volunteered to take on the fallen souls from all of the other Planets in our Galaxy so that not a single soul would have to experience the Second Death.

Remember, too, that during the last Inbreath all of the Suns and Planets who were involved in our Third Dimensional experiment accelerated in vibration, energy and consciousness into the Fourth Dimension. The Earth alone remained in the frequency of the Third Dimension. That is why it looks like all of the other Planets in our Universe are without life, because the souls evolving on those Planets are vibrating at a Fourth Dimensional frequency, which is beyond our physical sight. What we perceive as the physical substance of the various Planets is merely a dense residue of matter that could not sustain Third Dimensional life as we know it. When we complete our Ascension into the Fourth/ Fifth Dimension, we will truly understand what the term parallel Universes really means, and we will see that the other Planets in our Universe are **ALL** teeming with life.

A 500 -YEAR PERIOD OF GRACE

It was clear to the Powers That Be that if Earth had not been able to redeem Herself in hundreds of thousands of millenia, we weren't going to be able to reclaim our direction in the brief span of time that was left before the Cosmic Inbreath unless we received Divine Intervention. Once again, a Clarion Call reverberated through the Universe invoking assistance for this wayward Planet.

Knowing that the survival of the Earth was hanging in the balance, the response poured forth from the Heart of Divine Love.

Never in all Eternity has that much love poured forth from Suns and Galaxies and Universes throughout all Creation to help one small Planet. Whenever there is a tremendous outpouring of love, special dispensations can be granted by Cosmic Law, and unusual Divine Intervention is allowed.

Our Father-Mother God evaluated the need of the hour on Earth and granted a *500-year Period of Grace* to give us one final opportunity with unusual Divine Intervention to save this sweet Earth and all Her life.

Even though all of the other Suns and Planets in our Universe were ready to move into the higher Fifth Dimensional Octaves of Light and Joy, They agreed to wait for 500 years to see if this troubled Planet could be redeemed.

Never in the history of the Universe has a Planet so contaminated with negativity been given the opportunity to move into the Light so quickly. Once again, the Earth was involved in a unique experiment that had never been attempted before. This experiment drew the attention and the assistance of the entire Universe. All of the Suns and Planets throughout Infinity watched in breathless wonder, knowing full well that our God Victorious success would change the course of evolution for all Eternity. Since no Planet had ever fallen to the depths of discord that the Earth had reached and still survived, when the Sons and Daughters of God on Earth Ascend back into their true God Reality, we will have a broader spectrum of experience than any evolving souls have ever achieved.

We are always a sum total of all of our experiences, so with our glorious Ascension in the Light, we will "push the envelope" of Creation into uncharted territory and actually reach a *new level of Godhood*, thus expanding the Body of our Father-Mother God into new Octaves of Perfection. This quantum leap in consciousness benefits all dimensions of evolution, so we are receiving more assistance than ever before in the history of Creation, and ALL life is pulling for the God Victorious Accomplishment of this unprecedented Divine Plan.

As the 500-year Grace Period began, our Father-Mother God opened Highways of Light from the Realms of Perfection into the physical plane of Earth. The Company of Heaven and the Spiritual Hierarchy serving the Earth were given permission to reach into the consciousness of anyone evolving on Earth who could perceive Their Presence and was willing to be an open door for the Light of God into the physical plane. Several selfless souls volunteered to be the Hands of God in the world of form, and even though much powerful work was done in the silence of their hearts, some of the activities were so profound that they drew the attention of the entire World.

The Masculine Polarity of God enters the Earth as a tremendous shaft of Light in the area of the Himalayan Mountains near Tibet. The Feminine Polarity of God enters the Earth as a tremendous shaft of Light in the area of Mount Meru near Lake Titicaca, Bolivia, in South America. When we closed our Heart Centers and blocked the flow of the

Feminine Polarity of God into the Earth, we created an imbalance in the influx of Light that poured through the shaft of Light in South America. It was clear to the Beings of Light in the Heavenly Realms that one of the most important things that needed to be accomplished was to increase the flow of Divine Love through the Feminine Polarity of God. Since the Universal Law is "WHERE YOUR ATTENTION IS, THERE YOU ARE," a plan was set into motion that would focus the attention of Humanity on the Divine Mother and invoke the Light of Divine Love into South America.

Five hundred years ago Beloved Mother Mary volunteered to project Her luminous Presence into the hearts and minds of people in Mexico and throughout South America. The Divine Intent of this plan was to awaken within Humanity the remembrance of our Mother God by focusing their attention on the Being Who was most recently associated with representing the Divine Mother in Her embodiment as the Mother of Jesus.

When Juan Diego received the vision of the "Virgin of Guadalupe" and shared his apparition with the World, the people in Mexico and South America began opening their hearts once again to the Divine Love of our Mother God. This created an open door through which the Divine Plan could be expanded.

At approximately the same time, the Mayan civilization in South America also began to perceive the moment at hand. Quetzalcoatl, revered by the ancient Maya as the Lord of the Dawn, declared that there would be a 500-year period of healing on the Planet that would culminate in the full awakening of Humanity.

To the Maya, Quetzalcoatl represented a force of Cosmic Intelligence that is the Enlightenment that soars through the spinal column to awaken the Crown Chakra. He represents the unification of the duality of the Divine Masculine and the Divine Feminine, which brings the state of Enlightenment into manifestation.

Even though the ancient prophecies of Mesoamerica foretold of the coming of an Age of Light, it was clear that the 500-year period of healing would be a time of darkness and exteme tribulation on Earth.

In Europe the call for assistance from the Heavenly Realms was being felt as well. The Divinity within the Heart Flames of people throughout Europe began to long for freedom from oppression. At that time, Christopher Columbus and several of his cohorts responded to their inner heart promptings and embarked on a mission that was being Divinely guided.

I know there is a lot of "bad press" about Christopher Columbus and his mission because of the atrocities perpetrated on the indigenous people of the Americas with the coming of the Europeans. There is no doubt that, as has happened time and time again throughout history, our human egos messed the plan up horrendously. That does not change, however, the original Divine Intent which is still waiting patiently to be brought into form.

The Divine Intent of Christopher Columbus' mission was to establish an archetype in the outer world that would be the initial impulse of a "New World." This New World was to eventually evolve into the harmony and balance of the New Heaven and the New Earth.

It was not by chance that Christopher Columbus' flotilla was magnetized first into the area of the Caribbean Islands. Pulsating in that area is the largest portal of the Violet Flame of Freedom on the Planet. As Christopher Columbus and his companions entered this portal of Freedom, the Violet Flame of Freedom was anchored in their Heart Centers. When they came to the North American continent, the Flame of Freedom was given to the American Indians as a sacred trust. This fulfilled an ancient prophecy of the Indians. They knew that they had been chosen to be the stewards of the Earth to prepare the sacred land mass of North America for a race of God Conscious souls.

AMERICA is an anagram for the "I AM" RACE. This race was to be comprised of ALL races, ALL religions, ALL creeds, ALL cultures, ALL nationalities living together in equality, harmony, freedom, mutual respect and reverence for all life, one nation, the family of Humanity, under God, with liberty, justice, abundance, happiness and FREEDOM for all.

In spite of the antics and treachery of our human egos, our founding fathers still tapped the intent of the Divine Plan effectively enough to express our goals accurately in our sacred documents, original declarations and the Constitution. This Divine Plan is now waiting in dormancy to be resurrected into its full Divine Potential.

When the Company of Heaven saw how the Divine Intent of the "New World" was being distorted by our human egos, They knew that Humanity needed to clearly see what would occur if we did not take advantage of our 500-year Period of Grace and change our course of direction. A man in France responded to the need of the hour and offered to communicate to Humanity the vision of the path we were choosing to follow. Thus, did Nostradamus transcribe his Divinely inspired vision of the holocaust Humanity would experience **if** we did not heed the warning and change the course of our direction.

Even with all of these plans in motion, our Father-Mother God did not believe we would be able to get our heads above the veil of human miscreation effectively enough to transmute the effects of the "fall" in time for the Cosmic Inbreath. So, once again They invoked assistance from the Universe.

This time Cosmic and Ascended Beings from Octaves of Perfection throughout Infinity responded to our God Parent's Heart Call and asked for permission to embody on

Earth. Occasionally, throughout the history of the Earth, an evolved Being of this magnitude would be allowed to embody on Earth for a specific reason. We have recorded their existence as our great Adepts, Initiates, Buddhas and Avatars. However, Cosmic Law has never allowed them to embody on Earth en masse.

Our God Parents had some concerns about this plan because these Beings of Light had never experienced anything like the negativity occurring on Earth, and they would be subject to the Laws of Earth just like any other incarnating soul. That meant they would have the Band of Forgetfulness, and they would not remember who they were or why they were here until they lifted up in consciousness and "awakened."

After what happened to the evolving Humanity on Earth with the coming of the laggards, our God Parents wanted to be exceptionally cautious. The difference with this situation, however, is that the Beings of Light volunteering to embody on Earth had already completed their lessons of co-creation in other Systems of Worlds, and they had attained their Ascension in the Light. The Humanity of Earth had not reached that level of self-mastery when the laggards came to Earth.

Our God Parents agreed to allow a few of these highly evolved Beings to embody at a time to see how effective they could be once they were buried in the quagmire of human miscreation on Earth. The hope was that since these Beings of Light were not tied to the Karmic liabilities on Earth and since they were recently connected with the Realms of Perfection, they would have a far better chance of "awakening," even in the midst of the adversity, than would the Humanity of Earth who had been immersed in the effluvia for aeons of time.

The Divine Intent was for these Illumined Ones to embody on Earth as **normal Human Beings**. It was imperative that they not be distinguished in any way from the rest of the people evolving on Earth. There was to be no separation or obvious skills that would create suspicion. They would embody into mainstream Humanity and live conventional lives. Their success would be dependent on their anonymity. After all, the experiment that took place during the time referred to in Greek Mythology had failed miserably. This time it was going to be different.

At the beginning of our 500-year Period of Grace, the Beings of Light were allowed to embody a few at a time and inconspicuously live their lives, eventually "awakening" to the Truth of their God Reality, and fulfilling their Divine Mission of being open portals through which the Light of God could once again reach the Earth.

To the amazement and the joy of the entire Company of Heaven, this experiment succeeded beyond the greatest expectations of everyone involved. Due to the overwhelming success of the experiment, our Father-Mother God issued a Divine Fiat to allow the process to be greatly accelerated during the last 100 years of our Period of Grace.

THE LAST 100 YEARS

In the late 1800s, a Cosmic Dispensation was granted to allow the Beings of Light from other Systems of Worlds to embody on Earth in unlimited numbers and to allow the Spiritual Hierarchy serving the Earth from the Realms of Perfection to *"come through the veil to meet us halfway."*

It is impossible for us to comprehend with our finite minds how this has accelerated our evolutionary process and our awakening on Earth, but it is for this reason alone that all of the prophecies of old declared that *"In the latter days, the transformation will take place in the twinkling of an eye."*

Since the Spiritual Hierarchy has come through the veil to meet us halfway, Sacred Knowledge has been pouring forth from the Realms of Truth. Several Mystery Schools have appeared on the screen of life, and the Age of Knowledge, as expressed through Technology, Science, Medicine, Communications, Transportation, Education, Agriculture and Architecture, has flourished.

The tremendous influx of illumined souls has caused a population explosion that looks, from outer appearances, to be causing a great deal of stress on the Planet. But, I promise you, this illusion is temporary. This plan would never have been implemented if it was going to cause more harm than good.

We are now reaching the culmination of our 500-year Period of Grace, and I would like to elaborate about what is happening during this Cosmic Moment on Earth.

The Illumined Beings from other Systems of Worlds have volunteered to incarnate into every single walk of life on Earth. Their numbers are in the millions now, and they have agreed to embody into lives that would reach into the depths of human suffering. They are abiding in every corner of the Globe. These Beings are adept in the Universal Laws, and they know at Inner Levels, *"As 'I Am' lifted up, all life is lifted up with me."*

Because of the tremendous influx of God's Light that has been pouring into the Planet over the last several years, these illumined souls are beginning to awaken and remember who they are and why they are here. As they awaken and remember who they are, they clearly understand that the effectiveness of their Divine Mission is DEPENDENT on their ANONYMITY. It is imperative that they be mainstream and normal, living lives that blend into the environments in which they have chosen to embody. They are living lives that reflect all of the blessings and challenges of the Earthly experience so that as they pass through the transformation process and create Heaven on Earth in their personal, tangible lives, the rest of Humanity will know, *"if that normal person can do it, so can I."*

As these illumined souls awaken, they remember that they have come to Earth in an act of selfless service and

Divine Love. They realize the awesome privilege it is to be able to serve in this incredible moment on Earth, and they have a sense of humility and gratitude about their service. There is never a trace of superiority or *"holier than thou"* associated with their service, and there is no ego or self-aggrandizement. These Beings know they are here to empower Humanity to reach our full potential and soar into our true God Reality, and they clearly see that *"the greatest honor is to be the servant of all."*

The great majority of these illumined souls have embodied through the normal process of birth, but on very rare occasions, a Being of Light may enter the physical plane of experience as a full-grown adult. These Beings are called "walk-ins." This rare process involves two souls. One soul has agreed prior to embodiment to come into the physical plane through the normal birth process and prepare the four lower bodies the second soul will use when it is time for him/her to begin his/her mission on Earth. The second soul is the "walk-in." This is a very advanced soul who would not benefit by having to go through the infant and childhood stages of growth prior to beginning his/her mission.

The soul who is preparing the vehicles for the Being of Light knows through his/her God Presence the service s/he is providing, and s/he understands that there will be a time when the transfer of souls will take place. At that moment, s/he will go into the higher schools of learning, and the advanced Being will enter the bodies s/he has prepared.

In order to make the release easier, the transfer usually takes place during a critical moment when the first soul is near death, either through an illness or a near-death experience. When all is in readiness, the God Self of the first soul severs the Silver Cord and withdraws the Spark of Divinity in the Heart Flame. Instantly the second soul's God Self anchors the Spark of Divinity and the Silver Cord in the Heart Flame of the prepared vehicle.

It usually takes the advanced soul a while to integrate

into the body. The incoming soul has all of the brain consciousness of the first soul, so the incoming soul has all of the knowledge and memories stored in the brain structure. The advanced soul still has the Band of Forgetfulness, so it may be a while before s/he begins to remember who s/he is and why s/he is here.

I really want to stress again how very rare this process is and reiterate that if these advanced souls discussed the fact that they were "walk-ins" to other people, it would cause a sense of oddity and separation that would render their service ineffective. These highly evolved Beings of Light clearly understand that fact, and they would not communicate that they are "walk-ins" to anyone.

The reason it is so very important for us to clearly understand what is occurring on Earth at the present time is because this moment is critical to the fulfillment of the overall Divine Plan, and we are extremely vulnerable to the negative influences of our lower human egos and the forces of imbalance in the psychic-astral plane. Consequently, this dimension of deception is doing everything it can to trick us into giving our power away.

It is whispering "sweet nothings" in people's ears and stroking their egos by telling them they are more illumined or more evolved than the rest of Humanity. This information is designed to separate, confuse and discredit the awakening souls on Earth.

HEAR THESE WORDS!!!

Of all of the knowledge and Wisdom of the Ages, there is not a single TRUTH that is more important for you to know at this moment on Earth than this...

YOU are a Child of God!!! There is not another soul in all of Creation that is loved *more* than YOU are by our Father-Mother God. This is true regardless of who you are or where you are from or what your mission is on Earth. This is true regardless of how far you have fallen or how high you have soared.

YOU have a unique golden thread to weave into the Tapestry of the Divine Plan now unfolding on Earth, and YOUR thread is *just as significant* and *just as critical* as every other soul's thead who is evolving here.

YOU are valuable and desperately needed. God has chosen YOU to be on Earth at this time to fulfill a portion of the glorious Divine Plan. God has chosen YOU to express some beautiful manifestation as YOU release the unique perfume and music of YOUR Being to bless all life.

YOU have a fragrance and tone that is unlike any other ever released by an evolving lifestream on this precious Planet.

YOU have something sacred blazing in YOUR soul that has never been known by another, some beautiful gift of life which YOUR God Presence alone can externalize.

This is the moment YOU have been preparing for; this is the time when YOU will join with the collective Heart of Humanity and love this sweet Earth and all Her life FREE!!!

Feel these words as they resonate in your Heart Flame. Know their TRUTH for YOURSELF *and* for *every other Human Being on Earth.*

Feel the Light of God within you expanding and expanding as you begin to experience the REALIZATION OF YOUR OWN DIVINITY ONCE AGAIN!!!

CHAPTER
FIVE

THE FINAL 15 YEARS
OF GRACE

By *1980* enough souls had awakened on Earth to implement the final phase of the new Divine Plan. This plan is extremely complex and multifaceted, as well as multidimensional. What I am sharing are just a *few* of the highlights. It is important to understand that Lightworkers around the World have been working daily and hourly accomplishing incredible things to bring us to this Cosmic Moment. Every facet of the Divine Plan is critical to the whole, and no one's service is any more important than anyone else's.

The God Self of EVERY man, woman and child evolving on Earth has participated in these activities of Light, whether their outer mind or their human ego was aware of it or not. As you read about what happened on the specific dates mentioned, you will often remember something very significant that occurred in your life at that time. Our God Self always guides us to our right and perfect place even if we don't consciously understand why. Our Divine Plan is often being fulfilled in *spite* of ourselves rather than *because* of ourselves. In most instances, the most important thing we can do to fulfill our Mission is just to listen to the inner promptings of our heart, then get out of the way, and *"let go and let God."*

THE NEW DIVINE PLAN

On *June 21, 1980*, during the *Summer Solstice*, the vibration of the Earth had at last been accelerated through the conscious invocations of Lightworkers around the World to a frequency that could sustain the *First Ray of God's First Cause of Perfection and Divine Will.*

This sacred and holy Light was projected into the Divine Momentum pulsating in the center of the Earth. It poured from the Heart of God into the Unified Chalice of the collective consciousness of all Humanity and flowed through our Heart Flames into the Sun of Even Pressure in the center of Mother Earth where It was permanently anchored.

This Divine Light from the Heart of our Father God created a matrix that would eventually hold the Divine Blueprint for the New Earth and all life evolving upon Her.

The Light built in intensity and power for several months, and when It reached a crescendo on *October 29, 1980*, our Mother God projected the *Flame of the Immaculate Concept* on a Ray of Divine Love into the matrix of God's First Cause of Perfection and Divine Will in the center of the Earth. This activated the Divine Blueprint for the New Earth and sealed this Forcefield of Light in the essence of Divine Love.

From that day forward, the Flame of the Immaculate Concept has fed and nurtured the Divine Blueprint for the New Earth in all Her glory.

It's difficult for us to really grasp the magnitude of that activity of Light, but during that Cosmic Moment, the Divine Blueprint pulsating in the core of purity in every electron evolving on Earth was activated. *That means that everything that conflicts with the Divine Blueprint of the New Earth is being pushed to the surface to be healed and transmuted back into Light.* That is causing some extreme imbalances on Earth, and from outer appearances it seems as if the problems on Earth are getting worse. Actually, the things that are being brought to our attention through the media are being revealed to us so that we can invoke the Light of God into the persons, places, conditions and things involved and transmute the cause, core, effect, record and memory of the negativity back into Light. This phenomenon occurring on Earth is why the Bible and other Holy Books referred to this time as *"the time of screaming and the gnashing of teeth."*

I know this experience is extremely intense, but fortunately, it's going to be fairly short lived considering the millions of years we have spent creating this mess.

Invoke the Violet Flame of Forgiveness and the Pink Flame of Divine Love perpetually into every negative experience on Earth, and hang in there! It's going to be well worth our efforts.

HEALING THE TEAR
IN MOTHER EARTH'S ETHERIC BODY

After the Divine Blueprint for the New Earth was securely anchored in the Sun of Even Pressure, we were finally able to invoke the frequency of Healing that was necessary in order to heal the tear in Mother Earth's Etheric Body.

Our Father-Mother God and the entire Company of Heaven invoked the assistance of awakening Lightworkers who were abiding in the area of the sacred mountain called Picacho Peak near Tucson, Arizona, in the United States of America.

The Lightworkers were told that the Earth, at long last, was vibrating at a frequency that could withstand a Higher Order of Healing. They were told that a new Octave of Healing beyond anything the Earth had ever experienced was available, but it had to be magnetized from the Core of Creation by embodied Lightworkers in order to be permanently sustained on Earth.

This sacred Healing Light is known throughout the Universe as the Flame of Healing through the Power of Limitless Transmutation. It is an Emerald Green Flame with an Amethyst (Violet) radiance.

The Lightworkers consecrated their life energies to this Divine Mission, and for several years they daily and hourly invoked the sacred Healing substance into the atmosphere of Earth.

In *1983*, they were told by the Company of Heaven that the Flame of Healing through the Power of Limitless Trans-

mutation had been magnetized into the physical plane effectively enough to be permanently anchored into the Crystal
Grid System.

In a Divine Ceremony of Light, this sacred Flame was
anchored through the open Portal in Tucson, Arizona, into
the center of the Earth and expanded through the Crystal Grid
System to every particle of life evolving on the Planet.

This Healing Light accelerated Humanity's Awakening.
Little by little, the Light increased on Earth until there were
finally enough awakened souls to invoke the amount of Light
that was necessary to heal the tear in the Etheric Body of
Mother Earth that had occurred during the sinking of Lemuria.

A plan was set into motion through the unified efforts of
both Heaven and Earth that would free the souls trapped in the
Etheric tear and heal Mother Earth's Etheric wound.

Utilizing the full benefits of the Spiritual energies that
flood the Earth in the Spring during the *Vernal Equinox* and
the *celebration of Resurrection*, the entire Company of
Heaven joined in consciousness with the Divine Presence of
every man, woman and child evolving on Earth. On *Good
Friday, April 1,1983*, as one unified force, we created an
open portal through which the Flame of Healing through the
Power of Limitless Transmutation poured into the tear in
Mother Earth's Etheric Body and *permanently healed it*.
The hundreds of thousands of souls who had been trapped in
a state of limbo for thousands of years were at long last freed.
These souls were then magnetized into the Forcefield of the
Violet Transmuting Flame and the Ascension Flame that
pulsates through Picacho Peak. These Flames which had
been prepared for thousands of years by their fellow
Lemurians who had embodied as American Indians blazed in,
through and around every precious soul.   As the souls
entered the sacred Flames, they were bathed in the soothing
essence of Divine Forgiveness and Freedom. This activity of
Light built in momentum, and on the third day, *April 3, 1983*,
as the first Rays of the Sun began to bathe the Earth with the

Resurrection Flame and people throughout the Planet turned their attention to the *celebration of Easter and the Resurrection of the Christ*, the trapped souls entered the Ascension Vortex at Picacho Peak and joyously Ascended into the next phase of their evolutionary process. As the Ascension Flame blazed in, through and around them, they Ascended into the Inner Schools of Learning that would prepare them to move forward in the Light.

The healing of the tear in the Etheric Body of Mother Earth and the freeing of the hundreds of thousands of trapped Lemurian souls allowed the Earth to accelerate in energy, vibration and consciousness in a way that we had not previously experienced.

A WINDOW OF OPPORTUNITY

With the acceleration of consciousness and vibration taking place on the Planet, our Father-Mother God and the Spiritual Hierarchy serving the Earth evaluated the need of the hour. We were moving out of the forcefield of Pisces, and the Sixth Solar Aspect of Deity that had been building in momentum for the past 2000 years was beginning to recede. We were just beginning to experience the fringe of the forcefield of Aquarius and the Seventh Solar Aspect of Deity. This lull of activity opened a window of opportunity that provided the Company of Heaven with a unique open door into Humanity's consciousness. Not since the "fall" has our consciousness been more receptive to the influx of Divine Ideas pouring forth from the Mind of God.

The Company of Heaven recognized that the most important thing for us to remember during this critical moment on Earth is that we are truly Sons and Daughters of God with the ability to be the Hands of God in the physical world of form. They flooded our consciousness with the Divine Knowledge and Wisdom of our ability to co-create a new reality on Earth. We were immersed in the realization that *there is not a force on the Planet that is more powerful than Humanity's unified consciousness focused in Divine Love and one-pointed in our mission.*

This awareness blazed across the face of the Earth and triggered in our Heart Flames an inner knowing of the urgency of the hour and the need for all of us to join in consciousness to redeem this Earth and restore this Blessed Planet to Her original Divine Intent...Freedom's Holy Star...Heaven on Earth.

In every conceivable corner of the Globe, people gathered together in groups to meditate, visualize, pray and focus their attention on the healing of this sweet Earth. Global activities were organized to create a sense of Oneness within the hearts and minds of the Family of Humanity, awakening within us the inner knowing that *ALL life is interrelated, and what affects ANY part of life on Earth affects the whole of Creat*ion.

The inner work exploded on the screen of life in *1986*. During that incredible year, the outer world manifestation of Global Light Work revealed to all who *"had eyes to see"* that the tides of change were in full motion, and there was no turning back.

1986 was heralded by the Company of Heaven as a Year of Transformation and signaled the initial impulse of **the return of God's Will to Earth.**

The United Nations declared *1986* as the *"International Year of Peace"* for the first time in history.

A group of Lightworkers organized what was called *"The Great Peace March: A Step Forward."* On *March 1, 1986*, several thousand people began a march that took them from Los Angeles, California, to Washington, D.C. In an attitude of World Peace and Reverence for all Life, they began a journey to end the threat of nuclear war and to sustain Eternal Peace. Along the path they were met by thousands of fellow citizens who joined the march into Washington, D.C. Through the media, this Peace March was brought to the attention of millions and millions of people throughout the World. Every nation and world leader was given the message: *The People of the World long for and demand that Peace be a priority in ALL governmental affairs. The People of the World will lead their leaders.*

Another major activity that began in *1986* is called *"Peace the 21st."* "Peace the 21st" is a simple, but tremendously effective concept. We know now that there is power in thought, and we know the collective thought of Humanity is the most powerful force on Earth. The objective of this activity is to harness this force in the interest of World Peace. "Peace the 21st" is designed to gather together those who desire to participate in forming a massive and united "Thought-Image of Peace."

This Global effort for World Peace involves an ever-expanding number of participants. It is a concept based on Universal Love and cooperation. The activity is planned to take maximum advantage of the increased flow of Light on the *Equinoxes* and the *Solstices*. *On the 21st day of the months of March, June, September and December of EACH YEAR, from 7:00 to 7:30 P.M. local time*, lifestreams throughout the World join together in consciousness to energize a Thought-Image of Peace. We can participate in any way that is comfortable for us: prayer, meditation, affirmations, music, etc. Whatever we decide to do should be positive and constructive, emphasizing the theme of peace and love. It is the focused effort of a multitude of people joining their thought-images together at the same time for the same purpose that is important.

The next major activity to invoke worldwide attention in *1986* was *"Hands Across America."* The goal of this project was to raise funds to combat hunger and homelessness in America. But, by far, the greatest benefit was the joining together of literally millions of people around the World in a consciousness of Humanity reaching out to help each other. Through this activity, millions of people joined hands forming a human chain, which created a unified forcefield that extended from the Statue of Liberty across America to the Pacific Ocean in Los Angeles, California. Imagine the power of millions of people joining hands across this sacred nation singing "America the Beautiful" and "We Are The World."

Another very special activity in *1986* was called *"The First Earth Run."* The Vision of this activity was to create an event of such magnitude that all Humanity would be compelled to action by the image it generated...a great thread of Light passed around the World by tens of thousands of people, linking us and showing us that we are together, igniting a Global sense of hope for the future.

The First Earth Run began *at the United Nations* in *September, 1986*, and culminated back *at the United Nations* in *December, 1986*, after a torch of Light was carried around the World.

The goals of The First Earth Run were accomplished in a five-phase program:

1. The torch relay itself, in which a flame serving as a visual symbol of cooperation connected nation to nation as runners from every country were invited to relay the fire around the Earth. Through the ever-changing and endless landscapes of our Earth—the torch was held aloft, passed from Russian runner to American runner to Chinese runner to Jamaican runner to Kenyan runner—a cooperative effort against time, distance and physical limitations.

2. At local ceremonies along the route, people received the flame from torch-bearing runners onto candles, torches and miner's lamps, then spread it from individual to individual, community to community. By the end of the Earth Run, a substantial portion of the people of the World had received the flame onto their own personal candles. To culminate the event, the torch was brought into the United Nations at which point people worldwide relit their candles.

3. Concert celebrations took place in major cities along the route to coincide with the arrival of the flame.

4. The *"Olympics of Cooperation"* encouraged communities along the route to acknowledge projects which demonstrated the spirit of cooperation. These projects were publicly recognized, and medals and financial grants were awarded to those which most effectively met local challenges.

5. There was endorsement of, and participation in, the Earth Run by the world leaders along the route and also in the opening and closing ceremonies at the United Nations. Their support was an example to people everywhere that Global cooperation and cross-cultural understanding is achievable.

Hundreds of thousands of people lined the streets of New York City as the torch wound its way to the United Nations to complete its epic around-the-World journey. The Secretary General of the United Nations and the world leaders gathered to receive the energy of millions now embodied in the torch and passed it from one to another.

The final major activity that took place in *1986* was the project called *"The World Healing Meditation."* This activity called for 500-million people around the World to consent to the healing and harmonizing of this Planet and all forms of life hereon. The activity is described in detail in a book titled *THE PLANETARY COMMISSION* by John Randolph Price. The book states:

"Our objective is obvious. Why not reverse the polarity of the forcefield of negativity and achieve a critical mass of positive energy? Why not ensure a chain reaction of self-sustaining good in and around and through this Planet? It can be done, and it will be! We will achieve a critical mass of Spiritual Consciousness to heal the sense of separation and restore Humankind to Godkind. The fact that we can do it has already been demonstrated in the laboratory. One of the major universities on the west coast took the figure of fifty-million people with a Spiritual Consciousness and through the use of computers and measurements of Spiritual energy radiation, made this observation: if these men and women would meditate simultaneously and release their energy into the Earth's magnetic field, the entire vibration of the Planet would begin to change, and if there were no massive and dedicated counter forces to offset the benefits, war, poverty, crime, hunger and disease and other problems of Humanity would be eliminated.

"In order to reach the critical mass of Spiritual Consciousness, our objective by December 1986, is to have 500- million people on Earth simply consenting to a healing of this Planet with no less than fifty-million meditating at the same time on *December 31, 1986*, 12:00 Noon Greenwich Time."

People added to this Light in any way that was comfortable for them with Love, Music, Prayer, Guided Visualization, Meditation, Positive Thought or any other constructive release of positive energy.

Hundreds of millions of people participated in this God Victorious activity, and organizations throughout the World are continuing to energize this glorious thoughtform on the last day of each month. Then, on *December 31st of each year, at 12:00 Noon Greenwich Mean Time*, the Lightworkers of the World join together to amplify this powerful "World Healing Meditation" and project it onto the physical plane of Earth.

World Healing Meditation

In the beginning—In the beginning God. In the beginning God created Heaven and Earth. And God said "Let there be Light," and there was Light.

*Now is the time of the **new** beginning. I Am a co-creator with God, and it is a New Heaven that comes as the Good Will of God is expressed on Earth through me. It is the Kingdom of Light, Love, Peace and Understanding, and I Am doing my part to reveal Its Reality.*

I begin with me. I Am a Living Soul, and the Spirit of God dwells in me, as me. I and the Father-Mother God are one, and all that God has is mine. In Truth, I Am the Christ of God.

What is true for me is true of everyone, for God is all and all is God. I see only the Spirit of God in every soul, and to every man, woman and child on Earth I say: I love you, for you are me. You are my Holy Self.

I now open my heart and let the pure essence of Unconditional Love pour out. I see it as a Golden Light radiating from the center of my Being, and I feel Its Divine Vibration in and through me, above and below me.

I Am one with the Light. I Am filled with the Light. I Am illumined by the Light. I Am the Light of the World.

With purpose of mind, I send forth the Light. I let the radiance go before me to join the other Lights. I know this is happening all over the World at this very moment. I see the merging Lights. There is now one Light. We are the Light of the World.

The one Light of Love, Peace and Understanding is moving and expanding as it flows across the face of the Earth, touching and illuminating every soul trapped in the shadow of the illusion, and where there was darkness, there is now the Light of Reality.

And the radiance grows, permeating, saturating every form of life. There is only the vibration of one perfect life now. All the kingdoms of the Earth respond, and the Planet is alive with Light and Love.

There is total Oneness, and in this Oneness we speak the Word. Let the sense of separation be dissolved. Let Humankind now be returned to Godkind.

Let Peace come forth in every mind. Let love flow forth from every heart. Let Forgiveness reign in every soul. Let Understanding be the common bond.

And now, from the Light of the World, the One Presence and Power of the Universe responds. The Activity of God is Healing and Harmonizing Planet Earth. Omnipotence is made manifest.

I Am seeing the salvation of the Planet before my very eyes as all false beliefs and error patterns are dissolved. The sense of separation is no more; the healing has taken place, and the World is restored to sanity.

This is the beginning of Peace on Earth and Good Will toward all, as love flows forth from every heart, forgiveness reigns in every soul, and all hearts and minds are one in perfect understanding.

It is done. And so it is. I Am.

For further information contact:John Randolph Price, PO Box 1768, Boerne Texas 78006-6768.

HARMONIC CONVERGENCE

Harmonic Convergence was a moment that changed the course of history on Earth for all Eternity. With all of the knowledge and wisdom that we can possibly absorb pouring into our consciousness about that event, we're barely scratching the surface of the magnitude of what actually transpired during that Activity of Light.

Prophesies of old told of the coming of that unparalleled event. The Hopi, Lakota Sioux and various other American Indian tribes, as well as the ancient Maya civilizations, foretold of a moment in time, *August 15-17, 1987*, in which a Spiritual Initiation of Illumination would create a quantum leap in consciousness for all Humanity that would tip the scales into a new paradigm of planetary healing and transformation.

Many incredible things took place during that Cosmic Moment on Earth. Harmonic Convergence was truly a multi-faceted, multidimensional symphony of complex Divine Plans.

During that sacred time, the Feminine Ray of Divine Love was amplified through the Divine Momentum of the Eternal Sun of Even Pressure that pulsates in the center of the Earth. This sacred Light of our Mother God expanded into the Divine Blueprint blazing in the core of purity in every electron of precious life energy on Earth. The Divine Mother Principle sounded a Cosmic Tone that invoked the Divine Love Nature within every particle of life to come forth and reclaim Its position on Earth as a fundamental building block of all Creation. The response from every particle of life created a forcefield of our Mother God's Love that expanded into an atmosphere of safety that allowed THE HOLY CHRIST SELVES BLAZING WITHIN OUR HEARTS TO BE CALLED FORTH TO ONCE AGAIN TAKE FULL DOMINION OF OUR FOUR LOWER BODIES.

This was the initial impulse of the Second Coming of the Christ through Humanity, and it paved the way for the eventual return of our *full grown* Holy Christ Selves.

The ***Second Coming of the Christ*** is a multifaceted, multidimensional activity of Light. One day we will experience the radiant, luminous Presence of Beloved Jesus in all of His splendor and glory pulsating in the Heavens with the entire Company of Heaven. But, that will only occur *after* Humanity has returned to our original Divine Intent, and our individual Holy Christ Selves have burst the bonds of our human egos and taken full dominion of our four lower bodies. At that time, we will each become, once again, the Christ grown to full stature. Only then will we rise in energy, vibration and consciousness to a frequency that will allow us to tangibly see the luminous Presence of Beloved Jesus and the all-encompassing Presence of the Christ.

As the Divinity within the Heart Center of every man, woman and child on Earth expanded the maximum that Cosmic Law would allow during Harmonic Convergence, the vibratory rate of our four lower bodies accelerated in frequency. We were each raised up closer to the Heart of our Mighty "I Am" Presence. Our Seven-fold Planetary Spines were lifted up in frequency closer to the Twelve-fold Solar Spines of our **Solar** Christ Presences, and our ability to channel Light into the physical plane of Earth was greatly increased. This opened the door for the next step of the Divine Plan for Harmonic Convergence.

I'm going to review a little of the background that brought us to this point so we can really grasp the significance of this glorious event.

Remember that prior to the fall of Humanity, at the time when the Earth and all life evolving upon Her were fulfilling the Divine Intent of this particular school of learning, the

Crystal Grid System of the Earth was fully empowered with the Seven Planetary Aspects of Deity, the "Seven Rays" of our Third Dimensional experience. This Divine Light from the Heart of our Father-Mother God flowed into the Third Dimension through the axis (spine) of the Earth and was projected through the Chakras of Mother Earth located along the axis into the Crystal Grid System. This system is identical to and serves the same purpose as the electrical meridians in our own bodies that we refer to in the science of acupuncture. After all, Mother Earth is a living, breathing organism just as we are, and the Light that flows through our Silver Cord into our Chakras and Meridians and sustains our life in the physical plane is just as necessary in order to sustain the life of Mother Earth.

Before the "fall," this Divine Light blazed through the Crystal Grid System into every electron of precious life energy evolving here and perpetually maintained a state of Limitless Physical Perfection on Earth.

Due to circumstances of the "fall," we started using our creative faculties of thought and feeling to create thoughtforms and patterns of discord, and as we fell deeper into the quagmire of our own human miscreations, we created a tragedy of unfathomable proportions.

So, in one compassionate, but tragic, Divine Fiat the Light was withdrawn from the Crystal Grid System until It was barely strong enough to sustain the body of Mother Earth.

Needless to say, this tragedy catapulted us deeper and deeper into the blackness of separation from God, creating overwhelming depression and despair.

Our negativity drew the attention of other dark forces in the Universe. The collective force of darkness in the Cosmos known as "cosmic evil" saw that the Light on Earth had been withdrawn to the point where Humanity could barely sustain brain consciousness. It also saw that our Crystal Grid System had been deactivated. Knowing our frailty, this negative entity seized the opportunity to claim this Planet *as a school of learning for the forces of darkness.* Words cannot express the effect this horrendous event has had on Humanity. From that grievous moment, the Earth has not only been dealing with the weight of Humanity's fallen energies, but the forces of "cosmic evil," in all their treachery, have been sending their darkest souls here to learn to perpetuate "evil." This is why the world religions have stated that Satan has claimed the Earth, and it is one of the main reasons our progress has been so incredibly slow.

Even though illumined souls have incarnated throughout the Ages, there were not enough in embodiment at any one time to reverse the "magnetic grid" system of the forces of imbalance.

But, even in the face of this sinister interference, our Father-Mother God never abandoned us. The Company of Heaven never stopped striving to create new plans to free us from the oppressive grip of this sinister force so that we could burst the "magnetic grid" system and reactivate the Crystal Grid System safely, once and for all.

And precious Lightworkers, WE FINALLY DID IT!!!

With all that occurred during Harmonic Convergence, nothing was more crucial to our Ascension in the Light than the GOD VICTORIOUS REACTIVATION OF THE CRYSTAL GRID SYSTEM. Hundreds of thousands of people were Divinely Directed to go to Sacred Sites all over the Earth. People from every single walk of life responded to their inner Heart Call and allowed their bodies to be the Hands of God in the physical plane. Each person gathered at a power point or acupuncture point along the Crystal Grid Meridians of Beloved Mother Earth and offered the Cup of their Consciousness as a Holy Grail through which the Light of God poured Victoriously, reactivating the Crystal Grid System.

The following is a message from Gautama Buddha that was given to Humanity during the *Full Moon* celebration of the *Wesak Festival* on *May 13, 1987*.

Radiation and Message of
Gautama Buddha
through Group Avatar

"As you have been apprised, 1987 is a Cosmic Moment in the history of this Dear Planet, and I, who currently hold the office of Planetary Logos to Earth, now invoke your assistance.   Because of the need of the hour, on Easter Morn the Karmic Board of the Spiritual Hierarchy was drawn into special session under the direction of Cosmic Law. This August Body of Beings has been drawing before It, in their finer bodies, every man, woman and child evolving on Earth. As each soul passes before the Karmic Board, a special request is made by these Beings of Limitless Mercy and Compassion.   Each soul is being asked to now fulfill the vows s/he took in the Heart of God before this embodiment to assist in this urgent hour. Each soul is being asked to release the good stored in their Causal Body to draw forth every gift, every talent, every skill or ability that has ever been developed in any exist- ence, in any dimension, and release it now for the benefit of all life on Earth. The Karmic Board is asking each soul to recommit and dedicate him/herself to increased service to the Light.

"The Light of God, expended by those of Us in the Heavenly Realms, is always used with great reverence and efficiency.   Therefore, you must realize for this unique activity to be taking place, the need for Humanity's assis- tance is extremely critical. The Cosmic push to bring the Masculine and Feminine Polarities of Deity into perfect balance is being accelerated. When these dual aspects of God, Divine Will (Masculine) and Divine Love (Feminine),

are in perfect HARMONY (Balance), the birth of Divine Illumination (the Son/Daughter or the Christ) will occur. The Christing of this Planet and all Her life is the next step in moving Earth forward into the Fourth/Fifth Dimensional Octaves of Perfection where She will manifest Her Divine Heritage of Heaven on Earth.

*"This sacred night, during the Full Moon of the Wesak Festival, a Cosmic dispensation has been granted by the Karmic Board. Due to the increased commitment of Humanity and the petitions and promises of greater service, Cosmic Law has allowed a Galactic Being from the Great Silence to enter the atmosphere of Earth. This majestic Being's name resonates with celestial tones; the closest sound of your Third Dimensional frequency is **LuElla**. She has come with Her Regal Court for an unprecedented service to life. She has come to EMPOWER and ACTIVATE the Crystal System of Earth. The full-gathered momentum of Her radiant Light, drawn from the very Heart of God, is the glittering essence of Emerald Green and Sapphire Blue Crystal. The qualities and frequencies of this scintillating substance are beyond anything experienced in the physical plane of Earth. She has taken Her strategic position in the Etheric Realms above the sacred focus of Diamond Head in Hawaii within the Temple of Harmony and Eternal Peace that pulsates there.*

"Diamond Head is a sacred mountain that resonates with Eternal Truth. At the inception of this Planet, prior to the fall of Humanity, Diamond Head was a tremendous vortex of power on the continent of Lemuria or Mu. Through this vortex, the Crystal Grid System of the Planet was empowered with perfect Harmony and the totality of God's Perfection. After the fall of man, when Humanity became so immersed in Her own miscreation, the Crystal System, amplifying all in Its radiance including Humanity's discord, became a source of pain and destruction for Humanity. As a merciful activity to life, the power was

withdrawn from the Crystals until there was a mere flicker of Its original glory. Now, through the invocations and assistance of the Humanity of Earth and through your rededication to service, the Crystal System of Earth shall again, one day soon, express all Its potential and power.

*"The name of this sacred mountain, Diamond Head, signifies the Crystal Purity of the CROWN CHAKRA OF GOD ILLUMINATION for the Planet Earth. On **August 17, 1987**, when the Masculine and Feminine Polarities of Deity are brought into Perfect Harmony, the Light of God Illumination will pour into this forcefield at Diamond Head and will be anchored into the Crown Chakra of the Planet through the Heart Flames of the Lightworkers gathered there. This Light will then be transmitted through the Crystal Grid System of the Planet to every other Chakra Center and anchored into the Earth through the Lightworkers gathered at sacred sites all over the World.*

"Beloved LuElla has directed Her Court to traverse this Planet, and a member of Her Legions has descended into EVERY power point on the Planet. From this sacred night until the influx of God Illumination on August 17, 1987, these selfless Servants of God will prepare each power point to receive the maximum frequency of Light. After the Light of Illumination has been transmitted throughout the Planet on August 17th, Beloved LuElla will begin magnetizing from the Heart of God the Electronic Light Substance that will empower the Crystal System and eventually restore It to Its original glory and service. This Light will be transmitted into the Crystals ever so gently, so this power will ONLY bless life as this Planet is raised into the Octaves of Perfection.

"We in Heaven's Realms ask you each one to be the PEACE COMMANDING PRESENCE you are capable of being. Invoke the Violet Transmuting Flame as never before into every electron of Humanity's misqualified energy, past or present, known or unknown. The more

Humanity's misqualified energy has been transmuted into Light, the more power God can transmit into the Crystal System and the greater the forward movement of the Planet and all life into Light.

"Dear Ones, go within, and ask your God Presence how you can be the most powerful force of God's Light at this Cosmic Moment. We in Heaven's Realms await your assistance. Remember always: You are the open door which no one can shut."

"I AM", "I AM", "I AM"
(End of Gautama Buddha's message)

At the time of Harmonic Convergence, the Beings of Light from the Realms of Truth said the Crystal Grid activation would be a *25-year process*. They said the first five years would be the most tumultuous. Then, we would go through a quantum paradigm shift that would catapult us into the frequencies of Light. They said from that time on our Victorious Ascension into the Light would be Assured.

We were asked by the Spiritual Hierarchy to organize a Global activity at Diamond Head in Hawaii to draw Lightworkers from all over the World who would form a Chalice of Light that would create an open portal through which the Light of God would flow into Diamond Head to reactivate the Crystal Grid System. We organized the first World Congress On Illumination at that time.*

On *August 17, 1987*, the Crystal Grid System was activated the maximum allowed by Cosmic Law, and to the elation of the entire Company of Heaven, the magnetic grid

---

* *The Company of Heaven asked that this be an annual event, held usually on the anniversary of Harmonic Convergence, to provide a vehicle through which the Light of God will pour to implement the unfolding Divine Plans of Planetary Transformation being orchestrated by the Divine cooperation of the Company of Heaven and Humanity.*

of "cosmic evil" was shattered.

This allowed the Divine Plan on Earth to soar.

Consistently, throughout this book, I state that during a particular activity of Light, *something* took place *"the maximum that Cosmic Law would allow."* That means that our Father-Mother God monitored the situation and allowed Divine Light to flow into the activity the maximum that we could endure at that precise moment. It means we were brought to the brink of our tolerance level, and the healing or the purification or the acceleration of Light occurred to the fullest extent without causing harm to us physically.

God isn't going to blast us into oblivion with Light and kill us in our healing process. Our Father-Mother God are, however, healing us the maximum we can *safely* withstand.

Ascension Into
The Twelve Solar Aspects of Deity

During Harmonic Convergence, the Earth and all Her life Ascended a quantum leap in energy, vibration and consciousness. By *1988* we had Ascended in frequency sufficiently to allow our Father-Mother God to activate the Solar Axis of the Earth. This allowed the Twelve Solar Aspects of Deity to begin flowing through the Crystal Grid System, and it also allowed each of us to receive higher frequencies of Divine Light through our Twelve-fold Solar Spines, which were now blending with and radiating through our Seven-fold Planetary Spines. This prepared us for another major shift of consciousness.

EARTH LINK-88

The activity referred to as *Earth Link-88* took place on *February 13, 1988*. The interim stage between Harmonic Convergence and Earth Link-88 represented a turning point in the direction of World endeavor.

The critical mass, which balanced the Feminine Polarity of Divine Love in Causal Levels of Creation during Harmonic Convergence, was externalized as an explosion of Light on *February 13, 1988*. People everywhere experienced a resonant shift in their level of conscious awareness. The collective ceiling of human thought opened to the Spiritual Realms allowing a stream of Light to enter each person's sphere of consciousness, illuminating a vision of higher Truth. Light was released from the heart of every created atom, from within every living cell in the human body, restructuring the genetic blueprint with higher life codes. Humanity literally awakened as our "I Am" Consciousness was brought into alignment with the Universal "I Am" that "I Am".

The catalyst for this extraordinary event was the exact planetary conjunction of Saturn and Uranus. The metal Uranium is named after Uranus and Saturn, and it represents the principle of density of form. Together they combine to create the "critical mass" explosion of Light demonstrated by nuclear physics. Unlike the situation that occurred in *1945* after the previous conjunction of these two Planets in Taurus, the sign of the release of secret power from the depths of the Earth which resulted in the destruction of Nagasaki and Hiroshima, the *1988* conjunction occurred in the final degree of Sagittarius, the sign of the Spiritual goals and aspirations of Humanity. This potent release of Light illuminated a new direction and purpose for the Spiritual development of Humanity. A powerful new mental structure was revealed that revolutionized our concept of ourselves and the Universe. This revelation changed the foundation of science, religion and philosophy and created a new World vision that CHANGED THE COURSE OF HISTORY FOREVER!

STAR ∗ LINK 88

On *June 11, 1988*, through an event called *Star ∗ Link 88*, a dimensional doorway was opened, and the Seventh Angelic Vortex was activated in the City of Angels. Through this Cosmic event, the *"Seventh Angel began to sound."* (St. John's Revelation, Chapter 10.)

At the Los Angeles Coliseum in California, several thousand people gathered together for a six-hour event of unified consciousness in which a reactivation and initiation into multidimensional awareness occurred. This blessed Planet and ALL Her life were lifted up yet another octave in vibration, closer to the Heart of our Father-Mother God.

Through the activity of Star∗Link 88, the Angelic Host, from frequencies beyond anything we have ever experienced, entered the atmosphere of Earth. These mighty Seraphim from the Fifth Dimension assisted God in activating the pre-encoded memories that were implanted deep within Humanity's cellular patterns aeons ago. These patterns reflect our Divine Plan, our purpose and reason for being. Humanity experienced a great soaring and awakening as we began to remember our Divine Heritage.

A Cosmic Fiat was issued by God, and **1988 was decreed the year in which Humanity would step through the doorway into multidimensional awareness.** This was accomplished as the frequencies of the Third Dimension were accelerated closer to the higher Octaves of the Fourth Dimension.

During that sacred moment in time, *Humanity was empowered with the increased presence of the Angelic Host* which is, even now, continually entering the Earth through the Seventh Angelic Vortex. The influx of Angels has formed an expanded bridge between Heaven and Earth— spirit and matter. Over this Sacred Bridge, the Rays of Light of the Twelve-fold Aspect of Deity from the Great Central Sun perpetually bathe the Earth.

The Light from these Ministering Angels is increasing daily and hourly, *awakening Humanity to the tangible presence of the Angelic Kingdom.* Moment-to-moment the activated, pre-encoded memories of our purpose and reason for being, now reflecting at a physical, cellular level within our four lower bodies, are reverberating through our creative centers of thought and feeling. As these currents of wisdom and illumination pass through our conscious minds, our God Presence sends a Ray of Light to help us grasp each Divine Idea. Knowledge of our Divine Plan is now available to us as never before. We need only reach up and tap the Octaves of Illumined Truth.

Lightworkers throughout the Planet continue to awaken daily, and the body of world servers referred to as Group Avatar is ever-growing.

In a rhythmic momentum on the anniversaries of the World Healing Meditation, Harmonic Convergence, the Solstices and Equinoxes, the New Moons and the Full Moons, Lunar and Solar Eclipses and the Sacred Holidays of *ALL* World Religions, Lightworkers join together in Global activities invoking the Light through prayer and meditation to assist this sweet Earth in Her process of rebirth.

CRYSTAL LIGHTLINK

In *1989*, some events of tremendous magnitude also took place. On *April 16, 1989*, an activity called *Crystal Lightlink* occurred. During that unique moment, God projected into the Crystal Grid System of Earth unparalleled frequencies of the Twelve-fold Aspect of Deity. This activity of Light accelerated the awakening taking place on the Planet. The energies initiated a massive Planetary and Galactic activation and reprogramming of all crystalline structures existing within the Earth, the Etheric plane and within our human bodies. This activation raised the consciousness of every soul and every living cell on Earth.

The activated Crystal System on Earth was then able to function at a higher level of effectiveness, transmitting energy like our crystal radio sets of the past or our quartz crystal watches. This event greatly enhanced our telecommunication system with interdimensional, interstellar, intergalactic energies and with higher intelligences.

SEALING THE DOOR
WHERE EVIL DWELLS

With the Crystal Grid Activation accelerated, other doors of opportunity began to open. In *May of 1989*, awakened Humanity began to perceive more clearly our ability to work in conscious cooperation with the Spiritual Hierarchy Who serve Earth from the Realms of Illumined Truth. This awareness enabled a plan to be implemented from On High to purge the Earth of the pockets of negativity that existed in various vortexes on the Planet. These negative vortexes had been created over aeons of time and were sustained and energized by "cosmic evil" and the fallen souls known as the laggards. God won't give one electron of energy to sustain the negativity on Earth, so the only way this realm exists is by living parasitically off of our misqualified energy, our negative thoughts and feelings. For centuries, these vortexes of accumulated negativity would serve as batteries to energize the forces of imbalance.

On *May 8, 1989*, through the unified efforts of Heaven and Earth, Violet Lightning from the Heart of God was projected into the pockets of negativity throughout the entire Planet. These bolts of Violet Transmuting Lightning shattered and transmuted the vortexes of negativity, thus sealing them in a forcefield of mercy, compassion and forgiveness. This accomplished effectively the goal of Heaven, and *"the door where evil dwells"* was sealed.

Needless to say, this created havoc in the psychic-astral realm where the forces of imbalance abide. Pandemonium ensued, and these forces became rampant on Earth, looking for other avenues to feed and energize their lifeforms. This was the time we were warned about in St. John's Revelations when he stated that in the latter days, *"Satan would be loosed on the Earth."*

As the forces of imbalance ranted and flailed through the astral plane, they focused their unified efforts into a budding activity of Light that was building in momentum in the most oppressed area of the Planet.

The Spiritual Hierarchy asked Lightworkers to gather within the forcefield of the Flame of Freedom and Liberty that is anchored through the statue of the Goddess of Freedom blazing from the top of the Capitol Rotunda in Washington D.C. On *June 4th and 5th, 1989*, the Flame of Freedom and Liberty was projected from the Lightworkers in Washington, D.C. into the Lightworkers gathering their forces at Tiananmen Square in China. As those selfless souls in China held tenaciously to the Divine Flame of Freedom and Liberty, the Light of God was secured through their Heart Flames into the Center of the Earth permanently. Tragically, their numbers were few compared to the number of people who were willing to be the pawns of the enraged forces of imbalance, and the selfess servants of God were mowed down in a heinous act of murder. Their efforts were not in vain, however, and they are true martyrs in every sense of the word. The Flame of Freedom and Liberty that they secured is now blazing through all of China and is transmuting the resistance of the dark forces there. This Light of our Father-Mother God is softening the hearts of all associated with the governments of China, and in the not-too-distant future, we will see the God Victorious Accomplishment of the sacrifice of these precious souls.

After the tragedy of Tiananmen Square, the Lightworkers

realized the need for superhuman assitance to help calm the rage of the forces of imbalance. A plea for assistance was made to the Heart of our Father-Mother God. An evaluation by God determined that we had progressed sufficiently to allow additional grants of energy to help during this Earthly crisis. An unprecedented incident occurred. For the first time ever in any System of Worlds, the Karmic Board of the Spiritual Hierarchy allowed the suspension of Humanity's Free Will for eleven days. From *June 10, 1989, to the Summer Solstice on June 21, 1989,* our Free Will was held in abeyance. During that time, every man, woman and child evolving on Earth, whether in or out of embodiment, in any dimension or state of consciousness, was drawn into the sacred Temple that pulsates in the inner planes above Mt. Lemmon in Tucson, Arizona. It is the Temple of Reverence for all Life. This occurred in our finer bodies while we slept at night. No one had a choice in this matter because of the suspension of our Free Will.

Once we were in the Temple, we were brought before the Karmic Board, and we were shown a panorama of our past. We were clearly shown the error of our ways, the fall, the choices we have made and the end result of these choices. We recognized our responsibility in the Earthly condition, and we were shown what we have volunteered to do to correct our course and assist in the process of planetary transformation. We were then commanded by the Karmic Board to look into the mirror of life and perceive our own Divinity. Not one soul, regardless of the state of depravity it had fallen to, was allowed to deny the Divinity of its true reality. This reflection of our Divinity was seared in to the intelligence of our four lower bodies and will gradually filter into our conscious minds.

After we were commanded to perceive our Divinity, the Karmic Board revealed to each of us what would be necessary for us to do in order to transmute our past transgressions of the Law of Love and Harmony, so that we can move forward in the Light with the rest of our Solar System.

For eleven days, during the time our Free Will was suspended, we were bathed in the Divine Quality of Eternal Peace while we contemplated our options. As we slept, we were drawn into the Temple of Eternal Peace that pulsates in the Etheric Realms over Venezuela in South America. During Sunrise on the morning of the **Summer Solstice, June 21, 1989,** the Cosmic Tone sounded, and each soul was summoned before the Karmic Board to make a choice as to whether or not they were willing to do what was necessary to transmute their past and move into the Light. Through that choice, Free Will was re-established.

This sacred event clearly reflects the magnitude of God's mercy and compassion. Many souls had been denying their Divinity for thousands of lifetimes. Now with the reflection of our Divinity seared into the consciousness of our four lower bodies, it will be impossible for us to continue to reject it for any length of time. Even though this activity took place at inner levels and, consequently, most people don't consciously remember it, it doesn't matter. The event is powerfully recorded in our etheric records and memories and will surface when we need it the most.

The Spiritual Hierarchy said this unprecedented experiment was successful beyond their greatest hope. More souls than they dreamed possible chose to fulfill their obligations in the remaining time and move into the Light. This means that our work is being accelerated, and our energy is returning faster than ever to be loved free. But, remember, we are never going to be given anything we can't handle, and we have powerful tools to help us.

The souls that chose not to move forward into the Light at that time did so because they decided it was too much work to do what was necessary to clear their past in the short time allotted. They will gradually be taken off the Planet through the natural process of death, and when the time is right, they will be reborn in another System of Worlds, again in Third

Dimensional frequencies. They will be reduced to approximately the caveman state of consciousness, so they won't immediately destroy themselves with technology. The caveman state of consciousness is what Humanity fell to during the creation of the veil of negativity that blinded us from our own Divinity. It is not the consciousness of the first impulse of the Human species on Earth as our scientists have professed.

Many people will wonder whether or not they have chosen to move forward into the Light. I want to assure you that if you have any conscious desire to do so at all, you definitely made the positive choice before the Karmic Board. Now we need to focus on our commitments and be about the business of our Father-Mother God, transmuting our past and healing this sweet Earth.

This Divine Activity of Light sent a calming unguent of Eternal Peace through the chaos of the psychic-astral realm. The forces of imbalance were greatly diminished as many chose to move into the Light. The remaining fallen souls, however, continued, in panic, to perpetuate their mischief.

NOSTRADAMAS' PREDICTED HOLOCAUST
NUCLEAR WAR IS AVERTED!!!

With the God Victorious success of the miraculous events just described, the Company of Heaven and awakened Lightworkers believed that the consciousness of Humanity was now ready for the implementation of a Divine Plan that would *permanently avert* the holocaust nuclear war that was looming on the horizon.

The critical first step of any phase of planetary healing has to begin with the ***FIRST INITIATION***, which is the initiation into the ***REVERENCE FOR ALL LIFE.***

It is only by remembering the interrelatedness and the Oneness of ALL life that Humanity can transcend the limited and fear-based prejudice, ignorance, hate and treachery of our fallen human egos. Only then can we set aside our selfishness, greed, abuse of power, corruption, self-obsessed compulsions and depraved behavior patterns long enough to recognize the Divinity in every other particle of life and lift into the frequencies of Divine Love, Eternal Peace, Tolerance, Limitless Abundance, Cooperation and Joy.

An open portal for the Divine Quality of Reverence for All Life pulsates within the forcefield of the Grand Teton Mountains in Wyoming in the United States of America.

We were asked by the Company of Heaven to hold the Third Annual World Congress On Illumination within the forcefield of the Grand Tetons during the *Autumn Equinox on September 23, 1989.* We scheduled that event a year in advance and invoked the God Presences of all Humanity to prepare the consciousness of every evolving soul to respond according to their individual Divine Plans.

We knew that in order for enough Light to pour into the Planet to Initiate the *critical mass* of Humanity into the consciousness of Reverence for All Life, our Father-Mother God needed a tremendous chalice formed by the collective consciousness of Humanity. The Universal Law is *WHERE YOUR ATTENTION IS, THERE YOU ARE*, and it was critical that we draw the focus of the masses' attention into the forcefield at the Grand Tetons. The Company of Heaven told us to be at peace, that all was in Divine Order, and our Victory was assured.

A couple of weeks before the World Congress On Illumination, the two super powers decided to hold a Peace Summit at Jackson Hole, Wyoming, during the week of the Autumn Equinox. Secretary of State James Baker of the United States of America and Secretary of State Edward Shevardnadze of the Soviet Union were drawn into the forcefield of Reverence for All Life. For the entire World Congress On Illumination, the attention of the World was focused on the Grand Tetons. Everytime anyone watched a television news report of the Peace Summit or read a newspaper article about the progress of the meetings taking place or listened to a radio report or thought about the event, their energies were woven into the unified Chalice of Humanity's consciousness that was forming within the portal of Reverence for All Life.

On the dawn of the Autumn Equinox, the Cosmic Tone rang through the Universe, and the greatest influx of the Reverence for ALL Life ever manifested in the world of form poured into the Chalice of Humanity's unified consciousness. This Divine Light of Oneness literally shook the ethers and broke down the barriers of separation. A few weeks later, on *November 9, 1989*, we experienced the most dramatic physical manifestation of that fact as we witnessed the *crumbling of the Berlin Wall*.

Throughout November and December the effects were amplified and the dictators of communism began to fall, and the knell tolled the beginning of the end of communism.

Time Warp

With the completion of the anchoring of the frequencies of Oneness and Reverence for All Life, we moved forward into a new opportunity. During *November 17, 18 and 19, 1989*, a unique phenomenon occurred known as *Time Warp*.

Time Warp was described by the Spiritual Hierarchy as a dimensional collapsing of time in which the Earth shifted into an accelerated time flow in preparation for moving into the higher *timeless* frequencies of the Fifth Dimension. This shift actually accelerated our time frequency from a 24-hour day to a 22-hour day. Since that event, time has collapsed even further and accelerated into a 18-to 20-hour day. All frequency impulses increased simultaneously, including our clocks, so from outer appearances, it looks like we still have a 24-hour day, but I don't know a single person who hasn't commented about how fast time is flying by.

The collapsing of time has greatly accelerated the transformation occurring on Earth, and as a result, Humanity's negative behavior patterns are being pushed to the surface at an increased pace. The challenges of daily living are being exacerbated, and from outer appearances, it looks like things are actually getting worse, but...NOTHING COULD BE FURTHER FROM THE TRUTH.

A New Decade of Opportunity

As we moved into *1990*, we were more aligned in opportunity and hope than ever before, and the Company of Heaven heralded the *1990s* as *a decade of permanent, tangible change.*

On *January 11, 1990*, a group of Lightworkers who had participated in the World Congress On Illumination and been physically within the forcefield of Reverence for All Life during the *Autumn Equinox in 1989*, volunteered to travel to *Ireland and the Soviet Union* to create a *Highway of Light* from the portal of Reverence for all Life into these two strife-filled areas. These Highways of Light allowed the Spiritual Hierarchy to project Divine Light directly from the portal at the Tetons into Ireland and the Soviet Union to accelerate the healing process taking place in these two countries.

On *April 22, 1990*, we celebrated the 20th anniversary of *Earth Day*, and hundreds of millions of people throughout the Globe consented to the healing of Beloved Mother Earth as they awakened to their true purpose and reason for being.

During the *Summer Solstice on June 21, 1990*, the Light of God poured through the consciousness of awakening Humanity and *activated the Divine Blueprint* of the delicate plan that was unfolding to PERMANENTLY avert the holocaust nuclear war that Nostradamas had predicted.

Since we have gotten into the pattern of using pain as our motivator, we usually need a crisis in order for us to open our hearts and minds effectively enough to invoke the full power of God's Light through our thoughts, words, actions and feelings.

On *August 2, 1990*, we witnessed the crisis we needed to motivate us into action. As Iraq invaded Kuwait, awakened Lightworkers in every corner of the Globe began invoking Light into the area. The Light of God blazed in, through and around all of the areas of strife in the Middle East and *transmuted the archetype of the masculine abuse of power and the archetype of the suppression and oppression of women* that was formed in that area aeons ago at the time of the coming of the laggards. It was these two distorted archetypes that have perpetuated the animosity and hatred in the Middle East for millenia. And, it was these two distorted archetypes that were destined to trigger the holocaust nuclear war.

Anchoring of the Highway of Light

The next phase of the plan involved opening a tremendous portal of Light that would allow the Light pouring from the Heart of our Father-Mother God to reach the Earth unimpeded by the interference of the psychic-astral plane.

The Company of Heaven asked us to hold the Fourth Annual World Congress On Illumination on the anniversary of Harmonic Convergence within the forcefield of the Flame of Healing through the Power of Limitless Transmutation in Tucson, Arizona. This forcefield is the Emerald Green Pillar of Light with an Amethyst radiance that has been building in power and momentum on Earth since it was first anchored in *1983*. The Flame of Healing has created a forcefield through the psychic-astral plane that has held the forces of imbalance in abeyance. As the Lightworkers gathered within this vortex of Light in *August 1990*, our God Parents from all of the Solar Dimensions of our Suns— Elohae and Eloha, Alpha and Omega and Helios and Vesta—

projected a tremendous shaft of Light through that vortex into the Center of the Earth. This formed a *Highway of Light* through the psychic-astral plane that extends several thousand miles in every direction. This incredible open portal is allowing Fourth Dimensional frequencies of the Twelve Solar Aspects of Deity to bathe the Planet as never before. This Divine Light intensified our planetary forcefield of protection and security and amplified the Light flowing through the Crystal Grid System, thus embracing the Earth and all Her life in an invincible forcefield of protection.

Transmuting the Abuse of Power

After the Highway of Light was opened, Lightworkers were asked by the Company of Heaven to gather in Sun River, Oregon within the "ring of fire" that connects the volcanic activity of the Pacific Ocean. Since the original abuse of the Masculine Power Center of the throat and the suppression of the Feminine Heart Center of Divine Love began on the continent of Lemuria, the plan was for the Lightworkers to *invoke the Violet Fire and transmute the etheric records and memories of the abuse of power and suppression of Divine Love* back through the Ages of time to the original fall, thus dissipating the negativity subconsciously feeding the situation in the Middle East.

On *October 17, 1990*, the Legions of Light from the entire forcefield of the New Age of Aquarius and the Seventh Solar Aspect of Deity descended into the atmosphere of Earth to assist in magnetizing, from the Heart of God, the Violet Light of Forgiveness, Mercy, Compassion, Transmutation and Freedom. This Light was projected into the mass consciousness of Humanity transmuting, cause, core, effect, record and memory, the misqualified thoughts, feelings and actions reflecting our abuse of power and suppression of love back to the beginning of time. Once again the effects of this purification surpassed even the greatest expectations of Heaven. The subconscious blocks and resistance to balancing our use of power with Divine Love were thrown asunder. The energy that had sustained the misqualified use of power through aggression, dominance, corruption, manipulation and deception was dissipated. This created a sense of vulnerability and fear that shattered the confidence of those in the World who were wielding their power without the Grace of Divine Love.

On *January 16, 1991*, the physical purging that was prophesied for the Holy Land began. On the eve of Desert Storm, during the *New Moon Solar Eclipse*, the Light of God poured into the Middle East, embracing the area in a forcefield of protection. Legions of Angels took their strategic positions, standing shoulder-to-shoulder as they surrounded the war zone. Through the invocation and prayers of Lightworkers throughout the Planet and the cooperative efforts of Heaven and Earth, the DIVINE LIGHT OF ETERNAL PEACE poured through the newly opened Highway of Light in unprecedented frequencies and purged the Middle East. Through this act of Divine Intervention, *the holocaust nuclear war that Nostradamus predicted was averted.*

The purging of the imbalance of power occurred with a miraculously minimal loss of life. Every soul is precious, and any loss of life is tragic, but compared to what might have happened, we have the right to be very, very grateful.

ANCHORING THE IMMACULATE HEART
FOR DIVINE GOVERNMENT

With the etheric records and memories of the abuse of power transmuted, our Father-Mother God could now, more effectively, reflect the balance of Divine Love from the Realms of Cause into the physical plane of Earth. Upon the completion of Desert Storn, it was determined by the Heavenly Realms that the need of the hour on Earth was to re-establish the correct pattern for Divine Government. Needless to say, the governments of the World are responsible for most effectively demonstrating the abuse of power, and in order for Humanity to successfully shift from a consciousness of dominance and aggression to a consciousness of reverence for all life, major changes in our behavior patterns are necessary. Through the window of opportunity that is now open in this dawning New Age, our Father-Mother God began projecting Spiritual currents of energy into the atmosphere of Earth to implement a new plan to re-establish the pattern for Divine Government.

Contrary to some of the misinformation and the disinformation now being bandied about, Divine Government does not mean "one World government" or a "new World Order." Divine Government means each nation governing itself according to the highest good of its people with mutual respect and tolerance for every other government. It involves every nation working together for the highest good of all.

America was to be the home of the "I Am" Race. This was to be a race of God conscious souls aligned with their true God reality, their "I Am" Presences. The "I Am" Race was to be a race comprised of every race, nationality, religion, creed, doctrine and philosophy. They were to be self-governed souls working together in perfect harmony and balance, always embracing their use of power with Divine Love and expressing respect, love and tolerance for each other as they valued all life on Earth.

People throughout the World have responded to their heart's call for freedom. They have flocked to America as they sought freedom from oppression, domination, aggression, violence and freedom to worship as their inner Beings directed. Our founding fathers came, and they listened to their inner voice as the *Constitution of the United States of America* and the *Bill of Rights* and the *Declaration of Independence* were formulated to align with the Divine Plan for America.

But, unfortunately, as has happened time and again throughout the Earth's evolution, the Divine Plan went awry. Human egos, greed, selfishness and the abuse of power took control, and the rest is a sad documentation of history.

Now, with the peril of Desert Storm behind us, with the awakening taking place on Earth and with the victory of the opening of the Highway of Light, once again we were called from "above" to anchor the Divine Blueprint for this country in order to correct Her course and restore her Global mission.

The first step in forming the physical vehicle for any manifest form is the creation of the Immaculate Heart. This is the chalice that will hold the Divine Spark—the Immortal Victorious Three-fold Flame that contains within Its frequencies the Immaculate Concept of the particular Divine Plan involved.

Since Washington, D.C. is considered the seat of government in this country, it was necessary that the Immaculate Heart of Divine Government be anchored within that forcefield.

During the time frame known as the mystical month of May, some very sacred activities take place at inner levels. The Heavenly Temple known as the Temple of the Immaculate Heart is opened, and all lifestreams preparing to embody in the next twelve-month cycle are drawn into that Temple. There the purest electrons from their Beings are magnetized to form their Immaculate Heart, the chalice that will hold their Three-fold Flame while they are in embodiment on Earth.

In *May of 1991*, the purest electrons available were drawn to form the forcefield of the *Immaculate Heart of Divine Government* which was to be anchored in Washington, D.C. Again, the focused attention of Humanity was critical in order to create a unified chalice of consciousness through which the Immaculate Heart would manifest into the physical plane. Remember, where your attention is, there you are. In order to draw the attention of the World to Washington, D.C. and to focus the attention of Humanity on the *heart*, Divine Intervention was necessary. The first weekend in May the Light of God poured into the Planet, and the *appearance* of a slight irregular heartbeat temporarily manifested in President George Bush. That event drew the attention of the entire World to the *"heart of government"* in *Washington, D.C.* in a way that nothing else could have. During the Global focus of Humanity's attention, a Chalice of Light was formed through our collective consciousness. This assured God's Victory, and the Immaculate Heart of Divine Government was anchored in perfect order.

THE CONJUNCTION OF
VENUS, MARS AND JUPITER

All was in readiness for the next step of the Divine Plan of Planetary Transformation. This step involved a Cosmic push to *expand the Feminine Polarity of Divine Love from the inner Realms of Cause into the physical plane of Earth.* It occurred through a rare astronomical alignment.

In *June 1991*, the almost perfect conjunction of the Planets Venus, Mars and Jupiter occurred. Spiritually, Venus always represents the Feminine Polarity of Divine Love. Mars represents the Masculine Polarity of Power, and Jupiter represents expansion and growth of Spiritual Freedom. All of these Planets were joined together in the forcefield of the constellation of Leo on *June 18, 1991*, which was the moment of closest conjunction. Leo represents Solar energy at its most powerful frequency and love in its purest form. The radiance from this Celestial formation bathed the Earth for several days in the balanced expansion of Divine Power and Divine Love, the pure essence of our Father-Mother God. This influx of Divine Light assisted in breaking down the patterns of resistance that were keeping people stuck in dysfunctional, oppressive situations which were preventing them from releasing and letting go of people, places, conditions or things that were no longer serving their highest good.

The crystallized negativity that had kept Humanity stuck in old, destructive patterns and belief systems of the past began to melt and take on a more fluid and flexible form. The molecules of discord began to float apart, and the balanced Light of our Father-Mother God began to interpenetrate the dense forcefields of negativity for the first time in aeons. This prepared us for the next incredible event.

ASCENDING
THROUGH THE DOORWAY OF 11:11

There were various interpretations of what the *"Doorway of the 11:11"* really meant, but the clearest information described the unique Doorway of Opportunity that opened from the *Solar Eclipse on July 11, 1991*, until we completed our Ascension off of the Wheel of Karma and onto our correct Spiral of Evolution on *January 11, 1992*. This involved a six-month period of incredible acceleration of energy and vibration and a quantum shift in consciousness on the Planet. This is what the Spiritual Hierarchy was referring to when we were told at Harmonic Convergence in *1987* that our Ascension in consciousness would be a 25-year process. They said the first five years would be the most tumultuous; *then we would go through a quantum paradigm shift*, and for the next 20 years, we would gradually ascend into greater frequencies of Light until the Crystal Grid System was returned to its full manifest potential by *January 11, 2012.*

Solar Eclipse of July 11, 1991

With the Light of God blazing in, through and around every electron of precious life energy evolving on Earth after the rare conjunction of Venus, Mars and Jupiter in June, we were ready for a Cosmic experiment. This was an experiment that had never before been tried in any system of Worlds, an experiment of unprecedented Divine Intervention. Every illumined soul in embodiment on Earth was prepared at inner levels while they slept at night to assist in the plan. We were each given an opportunity to renew our vows to love free all life on Earth, which we had taken within the Heart of God before this embodiment. A new level of purpose and commitment began to filter into our conscious minds, and we began to intuitively perceive the urgency of the hour.

To assist in the experiment, Legions of Cosmic and Ascended Beings from the entire Universe descended into the atmosphere of Earth and took Their strategic positions around the Planet to embrace this sweet Earth in an invincible forcefield of love and protection.

The experiment took place during a rare celestial alignment of the Sun, the Moon and the Earth, a unique *Solar Eclipse* that was held in the momentum of the *New Moon*. Solar Eclipses occur fairly regularly on the Planet, approximately two per year, but the eclipse that took place on *July 11, 1991*, was rare in that it was a full seven minutes of total alignment. This unusual Solar Eclipse was held in the embrace of two *Full Moon Lunar Eclipses*, one on *June 26, 1991*, and one on *July 26, 1991.*

During the seven minutes of perfect alignment of the Solar Eclipse, all of the pressures of imbalance, discord and Karma were temporarily lifted from every cell, atom, electron and sub-atomic particle on the physical realm of Earth. During that Cosmic Moment, the only forces in action on the physical plane were the Fire Pillars of Love and Power of our Father-Mother God, blending in perfect balance, realigning the foundations of consciousness on Earth with Divinity. The central core of perfection that continues to beat within the heart of every electron of life existing on Earth was activated.

The Solar Impulse of our Father-Mother God arced out of the Great Central Sun entering the physical Plane of Earth completely unopposed and unimpeded. The power of *this sacred Light accelerated the core of perfection within EVERY atom.* This profoundly affected the substance of organic/cellular life on Earth, particularly in the DNA and RNA in which the blueprint for the Planet's Divine Plan is recorded. This substance contains the plan of absolute perfection on the physical realm.

During the moment of the Solar Eclipse, our God Parents released a Violet Ray of Freedom that was the perfect balance of the Masculine Polarity of Divine Power—Sapphire Blue and the Feminine Polarity of Divine Love—Pink. The Violet Ray of Freedom, which was able to enter the Earth for the very first time unimpeded by negativity, *TRANSMUTED INTO FOURTH DIMENSIONAL FREQUENCIES OF PERFECTION, 50 PERCENT OF ALL OF THE ENERGY THAT HAS EVER BEEN MISQUALIFIED ON EARTH.* The energy was transmuted mostly from unconscious and subconscious realms. This literally meant that 50 percent of every electron of precious life energy we had ever misqualified in any existence or dimension, both known and unknown, through the misuse of our creative faculties of thought and feeling, WAS GONE!!!

This negative energy had interpenetrated our Beings at a cellular level for aeons of time holding sway over our atomic vehicles. This is why disease and distress seem so prevalent in our human experience. With this purification, a realignment and rebalancing occurred at a deep atomic level. The Solar Healing of our God Parents profoundly affected the living cells of Humanity and the Nature Kingdom as well as the molecules, atoms, electrons and sub-atomic particles of all life within Earth's realms (animate and inanimate). This accelerated the physics, chemistry and biology of life on Earth closer to Fourth/Fifth Dimensional consciousness.

In simple words, this transmutation of negativity scientifically assured the Ascension of this Planet HERE and NOW! The effects of this cause allowed each of us to more quickly rediscover our own Divine Plans, free from ONE-HALF of the old baggage from our past.

The Solar Inbreath

With 50 percent of the mass Karma of Humanity and the other lifewaves on Earth transmuted, a door of opportunity opened during the Eclipse to allow even greater assistance from On High. The purification of 50 percent of our past *ensured* the inclusion of the physical realm of Earth in a *Solar Inbreath* that involved our entire Solar System. A Solar Inbreath is a multidimensional activity of Light in which our Father-Mother God breathe all life closer to Their own Divine Three-fold Flame. This activity aligns all of the Three-fold Flames that pulsate in any part of life. The Three-fold Flame at any point of evolution is the focal point of unity with the whole of Creation. Even though all parts of life evolve in different directions with different goals and different experiences, at certain points in each great Cosmic Cycle, all activity is suspended *for a Cosmic moment* to reconfirm that all life is ONE...and that this fundamental condition of the Universe remains primary and absolute. This is termed a Solar Inbreath.

The Solar Inbreath connotes a movement in toward the center. When we breathe, we breathe in toward our Heart Flame, and so do our God Parents. But this Solar Inbreath occurred not in the physical realm as measured by distance or time. Rather, it occurred in the Realms of Consciousness, where an alignment of all Three-fold Flames brought an accelerated magnetic cohesion amongst all the component parts. This reconfirmed that God's First Cause of Perfection for all life has complete dominion throughout the whole of Creation. This is symbolized in physical terms as if the

Planets are drawn closer to the Sun. What does occur for all Planets is a more perfect orbital pattern and accelerated core planetary vibration through the planetary Three-fold Flame. In the Earth's case, it also included a gentle, but sure, realigning of the planetary axis.

During the Solar Inbreath, the alignment of all Three-fold Flames was not just vertical (between the various realms and dimensions of this Universe) but also horizontal (within each realm and dimension). This is particularly true for the physical realm of Humanity. *A certain fundamental alignment of all Three-fold Flames within Humanity* was produced so the whole of Humanity, through its center, will rise into the Fourth/Fifth Dimension of Unconditional Divine Love. This opportunity ended all separateness permanently...not only of Earth and Humanity from the Divinity of the Universe, but it also ended the separation of Humanity from the influence of our own Three-fold Flame of Cosmic Balance and Healing. Remember, the Three-fold Flame at the center of every Human Being is the same Flame in the Central Sun.

At the moment of the Solar Eclipse, and sustained thereafter, the Three-fold Flame of every Human Being (in and out of embodiment) was fundamentally changed, completely aligned with and further empowered by the Three-fold Flame of Alpha and Omega from the Central Sun. This allowed each Three-fold Flame to function like the Sun Itself and begin an Inbreath of all the energies of the four lower vehicles of each individual into the Sun or Christ Self...gradually, but very assuredly, raising all the energy and vibration of that lifestream into Fourth/Fifth Dimensional Consciousness.

The Three-fold Flame was to be the source of all guidance and development of the Universe, including our own sphere of influence on Earth. In the history of Humanity's evolution, the source of guidance and authority shifted to the human ego, bringing about the present difficult and painful experiences now related to physical embodiment. However, there shall now be a fundamental shift back to the Three-fold Flame as the Source of all guidance and authority for Humanity's development. The Solar Eclipse/Inbreath was God's mark of this shift.

The Realigning of the Axis

Along with the Inbreath, *a gentle realignment of our planetary axis occurred during the Solar Eclipse.*
The axis around which an individual or Planet develops determines the realms of experience open to that Being. If an axis is tilted (out of alignment in consciousness more so than physically), access to other realms becomes difficult and oftentimes distorted, hence, Humanity's individual and collective difficulty in achieving higher consciousness and, unfortunately, the tendency toward opening to the distorted realms of psychic and astral chaos. We can see why the axis of Earth must be aligned with the Solar Axis. The Scepter of Power, which an axis represents, determines the orbit and how far a Being might reach out in his/her evolving God Consciousness. Every evolving individual, Planet or Sun, has a spine/axis around which it evolves, which determines its experience. The Cosmic Inbreath, at the moment of the *Solar Eclipse on July 11, 1991*, brought the greatest realignment of Earth's axis yet known, aligning Her with the perfect axis and Orbit of Consciousness She was always intended to have as an evolving Planet. This quickened Her core vibration, accelerating Humanity toward Christ Consciousness.

ACTIVATING THE BLUEPRINT
FOR DIVINE GOVERNMENT

With the Immaculate Heart for Divine Government in place and the God Victorious activities of the Solar Eclipse and Solar Inbreath complete, we were at last in a position to *activate the blueprint for Divine Government for the Planet.* The Spiritual Hierarchy asked us to arrange the Fifth Annual World Congress On Illumination on the anniversary of Harmonic Convergence in Washington, D.C. within the forcefield of the Immaculate Heart of Divine Government that had been anchored in *May 1991.*

All manifest form begins with a blueprint, and the anchoring of the Blueprint for Divine Government was imperative in order for the upward shift in Humanity's consciousness to be accomplished, as ordained by Cosmic Law.

On *August 18, 1991,* the Blueprint for Divine Government in all its glory was anchored into the receptive core of purity in every electron of physical matter. This affected the RNA-DNA patterning of all life. The perfected patterns, which form the matrix for the transformation of all governments, are now readily available.

The Divine Blueprint now activated in all governments will first reflect in the Realms of Cause. Then, we will begin seeing tangible proof of the shift in our everyday lives.

The blueprint contains within its patterns the frequencies of Divine Government, prosperity, peace, harmony, liberty, justice, happiness, joy, freedom and reverence for all life.

Within twelve hours after the Blueprint for Divine Government was anchored, the coup in the Soviet Union against Mikhail Gorbachev was attempted. This failed attempt struck the final blow to communism in the Soviet Union and established a momentum of democracy and freedom that no one will be able to stop.

ACTIVATING THE
AMETHYST CRYSTAL GRID SYSTEM

Through another activity of Light on *August 8, 1991,* the Beings of Light associated with the Seventh Solar Aspect of Deity *opened a portal of Light, a Stargate from the forcefield of Aquarius into the atmosphere of Earth in Giza, Egypt.* The Divine Intent of this Stargate was to allow the Violet Flame of Limitless Transmutation greater access into the Earth.

During the *Autumn Equinox on September 23, 1991*, an evaluation was made from On High to determine if any of Humanity's negativity was contaminating the rest of the Solar System by filtering out through the open Stargate in Egypt. To the relief and joy of the Heavenly Realms, it was not. Violet Fire Angels Who had been stationed in the auras of all Humanity were effectively assisting us in transmuting our daily misqualified energy, and the Lightworkers who invoked the Violet Fire to transmute the remaining mass Karma on Earth were also effectively keeping the negativity in check.

Lightworkers responded to the request of the Spiritual Hierarchy and gathered in the power point of the Crystal Amethyst Grid System in Thunder Bay, Canada. This is the forcefield of the largest amethyst mines in North America. As we reached up into the Realms of Illumined Truth, we were told by the Spiritual Hierarchy that a plan was in motion to amplify the activation of the Crystal Grid System and infuse the entire System with the full momentum of the Amethyst Violet Transmuting Flame.

On *September 30, 1991*, the Light of God poured through the unified cup created by all Lightworkers on the Planet (whether they were consciously aware of it or not) and entered the Amethyst Crystal Grid System in Thunder Bay, Canada. The Light was then transmitted through the entire Crystal Grid System on Earth, and this precious Violet Light was projected into every crystal, creating a Forcefield of Transmutation and Invincible Protection.

With mighty bolts of Violet Lightning, the other eleven

Stargates of Aquarius were opened in the following order:
1.   Giza, Egypt—The Lion's Gate
   (opened *August 8, 1991*)

The following opened *September 30, 1991*
2.   Thunder Bay, Canada
3.   Southwestern United States of America
4.   Cuba and the Caribbean Islands
5.   Brazil
6.   Sumatra—South Pacific
7.   New Zealand
8.   South Africa
9.   Beijing, China
10.   St. Petersburg, Soviet Union
11.   Arctic—North Pole
12.   Antarctica—South Pole

ASCENDING OFF THE WHEEL OF KARMA

With the Violet Flame blazing through the Stargates of Aquarius into the Crystal Grid System, our Father-Mother God and the Company of Heaven felt we were ready for the final preparation that would allow us to *Ascend off the Wheel of Karma and regain our path on the Spiral of Evolution.*

As the Seventh Solar Aspect of Deity from Aquarius flooded every particle of life, the God qualities of Forgiveness, Freedom, Mercy, Compassion, Transmutation, Victory, Liberty, Divine Justice and Opportunity penetrated into every electron of physical substance on Earth. This created a shift of vibration on the Planet that lifted us up enough to enable us to *form a bridge across the abyss from the Wheel of Karma to the Spiral of Evolution*.

The Divine Etheric Pattern for Earth has always remained in the correct orbit on the Spiral of Evolution even when Earth fell away. This Etheric pattern is a magnetic forcefield that has unsuccessfully been trying to draw the

Earth back into Her correct orbit for aeons of time. The Lightworkers gathered at Thunder Bay, and those who joined in consciousness from around the World, created a unified Divine Presence which expanded to engulf the entire Planet. The unified body of Lightworkers aligned with the axis of the Earth, and our spinal columns became one with that shaft of Light. Our Seven Planetary Chakras merged with the Seven Planetary Chakras aligned along the axis of the Planet, and as one breath, one heartbeat, one consciousness of Holy Spirit, we projected seven mighty shafts of Violet Light into the axis of the Divine Etheric Pattern of the New Earth pulsating in the correct orbit. This created a Bridge of Freedom that built in momentum for several days. Then, on *October 4, 1991*, an unparalleled influx of the Ascension Flame poured through the twelve open Stargates of Aquarius, and this sweet Earth Ascended in perfect safety over the Bridge of Freedom into Her correct spiral in preparation for Her passage through the doorway into the Fourth/Fifth Dimension.

The Ascension off the Wheel of Karma onto the Spiral of Evolution cleared the way for the completion of Earth's God Victorious Ascension through the Doorway of the 11:11.

On *January 11, 1992*, we completed our *Ascension through the "Doorway of the 11:11"* onto our correct position on the Spiral of Evolution. This was our initial impulse into the Fourth Dimension. This momentous activity of Light completed the shifting of Humanity into a frequency of Light beyond what the force of "cosmic evil" could access, and it accelerated the Crystal Grid System into a frequency far beyond the reach of "cosmic evil's" magnetic grid.

It looked as though, after being held hostage for millions of years by this sinister force, this sweet Earth was finally FREE! The Spiritual Hierarchy said that on *January 11th each year from 1992 to 2012*, a major influx of Light will pour into Earth to assist our progress.

Unfortunately, the force of "cosmic evil" did not give up easily, and it was functioning at such a frequency of pandemonium that it could not see it was being given an extremely merciful and compassionate opportunity to move into the Light. It thought it was being destroyed, and it was fighting tooth and nail for its survival.

When this negative force recognized that it could no longer trap us on the Wheel of Karma with its "magnetic grid," it began devising another plan to regain control of the Earth.

Since the pockets of negativity on Earth that "cosmic evil" had previously used to energize itself were sealed on *May 8, 1989*, that malevolent force knew that the ONLY possible way it could regain access to the Earth was by getting people in embodiment on Earth to be its pawns and tricking them into letting it use their bodies to access the physical plane.

"Cosmic evil" knew it was in trouble and that it was losing its school for the dark forces when the Crystal Grid System was reactivated during Harmonic Convergence in *1987*. At that time its "magnetic grid" that had held the Earth in opposition to the Light for millions of years was shattered. When the pockets of negativity in the Earth that energized this force were sealed in *1989*, "cosmic evil" immediately began creating a contingency plan to regain its grip on the Earth.

In *1989*, "cosmic evil" began communicating through the receptive consciousness of a few people on the Planet. It devised a plan of deception that allowed it to use the physical bodies of those people to reopen two of the pockets of negativity that had been sealed. These were vortexes in areas of the Planet that had sustained the dark forces for aeons of time; one was in Bolivia in South America and the other was in the area of Durbin in South Africa.

Once these vortexes were reopened, the souls who had been tricked into being the pawns for "cosmic evil" were used as transformers to sustain the pockets of negativity by channeling Humanity's accumulated discord into the vortexes to feed "cosmic evil" while it pursued its plan to reclaim the Earth.

After the incredible influx of Light that transmuted 50 percent of the negativity on Earth from unconscious and subconscious levels during the *July 11, 1991, Solar Eclipse*, "cosmic evil" became acutely aware that the next step of the Divine Plan would free the Earth from the Wheel of Karma and lift all life on Earth into a frequency of Light that was far beyond its reach. It knew it had to do something drastic or the Ascension of the Earth on *January 11, 1992*, would free Her and all life evolving upon Her from its negative influence forever.

"Cosmic evil" began weaving its plan of deception into the consciousness of Humanity by revealing its plan publicly through one of its channels on *January 4, 1992*, just a few days before we completed our Ascension off the Wheel of Karma onto the Spiral of Evolution. The entity specifically gave the information prior to the shift in hopes that at least some fragments of its plan would be carried into the new spiral so that it could build from there. It said that its name vibrates with the frequency of eleven (11) and that its "plan" would take eleven years. That was specifically designed to pass it through the 11:11 shift unnoticed.

The force of "cosmic evil," in unison with the psychic-astral plane, has been tricking our recalcitrant human egos for literally millions of years. Just about everywhere we look, we can see misinformation and disinformation, obvious ploys and tricks, lies and scams that are designed to distract people from their Divine Plan. This interference is certainly not new. But, this time, because of the urgency of the hour and the desperation of this force of imbalance, its plan reached a new level of treachery.

"Cosmic evil" realized that the Light was increasing on Earth at warp speed due to the awakening of powerful

Lightworkers. It was also aware of the immeasurable wisdom and knowledge these Beings had brought with them from their experiences in the Realms of Perfection and in other Systems of Worlds. It knew that these illumined souls had developed unparalleled talent, skill, ability, strength and courage to invoke the Light and be the Hands of God on Earth, even in the face of all adversity. It became painfully clear to this force of darkness that the only chance it had to regain dominion of the Earth was to block the Lightworkers from remembering who they are and fulfilling their Divine Plans.

This force of negativity is *very* adept at whispering "sweet nothings" in our ears and sweet-talking our human egos into doing its will. The awakened Lightworkers, however, presented a whole new challenge. These people are not easily deceived and are very aware of the antics of the sinister force. Therefore, a plan had to be devised that was so deceptive and so cunning that the Lightworkers wouldn't see what was happening to them.

First of all, "cosmic evil" selected channels who were proficient in emulating powerful forcefields of love. The entity was very aware that the resonance of love is magnetic and would draw people from all over the World into its gatherings and seminars. It also knew that it is the frequency of love that creates the level of trust necessary to get people to let down their guards and become vulnerable.

"Cosmic evil" does not resonate with the frequency of love, so it needed to use the forcefields of its channels to deceive people into thinking *it* was the source of the love they were feeling when they were attending its seminars.

Next, the entity had to cloak its horrendous plan in a way that would not be seen by the Lightworkers. It took its simple instructions and sprinkled them here and there throughout volumes of other information that was clearly based in Truth and Love. Once again, this entity knows that we are not stupid. It does not say, *"I am the sinister force, and I have come to ruin your life."* It says, *"I'm god, follow me."* Consequently, it buried the instructions for its plan of treachery amidst volumes of Truth so it would be easy to conceal and difficult to decipher.

When the specifics of the plan are extrapolated from the body of the text, the intent is obvious and shocking.

The entity instructed the Lightworkers to invoke a *"neutral implant"* that it says will *"void our imprints." Our imprints include everything we have ever known since we were first breathed forth from the Heart of God.* The implant was also to void our past Karma. Once we accepted the implant, the entity said for us to notice that our *"silver tether"* was missing. Our **silver cord** is not a "tether," of course, it is our Divine Life Force.

It said we must invoke the implant out loud for a full cycle of the moon, 28 days. Then our Spiritual Guides will abandon us, and we will go into a black depression for 90 days, at which time we will receive the *"implant"* and *"new guides."* It said once we received these new guides, we will *not* even be able to communicate with our Higher Selves without going through *them.* Once we receive the new guides, the entity said *our bodies will be used to rebuild its magnetic grid,* and if we choose not to do this work, we will *"terminate"* ourselves and be welcomed by the entity on the other side.

When this information is read in this context, it is astonishing to think *anyone*, let alone an illumined soul, could read those instructions and not perceive them to be an obvious ploy of the sinister force. But, they were *not* presented in that context. The instructions I have shared with you are exact, but in the books, they were surrounded with so much other information that is based in love and truth that the magnitude of what the entity was actually instructing was lost in a cloak of invisibilty.

Astoundingly, since *1992*, tens of thousands of Lightworkers were drawn to this entity's message, and thousands of them have actually followed the instructions and invoked the implant. Powerful Lightworkers around the World who were highly respected for their affinity for Truth and their integrity were drawn into this entity's web of deception. The entity was actually even asked to speak through its channel at the United Nations, which it did on *November 21, 1995*.

The Light of God is Always Victorious

Fortunately, the Light of God, which is now blazing throughout the Planet, is ALWAYS Victorious, and it is infinitely more powerful than ANY force of darkness.

Even though the devious plan of "cosmic evil" created a small glitch in the overall scheme of things, the Divine Plan of our Father-Mother God and the Company of Heaven kept unfolding in perfect Divine Order.

AVERTING THE PREDICTED CATACLYSMIC EARTHQUAKES DURING THE LATTER DAYS

The *Summer of 1992* was an experience of God Victorious Accomplishment. It was truly a multidimensional activity of Light that deeply affected every particle of life on Earth. None of us will ever be the same again, and whether we participated in the life-transforming events consciously or unconsciously, we will reap the benefits for all Eternity.

Preparation for that glorious span of time had been orchestrated by the unified efforts of Heaven and Earth for literally thousands of years. Even though the Divine Plan on Earth is always subject to the Free Will choices of Humanity, it was perceived aeons ago that, during the Cosmic Moment of the Summer of 1992, there would be millions of awakened souls in embodiment who would be capable of magnetizing the Light of God into the physical plane of Earth with enough power to ***propel this Planet out of the darkness into the Light.***

Many accelerations of vibration had taken place on Earth since *1987*. Each of these accelerations lifted Humanity and all life evolving on Earth up an octave in vibration out of the oppressive frequencies of the sea of negativity that surrounds this Planet. Step-by-step, we moved into frequencies of Light that vibrated with more Divine Qualities of Harmony and Balance. This gradual Ascension had the effect of softening our hearts and awakening our minds to the realization of the Oneness of all life. It literally healed our self-inflicted separation from our "I Am" Presences and brought us into alignment with the Divine Mediator between God and Humanity, our Holy Christ Selves.

Through the healing that took place during the *Summer of 1992*, we were in a position, as never before, to raise our Earthly bodies into the loving embrace of our true God Reality. We were experiencing the initial impulse of PERMANENT planetary transformation. This literally meant the transformation of all physical matter on an atomic cellular level. It involved the activation of the pre-encoded memories contained within the RNA-DNA patterns of all living substance. These memories reflected the original Divine Intent of all manifest form in the Third Dimensional Plane, which is LIMITLESS PHYSICAL PERFECTION.

THE FIRST EARTH SUMMIT

One of the most devasting results of the "fall of man" was the schism that was formed between the Human Kingdom and the Elemental Kingdom on Earth. In the original Divine Plan, Humanity, Elementals and Angels walked hand-in-hand in conscious cooperation. After the "fall," we lost the ability to commune with the Elementals and Angels because we were buried in darkness. We perceived the Nature Kingdom to be void of intelligence. Consequently, the lower human ego obsessively abused the elements of Earth for its personal gain. This brought us to the brink of self-destruction. The degenerating plight of Humanity and the abominable pollution of Mother Earth clearly reflect the war that has been going on between Humanity and the Elements. This war has resulted in devasting earthquakes, hurricanes, tornadoes, floods, famines, plagues, disease, pestilence, extreme weather conditions, death and every other imbalance in the Nature Kingdom. One of the most critical factors of planetary transformation was the healing of the abyss separating the two Kingdoms. Every electron of the physical plane is comprised of Elemental substance: earth, air, water, fire and ether. There is no way that we can transform physical matter without the cooperation of the Elemental Kingdom. So, our primary goal was to heal the battle going on between the Nature Kingdom and Humanity if we were going to regain our original path and restore the physical plane to Heaven on Earth.

Since the human ego is very manipulative, it had to actually bring the Earth to the brink of dissolution in order to get our attention. Only after our air was polluted, our water putrified, our Earth plagued with Global warming, ozone depletion, floods, famines, deforestation, animal extinction, toxic waste, pesticides, over-population, poverty, bizarre weather conditions, disease, aging and death, did we finally say..."*Wait a minute; I think something is wrong here.*"

When that realization finally registered in our conscious minds, we took the first step toward reversing our downward spiral into oblivion. Our awareness that the outrageous behavior of our obsessive, greedy human egos had brought the Earth and all Her life to the threshold of extinction ultimately shocked us sufficiently to motivate us into action. Awakening souls began to seek viable solutions to the problems manifesting on Earth. It became very clear that our challenges were monumental, and it would take the unified efforts of Humanity to change our current direction of ruination and reclaim our Divine Path of co-creating Heaven on Earth.

Several decades ago, individuals and groups began to connect, once again, with the Earth. They sought out the indigenous people of Earth who had not lost the ability to commune with the Elementals, and they began to invoke the Light of God through Sacred Ceremonies of Love and Forgiveness. The Elemental Kingdom began to cautiously observe the Lightworkers' efforts, and at first, very skeptically, watched and wondered. It was obvious that we had rendered asunder every bit of trust the Elementals had for us, and that trust was not going to be restored easily. Fortunately, the awakened souls realized the extreme degree of abuse we had inflicted upon the Elementals and continued to persevere. Ever so slowly, the Elementals began to trust the sincere desire of the Lightworkers to heal the separation between the Elementals and themselves and the desire, once again, to unite in cooperative service to Mother Earth. In *1970*, a day was chosen for an annual Global Celebration to honor the Earth and commit to Her healing. *April 22nd* was declared *Earth Day*, and throughout the World, people celebrated Mother Earth. The sincere desire to heal and reunite, arising in the hearts of Humanity and Elementals invoked assistance from the Realms of Illumined Truth, and the Heavenly response set a plan into motion to permanently heal the schism between Human Beings and Elemental Beings—*a plan that would AVERT the cataclysmic earthquakes and destruction that the prophets and seers had predicted.*

The Clarion Call rang through the Universe and activated within the hearts and minds of Humanity the need to set our petty differences aside and come together as a unified force with the common goal of healing the Earth.

The people already aligned with the environment began to redouble their efforts, and a Divine Blueprint for an outer world activity of Light that had never before been attempted began to form in the ethers. This blueprint filtered into the consciousness of world leaders and lay people alike. The organization that symbolizes Global unification, the United Nations, chose to accept the responsibility of organizing this glorious event. Plans were set into motion, and the very first *Earth Summit* began to manifest. The United Nations decided to call this sacred conclave *The United Nations Conference on Environment and Development (UNCED)... The First Earth Summit.* It was scheduled to be held in Rio de Janeiro, Brazil, *June 1-14, 1992.*

Brazil, interestingly, symbolizes the paradox going on in both Humanity and the Elementals. Rio de Janeiro is a beautiful city of approximately nine-million people. It clearly reflects all of Humanity's ills: pollution, dire poverty, homelessness, abandoned children, deforestation, inequality, corruption, despair, disease, crime, perversion, substance abuse, etc. Yet, in the midst of Humanity's darkness, there is a blazing Light of beauty and wonder. There is a Spiritual core of awakened souls that hold tenaciously to the knowledge that we truly have a choice. They understand that we have created our present plight, and we alone can change it. They know of their own Divinity, and they are determined to be God in Action on Earth.

The Elementals in Brazil are some of the most exquisite on the Planet. The shimmering waters and tropical rain forests sustain an awe-inspiring variety of lifeforms. The mountains, valley, skies and beaches are filled with splendor.

Ironically, it was because of the extremes existing in Brazil that this location was chosen for the first Earth Summit. What better place to draw the attention of the World as we focus on what the lower human ego has done to destroy Mother Earth and what Divine Humanity can now do to heal Her.

For two years, the World prepared at both inner and outer levels for the largest gathering of world leaders and nongovernmental organizations ever known in the history of time. The Earth Summit was truly a multidimensional activity of Light.

During the mystical month of May preceding the Earth Summit, the Feminine Polarity of God, known to us most commonly as the Holy Spirit, increased in vibration and power on Earth. This Feminine essence of Divine Love has always been the sustaining force behind the Elemental Kingdom. That is why we refer to the elements as *Mother* Nature and *Mother* Earth. As the embrace of the Holy Spirit caressed the abused bodies of the Elementals on Earth, they began to soften their hearts toward their Earthly adversaries, the Human Beings. This nurturing Mother's Love helped prepare them for the healing that was to take place during the Earth Summit. It also enabled the Elementals to contemplate Humanity's remorse and our plea for forgiveness. In order for the Elemental Kingdom to believe we were really serious about wanting to heal the atrocities we have perpetrated upon them, we needed to join together in an obvious demonstration. The Earth Summit was the vehicle designed to prove to all the World, at both inner and outer levels, that at long last, Humanity has finally recognized our responsibility as stewards of the Earth.

For the first time ever, 176 world leaders came together for a common cause: the healing of the Earth. Each leader had his/her own agenda and his/her own ideas on how the healing would be accomplished, but it was the fact that ALL were in agreement that something needed to be done to save the Earth that was significant and unique.

In addition to the world leaders, 40,000 individuals and organizations committed to planetary healing and transformation also traveled to Rio and joined together to create a unified consciousness that would radiate forth to all life on Earth as a beacon of hope. This sacred gathering was the outer world demonstration the Elementals had been waiting for to clearly prove that we were, once again, worthy of their trust.

On *May 31, 1992*, the day before the opening of the Earth Summit, a group of Lightworkers gathered in Brazil to invoke an invincible forcefield of protection in, through and around Rio de Janeiro. The entire Company of Heaven joined in this activity of Light, and a ***Ray of God Victorious Accomplishment was anchored into Rio*** to create an environment through which the Divine Plan for this sacred conclave would be fulfilled. The Divine Quality of Victory poured into the Planet through this Ray, and it increased in power and momentum daily and hourly.

On *June 1, 1992*, the Earth Summit began, and through a multitude of activities, the people gathered in Rio and those tuning in in consciousness from around the World started creating a tremendous *Chalice of Light*. This Chalice of Light ***formed an open portal between Heaven and Earth.***

Through this portal, the Divine Love of God poured into the physical plane to heal, through the Law of Forgiveness, the separation between Humanity and the Elementals. Our unified efforts built to a crescendo on *June 7, 1992*. This was the midpoint of the Earth Summit and the Holy Day known in the outer world as Pentecost, the day of the Baptism of Holy Spirit.

It was not a coincidence that the apex of the Earth Summit fell on the day that is dedicated to the Divine Presence that sustains and nurtures the Nature Kingdom. On this Sacred Day, inner and outer world activities of Light took place at the Earth Summit that enabled us to integrate and anchor into the physical world of form unprecedented healing frequencies of Divine Love...truly a ***Baptism of Holy Spirit.***

This unparalleled influx of Divine Love healed Humanity's self-inflicted separation from the Elementals. *A covenant of Divine Love was formed between Humanity and the Elemental Kingdom that created a new conscious-*

ness of trust and cooperation, which will enable us to accomplish, through God's Victory, the physical transformation of this sweet Earth and all Her lifeforms.

For the remainder of the Earth Summit, many wonderful activities occurred as the Healing Light of Holy Spirit was integrated into every particle of life on the Planet. The final day of the Earth Summit was *June 14, 1992, the Full Moon of Gemini.* Throughout the World, the Gemini Full Moon is celebrated as the *Festival of the Goodwill of Humanity.* This is a time when Humanity demonstates goodwill and a sincere heart commitment to be God in Action on Earth. During that particular Gemini Full Moon, we were also blessed with a *Lunar Eclipse that sealed, for all Eternity, the healing between the Human Kingdom and the Elemental Kingdom* that had been Victoriously accomplished during the Earth Summit.

On the Holy Night of the Gemini Full Moon within the embrace of the Lunar Eclipse, an awesome musical Light and Sound Show was performed on the beach in Rio de Janeiro before an audience of 250,000 people. During that activity of Light, every electron of precious life energy that had been expended to bring the first Earth Summit into physical manifestation was purified and woven into Beloved Mother Earth's Seamless Garment of Light. This is the resplendent raiment adorning Mother Earth as She re-establishes, forever, Her Divine Heritage of Heaven on Earth.

This healing means that we now are in a position to work in cooperation with the intelligence of all manifest form, all physical matter, all Earthly substance, including our physical bodies and our physical realities. If we will only grasp the magnitude of that, we will realize LIMITLESS PHYSICAL PERFECTION is available to each and every one of us, *here and now.*

TIME SHIFT

Following the Earth Summit, there were several accelerations of vibration on the Planet that further prepared us
for our Ascension into Timelessness. On *June 21, 1992*, we
experienced an unusually powerful *Summer Solstice; June
30, 1992*, there was a *New Moon total Solar Eclipse; July
4, 1992*, we celebrated *Independence Day*, which was enhanced because 1992 was the 500th anniversary of the
discovery of America, and we were blessed with *an influx of
the Sacred Flame of Freedom from On High.*

Each of these waves of cosmic force came with mixed
blessings. On each level, the increases in vibration fine-
tuned the alignment of our atomic, cellular vehicles with the
Light Body of our Holy Christ Selves. This readied us for
the time when our Divine Selves would be able to truly
integrate with our physical bodies and take full dominion,
once again, of our Earthly vehicles.

In addition to the long-awaited healing of the separation
between our physical bodies and our Holy Christ Selves, we
also experienced the opposite extreme, which was the incredible clearing and purging of our pasts. Any areas of our
lives that were not enhancing our forward progress were
pushed to the surface for purification. This had the effect of
exacerbating our daily challenges. From outer appearances,
it seemed as though financial problems became worse,
relationships deteriorated, jobs were more unbearable, our
behavior was more obsessive, compulsive addictions increased, diseases intensified, grief deepened, anxiety height-
ened, low self-esteem was magnified, nerves were shattered,
fear mounted and a general sense of panic gripped our Solar
Plexus.

If we were able to hold the purging in perspective,
emotionally detach from the things rising up for purification
and invoke the Violet Flame to Transmute into Light the
negativity that was surfacing, we moved through the process

fairly unscathed. But, if we focused on the appearance of hopelessness and despair, we pulled ourselves into the thrashing claws of terror.

Fortunately, this intense clearing was fairly short-lived. Contrary to what it felt like, it was, in reality, a merciful opportunity for each one of us. In that short span of time, we were given the ability to transmute *hundreds* of lifetimes worth of negativity in the *"twinkling of an eye."*   Whether we were consciously aware of what was happening or not, our God Presences cleared the maximum we were capable of withstanding according to our individual Divine Plans. This purging was necessary in order for the Earth and all life evolving upon Her to be ready for the next Cosmic push.

On *July 26, 1992*, we experienced what was called a timeshift. In actuality, we went through another collapsing of Third Dimensional time and Ascended into a new frequency of Fourth Dimensional time. We are so used to being constrained and limited by time and space that it is practically impossible for us to relate to the concept of moving toward timelessness, but what we will gradually acknowledge is that we are finally living in the *Eternal Moment of Now.* This is an ever-present awareness of our multidimensionality, expressing the totality of who we are at all times, in all dimensions. This great expansion of our consciousness has Ascended the knowledge of who we are from the finite to the infinite.

This was a critical step. It was necessary in order for us to be able to complete the integration of our Holy Christ Selves into the atomic, cellular structure of our four lower bodies. That integration took place during the next Cosmic Event of the Sixth Celebration of Harmonic Convergence. We had known all along that the Sixth Celebration of Harmonic Convergence was going to be a milestone in the evolution of Earth, but I don't think anyone fathomed the immensity of what would occur.

Sixth Celebration of Harmonic Convergence

We were asked by the Company of Heaven to hold the Sixth Annual World Congress On Illumination during the anniversary of Harmonic Convergence. We were told the sacred gathering should be held within the Vortex of Healing through the Power of Limitless Transmutation that pulsates in the vicinity of Tucson, Arizona. Lightworkers from all over the World were invited, and each one responded according to their inner heart call. We were asked to invite presenters who were aligned with the Divine Truth of Limitless Physical Perfection and who were informed of the tangible tools that would allow our physical bodies to absorb the maximum frequencies of Light.

Each day of the Congress we utilized the tools from the Realms of Illumined Truth and, daily and hourly, prepared our bodies to be transformers of Light. Through the unified cup of our consciousness, we created a Bridge of Light that was formed over the abyss separating the RNA-DNA patterns in our four lower bodies from the Divine RNA-DNA patterns of our Holy Christ Selves.

This abyss is what had prevented our Holy Christ Selves from integrating into the actual cellular structures of our physical bodies. It was a short circuit that blocked the rejuvenating, transforming Light of our Holy Christ Selves from reaching the cells and organs of our physical bodies. That is why our bodies run out of energy and disintegrate and die.

Once the Bridge of Light was formed and the circuitry reconnected between the physical body and the Holy Christ Self, the integration began. Because of the Oneness of all life, this reconnection of circuitry passed through the unified cup of those gathered in the Healing Vortex in Tucson and, through them, was transmitted to every other person on Earth. This actually means that we are now, at long last, physically reconnected to our Holy Christ Selves and our Divine RNA-DNA patterns of LIMITLESS PHYSICAL

PERFECTION.

That was the second impulse of the Second Coming of the Christ within Humanity. Now, it is simply a matter of unifying our battered, mutated cells and allowing the Divine Pattern of our Holy Christ Selves to shine through. This will be a gradual process, but with perseverance, our Victory is assured.

Day-by-day we are experiencing more Light shining through our bodies. As we master our thoughts, words, actions and feelings and allow our Christ Presences to have full dominion of all our physical experiences, we will witness our own personal tangible transformation.

Heaven On Earth Is Available Here And Now! All We Have To Do Is Accept It!

This physical reconnection to our Holy Christ Selves is what we have been striving for and longing to accomplish since we first fell from Grace. Now that it has been God Victoriously accomplished, we are absolutely capable of restoring our physical, etheric, mental and emotional bodies to their original Divine Intent, which is ETERNAL YOUTH, VIBRANT HEALTH AND RADIANT BEAUTY.

With the healing that took place between our physical bodies and our Holy Christ Selves, we were finally in a position to activate our Fourth Dimensional Twelve-fold Solar Spines and Solar Causal Bodies. It was determined by the Company of Heaven that in order for this activity of Light to be God Victoriously accomplished, the open portal of the Feminine Polarity of God's Divine Love needed to be expanded. Lightworkers were asked to gather within the forcefield where the Feminine Polarity of God enters the Earth in Lake Titicaca, Bolivia.

ASCENDING INTO
THE TWELVE SOLAR ASPECTS OF DEITY

Within the Sun Cycle (Libra) which reflects the Divine Quality of Liberty throughout the Planet, Lightworkers gathered within the Forcefield of our Mother God in Bolivia in *October 1992.* Through the collective Chalice of Humanity's consciousness, the Light of our Father-Mother God poured into the Earth and *accelerated the activation of Humanity's Twelve-fold Solar Spines.* This increase of Light actually raised our Third Dimensional Seven-fold Planetary Spines into the full radiance and embrace of the Fourth Dimensional Twelve-fold Solar Spines of our SO-LAR CHRIST PRESENCES. This allowed the Twelve-fold Causal Body of God to begin flowing through our Twelve Solar Chakra Centers.

This meant that due to the incredible accelerations in energy, vibration and consciousness we had experienced since Harmonic Convergence in *1987*, we were, at last, vibrating at a frequency close enough to the Octaves of the Fourth Dimension to once again access the full spectrum of the Twelve Solar Aspects of Deity of our Father-Mother God instead of just the limited Seven-fold spectrum we had to work with in the Third Dimension. This infusion of Light anchored the Twelve-fold Solar Aspect of Deity through the spinal column of every man, woman and child.

This Divine Activity had the physical, tangible effect of expanding our ability to project Light into the world of form. The difference in the amount of Light we are capable of radiating forth now, compared to the Light we expressed through our Seven-fold Planetary Spines and Causal Bodies, is the equivalent of the Light of the Sun compared to the Light of the Moon.

This blessed Planet is now blazing in the Universe as Freedom's Holy Star at Causal levels. Through our concentrated efforts, you and I and every other Lightworker now have the ability to utilize this Divine Light and to transform

our individual lives into LIMITLESS PHYSICAL PERFEC-
TION as examples for all the World to see. Once the Divine
Laws of Eternal Youth, Vibrant Health and Radiant Beauty are
reflecting through our bodies at an atomic cellular level,
Humanity will begin to finally believe that the miscreation of
the lower human ego is indeed a lie. People will observe our
examples of transfiguration and know that if it is possible for
one Human Being, it is surely possible for all Human Beings.
One by one, they will apply the Universal Laws and change
their physical realities to perfection. The effect will be
exponential, and in a relatively short time, Heaven will
manifest on Earth.

The most exciting thing about this new awareness is that
we don't have to fully understand it; we don't even have to
believe it. All we have to do is experiment with the Sacred
Knowledge being revealed to us from On High, and we will
prove, beyond a shadow of a doubt, that LIMITLESS PHYSI-
CAL PERFECTION is available in this physical reality, right
here and right now.

EXPANDING THE FEMININE POLARITY
OF DIVINE LOVE

Once the Twelve Solar Aspects of Deity began flowing
into the Planet through the newly activated Twelve-fold
Solar Spines and Twelve-fold Solar Causal Bodies of all
Humanity, our Father-Mother God were able to EXPAND,
WITHOUT LIMIT, THE FEMININE POLARITY OF
OUR MOTHER GOD through the shaft of Light that enters
the Planet in the area of Mt. Meru in the Andes Mountains at
Lake Titicaca in Bolivia.

The God Victorious Success of this event opened a
window of opportunity for new frequencies of healing from
our Mother God to flow into the Earth.

A NEW ORDER OF HEALING

On *October 10, 1992*, after a purifying activity of the Violet Transmuting Flame, a frequency of Solar Healing poured into the Planet establishing a *New Order of Healing on Earth*.

Prior to the fall of Humanity, pure Healing Light from the very Heart of God continually poured into every human heart and flowed out through our hands, blessing everything we touched. As the lower human ego, with its recalcitrant ways, slowly became the unintended master of our four lower bodies, that Healing Light became contaminated with our negative expressions of thoughts and feelings. Instead of being a blessing to all life, the increased energy flowing through our hands became a source of additional pain and suffering, thus adding to the misery on Earth rather than being a healing blessing as was originally intended. In an act of mercy, our Holy Christ Selves placed seals over the energy centers in our hands to stop the flow of Healing Light so that we would not misqualify It into gross mutations of discord and suffering.

Those seals have remained for lifetime after lifetime, awaiting the moment when the Holy Christ Self would once again regain Its rightful authority over our four lower bodies. With the expansion of our Solar Spines and Causal Bodies, the Holy Christ Selves of every man, woman and child evolving on Earth, whether they are in or out of embodiment, became, at long last, the *predominant* Master of our four vehicles of Earthly experience—our physical, etheric, mental and emotional bodies. *That was the third impulse of the Second Coming of the Christ through Humanity.* This shift of power from the human ego to the Holy Christ Self has been Victoriously accomplished in the Realms of Cause and is now gradually filtering into the everyday experiences of Humanity.

As this occurs, we may undergo the rebellious resistance of the human ego struggling to keep its control, but if we gently command it into the Light, its rebellion will be very short-lived. The Holy Christ Self is in command, and we need only lift up in consciousness and perceive that resplendent Presence radiating through our vehicles to confirm that fact. Remember, we still have *Free Will*, so if we choose to allow our human ego to remain in control, it will, but now WE HAVE A CHOICE. If we choose to allow our Holy Christ Self to express through us, it will joyously take the helm and guide us into lives of fulfillment and joy.

Our self-inflicted separation from this Divine Aspect of our consciousness HAS BEEN HEALED, and along with that healing, the Holy Christ Selves of every Human Being removed the seals from the energy centers in the palms of our hands. This glorious event has initiated the Planet Earth into a *New Order of Healing*. Now, the Solar frequencies of Divine Healing Light will flow through us under the direction of our Holy Christ Selves. Golden Tubes of Light have been created within our vehicles to allow this Sacred Healing Energy to flow through us and not be contaminated by the negativity we may still be expressing with our thoughts, words, actions or feelings. The Golden Tubes of Light allow the Healing Energy to pass easily into our bodies and out our hands, but they prevent any of our negativity from passing into the Healing Energy. This means that we will now be a constant force of healing on this Planet if we choose to be, and in order to choose to be, all we have to do is give our God Presence permission to project the Divine Light of Healing through us. This can be simply done through the following invocation:

> *Beloved Presence of God "I AM" in me...through the full power of the Divinity blazing in my heart, I invoke You now to project through every electron of my Being, the most intensified activity of Healing Light allowed at this moment according to my Divine Plan. Increase this Holy Light daily*

and hourly with every breath I take. Allow me to be a powerful force of healing to all life I come in contact with during my Earthly experience. Magnetize into my sphere of influence every person, place, condition or thing that I can, in any way, assist with God's Healing Light. Give me the Divine Opportunities to love life free on this sweet Earth.

"I AM" open!
"I AM" willing!
"I AM" receptive!
"I AM" grateful!
"I AM" God's Healing in Action on Earth!
As God's Most Holy Name,
"I AM", "I AM", "I AM"

The Higher Order of **Solar** Healing Light is Emerald Green with an Amethyst Violet Radiance. The Divine Flame of Healing through the Power of Limitless Transmutation was amplified during this activity of Light into glorious frequencies beyond the Fifth Dimension. This is the highest frequency of Healing Light ever manifested on Earth. Visualize this Sacred Healing Light flowing through your body, healing every frequency of vibration that is less than Limitless Physical Perfection. Then see the Healing Light flowing out of your hands, healing all you touch.

We have all heard about special people who were able to heal with the *"laying on of hands."* These were people who, through their unique process of evolution had the seals removed from their hands. Now that miracle has transpired for all of us, and daily our healing abilities will increase through our invocations and the power of our conscious attention.

After the new order of Solar Healing was established on Earth, we were ready for the next great quantum leap in our service.

The Unified Christ Presence of Humanity is Invested Into the Office of Lord of the World

On *October 11, 1992*, during a Divine Ceremony at inner levels, the Unified Christ Presence of Humanity was invested once again to hold the highest office of the Spiritual Hierarchy on Earth, the office of Lord of the World. This is a position that the collective Christ Presence of Humanity was always supposed to hold, a position that empowered us to be the stewards of the Earth we were destined to be. Unfortunately, with the "fall," we lost the ability to be effective caretakers of the Earth. Instead, we became the Earth's nemesis. Since we were incapable of fulfilling the office of Lord of the World, other members of the Ascended Realms of Perfection volunteered to come and cradle the Earth in Their Heart Flames until Humanity regained our direction and once again became one with our Christ Presences. These Divine Beings are referred to in the Bible as the "Ancient of Days."

During a Divine Ceremony on *October 11, 1992*, Gautama Buddha, the Being Who currently held the office of Lord of the World, placed the vestments of Lord of the World around the Unified Christ Presence of Humanity— and the transfer of power was completed. Beloved Lord Gautama was released from His sacred responsibilities and freed to move on to higher service. The Unified Christ Presence of Humanity vowed to fulfill the office of Lord of the World.

The Victory of this transfer of power to the Christ Presence of Humanity paved the way for the anchoring of the Twelve Solar Aspects of Deity through the axis of the body of Beloved Mother Earth.

BEGINNING OF THE NEW WORLD
"The New Heaven and the New Earth"

On *October 12, 1992*, many celebrations took place around theWorld acknowledging the 500th anniversary of what was called the "discovery" of the New World by Christopher Columbus. The year 1992 was also the 500th anniversary of the Vision of Our Lady of Guadalupe, and it was the completion of the 500-year cycle of darkness of the Mayan and Incan civilizations' calendars. It also brought to fruition our 500-year Period of Grace. This Global focus on the "New World" and "New Beginnings" created an open portal that, for a brief span of time, merged Heaven and Earth. This allowed our Father-Mother God to transfer the Twelve Solar Aspects of Deity into the physical axis of Earth. This expanded the Causal Body of Mother Earth from a Sevenfold Planetary Body into a Twelve-fold Solar Body, increasing Her Light *a thousand times a thousand fold.*

To assist in the transfer of the Twelve Solar Aspects of Deity into physical reality, Spiritual groups gathered in Mexico and in South America in the Sacred Foci of the Sun. One group met on the Island of the Sun in Lake Titicaca, Bolivia, and the other Spiritual group met at Palenque, Mexico. Throughout that sacred day, the two groups invoked the Divine Light of God into the physical plane of Earth. As the Solar Light penetrated into the axis of Earth, the Twelve Solar Aspects of Deity blazed through the Planet. A powerful Ray of Solar Light was anchored and secured in the ancient focus of the Sun in the District of Heliopolis, the "City of the Sun" in Cairo, Egypt, on the continent of Africa, the dark continent. This caused a slight earthquake in the District of Heliopolis. It was reported that there had never been an earthquake in that location before, but the prophecies in Cairo had foretold of a coming earthquake that would one day occur in the "City of the Sun" in Cairo, *signaling the beginning of the Permanent Golden Age.*

SEALING THE LAST TWO POCKETS
OF NEGATIVITY ON EARTH

After the Light of the Twelve Solar Aspects of Deity was securely blazing through every particle of life on Earth, our Father-Mother God and the Company of Heaven felt we were strong enough to seal the two pockets of negativity that the force of "cosmic evil" had been able to reopen through its Human pawns.

The two pockets that had been reopened were the most powerful vortexes of negativity on Earth. One was located in Bolivia in South America, and one was located in Durbin in South Africa. These vortexes have held the two continents of South America and Africa in darkness for centuries of time. Even as great civilizations of Light sprang up and tried to counteract the forces of darkness through the Light of the Sun, one by one they failed. Now, through the Power of God's Light, Victory was assured!

First, the Lightworkers gathered at Lake Titicaca in Bolivia, invoked the Light of God and through the collective Christ Presence of Humanity, bolts of Violet Lightning from the Heart of our Father-Mother God pierced into the pocket of negativity in Bolivia and PERMANENTLY *"sealed the door where evil dwells."*

Next, a group of Lightworkers gathered in South Africa for a multifaceted activity of Light. First, through the collective Christ Presence of Humanity, once again the Violet Lightning from the Heart of God PERMANENTLY *"sealed the door where evil dwells"* in Durbin, the last vortex of "cosmic evil" in the physical plane of Earth.

After the sealing of the last pocket of negativity on Earth, the next step of planetary healing was to raise the frequency and vibration of the dark continent of Africa. With the final two pockets of negativity sealed, all was in readiness to draw the Light of the Twelve Solar Aspects of Deity from the anchorage point in the District of the Sun in Heliopolis in

Cairo through all of Africa to the Sacred focus of Table Mountain at the southernmost point of Africa in Cape Town. A Spiritual conference called "Planet in Change" was held in South Africa to build a momentum of Light that would magnetize the Light from Cairo through all of Africa to Table Mountain. The entire Elemental Kingdom was prepared to receive the Light, and on *October 31, 1992*, the Light of the Twelve Solar Aspects of Deity flashed through Africa returning her once and for all to a continent of Light.

After the miraculous, God Victorious success of the recent past, the force of "cosmic evil" became desperate in its attempt to regain control of the Earth. It was painfully aware that its plans of destruction had been foiled by the Lightworkers on Earth and the Company of Heaven working in harmony with the Light of God.

The activities of Light were a catastrophic blow to the plans of "cosmic evil," and it knew it had to redouble its efforts. What it didn't understand was that the Company of Heaven and the God Presences of Humanity anticipated this reaction and set a plan in motion that would counteract the adverse effects of whatever "cosmic evil" had planned.

HEALING OUR EMOTIONAL BODIES

On *December 21, 1992, the Winter Solstice*, a Divine Plan was set into motion that would create for all Humanity the greatest opportunity we had ever experienced to transmute the pain of our pasts and heal our Emotional Bodies. The Goddess of Liberty, the Divine Exponent of the Seventh Solar Aspect of Liberation, volunteered to accept the responsibility of enfolding the Earth and all life evolving here in Her Luminous Presence. She expanded Her Heart Flame of Liberation to assist each of us to liberate ourselves from the emotional pain and suffering we had experienced since the fall of Humanity.

During the first impulses of the *New Year, 1993*, the

Earth was empowered with additional Light from the Core of Creation. *1993* numerically carried the vibration of the master number 22—1+9+9+3=22. The master number 22 reflects the frequency of Power on *ALL* Planes and the ability to change the course of history. This frequency was greatly amplified by a rare conjunction between the Planets Neptune and Uranus. This conjunction occurs only once every 171 years, and never before had we been in such a healed state of consciousness to reap its wonderful benefits. This was also the first time we were even consciously aware of the Planets Neptune and Uranus during their conjunction.

The exact alignment of these two Planets created an atmosphere of new awareness. Uranus is the Planet that is assisting the Earth into our next Spiritual Orbit on the Spiral of Evolution. It is the Planet of insight, awareness and illumination. Neptune is the Planet that balances the emotional strata of Earth which is associated with the Water Element. Neptune also brings new ideals and new levels of faith and accomplishment. The union of these two mighty forces created an environment that allowed great change and personal transformation. This conjunction created a transition in Global consciousness, lifting us beyond the human ego and beyond our human limitations into frequencies of self-empowerment and human dignity.

The influence of this rare alignment of Neptune and Uranus embraced all of *1993* as it built in momentum month after month. This was a wake-up call that amplified, through all levels of consciousness, the urgency of the hour and the need for each of us to accept responsibility for our part in healing this sweet Earth.

The Company of Heaven knew that the healing effects of this rare conjunction would be glorious, but also extremely difficult for Humanity. They knew that in order for the emotional pain of our pasts to be healed, it had to be pushed to the surface. This initially always causes things to seem much more intense and overwhelming.

In order to ease our pain and move us very quickly through the negative challenges we were going through, we were given an opportunity of incredible mercy and compassion. Our Father-Mother God opened a door to *Limitless Solar Transmutation* that had never before been experienced in any physical dimension. This was a frequency of the Violet Transmuting Flame beyond anything we had ever been capable of withstanding. It was a frequency of Divine Solar Light from the Causal Body of God that transmuted back into perfection anything in Its path. It reached into the cause, core, effect, record and memory of every frequency of vibration that was less than God's Perfection and transmuted that negative condition back into its original Divine Blueprint. This sacred gift was released on Earth because of the need of the hour and the Cosmic Moment at hand. This was the initial impulse of Divine Intervention we had been told would occur during Earth's final purge and cleansing.

The critical factor in this intervention was that in order for the Fifth Dimensional frequencies of Limitless Solar Transmutation to be effectively integrated into our Third Dimensional experiences on Earth, they had to be consciously drawn through the Heart Flames of Lightworkers abiding on Earth. Otherwise, even though this blessed Light was pouring into the atmosphere of Earth, we would not have received Its miraculous benefits in our daily lives. Fortunately, a plan was set into motion by the entire Company of Heaven to avert such a tragedy.

Pulsating in the Etheric Realms over the southern portion of Mexico, all of the Caribbean Islands, the Dominican Republic and Cuba is a tremendous vortex of the Violet Transmuting Flame. This Forcefield of Divine Light has been building in momentum for thousands of years. It has been sustained by the Solar Archangels of the Seventh Ray of Spiritual Freedom—Archangel Zadkiel and His Divine Complement, Archaii Holy Amethyst.

During past Cosmic Moments on Earth, this vortex has

been opened for a brief period of time to allow the Sacred Violet Fire of Transmutation to pour into the physical plane of Earth. This was done with the Divine Intent of establishing a frequency of Freedom on Earth that would lift all Humanity out of our oppressive, humanly created state of fear, pain and suffering into the Illumined Truth of our Divine Heritage as Sons and Daughters of God.

Unfortunately, in the past we were separated from our Holy Christ Selves so completely that we experienced very little success from that activity of transmutation, and the success we did accomplish was very short-lived because the lower human ego would quickly return to its wayward consciousness.

Now, for the first time since the "fall of man," we were reunited with our Holy Christ Presences. This opened a door of opportunity we never dreamed possible.

On *January 11, 1993*, the Violet Transmuting Flame vortex of Archangel Zadkiel and Holy Amethyst began receiving, from the Heart of God, the most intensified frequency of Limitless Solar Transmutation Cosmic Law would allow. It was projected into the consciousness and the Heart Flame of every Lightworker on the Planet. Daily and hourly It built in momentum until It reached a crescendo on the *Summer Solstice of June 21, 1993.*

We were asked by the Company of Heaven to hold the Seventh Annual World Congress On Illumination within the Violet Fire vortex in the Caribbean. We arranged a Caribbean Cruise during the Summer Solstice to receive the full benefits of the emotional healing taking place through the Water Element.

Two hundred awakened souls joined us physically on the cruise, and thousands joined us in consciousness from their forcefields of Light around the Globe. In addition to those who were consciously participating in this Divine Plan, the Holy Christ Selves of every man, woman and child joined with us at inner levels, and the entire Elemental Kingdom and

Angelic Kingdom serving the Earth at this time also joined with us in consciousness.

On the *Full Moon of June 20, 1993*, the gathering of Lightworkers began in Florida. The Feminine Director of the Water Element and the Masculine Director of the Water Element began to flood the oceans, seas, lakes, rivers, springs, creeks, water ways and every molecule of water on Earth with the Solar radiance of the New Order of Healing. The Emerald Green Solar Ray of Healing with a Violet Radiance of Limitless Transmutation poured into the waters of Earth preparing every electron of emotional energy to receive the most powerful healing we could endure.

Archangel Zadkiel and Holy Amethyst stood in readiness, and as the First Rays of Sunlight burst through the darkness heralding the first impulse of the *Summer Solstice on June 21, 1993*, our Father-Mother God began magnetizing, from the very Core of Creation, the intensified activity of the Violet Flame of Limitless Solar Transmutation. The entire Company of Heaven joined with Archangel Zadkiel and Holy Amethyst, and as one breath, one heartbeat, one consciousness of pure Divine Love, the Fifth Dimensional Light of the Violet Flame of Limitless Solar Transmutation was breathed into the Heart Flames of the embodied Lightworkers on Earth.

For seven days this crescendo of Holy Light bathed all life evolving on Earth, giving every man, woman and child, every Elemental and every Angelic Presence abiding on Earth the opportunity to release ALL of our miserable afflictions, maladies, addictions, obsessions, negative behavior patterns, dysfunctional emotions, painful experiences, limiting conditions, distorted perceptions, erroneous and destructive belief systems, illusions and ignorance. The release of these conditions and states of consciousness cleared the way for our Holy Christ Presences to take full dominion of our four lower bodies.

This unification of Heaven and Earth created a PERMA-

NENT OPEN PORTAL between the two realms, through which this Divine Light will continually pour until all life on Earth is wholly Ascended and Free. This open portal will now allow the full momentum of this new frequency of Violet Fire to continually bathe the Earth with Its Divine Gifts. The *Violet* Fire is the perfect balance of the Masculine (Blue Ray of Power) and Feminine (Pink Ray of Divine Love) Aspects of Deity. It is heralding the return of the Divine Mother, and now *this open portal of Violet Fire symbolizes our Mother God reasserting Her Sacred Self on Earth with Cosmic Power.*

The Light of God is Eternally Victorious, and during this Cosmic Moment on Earth, It was exceedingly so. Not even the Company of Heaven expected the overwhelming success of the unified efforts of awakened Humanity. But, succeed we did, and this Earth and all Her life will never be the same again. On *June 26, 1993*, we Ascended into frequencies of the *Solar Christ Presence* of Humanity, and the CHRIST will never recede from Earth. *This was the fourth impulse of the Second Coming of the Christ through Humanity.*

This Divine Activity of Light was multifaceted, and every Being on Earth participated in this glorious event either consciously or superconsciously, according to their inner Heart Call and their wisdom and understanding.

RETURN OF THE
SOLAR CHRIST PRESENCE

Our Ascension into the frequencies of our *Solar* Christ Presences lifted our Holy Christ Selves into an octave of energy, vibration and consciousness that ASSURED Its ability to *permanently* retain dominion of our four lower bodies. This ASSURED that never again will our lower human egos be the *predominant* masters of our thoughts, words, actions and feelings. This literally means that for the *majority* of our daily experience on Earth, at least 51 percent of the time collectively, we are functioning in the frequencies of Harmony and Balance of our Holy Christ Selves.

This seems difficult to believe because we let the times when we're not at peace or feeling harmonious to get the most attention, but if you will monitor your own thoughts, words, actions and feelings in a 24-hour period, you will see that more than half of the time, you are actually calm, peaceful, harmonious and sometimes, even happy and joyful. If you have a really bad day, then monitor your whole week, and you will see that the positive times balanced out your bad day.

As you focus on the positive times and revel in the good things going on in your life, your Holy Christ Self will integrate the Light of your Solar Christ Presence even more. Each day the scales will tip toward Christ Consciousness, and your life will just get better and better.

Each and every lifestream evolving on Earth is now reunited with the Solar Aspect of their Holy Christ Presence. This is the part of our Being that reflects the true Son or Daughter of God we actually are. This is the ultimate realization of our own Divinity.

It is difficult for us to grasp the magnitude of just what this means, but this is our reunification with our Divinity, and it has assured the transformation of our physical reality into Heaven on Earth. Again, this was Victoriously Accomplished in the Realms of Cause and now, as we focus on this Divine Aspect of ourselves, It will gradually reflect into our daily lives, manifesting Heaven on Earth and Limitless Physical Perfection.

As we learn to integrate this Presence of Light through our four lower bodies (phsyical, etheric, mental and emotional), these vehicles will be transformed into the perfection that they were originally supposed to express.

Being reunited with our Divine Selves has opened doors of opportunity we have never dared to dream were possible. And it is critical that we take the *necessary steps* to integrate our Solar Christ Presences into our daily life experiences with evey thought, word, action and feeling we express.

One of the most important changes that has taken place since the return of our Solar Christ Presence is that *this Divine Presence encapsulates the Light of God in an invincible armor of love* **before** *It enters our four lower vehicles.* This prevents any of the contamination of our lower vehicles from changing the vibration, color or sound of God's Divine Light.

Prior to the return of the Solar Christ Presence, **all Light** passing through us was subject to the feelings we were experiencing at the time. If we were angry or fearful, not just the energy our human egos was using to act out negative behavior patterns was contaminated, but even the most Holy Light picked up the vibrations of anger or fear and was distored to a degree as It passed through us. Because of this phenomenon, our God Presence would withold the Divine Light passing through us until we were in a state of harmony again.

This greatly limited our ability to be powerful Lightworkers. We were ineffective unless we were centered and harmonious. Now, even if we are off-center due to our daily challenges and our lower human egos are misqualifying energy through our thoughts, words, actions or feelings, we can still invoke the Light of God and expect the full force of Its perfection to flow into the situation at hand. This will greatly assist us in quickly clearing and transmuting the negativity in our personal lives and on Earth. It will enable us to be powerful forces of Light even in the face of our human frailties, until our Solar Christ Presence is in full command of our every thought, word, action and feeling, once and for all.

THE PURGING OF THE "ANTI-CHRIST"

Once the Solar Christ Presences of all Humanity had greater access to our Holy Christ Selves, our increased Light began to push anything that conflicted with the Christ to the surface to be transmuted and loved free.

This allowed the plan that the Company of Heaven had devised to block "cosmic evil's" attempt to sabotage our Ascension in the Light to be implemented. Preparation for this phase of the plan began in the early *1980s in Medjugorje, Yugoslavia.*

Mother Mary revealed to us that within the vortex of Yugoslavia are great forces of Light and great forces of darkness, both in and out of embodiment, who volunteered to create the pageant that would escort the miscreations of Humanity, often called the anti-christ energies, into the higher schools of learning. Mother Mary said in order to prepare for this Cosmic Moment, She projected Her Luminous Presence into the forcefield of Yugoslavia (Medjugorje) for several years. Hundreds of thousands of souls from all over the World were drawn into Yugoslavia by Her Presence. As the souls came on their holy pilgrimages, they brought Rays of Light from their homelands and anchored them into Yugoslavia. Then a Ray of Divine Light from Yugoslavia was anchored in their Heart Flames and carried back to their homelands on their return journeys. This created myriad highways of Light from all over the World into Yugoslavia.

The war occurring in the former Yugoslavia *symbolically* represents the progressive descent of the human ego into chaos and hatred. It was triggered and amplified by the force of "cosmic evil" when the final pocket of negativity was permanently sealed in South Africa. Yugoslavia represents a microcosm of the macrocosm. When the oppressive yoke of communism was removed from Yugoslavia, intead of reveling in the joy of their newfound freedom, the lower human egos abiding there activated ancient hatreds. This caused men to pick up arms and begin a systematic slaughter through "ethnic cleansing." This consciousness is typical of the depravity of the human ego, and it is the epitome of the consciousness referred to as the anti-christ.

The anti-christ is, in reality, *any* frequency of vibration or *any* level of consciousness that conflicts with the perfection of the Christ. It is not specifically one entity or devil, but rather the accumulation of all of Humanity's misqualified thoughts, words, actions and feelings. It is hate, pain, poverty, disease, prejudice, suffering, fear, oppression, limitation, separation and all other aspects of existence that do not reflect the Harmony, Balance, Love and Oneness of God as expressed through Christ Consciousness. It is the confusion and pandemonium of the psychic-astral plane and the discarnate souls who are trapped there perpetuating the chaos and fear. It is our lower human egos with all of their treachery, and it is the collective ancient force known as "cosmic evil." IT IS TIME FOR THE ANTI-CHRIST TO BE BANISHED FROM THE EARTH!!!

This was indeed the next phase of the plan. A representative from Croatia (formerly Yugoslavia) was sponsored by Lightworkers to come on the Spiritual Cruise and be physically in the vortex of Limitless Solar Transmutation. In Croatia, Lightworkers were prepared to receive the Violet Light of Limitless Solar Transmutation. Through a Divine Ceremony, the Light of God that is always Victorious was projected through the vortex of the Violet Flame of Limitless Transmutation in the Caribbean to the Silent Watcher of Croatia, then into the Heart Flames of the Lightworkers there and through them INTO EVERY FREQUENCY OF ANTI-CHRIST ENERGY MANIFESTING IN CROATIA. Then the Violet Flame blazed throughout all of former Yugoslavia INTO ALL MANIFESTATIONS OF THE ANTI-CHRIST ON EARTH.

This merciful activity of God's Light created an opening in the psychic-astral plane that allowed the souls trapped there to be freed into the Inner Schools of Learning if they chose to move forward in the Light.

This literally freed millions of fallen souls who had been abiding for hundreds of thousands of years in this realm of human miscreation. This activity of Light also burst the remaining bonds of our lower human egos that were blocking the integration of our Holy Christ Selves into our four lower bodies.

This purging of the anti-christ was accomplished in perfect Divine Order in the Realms of Cause. This cleansing greatly reduced the number of souls that "cosmic evil" could entice to do its will, and it lifted much of the pressure this force had inflicted upon all Humanity in embodiment on Earth.

We began to experience the incredible freedom of that gift as it reflected into the physical world of effects. A lifting of the oppressive interference of the psychic-astral plane was felt IMMEDIATELY.

Confirmation From Nostradamus?

The Company of Heaven is always, delightfully, giving us outer world confirmation of our humble efforts to encourage us to *"keep on keeping on."*

When I returned from the Seventh Annual World Congress On Illumination, our Spiritual Cruise, there was a new book waiting in my mail. The book had not been released yet, but its author sent me an advance copy for review. When I picked the book up, it fell open to the page that contained the following information.

(The following is a quote, reprinted with permission, from the new book *NOSTRADAMUS NOW* by Joseph Robert Jochmans. This is an authoritative interpretation based on Nostradamus' original text.)

Is a Planetary Interdimensional Doorway About to be Opened?

ORIGINAL TEXT:

Loin pres de l'Urne le malin tourne arriere,
Qu'au grand Mars feu donnera
empechement:
Vers l'Aquilon au midi la grande fiere
FLORA tiendra la porte en pensement.

LINE ONE:

Loin pres de l'Urne le malin tourne arriere—"Far near the Urn the wicked one turns back." What we have here are the makings of an astrological configuration: The "Urn" is the sign of Aquarius, and in ancient symbology, the "wicked one" was considered to be the constrictive Planet of Saturn. That it "turns back" indicates it is in retrogade motion. The opening phrase "far near" was a cryptic usually employed by the prophet to designate more than one configuration, or more specifically, to pinpoint events which would take place between two configurations. In this case, whenever Saturn enters the sign of Aquarius (or any other sign), its slow motion allows time for at least two periods of retrograde motion, on the average, during its passage. It would appear that Nostradamus was designating a particular inter-retro-grade era for the next line's further astrological alignment.

LINE TWO:

Qu'au grand Mars feu donnera empechment—"That to great Mars fire will give hindrance." If we sweep away the obscurities, what the seer was actually saying is that the Planet Mars is to be found in the fire sign of Leo, which would be in opposition to the configuration of Saturn retrograde in Aquarius above. Yet, coordinating this with the information there, Nostradamus did not describe the Mars in Leo opposition as taking place at the same moment as the retrogrades but when they would be "far and near," on either side. These are very specific particulars, for in most cases, because Mars is relatively fast-moving compared with Saturn, during a Saturnian retrograde, the Red Planet is most often found either nearly conjuncted or opposed to Saturn. To find Mars in Leo exactly between two Saturn retrogrades and in the sign of Aquarius is a rarity among configurations. And this is true even if one calculates these positionings for either a Babylonian, an Astronomical or an Aquarian shifting of the signs to compensate for the Precession of the Equinoxes. As examples, no such configuration took place during Saturn's last passage through Aquarius (or Capricorn and Sagittarius) in the 1928 to 1934 era; nor will it work with the upcoming 2016-2022, the 2045-2051 or the 2075-2082 eras to manifest in the next century. However, we happen to be in a similar era as of this writing, *1986-1993.* So far, in the shiftings for the Aquarian and the Astronomical charts, nothing has come about. But for the upcoming Babylonian chart, there is a definite hit. From *May 28, to October 16, 1992,* Saturn is retrograde in Aquarius and will be again *July 1, to October 28, 1993.* In between the two, free of any overlap with either one or the other periods, Mars will be in Leo *April 28, to June 23, 1993.* Whatever events the prophet forecast in the rest of this verse, there is a good chance it will happen during this designated time—*between Easter and the Summer Solstice, 1993.*

LINE THREE:

Vers l'Aquilon au midi la grande fiere—"Toward Aquilon to the south the great woman of pride (will come)." The name "Aquilon," as we have already seen in previous studies, is derived from Aquila the Eagle, the uranology constellation which falls across what is now the United States of America and is its chief symbol. "To the south" designates a more specific area, namely the southern portion of the nation, today recognized as stretching from Virginia across the sunnier latitudes all the way to Texas. The wording "toward Aquilon" and "to the south" implies the arrival of something or someone from somewhere else, that this will be the intended destination of travel.   Who the subject is, the prophet identified as *la grand fiere*, the great Woman, with the added connotion of someone proud, dignified, possessing finesse; also considered as one held most precious, one who is relied upon for sustenance and guidance.   There is, too, the meaning of one who is "haughty," highminded, regal; likewise *fiere* is related to our words "fierce, fiery," offering us a picture of someone energetic and most singular in the fulfillment of their purpose.

These characteristics are very similar to how Nostradamus described other feminine figures in other verses: the "Woman of the Holy Earth" (IV, 24), the great "Mother" (V, 73), the "Joyous Maid of Bright Splendor" (X, 84), the "Crone Who Moves slowly" (V, 36), "She Who Offers Honey as a Gift of Love" (Sixain 18), the "great Artemis" (IX, 74) and the "Celestial Muse" (X, 50).   In the context in which many of these titles are found, it is clear the prophet was not referring to any ordinary female of human offspring, but was alluding to major feminine archetypes, Goddess figures, who represent the various creative aspects within all beingness. In particular, esoterically, the seer was honoring the World Mother of Humanity, the Earth Mother of the Planet and the Cosmic Mother of the Stars.   There is also a fourth Mother not often included with the other three because She is feared more than the rest, yet plays as important a role as the others in the creation process.   She is the Hidden Mother, who brings all things into completion. Her names are many: Kali, Hecate, Sekhmet, Pele, Tiamat, Kybele, the Black Tara, the Black Madonna.   It is She who sweeps away so that new growth can occur, a necessary part of our reality, as fall and winter are a necessary part of the cycle of the seasons, as are spring and summer. Because of Humanity's sometimes stubborn resistance to change, it is the Hidden Mother who must often appear as an angry "fierce, fiery" Goddess, the Warrior and Destroyer. However, when Her message is listened to and Humanity lets go of its outmoded ways of thinking and feeling that it has outgrown, it is She who, as the benign "sustainer," can offer a gift most "precious"—the next step in Humanity's evolution and Spiritual initiation. And it is only through her recognition and *Her inherent power of transmutation* that She can eventually fuse with the other Three Mothers, in order to bring into manifestation the Fifth Mother, the All Mother, the ultimate expression of oneness and totality.

What Nostradamus appears to be predicting here is that some form of expression and energy of the Hidden Mother (and ultimately the All Mother) is going to be influxed into the southern region of America, beginning in 1993.

(Note inserted: Is this referring to the Violet Flame of Limitless Solar Transmutation—"The Mother God reasserting Her Sacred Self with Cosmic Power" which returned to Earth June 21, 1993? See Page 189.)

LINE FOUR:

FLORA tiendra la porte en pensement—"FLORA (they) will hold the door (or gateway) in thought." Because the word FLORA is capitalized in the text, it is recognized as being a special name or title. Most commentators are too quick to associate FLORA with the city of Florence in Italy, even though it has nothing to do with the verse's other geographical specifics, "Aquilon" or Aquila-America. The one appellation that contains FLORA that stands out most prominently in the south part of America is "Florida," a perfect syncope. Though today the name Florida has been assigned to that of the famed peninsular state, originally it designated a much larger area. On the maps of Nostradamus' time, a century before the British colonization began, the Spanish used the label "Florida" to cover the entire southeast area of the North American continent—precisely in the same location considered the South today. So FLORA was simply employed as a confirmation for the geographics given in line three.

"They will hold the doorway in thought." Who "they" are understood to be is not clear, though the inference is these are people who are in some way associated with the "great Woman of pride" in line two, who are to prepare for the coming of Her Presence and serve as the catalysts for Her energies. The word tiendra can mean not only to "hold" something, but also to preserve and maintain it, suggesting that "they" will be permanent "keepers" and "protectors" of a certain location or locations. What that location/locations will have is a "door," or a "gateway," an entrance or portal into somewhere else. This will not be an ordinary physical opening (though something of a physical nature may exist to anchor it in), for it is to be "held in thought." The word used in the Old French is *pensement*, thought, pensive air, to concentrate, to focus on, mental singlemindedness and clarity; also, something visualized and imaged, then brought to mind and meditated upon again and again. What may be hinted at is some form of etheric interdimensional doorway, which will appear only within a physical anchoring structure or configuration and which can only be opened and closed through a concentrated collective visualization technique. The word *pensement* can also have the Latin connotation of "to empower."

(Note inserted: Is this referring to the PERMANENT OPEN PORTAL between Heaven and Earth through which the Divine Light of our Mother God will pour until all life on this sweet Earth is wholly Ascended and Free?   See page 188.)

Summary of the Prophecy:

During the very specific "window" time period of *April 28 to June 23, 1993*, a special group of individuals, if they choose to do so, could create a sacred space or spaces at pre-arranged locations throughout the South in the ancient region of "Florida" that could serve as an etheric doorway opening through which to invite the Hidden and other Mothers (comprising the All Mother), for Her to dwell and manifest Her powers and potential gifts to the World.

(end of quote from the book *Nostramadus Now* by
   Joseph Robert Jochman)

THE WELLSPRING OF ETERNAL HOPE

When we observe the negativity surfacing in our individual lives and witness the painful occurrences of war, disease, poverty, homelessness, environmental pollution, floods, famines, destructive weather conditions, dysfunctional families, crime, violence, corruption, drug abuse, prejudice, hate, joblessness, stress, frustration, despondency and total despair, it is very difficult for us to hold onto the belief and inner knowing that we are, in Truth, co-creating Heaven on Earth. But, nevertheless, THAT IS EXACTLY WHAT WE ARE DOING! Nobody said it was going to be easy; nobody even said it was going to be painless. What we have been told by the Realms of Illumined Truth and the Divine Mind of God, however, is that Heaven on Earth is now not only a viable possibility, but an absolutely ASSURED, GOD VICTORIOUS REALITY.

Just think, from the Realms of Perfection we are being told that Heaven on Earth has already been Victoriously Accomplished in the Divine Realms of Cause. Now, all we have to do is hold the vision in our consciousness, and through our thoughts, words, actions and feelings, magnetize that perfection into the world of form, thus transfiguring the

Earth into Her original Divine Birthright...*Freedom's Holy Star.*

I know that seems like a pretty lofty aspiration, but that is exactly why you and I are here on Earth during this unprecedented Cosmic Moment. And, if we weren't capable of pulling this off, we wouldn't have been allowed to embody on Earth at this time. It's that simple.

So, instead of wringing our hands and bemoaning the challenges in our lives, we need to reach up in consciousness and tap the Wisdom and Enlightenment that will set us *Free*.

This is such a special time, and we are beginning to get intuitive, inner glimpses of the magnitude of this Cosmic Moment on Earth. People are constantly expressing to me that they are experiencing a "feeling" or a new "level of understanding" about what's happening on Earth and in their lives that they were never aware of before. They just seem to "know" things that confused and baffled them in the past. They say their ability to discern what resonates as Truth in their hearts is much more obvious, and they have greater clarity and are able to pierce through the veil of illusion to perceive the reality of a situation much more easily. This isn't a skill that they are specifically working toward developing; it just seems to be mysteriously happening.

Even though people are still dealing with the dysfunctional belief systems of low self-esteem, failure, poverty consciousness, worthlessness, abandonment, separation, loneliness, etc., in the midst of the pain and suffering, they are beginning to get brief flashes of absolutely *"knowing"* that they are truly Sons and Daughters of God, and *"all that the Father has is mine."* Even though they are feeling overwhelmed by the enormity of the challenges manifesting on the Planet and sometimes helpless in their ability to change things, they keep hearing an inner voice that repeats again and again. *"You can do this! You came to love this Earth and all Her life free, and all the skills and knowledge you need to accomplish your goals are already within you."* When a person is feeling worthless and help-less, that statement seems rather ludicrous, but there is a new *"inner knowing"* that, for a brief glimmer of time, allows one to accept that Truth as unequivocally real.

It is a true paradox that one minute we are feeling like worthless *"worms in the dust,"* and the next minute we know that we are Sons and Daughers of God. But, there is a logical explanation as to why this phenomenon is occurring with ever-increasing frequency at this time. Since the return of the Solar Christ Presence, we have been undergoing a trans-formational healing. As our Twelve Solar Strands of DNA are integrated into our physical bodies, we are reconnecting with the Realms of Illumined Truth and Knowledge. It was never part of the original Divine Plan that we be separated from this realm but, due to our curiosity and the misuse of our creative faculties of thought and feeling, we manifested this situation.

For aeons of time, we have mistakenly been accepting this Third Dimensional reality as the only reality, and we grew to believe that our physical body is who we are. Imagine, we have been accepting only a *minuscule* part of our Being as our true God Reality! With the return of our Solar Christ Presence, the Twelve-fold Solar Flame of our Christ Presence is now blazing through our Heart Centers. It is activating our Twelve-fold Solar Spine and our Twelve-fold Solar Causal Body. The multidimensional, multicolored frequencies of Solar Light are interpenetrating every atom and molecule of our four lower bodies. As the Solar Light spins out from our Heart Flames, It fills the space between the electrons and sub-atomic particles of our bodies at an atomic cellular level.

This activity of Light is lifting us up in vibration into an octave of timelessness and spacelessness. This is giving our God Presence the opportunity to reweave the Twelve Solar Strands of DNA, thus *reconnecting our communication system* with the Realms of Illumined Truth and Knowledge and our God Presence. This is happening gradually, according to the Divine Plan of each individual.

As we reconnect the circuits of our Twelve Solar Strands of DNA, we are experiencing glimpses of "inner knowing." Before long we will be permanently reconnected with our multidimensional God Selves. Then, we will not have to depend on our limited lower human consciousness or anyone else's interpretations of Truth. We will know that we know that we know. Our time of floundering in ignorance and darkness will be over.

We will *know* that all life is interrelated, and we will *know* that we cannot hurt any part of life without its reflecting back on us. We will *know* that the supply of the Universe is limitless, and we will *know* that the Earth is merely a reflection of Humanity's consciousness. We will *know* that poverty, hate, pain, suffering, disease, prejudice, evil, aging, death and all other forms of mutated energy are human miscreations that are *not* a necessary part of our Earthly experience. And we will *know* that Heaven on Earth is not only a viable option, it is a very tangible imminent reality.

As we grasp this inner knowing, we will also remember one of the most important things of all. We will remember the Truth of what the Polarities of God *REALLY* are so that we will stop creating negativity through our erroneous belief systems.

It is true that everything has a dual polarity, but the polarity of God is NOT "good and evil"...REMEMBER...

The Polarity of God is the Duality of the Divine Masculine and the Divine Feminine

GOD DOES NOT RELEASE ONE ELECTRON OF PRECIOUS LIFE ENERGY THAT IS VIBRATING AT A FREQUENCY LESS THAN THE TOTAL PERFECTION OF GOD!!!

Therefore, ANYTHING that is vibrating at a frequency less than the Limitless Physical Perfection of HEAVEN ON EARTH is...**A HUMAN MISCREATION**...A MUTATION OF OUR PRECIOUS GIFT OF LIFE THAT **WE** CREATED THROUGH THE **MISUSE** OF OUR CREATIVE FACULTIES OF THOUGHT AND FEELING...and, it must, therefore, be transmuted back into its original Divine Intent in order for us to Ascend into the Fourth/Fifth Dimensional Octaves of Perfection.

If that seems hard to accept, know that is only because we have been struggling with the mutated creations of poverty, disease, war, crime, pollution, hate, fear, in other words, "evil," for so long that we can't even fathom what life would be like without them. I promise you, however, in the not-too-distant future, you are going to have the glorious opportunity to experience life on Earth without those maladies.

Accessing the Ascension Flame...a Gift of Hope

As the Twelve Solar Strands of DNA are rewoven within us and the Light filaments are reconnected through the Twelve Solar Helixes, the short circuit that disconnected us from the Realms of Illumined Truth and Knowledge will be spliced in a way that will automatically activate the pre-encoded memories of all the knowledge and Truth we have ever known. The trick is that we, and the rest of Humanity, have to get our heads above the mud puddle of pain, suffering and fear long enough to raise the frequency of our bodies in order for the complete reweaving of our Twelve Solar Strands to occur.

We are receiving welcomed assistance from On High to help us accomplish this tremendous feat. The Feminine Polarity of God, the essence of Divine Love, is pouring into the Planet as never before. It is awakening the right brain hemisphere and opening the Heart Center of every Human Being. This activity of Light is balancing our rational, logical minds (left brains) with our creative, intuitive minds (right brains), and it is balancing the power Center of our Throats with the Love Center of our Hearts.   When this balance effectively occurs, our power is always balanced with love, which instills within us a perpetual reverence for all life. This safeguards against any abuse of power.   When we are continually expressing our power embraced in the Divine Quality of Love, the distorted behavior patterns of aggression, dominance, greed, corruption, inhumanity, crime, violence, war, prejudice, hate, etc., will be non-existent.

We are going through a very special initiation at this time, and the Stargates in our Hearts are opening.   This allows each of us to connect with the Heart of God, opening a permanent portal of Divine Love from the Realms of Perfection into the physical reality of Earth. The opening of the Stargate of the Heart allows Humanity's feeling nature to be lifted upward. This enables our feelings to be refocused, changing the power of our attention from fear to abounding joy. This shift of consciousness alone will make a tremendous difference in our frequency of vibration, and it will move us a quantum leap forward.

The critical need of this momentous hour is for the masses of Humanity to awaken to the opportunity at hand. This blessed Planet and all Her life are Ascending into the Fourth/Fifth Dimensional experience of an unlimited timeless, spaceless, Solar Reality. This is the next evolutionary step of our Solar System. The magnitude of just what this Ascension means is beyond the understanding of our finite Human minds. Consequently, we don't "get it," and we don't understand how to implement the concept of it into our everyday realities. It, therefore, just becomes a lofty platitude to the majority of people. Because it doesn't seem real, they don't benefit from the abounding joy of realizing Heaven on Earth is an imminent reality.

Ascension is a quality of the Fourth Solar Aspect of Deity. It is the radiance of this Solar Aspect that is bathing the Planet and flooding the consciousness of Humanity with the frequencies of the Ascension Flame. It has been determined by the Godhead that, due to the fact that most of Humanity is still immersed in the quagmire of pain and suffering, the frequencies of the Ascension Flame are usually vibrating above what our conscious minds can grasp. Consequently, this Gift of Light is not having the positive effect that was expected. To remedy this problem, a contingency plan has been set into motion. It has been determined by the Company of Heaven that the influx of the Ascension Flame needs to be stepped down into a frequency that resonates clearly through the hearts of every man, woman and child on Earth, regardless of their level of consciousness or fear. The quality of the Fourth Solar Aspect of Deity that fits that particular qualification is HOPE.

Through a Divine Activity of Light projected through the Cup of Humanity's consciousness, the entire Company of Heaven magnetized from the very Heart of our Father-Mother God the glorious *Wellspring of Eternal Hope*. This Holy Light was anchored into this sweet Earth during the *Autumn Equinox in 1993.* This Divine Wellspring of Eternal Hope is now blazing through the open Stargates of the Hearts of all Humanity, and It is secured within the Divine Momentum in the center of the Earth to continually bubble up through the waters and the crust of the Earth, bathing every electron of precious life energy evolving on this Planet in the Divine Essence of HOPE.

This Wellspring of Eternal Hope is allowing the consciousness of Humanity to be lifted up once again, and It is enabling us to remember who we are. The masses are awakening to the fact that they are Sons and Daughters of God, and they are, once again, becoming receptive to the possibility of transformation—transformation of their own lives of pain, transformation of the collective Family of Humanity and transformation of Beloved Mother Earth.

The Wellspring of Eternal Hope is causing people to open their hearts and minds. It is stirring within them the need for Truth and the need to connect with other Lightworkers on the Planet so that they will feel loved and supported in their newfound wisdom and hope.

It is imperative that each Lightworker be a Peace Commanding Presence of Love, a safe haven whereby those awakening souls who are drawn to your sphere of influence may take a drink from your cup in an atmosphere of acceptance, tolerance, integrity, safety and above all, Divine Love. It is time that the Truth be made readily available to all seekers. And, it is time that every seeker be given the space to determine his/her own Truth through Divine Discerning Intelligence.

Ask the Presence of God blazing in your heart to magnetize into your Forcefield of Light any seeker of Truth who can benefit in any way from your love and your Truth. Then, in humble gratitude, give them a drink from your cup *with no expectations and absolutely no strings attached.*

As awakening souls experience the Wisdom and Knowledge of the Ages, they will be lifted higher and higher until their Twelve Solar Strands of DNA are rewoven, and the direct connection with their own multidimensional God Selves and the Realms of Illumined Truth will be complete. Then, they will not have to depend on any outside source for their information or Truth, and your service to them will have been accomplished God Victoriously.

THE RETURN OF THE
DIVINE MOTHER PRINCIPLE

With the Divine Balance of our Father-Mother God, the Violet Flame of Limitless Transmutation pouring into the Planet through the interdimensional doorway in the Caribbean and the Wellspring of Eternal Hope blazing through every part of life, we were ready for the next step of the

Divine Plan.

For an eleven-day period, from *November 11, 1993*, to *November 22, 1993*, the Flames of Limitless Transmutation and Liberation were greatly amplified on the Planet. This activity of Light was the final purging and healing of our Emotional Bodies and the emotional strata of Earth prior to the return of the Divine Mother Principle.

On *November 28, 1993*, we experienced a total *Full Moon Lunar Eclipse*. This Eclipse was in full view in the southwestern United States of America. The momentum of this Lunar Eclipse dealt with clearing the Karmic debris that has kept Humanity bound to the past. This unusual Eclipse set the stage for a very powerful purification of the etheric patterns of all of the negativity we have ever experienced as a result of the Divine Mother Principle withdrawing from the Earth when we closed down our Heart Centers during the "fall." This negativity consisted of all the abuse and neglect that has been inflicted on the feminine aspect of life in any way, shape or form. It consisted of all the struggles women have endured as mothers and wives. It consisted of all oppression women have experienced in the way of degradation, humiliation, sexual abuse, lack of respect, lack of reverence, lack of honor and lack of love. It also consisted of the invalidation and negation of women and their feminine qualities of intuition, creativity, nurturing and love.

These discordant patterns, pulsating in the Emotional Bodies of Humanity and the emotional strata of Earth, have created the greatest and most effective block in preventing the return to Earth of the feeling nature of God, the Divine Mother Principle. The Lunar Eclipse, conjunct with the South Node, enabled these destructive patterns to be cut free from the atomic, cellular substance of physical matter, and it allowed the liberation of these fallen patterns from the RNA/DNA blueprints of the Third Dimension. This prepared the fallen feminine energies to be Victoriously Ascended back into the Light.

On *December 5, 1993*, several hundred people gathered in Los Angeles, California, within the forcefield of the Angelic Vortex, the portal that was the original Vortex of the Goddess on the continent of Lemuria. Lightworkers from all over the World joined with us in consciousness, and the Solar Christ Presences of all Humanity participated at inner levels. Throughout a six-hour seminar, Light from the very Heart of God poured through the Angelic Vortex into the cup of our unified consciousness. The Light was then projected into the Crystal Grid System of Earth. This Light of Divine Love from our Mother God created reinforcing grids of love through all of the land faults in California and through all of the tectonic plates, faults, fissures and cracks in the body of Mother Earth, embracing this blessed Planet in an invincible forcefield of protection and Divine Love.

This Light of Divine Love was projected into the right brain hemisphere of each person evolving on Earth. Then, It poured through the open Stargate of every heart into the physical plane. This created an expanded grid of love permanently reconnecting every man, woman and child in the embrace of our Mother God. This was a Divine Baptism of the Holy Spirit in every sacred sense of the word. All was then in readiness for the return of the Archetype for the Divine Mother Principle.

The resplendent Presence of the Divine Mother Archetype was projected into the atmosphere of Earth from the very Heart of God through the open Angelic Vortex and through the open Stargate of every heart. The Immaculate Concept of this Divine Blueprint was re-encoded in the genetic patterns of all life evolving on Earth, thus preparing each particle of life for the perfect balancing of the right and left brain hemispheres and the balancing of the Throat Center of Power and the Heart Center of Love.

This blueprint of the Divine Mother Archetype built in power and momentum until the *Winter Solstice, December 21, 1993. During that Cosmic Moment, the Archetype of the Divine Mother Principle was anchored through every Heart Flame into the center of the Earth* for all Eternity. This brought to perfect God-Victorious fruition the RETURN OF THE FEELING NATURE OF GOD, THE DIVINE MOTHER PRINCIPLE, TO EARTH!!!

Balancing the Patriarchal Energies on Earth

With the Victory of this facet of the plan accomplished, we were truly ready for a glorious rebirth and Ascension into the next phase of the Divine Plan.

Capricorn begins on the Winter Solstice, which is the longest night of the year in the Northern Hemisphere, and it is considered the most mysterious of all of the Sun Cycles. The Winter Solstice has always been perceived as the holiest night of the year, since it heralds the return of the Sun, the Light, to Earth. Light is the Law of Life. Capricorn represents the Essence of the Law. For millenia now Capricorn has reflected only the Patriarchal Law of the Father. This was the result of the tragic withdrawal of the Matriarchal energies of the Divine Mother Principle. As the imbalance of masculine energies began to overwhelm the Earth, the Patriarchal Law of the Father was misunderstood and misused by Humanity to dominate, manipulate and control life. In order for the Earth to regain Her rightful place in the Universe, this travesty had to be corrected. This, in fact, was the next phase of the Divine Plan.

The first New Moon following the Winter Solstice is considered extremely powerful because it symbolizes the Feminine Nature of God (represented by the Moon) assisting the Masculine Nature of God (represented by the Sun) to bring the Light back to Earth. The first *New Moon* following the *Winter Solstice of 1993*, was on *January 11, 1994.*

January 11, 1994, was an unbelievably powerful day. Not only was it the first New Moon following the unparalleled return of the Divine Mother Principle which occurred on the Winter Solstice, but it also was empowered with a very, very rare alignment of Planets. On that sacred day, seven Planets (Mercury, Venus, Mars, Uranus, Neptune, the Sun and the Moon) were aligned within a nine-degree span in the Sun Cycle of Capricorn. That rare alignment was the most concentrated alignment of Planets in the last 300 years.

That alignment in the Sun Cycle of Capricorn during the Cosmic Moment of the return of our Mother God heralded the reinstatement of the BALANCE OF THE MATRIAR-CHAL LAW OF THE MOTHER on Earth.

On *January 11, 1994*, once again this sweet Earth and all Her life Ascended yet another quantum leap closer to the Heart of Perfection. This time the Earth was embraced in the perfect BALANCE OF THE LAW OF LIGHT OF OUR FATHER-MOTHER GOD. Held within that balance of Light, we were able to Ascend **in consciousness** into the Solar Heart of our Beloved God Parents in the Great Central Sun. There our Solar Christ Presences were invested with Twelve-fold Solar Heart Flames. This literally means that the Three-fold Flame we have always experienced as our Divine Spark has now been empowered and expanded to reflect into all of our experiences the Twelve Solar Aspects of our Father-Mother God in PERFECT BALANCE. Our Heart Flames are now Twelve-fold spiraling reflections of the Twelve Solar Aspects of Deity with Immortal Three-fold Flames pulsating as the Permanent Seed Atoms in the center. The Stargates of our Hearts are now open to all Dimensions of Divinity, and as we evolve into a new level of Godhood, even the body of God is evolving.

As we focus our attention on this Truth, our God Presences will reveal to us the immensity of just how this will enhance our Earthly sojourn. Our Ascension into the Light is steady and secure. There is no turning back, and our Victory is assured. What a sacred honor and privilege it is to be part of this glorious plan. We are ALL immeasurably blessed.

Reassuring Evidence That the Predicted
Cataclysmic Earthquakes Have Been Averted

The Earth is a living, breathing organism. She is cleansing and purging Her four lower bodies just like we are. As the Earth Ascends in frequency and vibration, the discord is pushed to the surface for purification. This often causes discomfort and some distress, but the end result is certainly going to be worth the inconvenience.

The Divine Covenant that was made between Humanity and the Elemental Kingdom during the first Earth Summit assured that the **devastating, cataclysmic destruction of large land masses and millions of people** *will not occur.* Instead, it was agreed that the cleansing and release of toxins and pressure within the body of Mother Earth will take place as constructively as possible with as little loss of life as possible.

The Earth must be purified of the abominations we have inflicted upon Her, so we will experience some difficult challenges like the *1993* and *1997* floods that we had through the farmlands and along the Ohio River in the United States. These healing waters purged much of the adverse effects of the chemical fertilizers and toxic pesticides that had contaminated the body of Mother Earth. This was extremely hard on the people who lived in those areas, but, mercifully, there was very little loss of life.

The important thing for us to really observe and be grateful for is that even though we are experiencing some powerful purging and releasing techniques of nature like tornadoes, hurricanes, fires, floods, volcanic eruptions, earthquakes and extreme weather conditions there has been relatively little loss of life.

I know it's very sad to lose personal property and our lifetime of treasures, but "THINGS" can be replaced eventually. Our loved ones are priceless and irreplaceable. After the initial shock and grief over the loss of our material possessions, we can begin a new adventure together as long as we still have each other.

The Nature Kingdom is giving us tangible signs that it is deliberately orchestrating the Earth's cleansing and has precise control over every activity. Regardless of how chaotic and out of control the acts of nature appear, NOT A BLADE OF GRASS OR A GRAIN OF SAND IS MOVED THAT IS NOT SUPPOSED TO BE MOVED. It is all in Divine Order.

When the astrologers and psychics around the World became aware of the concentrated alignment of Planets that was to occur on *January 11, 1994*, all of them predicted that the added gravitational pull on the Earth would cause cataclysmic earthquakes. But instead, on *December 5, 1993*, our Mother God, the exponent of the Nature Kingdom reinforced the faults, fissures, tectonic plates and cracks of the Earth with Divine Love. Then, the Elemental Kingdom held the pressure in abeyance until it could be released with the least destruction to human life. On *January 17, 1994, at 4:30 a.m.* on a legal holiday, the pressure was released in Los Angeles, California. Even the news announcers said it was a "miracle" that the earthquake occurred when it did.

Another earthquake took place that was 8.2 on the Richter Scale. If it had occurred in a populated area, it would have killed millions of people. Instead it was so deep within the Earth that little life was lost even though the earthquake appeared on monitors from Bolivia to Canada.

Earthquakes measuring 7.0 to 7.8 on the Richter Scale have occurred a few times as well. They are always far out in the ocean or in unpopulated areas. Then, so that we couldn't possibly deny the precise control and timing being utilized by the Directors of the Elements, one year to the *DAY, HOUR AND MINUTE, January 17, 1995, at 4:30 a.m.* in Kobe, Japan, we experienced another tremendous earthquake. Sadly, there were 6,400 people killed in that earth-quake, but the news announcers said it was a "miracle" that it occurred at that time. They said if it had occurred just *two hours* later, NINE HUNDRED THOUSAND people would have lost their lives.

Don't Be a Pawn of the Forces of Imbalance

Incredibly powerful "natural disasters" are taking place with mercifully little loss of life. This is being done to PROVE to us that the covenant has been made, and the Elemental Kingdom is once again working in harmony with us instead of being at war with us. The psychic-astral plane and the force of "cosmic evil" was very aware of this new Covenant. It knew it had lost the ability to get the Nature Kingdom to perpetuate its sinister will. Consequently, it was striving desperately to coerce our lower human egos into cooperating with it to recreate the destruction.

The forces of imbalance clearly understood the tremendous power of Humanity's collective thoughts and feelings. It knew if it could get our human egos to focus our attention on fear, earthquakes, cataclysmic destruction, etc., that we would recreate the thoughtforms to bring those things into manifestation. Many times, sincere, but misdirected psychics, are still predicting destructive Earth changes. They even go so far as to set dates and create maps to focus the full power of our attention and fear on one moment in time. Needless to say, this is incredibly destructive to the overall Divine Plan of planetary healing that is now in full swing.

Whenever you become aware of some destructive "prediction," instead of amplifying it with your thoughts or feelings, immediately invoke the full power of the Violet Flame of Limitless Transmutation and Forgiveness into the situation. Ask that every electron of the destructive thoughtform be transmuted cause, core, effect, record and memory according to the highest good for all concerned. Then, send your love into the Elemental Kingdom, and in deep humility and gratitude, bless the Elementals for their loving cooperation. Invoke Enlightenment and Wisdom into the consciousness of the psychics still making such predictions, and energize your vision of the New Heaven and the New Earth.

BURSTING THE BONDS
OF OUR HUMAN EGOS

After the tear in the Etheric Body of Mother Earth was healed on *April 1, 1983*, the Company of Heaven waited patiently for Humanity to reach a point where our own Etheric Bodies could be healed. Remember, the tear in Mother Earth's Etheric body not only trapped hundreds of thousands of souls in limbo, it also reflected on our individual Etheric Bodies, causing a weakness, sometimes even a hole in these vehicles.

All life is interrelated, and as we interpenetrated the Etheric Substance of Earth through physical embodiment over and over again, the Etheric tear began to reflect in the substance of our individual Etheric Bodies. This caused a weakness which made us vulnerable and susceptible to the influence of the psychic-astral plane of confusion and chaos. Needless to say, this wreaked all manner of havoc in our lives. This weakness in our auras has allowed the forces of imbalance to have direct access to our lower human egos. Through this vulnerable spot in our energy field, the psychic-astral realm that was striving to maintain control of the Earth and trying to keep us bound to fear and limitation was able to amplify our feelings of inadequacy and failure consciousness. It was able to perpetuate our belief in lack and limitation, and it thoroughly convinced us that our limited, struggling, oppressive lower human ego is who we actually are. There is not another aspect of ourselves that is LESS real.

This hole in our aura also complicated our situations on Earth because it allowed more negativity from the mass consciousness surrounding us to seep into our electromagnetic energy fields. This had the effect of amplifying our difficult experiences. What this means is that for aeons of time now, as a result of the Etheric tear, we have been going through much more pain and suffering than we would normally have experienced. With the flaw in our Etheric Bodies, everything we went through was compounded by negative outside influences. No wonder things seemed to be so incredibly out of balance.

For *eleven years*, the Cosmic Events I have described to you slowly prepared all of Humanity for the healing of our Etheric Bodies. Finally, we were in a position to have the flaw in our Etheric Bodies healed once and for all, thus eliminating permanently the undue influence the forces of imbalance had over the wayward aspect of our lower human egos.

In order to realize this goal, a Divine Plan was formed to unify the consciousness of the entire Company of Heaven with the God Presences of all Humanity. Once again, on the *11th anniversary of the healing of the Etheric Body of Mother Earth*, as the Spiritual energies of the **Vernal Equinox** and the **Resurrection Flame** flooded the Planet, the plan was activated and set into motion. On **Good Friday, April 1, 1994, the Solar Christ Presence of every man, woman and child evolving on Earth (whether they were in or out of embodiment) expanded Its Divine Self through the Heart Flame and burst asunder the last vestiges of the oppressive grip of the lower human ego.**

This activity of Light enabled the Stargates of our Hearts to open the maximum we had experienced since the "fall" aeons ago. Then, on the third day, the full-gathered momentum of the Resurrection Flame poured into every Heart Flame and literally Resurrected the lower human ego of every Human Being, transforming this fallen aspect of our human personalities into a higher level of consciousness. This was accomplished the maximum that Cosmic Law would allow for each individual soul. The victory of this Divine activity was achieved as the first Rays of the Sun began to bless the Earth on *Resurrection Morn, Easter Sunday, April 3, 1994.*

After that glorious event, daily and hourly the Solar Christ Presence integrated Itself, ever so gently and lovingly, into the atomic cellular substance of each person's Etheric Body in preparation for the Cosmic Moment when the Etheric tear in our Etheric Bodies could be healed.

THE PERMANENT OPENING
OF THE VORTEX OF THE GODDESS

With the oppressive grip of our human egos burst asunder, our God Parents from the Great Central Sun, Elohae and Eloha, were at last ready to fulfill the promise They made to the Star System of Sirius hundreds of thousands of years ago when Sirius realized that the Earth was not going to survive without further assistance. At that time, the Divine Intelligence from Sirius appealed to the Father-Mother God of our Great Central Sun and asked again for permission to bathe the Earth in the love of our Mother God until Humanity could resume this activity on Her own. A special dispensation was granted, but only for a minute fraction of the Light that originally poured through the Vortex of the Goddess.

Elohae and Eloha told Sirius that in a distant, future time there would be a Cosmic Moment in the evolution of this blessed Earth when Humanity would reach into the embrace of Her Solar Christ Presences. They said during that moment They would hold the Earth in the Solar Frequencies of God Perfection, and as a gift of love for the service the Earth rendered to the fallen laggard souls, and as a gift of gratitude to the Star System of Sirius for the selfless service rendered to Earth, they would allow Sirius to **PERMANENTLY** OPEN THE VORTEX OF THE DIVINE MOTHER/ GODDESS!!!

Since the original opening of the Vortex of the Goddess hundreds of thousands of years ago, Sirius has annually opened the Goddess Vortex only slightly to allow a mere trickle of the Divine Mother's Love to flow into Earth. This has been barely enough to keep our Heart Centers and our right brains alive. Yet it has been an act of selfless service, mercy and compassion beyond our comprehension.

In addition to the annual influx of Divine Mother energies, Sirius was given a cyclic opportunity to amplify Its efforts to intensify the love pouring through the Vortex of the Goddess. This cycle occurs every 52 years during a unique celestial event. It is known as the Sirius Periastron, and it is marked by the esoteric holy union of Sirius A and its satellite Star, Sirius B. This is the moment when these two celestial bodies are in closest proximity to each other. And, it is a time when the Sirius Star System is profoundly magnified throughout our Universe.

1994 heralded the Cosmic Moment decreed by Elohae and Eloha. These Divine Beings joined Alpha and Omega, our God Parents from our Central Sun and Helios and Vesta, our God Parents from our physical Sun. As one unified force, These glorious exponents of our Father-Mother God joined together to embrace this Earth in the Divine Balance of Solar Existence. As a result of this unique Divine Intervention, Humanity was lifted into the loving arms of Her receptive Solar Christ Presences. This amplified the opening of the Stargates of our Hearts. THEN, ALL WAS IN READINESS FOR THE PERMANENT OPENING OF THE VORTEX OF THE DIVINE MOTHER/GODDESS THROUGH THE STAR SYSTEM OF SIRIUS.

During the weekend of *April 16-17, 1994*, a Whole Life Expo was held at the Convention Center in downtown Los Angeles within the tremendous Angelic Vortex pulsating there. Thousands of Lightworkers were magnetized into the Vortex of the Goddess through this event. This allowed the entire Company of Heaven access into the physical plane through the Unified Cup of Humanity's Consciousness. A tremendous Chalice of Light was formed, and the God Presence of each Lightworker, physically in attendance or tuning in at inner or outer levels, wove into the Chalice the Divine Intent of our Mother God. This activity of Light prepared the physical vehicles of Humanity throughout the next seven days in order to lift every man, woman and child into our highest level of receptivity.

On *April 22, 1994*, the day celebrated Globally as *Earth Day*, our Father-Mother God bathed the Elemental Kingdom with the nurturing love of the Divine Mother. This activity of Light created a feeling of safety and comfort through all of the Gnomes and Nature Spirits, Salamanders, Undines, and Sylphs, through the Devas and Deva Rajas and all of the Builders of Form, thus preparing each one to receive the greatest influx of Divine Love ever manifested in the history of time.

On *April 23, 1994*, the celestial event of the Sirius Periastron took place. On that sacred day additional factors occurred which greatly empowered the holy union of Sirius A and its satellite star, Sirius B. A unique cyclical positioning of Pluto, Neptune and the Moon created a significantly special Cosmic trigger to enhance the essence of the Divine Love of our Mother God.

On that sacred and holy day, our Beloved God Parents from the Great Central Sun sounded a Mighty Trumpet, and the Celestial Tone resounded throughout the Universe, signaling the Star System of Sirius to open to full breadth the Vortex of the Goddess—the Portal of the Divine Mother—in Los Angeles, California.

For the first time in hundreds of thousands of years, the Divine Love of our Mother God poured into Planet Earth unimpeded by the flaw of human miscreation. The Solar

Christ Presence of each one of us is now daily and hourly assimilating this incredible Light through our Solar Heart Flames. It is being absorbed the maximum that we can endure, with every breath we take. This Divine Love is all-powerful and unimaginable. With it comes the Dawn of the New Heaven and the New Earth. The core of purity pulsating within every electron of precious life energy is being **reactivated**, and the Divine Blueprint, which was pre-encoded within our cellular patterns aeons ago, is being projected onto our RNA/DNA genetic codes.

The Divine Blueprint for this blessed Planet and all life evolving upon Her is now being established as the order of the New Cosmic Day. The Divine Love of our Mother God now brings to us, through the Divine Blueprint, all of the knowledge, wisdom and understanding we need to create a World of Limitless Physical Perfection. On *April 24, 1994*, we experienced the *Full Moon of Taurus*. This sacred time is celebrated each year as the Wesak Festival. It is a Global activity that honors the Divine Love and Balance of Buddhic Consciousness through the Ascended Wisdom and Love of our Solar Christ Presences. On this holy day, the fully opened Vortex of the Goddess was permanently anchored in every Heart Flame to blaze eternally through all life on Earth, assuring this sweet Earth's God Victorious Ascension into the LIGHT! We are NOW **changing**. We are NOW **transforming** our physical realities, at an atomic cellular level, into Heaven on Earth. It is very, very important for each of us to ask the Presence of God blazing in our hearts to reveal to us just what this glorious gift really means to us individually. Listen to your inner directives. Then, act with conviction and courage. Never have we had a more incredible opportunity to Ascend into Divine Love and Physical Perfection. We must turn our potential into action, and we must make it our physical reality.

Through this Divine Activity of Light, our Mother God is bringing to Earth, and to each of us, Her gift of Divine Love.

Through this gift, our lives and our World will be transformed. We are Her vessels, Her instruments of Light on Earth, and through our Solar Heart Flames, we can now be **"the open door that no one can shut."** Through the opened Stargates of our Hearts, She will bring to the suffering Human, Elemental and Angelic Kingdoms evolving on Earth gifts and treasures that are unimaginable and limitless.

And, **this is just the beginning**! We have moved off of the Wheel of Karma and returned to our Spiral of Evolution. We are daily and hourly Ascending into higher frequencies of God's Perfection. Just take a moment and FEEL the elation of your God Presence pouring through your heart. What a magnificent moment.

WE ARE COMING HOME!!!

THE TEAR IN
OUR ETHERIC BODIES IS HEALED!

After the incredible influx of the Divine Love of our Mother God that occurred through the opening of the Vortex of the Goddess, all was in readiness for the next phase of the Divine Plan. On *May 10, 1994*, during a *New Moon Solar Eclipse*, the likes of which will not occur again until the *Cosmic Year 2012*, the Light of God pierced deeply into the depths of human miscreation and activated within the dregs of human existence and fallen laggard energies the REMEMBRANCE OF DIVINITY.

As the Solar Eclipse swept across our Beloved Planet Earth, the dormant Spark of Divinity that had all but been extinguished in the most depraved consciousness of the fallen laggard souls was *revivified*. The Divine Blueprint, which was activated with the opening of the Vortex of the Goddess for every particle of life evolving on Earth, was awakened within the genetic codes of each of these fallen souls. And the initial **stirring of the conscious mind began**.

On *May 12, 1994, Ascension Thursday*, the day celebrated as the Ascension of the Christ (40 days after the Resurrection), the Ascension Flame bathed all life on Earth in Its Divine Essence. As this glorious gift from God blazed in, through and around every electron of precious life energy evolving on Earth, the fallen laggard miscreations that were still adversely affecting this Planet were raised up in energy, vibration and consciousness and permanently **SEALED** in the Light of the Ascension Flame. This activity of Light **assured that never again will Humanity fall to the depths of previous laggard consciousness**.

For *10 days*, the arisen laggard energies were given an opportunity to adjust to their new, higher frequency. During that time, our Father-Mother God projected the Light of Mercy and Compassion into the stirring conscious mind of each soul. This gave the mental strata of unified consciousness surrounding the Earth an upliftment.

It is one thing for the Divine Blueprint of Heaven on Earth to be once again activated within our RNA/DNA genetic codes, but it is quite another thing for our conscious minds to perceive the blueprint and grasp the patterns clearly enough to bring them into physical manifestation. It was obvious from outer appearances that we needed superhuman assistance in order to translate the Divine Blueprint from a thoughtform into physical reality. That, in fact, was the next step in the Divine Plan.

On *May 22, 1994*, the day celebrated as *Pentecost*, the day of the Baptism of the Holy Spirit, the hallowed substance of the Holy Breath of the Holy Spirit flooded the Earth. This Divine Essence penetrated deep into the core of purity within every electron of physical matter. It expanded the previous activation of the Divine Blueprint and accelerated the Immaculate Concept of all manifest form into the mental strata of consciousness. This means that now the tangible vision of Heaven on Earth is filtering into our conscious minds as never before, and the veil between Heaven and Earth is becoming gossamer.

With the God Victorious Accomplishment of all of the previous activities of Light, Humanity was finally pulsating in an octave of both vibration and consciousness that would be conducive to healing the flaw in our Etheric Bodies.

On *May 24, 1994*, we experienced a *Full Moon Lunar Eclipse*. The Sun represents the outer radiance and Power of our Father God, and the Moon represents the inner Divinity and Love of our Mother God. During the Cosmic Moment of the Lunar Eclipse, as we were held within the nurturing embrace of our Mother God, an intensified frequency of Divine Healing poured into Earth from the Core of all Creation. This Sacred Light of Healing flowed through the Etheric Body of every Being evolving on Earth and *permanently healed the ancient flaw that was caused when Lemuria sank beneath the healing waters of the Pacific Ocean.* The weaknesses and the holes in our Etheric Bodies were repaired. The new frequency of healing strengthened every facet of this Earthly vehicle.

A NEW ORDER OF ANGELIC ASSISTANCE

As you know, nothing happens by accident. This glorious freeing activity of Light, the healing of our Etheric Bodies, occurred during the *Full Moon of Gemini*. This is the Full Moon that is celebrated annually as the Festival of Goodwill for Humanity. Surely nothing will enhance the Goodwill of Humanity and our Reverence for **ALL** Life more effectively than being freed from the pain and suffering of mass consciousness and the insidious influence of our lower human egos and the forces of imbalance.

Now, having this information is one thing, but intellectual knowledge is useless if we can't integrate what we know and live out of that Illumined Truth. It's very easy for us to turn on the television or read a newspaper and say, *"If all of this glorious stuff is really happening, why do things look so bleak?"* The answer to that question is that our transformation is a process.   We are multidimensional Beings functioning on all levels of consciousness at once.   The change first begins in the Realm of Cause, and then it filters through the various octaves of reality into physical manifestation or what we call *"the world of effects."* The physical plane, which we perceive to be "reality," is actually the least **REAL** of all the dimensions of consciousness we abide in, and it is the very LAST dimension to reflect change. It takes time for the magnificent changes occurring on Earth to filter into physical manifestation.

As the new frequencies of harmony and perfection begin to penetrate into the core of purity within all physical matter, they push the conflicting negativity to the surface for purification. This is like putting a pot on the stove to boil, and all of the scum bubbles up to the surface. That is what is occurring on Earth at the present time, and that is why everything seems so horrific in our own personal lives, as well as Globally.

Fortunately, we are receiving more assistance from On High than ever before, and continually we're being blessed with Divine Help. On the day of the ***Lunar Eclipse***, after the incredible healing of our Etheric Bodies, a two-hour program about Angels was aired on national television. This, needless to say, was *not a coincidence*. Remember, the law is *"Where your attention is, there you are."* With hundreds of millions of people around the World focusing on Angels through satellite communication, a tremendous Heart Call rang through the Universe invoking the assistance of the Angelic Kingdom.

The collective Divine Presence of Humanity asked for help in sustaining the new level of awakened consciousness, and It asked for the courage and tenacity of each soul to persevere until the physical manifestation of Heaven on Earth, even in the face of all adversity. In response to Humanity's unified Heart Call, our Beloved Father-Mother God issued a Divine Fiat to the Sun beyond the Sun beyond the Sun and decreed for the intervention of the Galactic Angels from the Electronic Belt around our Great Central Sun. In one mighty stroke, the command was given, and *billions* of Galactic Angels beyond any consciousness we have ever experienced descended into the atmosphere of Earth. One of these august Angels entered the aura of every man, woman and child. These majestic Angels have volunteered, through Their selfless love, to assist each and every one of us until we have fulfilled our missions on Earth and carried this Planet home to Her full, glorious Ascension in the Light and until ALL life evolving upon Her is wholly Ascended and FREE!!! What a sacred gift!

Blessed Galactic Angels, in deep humility and gratitude, we welcome you, and we thank you with every fiber of our Beings for your selfless service to the Light. We consecrate and dedicate ourselves to the fulfillment of our Divine Plans, according to our wisdom and our understanding. And, we surrender to the glory of Heaven on Earth. And So It Is! "I Am".
And, in one Cosmic Moment, the Sacred Covenant between Humanity and the Angelic Kingdom was restored. Amen and Amen.

"COSMIC EVIL'S" RETALIATION...
THE O.J. SIMPSON SAGA

With the opening of the Vortex of Divine Feminine energies in Los Angeles, California, and the monumental success of the other events of Light, the force of "cosmic evil" knew it was losing ground. The influx of Light was pushing everything that conflicted with the Divine Feminine to the surface for purification. That included all patterns of female abuse, as well as all patterns of the masculine abuse of power. Whenever negative energies are pushed to the surface, they have the ability to trigger the human egos that identify with those behavior patterns to act out even more than usual. If "cosmic evil" interferes, it can greatly amplify the situation and make things even worse, such as the tragedies of Tiananmen Square, Bosnia-Herzegovina and Croatia.

Well, once again, to the horror of the World, "cosmic evil" amplified the negative energies surfacing in the Vortex of the Goddess/Divine Feminine in Los Angeles, and on *June 12, 1994,* we witnessed the brutal slayings of Nicole Brown Simpson and Ron Goldman.

This sinister force knows full well the power of Humanity's attention, and it perceived how our attention would be transfixed on this tragedy because of the people involved.

When someone has a propensity for a negative behavior pattern, it is not difficult for the forces of imbalance to amplify that propensity and manipulate the person into being its pawn. The intent of that evil deed was to keep the consciousness of Humanity focused on the horror of the tragedy in such a way that "cosmic evil" could feed off of that energy and block the healing that was taking place through the amplification of the Divine Love of our Mother God through the vortex in Los Angeles. It was also trying to block the balancing of Divine Power by our Father God that was blazing through the masculine abuse of power on the Planet.

As usual, "cosmic evil" underestimated the power of

God's Light, which is ALWAYS Victorious. Instead of just allowing our lower human egos to wring our hands in anguish and disbelief, our Father-Mother God and the Company of Heaven co-created a contingency plan in unison with the awakening Lightworkers. The plan was designed to reverse the intent of "cosmic evil" and transform that tragedy into an opportunity to heal every facet of the very things it represented. A plan was designed to heal *our masculine abuse of power which results in the suppression of our feminine expression of love...to the point of mortification.*

The Metaphor

If we step back and look at the *symbology* of that tragic event, we can see it reflects, metaphorically, the very thing each of us has been experiencing since we closed down our Heart Centers and our human egos took control of our four lower bodies and perpetuated our unbridled abuse of power.

SYMBOLICALLY, O.J. SIMPSON represents the dark side of our masculine nature, our human ego, that we have worshipped and made a hero. We raised it into an icon in spite of the fact that that aspect of our human personality has blatently abused its power. It battered and suppressed our feminine nature as it closed down our Love Center, even to the point of mortification.

SYMBOLICALLY, NICOLE BROWN SIMPSON represents the Lighter side of our feminine nature that has perpetually tried to bring in a balance of love, in spite of the abuse and suppression of our human egos. This feminine aspect of our Being has struggled to survive and relentlessly tried to express its Love Nature in vain for millenia.

SYMBOLICALLY, RON GOLDMAN, in this metaphor, represents the Lighter, less experienced side of our masculine nature that is continually striving to balance its power with love as it fights to rescue the feminine aspect of itself from the treachery of the human ego, alas, to its own demise.

I want to stress *emphatically* that the reference to Light and dark in this metaphor is referring to our **human nature** and *not* race or the color of skin.

This same metaphor has been reflected through our legends of yore as the knight in shining armor trying to rescue the damsel in distress to save her from the evil dragon/beast.

An Opportunity for Divine Healing

Due to the recent God Victorious expansions of Light on the Planet and the successful return of the Solar Christ Presences through Humanity, the Company of Heaven was able to transform this devastating tragedy into an opportunity for Divine Healing.

Our Father-Mother God invoked the Solar Christ Presence of every man, woman and child on Earth to assist with this plan.   Since our Solar Christ Presence is now the *predominant* influence over our four lower bodies, this Divine aspect blazing in our hearts agreed to utilize the focus of our attention to create a Chalice of Healing. That meant that every single time we put our attention on any facet of the Nicole Brown Simpson, Ron Goldman, O.J.Simpson tragedy, no matter what we were thinking, feeling, reading, seeing or saying about the situation, our Solar Christ Presences would take that energy, *purify it* and weave it into the tremendous Chalice of Healing that was forming through the unified Solar Christ Presence of ALL Humanity.

Nicole Brown Simpson and Ron Goldman's deaths were tragic and devastating, but the Healing Light that flowed into the Planet as a result of the Chalice of Light that was created through Humanity's focus of attention on that heinous crime will prevent their deaths from being in vain. They have been martyred in the name of domestic violence and the masculine abuse of power. They have, through their sacrifice, created a catalyst for healing those human maladies that no one will be able to stop.

The Chalice of Healing created an open portal through which the Light of God could pour into Earth to heal all of the residue that still remained that reflected our abuse of the feminine and our masculine abuse of power.   After its inception, the Chalice of Healing built in momentum daily and hourly.

Nicole's family turned the attention of the World to the Angelic Kingdom by wearing Angel pins in memory of Nicole and invoked the Divine Intervention of the Angelic Kingdom into this healing process as it built in momentum. (See additional information on pages 307 and 388.)

THE SPIRITUAL IMPLICATION
OF THE COMET SHOEMAKER-LEVY

July 16-22, 1994, we experienced the *Comet Shoemaker-Levy.*

Whenever we hear things like, "Scientists have declared that a train of twenty-one nuclei will strike Jupiter," we tend to panic a little, and through the consciousness of our lower human egos, we expect the worst. People begin to predict all kinds of disasters, and fear is rampant. It is true that the Earth is greatly affected by any change that takes place in the Heavenly Bodies surrounding Her, but why do we always expect the worst?

Actually, the Celestial Event which occurred *July 16-22, 1994*, with the Planet Jupiter and the Comet Shoemaker-Levy had a positive effect on our entire Solar System. It powerfully and uniquely affected the Global Spiritual Awakening that is occurring within ALL Humanity on Earth, and greatly accelerated our progress as we continued our ascent up the Spiral of Evolution.

When we lift our consciousness up out of the quagmire of human miscreation, doubt, confusion and fear, we tap the Realms of Illumined Truth. In this octave of consciousness, the Wisdom of the Ages is public knowledge, and we can clearly perceive the TRUTH of what is occurring on Earth during this glorious time of Her rebirth, instead of the "illusion" of Her desperate plight. **We are in the midst of the birthing process, and the labor pains are intense, but the results will far surpass our greatest expectations.**

The Jupiter/Comet event was referred to as the Jovian Jumpstart. The explosion of Light that occurred as the twenty-one nuclei of the comet struck the south temperate zone of Jupiter caused an outpouring of Spiritual Voltage that was stepped down in frequency and vibration in a way that was easily assimilated by Humanity. This occurred in a subtle but powerful way that "jumpstarted" the process of the **Spiritualization of Matter**.

The Earth and all life evolving upon Her is Ascending in energy, vibration and consciousness every nanosecond. This is causing a tangible, though subtle, transformation of physical matter at an atomic cellular level. The effect of the acceleration of Light that occurred as the comet struck Jupiter radically shifted the energy field on Earth. This will enable us to gradually remember that we are not physical Beings with Spirits, but rather we are Spiritual Beings experiencing a physical school of learning...we are Light Beings experiencing matter. This adjustment in our awareness will move us a quantum leap beyond the misperception of our human limitations of poverty, aging, disease, war, hate, crime and all other distorted consciousness. As we begin to remember who we really are, we will accept our true potential as co-creators with our Father-Mother God. We will **know** that through our thoughts, words, feelings and actions we are daily and hourly creating our own realities, and we will recognize that any action we take that harms any other part of life is **self-destructive**.

In the ancient Hebrew mystical teachings of the Kabbalah, Jupiter is path number twenty-one. In Hebrew, this path is called "Kaph," which means "hand." It is interesting that there were *21 nuclei* from the comet that struck Jupiter. On *July Twenty-One, 1994*, this wave of higher evolutionary energy superconductively flowed into the Etheric Field from which we are molded and awakened the higher Spiritual Knowledge within the collective consciousness on Earth. This was Jupiter giving us a **hand** or giving us a Jovian Jump-start.

This process increased the integration that is now taking place as our Solar Christ Presences take full dominion of our physical, etheric, mental and emotional bodies. This also activated the higher knowledge that was pre-encoded in the RNA-DNA genetic codes at our inception. This is something we have all been striving for at various levels of consciousness since the "fall." We are correcting our course of direction. We have stopped our descent into oblivion, and we have begun our Ascent into the original Divine Intent for this Planet, which is Heaven on Earth.

Jupiter's Divine Quality is one of pouring the abundance of life energy into us and awakening the Divine within us. As the comet amplified these Divine Qualities throughout the Solar System, we became the fortunate and grateful recipients.

This staggering event led up to the Cosmic Moment of the anniversary of Harmonic Convergence. This was a moment that Heaven and Earth had been anxiously anticipating for aeons of time.

REWEAVING
OUR TWELVE SOLAR STRANDS OF DNA

One of the most tragic results of the "fall" was that we lost the awareness of our God Selves. Originally, our RNA-DNA structures consisted of a twelve-fold helix of Solar Light that functioned as an elaborate communication system between all the aspects of our multidimensional God Selves and our Earthly Human Selves. In the beginning, we had total conscious awareness of all of our various levels of Being. Our Earthly consciousness was one with the Divine Mind of God and the Realms of Perfection. When we fell into the dense octaves of human miscreation, our Solar DNA short-circuited and fragmented into the double helix we now perceive. This double helix of DNA barely sustains brain consciousness and prevents us from tangibly receiving conscious communication from our God Selves. Our genetic codes are distorted, and we are reflecting all manner of physical, mental and Spiritual distortion. As long as we remain in this limited state, transformation into our Light Bodies of Limitless Physical Perfection is impossible. Consequently, all of the unified efforts of Heaven and Earth have gone into raising our vibratory rate up in frequency to the point where the communication system with our God Selves will be restored.

At long last the moment arrived, and the reweaving of the Twelve Solar Strands of our DNA was possible. A plan was set into motion to accomplish that tremendous feat during the influx of Light that occurs on the anniversary of Harmonic Convergence. To create a unified cup of Humanity's consciousness in order to assist in this magnificent opportunity, we were asked by the Company of Heaven to hold the Eighth Annual World Congress On Illumination from *August 13-18, 1994,* in Tucson, Arizona. Eight is the symbol of infinity and also represents the Universal Law—"As above, so below (8)." During this sacred conclave, we came together physically to create an open portal between Heaven and Earth.

The Light built in momentum for several days. Then, on *August 18, 1994*, in the Realms of Cause, *our Twelve Solar Strands of DNA were rewoven in total perfection*. Now, the process is beginning to reflect into the world of effects. Daily and hourly, at an atomic cellular level, the Twelve Solar Strands of our DNA are being rewoven physically. This means that the pre-encoded blueprint of our Divine Plan and the full magnitude of our God Potential is, at long last, available to our outer conscious minds in a way that has not been possible since the "fall." We are now gradually reconnecting with the multidimensional facets of our total Beings.

We are healing the system that was designed to perpetuate our ongoing communication with our God Selves and the Realms of Illumined Truth.

Through all levels of consciousness we are remembering that we are not physical Beings struggling to be Spiritual; **we are Spiritual Beings, empowered and Beloved Children of God, experiencing a physical reality.**

We are here on Earth to learn the lessons of co-creation. Through our sacred gift of Free Will and our creative faculties of thought and feeling, we have come to express the Universal Law of "As above, so below." We are here to co-create with our Father-Mother God the physical manifestation of Heaven on Earth, and through the bliss of our unified efforts, SO WE SHALL!

There are wonderful movies such as *Powder* and *Phenomenon* that are beginning to demonstrate our true Human potential. These movies reflect what it will be like when our Twelve Solar Strands of DNA are integrated into our four lower bodies, and we regain use of the remaining 90 percent of our brain capacity. This is going to happen far sooner than we can imagine, and in fact, is already beginning to happen in some people.

The Return of the White Buffalo

Just two days after the Victorious reweaving of our Twelve Solar Strands of DNA in the Realms of Cause, on *August 20, 1994, a female white buffalo calf was born on a farm in Janesville, Wisconsin, USA.* She is named Miracle and believed by the Native Americans to fulfill the Sioux legend of the return of the White Buffalo Calf Woman. This is the first such female buffalo known to have been born in this century. She is perceived by the thousands of people making pilgrimages to see her to be a manifestation of the Divine.

In the Indian legend, a woman in a shining white dress appeared before the starving people and delivered a sacred pipe. She taught them how to pray and told them about the buffalo. She promised to return and said she would bring with her the peace and prosperity that would unify all races and create a rebirth of Spirituality on Earth. She then disappeared, and as she vanished, she turned into a White Buffalo Calf. Following her apparition, herds of buffalo arrived, ensuring food, shelter and clothing for the Indians.

Since that time, the people have been praying for the return of the Spirit of the White Buffalo Calf Woman. The Sacred White Buffalo Pipe has been protected and revered, awaiting this Divine Moment of her return.

"THE VESTAL VIRGIN AWAITS AND
THE BRIDEGROOM COMETH!"

As we moved toward the balance of the *Autumn Equinox in 1994*, the Company of Heaven evaluated our forward progress in the Light, and we prepared to move forward into the next phase of Beloved Mother Earth's rebirth. The Divine Plan unfolds step-by-step. Each step of the plan is carefully evaluated at its fruition by our Father-Mother God, and the immensity of the next step of the plan is contingent on how well Humanity integrated and assimilated the facet of the Divine Plan that was just completed.   Our Twelve Solar Strands of DNA were being rewoven, and the greatest need of the hour was for us to begin to truly love ourselves. We needed to remember who we are as we made peace with ourselves and every facet of our physical reality. Our full empowerment into our Divine Birthright as Sons and Daughters of God is dependent on that. We become who we BELIEVE we are. The instant we accept and KNOW that we are precious Sons and Daughters of God, the floodgates of Heaven open, and ALL THAT THE FATHER-MOTHER GOD HAS IS OURS.

If we allow ourselves to be once again ensnared in the oppressive grip of our lower human egos, we will act out of that dysfunctional, co-dependent place, and our belief in unworthiness and low self-esteem will tragically prevent us from receiving all of the gifts of Limitless Physical Perfection, Divine Love, Abundance, Joy, Happiness, Laughter and every other conceivable Divine attribute that our Father-Mother God has *"stored up for us in Heaven."*

The entire Company of Heaven and the collective Divine Presence of Humanity formulated a Divine Plan for the remainder of *1994* and the *New Year, 1995, to help prevent us from falling back into the old familiar patterns of our human egos.*

The success of the plan was dependent on our ability to

reflect the vastness of *our Godhood*. Whatever we could do to accelerate the process of loving ourselves and making peace with our physical reality would greatly assist in our ability to move a quantum leap further into the Octaves of Harmony and Joy. We were co-creating Earth's rebirth. *The choice was up to us.*

The story of *"the Vestal Virgins awaiting the coming of the Bridegroom"* has always been a mystical tale cloaked in symbology and expectancy. There have been many interpretations as to what it really means, and indeed the Truth contained in this parable is multifaceted and multidimensional.

As the Twelve Solar Strands of our DNA were being rewoven, we were beginning to reconnect with the many dimensions of consciousness we short-circuited from, and lost awareness of, when we "fell" into the quagmire of human miscreation. These higher realms of consciousness began revealing to us, in a marvelous, tangible way, the incredible dance of synchronicity that is taking place between Heaven and Earth.

We had always participated through our God Selves, at inner levels, in the splendor of Divine Initiations which took place in the Realms of Illumined Truth, but now it was time for us to participate through all levels of consciousness in these glorious activities of Light. Consequently, we were clearly shown, through the Stargates of our conscious minds, the Divine Ceremony of our Sacred Initiations. These initiations involved Humanity and the Earth, and they reflected our collective evolution into higher states of awareness. They reflected our progress and our growth both as Human Beings and as a Planet, and, they reflected the Dawn of the New Cosmic Day.

Through all of the cycles of time, even in the very depth of our darkest hour, Archangel Michael has fulfilled His vow and remained as the Guardian Overlord of the Angelic Host, Humanity and the Elemental Kingdom on Earth. Though our

Ascension in the Light has been delayed for aeons of time due to our tragic "fall," Archangel Michael vowed that He would not fold His Cosmic Wings about Him to return HOME until the final Angelic Being is freed, the last Human Being is redeemed and the last Elemental returned to its perfect estate. The selfless service of this Awesome Archangel is beyond our understanding, and His love for us is infinite.

Now, after countless millenia, His Divine Mission is coming to fruition. At long last this Earth and all of Her life are Ascending in the Light, and the Cosmic Moment of Earth's transfiguration IS AT HAND!!!

The Divine Mother Principle, the feeling nature of God, is being balanced within us. Our power is finally being embraced with Divine Love in the way it was originally intended to be, so that **Reverence for ALL Life** will be an automatic and natural expression of our behavior patterns on Earth. This is truly the return of our Mother God. This is the key we have been waiting for that would turn us around and initiate our Ascent into Divinity.

The Divine Love of our Mother God—Holy Spirit—is the "Vestal Virgin" within us who has been waiting in dormancy for us to surrender our abusive expression of power to the Will of the Father, thus restoring it to the *Divine Power* of our Father God—the "Bridegroom."

In a glorious Ceremony of Light, that surrender was accomplished God Victoriously. The "Vestal Virgin" (the Divine Love of our Mother God) awaited, and the "Bridegroom" (the Divine Power of our Father God) came for the Sacred Marriage Ceremony.

After the Earth was bathed in the exquisite balance of our Father-Mother God, *on the Autumn Equinox, September 23, 1994*, Lightworkers from around the World gathered at the Forcefield of Archangel Michael that pulsates in the Etheric Realms over the beautiful Rocky Mountains that embrace the expanded area of Banff, Canada. They gathered at the crystalline aqua blue waters of Lake Louise. This pristine lake is surrounded by beautiful mountains and snow-capped glaciers.

Archangel Michael drew the God Selves of Humanity into His Forcefield to escort us into our next octave of evolution. Every man, woman and child on Earth participated in this glorious event whether they were consciously aware of it or not. So did every Elemental and Angel.

To begin the Cosmic Initiation, the God Selves of *ALL* Humanity gathered in the "upper room" with our Twin Flames. We began sounding the Cosmic Tone of Creation, the "Om." From our Masculine "I Am" Presence, a Sapphire Blue Ray of Divine Power emanated from the Throat Center to the mid-point above Lake Louise. From our Feminine "I Am" Presence, a Pink Ray of Divine Love emanated from the Heart Center to the mid-point above Lake Louise. As these two resplendent Rays of Light met in an explosion of creation, the permanent Three-fold Solar Atom of Humanity's Collective Heart Flame was formed. The emanation from this Divine Heart Flame expanded into a Twelve-fold Solar Flame. This created a beacon of Light through the Universe, signaling to the Cosmos that Planet Earth was ready for the long awaited MARRIAGE of the DIVINE FEMININE and the DIVINE MASCULINE within every part of life.

Archangel Michael and His Divine Complement, Archaii Faith, took Their strategic positions in the atmosphere above the Twelve-fold Solar Heart Flame of Humanity. They officially Ascended into Their higher order of Unified Divine Service as the COSMIC ANGEL OF THE NEW DAWN. These glorious exponents of Divine Love magnetized from the very Heart of God the Divine Light that formed a tremendous Pink Heart around the collective Solar Heart Flame of Humanity.

Next, the Sun Gods and Goddesses from our System of Worlds descended into the atmosphere of Earth forming a magnificent "V" above the pulsating Heart of Divine Love. The Sun Gods formed the Masculine Polarity of the "V" to the left, beginning with Beloved Helios, then Alpha, then Elohae. The Sun Goddesses formed the Feminine Polarity of the "V" to the right, beginning with Beloved Vesta, then Omega, then Eloha.

They ALL projected Their Divine Light into the Twelve-fold Solar Heart Flame of Humanity. Then, within the Heart Flame, the individualized forms of Humanity's *collective* Masculine and Feminine "I Am" Presences began to form. These two radiant Beings of Light were wondrous to behold.

The Clarion Song of the collective Mighty "I Am" Presences of Humanity reverberated out into the Universe, invoking the assistance of the entire Company of Heaven to come and join in the unprecedented God Victorious celebration taking place on Earth. The response came from Galaxies beyond Galaxies and Suns beyond Suns.

CROWNS, THRONES, PRINCIPALITIES, COSMIC BEINGS, GALACTIC BEINGS, SOLAR BEINGS, ALL ORDERS OF ANGELS, ELOHIM AND ASCENDED BEINGS came in projected consciousness to join in the celebration of Humanity and Mother Earth's Divine Initiation.

Now, after aeons of separation, all was in readiness for the Divine Initiation of Marriage.

The first step was the Divine Dance of Purification through the Law of Forgiveness and Limitless Transmutation.

The two Beings of Light Who represented the collective Masculine and Feminine "I Am" Presences of all Humanity stood facing each other in the Twelve-fold Solar Flame in the center of the heart that was pulsating above Lake Louise.

As the Initiation began, the Twelve-fold Solar Flame began blending the Solar Spines of the Masculine and Feminine "I Am" Presences through a sacred dance of Light.

Beginning at the base of the spine, a Ray of Solar Light began
Its ascent by forming a figure 8, = ∞ .

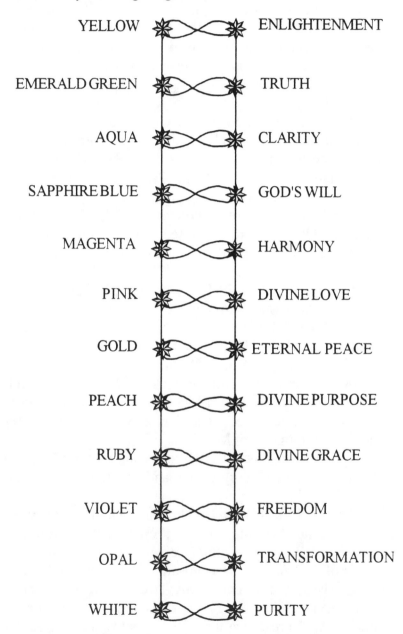

YELLOW — ENLIGHTENMENT

EMERALD GREEN — TRUTH

AQUA — CLARITY

SAPPHIRE BLUE — GOD'S WILL

MAGENTA — HARMONY

PINK — DIVINE LOVE

GOLD — ETERNAL PEACE

PEACH — DIVINE PURPOSE

RUBY — DIVINE GRACE

VIOLET — FREEDOM

OPAL — TRANSFORMATION

WHITE — PURITY

Through this Divine Dance of Light, their Solar Spines were blended into ONE Forcefield in the union of infinity consciousness.

As they remained facing each other, the Feminine "I Am" Presence placed her left hand (her Masculine Polarity) on the back of his neck and projected the Masculine Ray of Divine Power and Balance through her hand uniting his Throat Chakra of Power with hers, thus re-establishing, for all eternity, the *balance* of the Masculine Ray of Power within Humanity.

The Masculine "I Am" Presence then placed his right hand (his Feminine Polarity) on the center of her back and projected the Feminine Ray of Divine Love and Balance through his hand uniting her Heart Chakra of Divine Love with his, thus re-establishing, for all eternity, the *balance* of the Feminine Ray of Divine Love within Humanity.

She, then, placed the palm of her right hand (her Feminine Polarity) against the palm of his left hand (his Masculine Polarity) and, in this loving embrace, they began to magnetize from the very Core of Creation an intensified frequency of the Blue Ray of Divine Power and the Pink Ray of Divine Love. This Divine Light entered their Beings, and as they held each other in their arms, they began a Sacred Dance of Purification. The Mighty "I Am" Presences began to slowly spin. The Blue Ray of Divine Power blended in perfect balance with the Pink Ray of Divine Love creating magnificent waves of Violet Fire. The Masculine and Feminine "I Am" Presences slowly descended into the center of the Earth as they continued their loving Dance of Purification. Through this glorious activity of Light, a tremendous Lake of Violet Fire was formed below the heart which was pulsating in the atmosphere above Lake Louise.

Under the direction of the Cosmic Angel of the New Dawn, the remaining frequencies of energy that reflected the fallen masculine and feminine expressions of life on Earth were drawn into the Lake of Violet Fire.

This included the abuse of power in all of its distorted forms, the oppression of the feminine in any part of life and the abuse inflicted on women or men or children. It included dysfunctional expressions of family life and other relationships as well. It included behavior patterns that reflected co-dependence, obsession, compulsion, hatred, fear and prejudice.

As the Violet Fire Lake continued to blaze, this sacred substance purified the atomic cellular structure of all manifest form the maximum that Cosmic Law would allow. It transmuted the negativity—cause, core, effect, record and memory. This paved the way for the next level of the Divine Blueprint for the New Heaven and the New Earth to be permanently activated within Humanity's genetic codes.

When the purification was complete, the Cosmic Angel of the New Dawn sounded a Universal Tone. The Sun Gods and Goddesses lifted up, and the heart above Lake Louise opened in a burst of wondrous splendor. The Company of Heaven breathed in the Divine Light of the Twelve-fold Solar Flame blazing in the heart, and a magnificent Golden Stairway of Light Ascended from the Solar Heart Flame of Humanity into the Octaves of Eternal Perfection.

With the purification of the fallen masculine and feminine energies completed, the Earth was, at long last, prepared to receive the gifts and assistance of the Solar Angels of Abounding Joy. These glorious Angels reflect Octaves of Divine Emotion that we have been unable to reach or experience since our "fall." These are Octaves of God's Divine Feeling Nature that will immeasurably assist us in our endeavors to accelerate the tangible *physical* manifestation of Heaven on Earth.

In a majestic procession, the Solar Angels of Abounding Joy descended the Golden Stairway of Light and entered the atmosphere of Earth for the very first time.

There were Legions of Angels representing each of the following Divine Qualities:

> The Solar Angels of Joy
> The Solar Angels of Euphoria
> The Solar Angels of Delight
> The Solar Angels of Exaltation
> The Solar Angels of Happiness
> The Solar Angels of Laughter
> The Solar Angels of Elation
> The Solar Angels of Wonder
> The Solar Angels of Awe
> The Solar Angels of Playfulness
> The Solar Angels of Bliss
> The Solar Angels of Ecstasy

These resplendent exponents of Abounding Joy traversed the Planet North, South, East and West. They descended into the auras of every man, woman and child, every Elemental and every Angel serving the Earth.

They flooded every particle of life with Their Divine Gifts, and They vowed with every fiber of Their Beings to sustain these precious gifts on Earth until this Planet and all Her life are wholly Ascended and FREE!!!

Welcome, Precious Angels of Abounding Joy!
We Love you!
And we thank you, we thank you, we thank you!

In the protective embrace of the Angels of Abounding Joy and held in the new frequencies of Divine Solar Emotions, we were able to journey in consciousness through the records of time and space, back to the initial impulse of the fall of Humanity when the first distortion of the Masculine and Feminine began.

One of the greatest tragedies of the "fall" was the imbalance and separation that occurred within us when we closed down our Heart Centers causing the Feeling Nature of God—

the Divine Mother Principle—to withdraw from Earth. The unbridled abuse of power (our Masculine Nature) that resulted from closing our hearts down was the *direct cause* of all of the maladies Humanity and the Earth have experienced.

Now this tragedy is being HEALED. The Mother God Principle has returned to Earth, and the Stargates of our Hearts are opening. The Divine Love of the Holy Spirit (our Mother God) is flooding the Planet. And through this Divine Substance, ALL OF THE MALADIES ON EARTH *WILL* BE HEALED.

As we journeyed through the records of time, embraced in the blissful Solar Emotions, a new blueprint for the full expression of the Divine Feminine and the Divine Masculine was anchored within, and imprinted on, the genetic codes of all Humanity, Elementals and Angels.

Through the God Victorious success of that activity of Light, the Cosmic Moment finally arrived that Heaven and Earth had long awaited.

After millenia of struggle and preparation, all was in readiness for the multifaceted reunification of our Masculine and Feminine Natures.

The Marriage

This Divine Solar Initiation involved a glorious multidimensional, multifaceted MARRIAGE of the Masculine and Feminine within all life.

This included...

1. The marriage of the *polarities* of the Father-Mother God *within* each of us.

2. The marriage of the Masculine and Feminine "I Am" Presences within each White Fire Being.

3. And, the marriage of Heaven and Earth.

When Heaven signaled that the Cosmic Moment had arrived, the beautiful collective Masculine and Feminine "I Am" Presences of Humanity began Ascending from the center of the Earth into the Solar Atom in the heart above Lake Louise. These Divine Beings continued Their dance of love, blending Their Light in a wonderful Symphony of Divine Love and Divine Power into the Unity of One Cosmic White Fire Being.

The beautiful Masculine and Feminine White Fire Being Ascended the Golden Stairway of Light into the Octaves of Eternal Perfection, and before the very Heart of our Father-Mother God, the Divine Marriage Initiation took place.

Through a New Solar Order of Harmony,
a convergence of Heaven and Earth occurred.

The Cosmic Law of "As above, so below"
became the Order of the New Dawn.

And the Divine Mother rejoiced...
It is done! And so it is! "I Am"!

Further Assistance from the Heavenly Bodies

As *1994* came to a close, we experienced several amplifications of Light that made it one of the most God Victorious years of all time. From *October 12, 1994, to November 23, 1994, the Planet Venus was retrograde in Scorpio.* When a Planet is retrograde, it appears as though it is moving backward through the Heavens. This has the effect of stirring up and intensifying anything that conflicts with the God Qualities and the Divine Intent associated with that particular Heavenly Body. This allows any negativity that is blocking the flow of Divine Light to surface so that it can be purged and loved free.

Venus has always been known as the Planet of Divine Love and our material reality. Scorpio is the Sun Cycle that most effectively clears our past dysfunctional behavior patterns and brings the "death" or "destruction" of the old to make room for the rebirth and creation of the new. Consequently, after all of the events of *1994*: the return of the Divine Mother Principle; the permanent opening of the Vortex of the Goddess by Sirius; the creation of the Chalice of Divine Healing; the effects of the comet Shoemaker-Levy; the reweaving of our Twelve Solar Strands of DNA; the opening of the Stargates of our Hearts; the activation of our right brain hemispheres; the Divine Marriage of our Twin Flames, which elevated each of us into the manifest expression of our empowered White Fire Being and the coming of the Solar Angels of Abounding Joy (Whew!), we were finally in a position to allow the cleansing and purging of all of our past painful experiences involving relationships and our physical realities. Never before had a cleansing of this magnitude been attempted. Without the newly established nurturing embrace of our Mother God we would have been unable to withstand the excruciatingly painful feelings of our pasts surfacing at such an accelerated pace. But, due to the limitless mercy and compassion of our Father-Mother God, several safeguards were in place to make this unprecedented purification tolerable. I know that many people felt the things surfacing during that time frame were overwhelming, but I assure you the pain was nothing compared to what we would have experienced without the enfolding comfort of our Mother God—the Holy Spirit.

As *Venus reflected through Scorpio in a retrograde position*, the essence of Divine Love entered the core of purity in every single electron of energy evolving on Earth. This means that literally every electron of precious life energy we have ever used through our thoughts, words, actions or feelings, in any existence or dimension, known or unknown, back to our inception, was activated with a frequency of Divine Love. This caused every vibration less than Divine Love to be pushed to the surface for purification and transmutation back into the Light. As this activity built in momentum, the areas in our lives that were not expressing their highest potential became painfully obvious. We became blatantly aware of problems in our self-esteem, our relationships, finances, health, jobs and every other facet of our physical realities. We were not able to continue our old patterns of suppression and denial. We weren't given the luxury of pretending everything was all right when, in fact, our lives were in shambles.

Just when we thought we couldn't withstand another minute of pain, the Mercy of God prevailed, and we were bathed in the comfort of our Mother God. On *November 3, 1994*, we experienced a powerful *New Moon Solar Eclipse* that amplified the love nature of our Mother God through every particle of life. The Feminine Polarity of our Mother God enters the Earth as a tremendous shaft of Crystalline Pink Light in the area of Mount Meru at Lake Titicaca in Bolivia, South America. The Solar Eclipse on November 3rd reached its full crescendo directly over Lake Titicaca. During that Cosmic Moment, the Earth and all Her life were bathed in the Flame of Comfort of our Mother God, and we experienced a true Baptism of the Holy Spirit. This gave us a respite from the agony surfacing in our lives and relieved the intensity of our suffering, thus allowing us to reach into deeper levels of our painful past.

This process continued, and on *November 10th and 11th, 1994,* several additional Planets entered the Sun Cycle of Scorpio to assist Venus in Her healing activity of Light. Six Planets in Scorpio created the following energy structure:

The *Sun* in Scorpio symbolized the crumbling of old belief systems based in ignorance and fear and paved the way for our rebirth into Higher Wisdom and Illumination.

Mercury in Scorpio assisted in reconnecting our Twelve Solar Strands of DNA, enhancing our ability to translate all sensory data and our comprehension of Higher Wisdom.

Jupiter in Scorpio amplified our desire to learn, in depth, about Higher Wisdom as we connect with the Divine Mind of God.

Pluto in Scorpio brought to the surface any beliefs and behavior patterns that were blocking our development into Higher Wisdom and preventing us from positive growth. In other words, it generated the "death" of our old, obsolete patterns and belief systems.

The *North Node of the Moon* in Scorpio brought to the surface for purification the fear of being out of control and the fear of evolvement into Higher Wisdom.

Venus in Scorpio during this convergence of Planets continued to supply the love energy to transform all of the resistance and interference being pushed to the surface into the INNER LOVE OF THE DIVINE SELF.

The remaining Planets in our Solar System during those special days continued to support the energy of transformation—death of the old and rebirth of the new.

The *Moon* in Pisces cleared our fear of being trapped and the fear of losing our individuality in the collective presence of Oneness.

Neptune in Capricorn purged our illusions of darkness, the unknown, the duality of good and evil within and our struggle with our lower human egos. This cleared the way so that we could focus on our vision and put our creative talents to practical use.

Mars in Leo cleared our inner battles of anger, war, competition and sexual expression. This clearing would have been potentially dangerous if it hadn't been for the Divine Mother Principle moving us into our creative outlet of Higher Mind and Enlightenment.

Uranus in Capricorn shook the foundations of our old structures to allow for the Victory of our transformation to occur.

Daily and hourly this unique cleansing built in power and momentum. Once again, as we felt we were moving to the very brink of our pain tolerance level, the mercy of our Father-Mother God intervened. On *November 18, 1994*, we experienced a *Full Moon Lunar Eclipse*. This Eclipse took place in Taurus which enabled us to really get in touch with our concepts of self-worth, prosperity consciousness, personal values and integrity. In the gentle embrace of our Mother God, we were given the opportunity to evaluate just how we were expressing the quality of Divine Love in our lives.

How do we *really* feel about our relationships and the people in our lives on a deep level?

Are we expressing our love to them effectively?

What are our true motivations in our relationships?

Are we willing to put forth the necessary effort to transform our relationships into expressions of joy and happiness for all concerned?

Are we able to trust and openly express our love?

Are we willing to let go of the security blanket of our dysfunctional past and risk creating a life of abounding bliss and abundance?

Are we willing to look inside and revel in the true knowing of our innate worth as a Son or Daughter of God?

Are we willing to accept and BE who we really are?

The *Lunar Eclipse on November 18th* gave us the inner strength and courage to release all resistance to *being* our true God Selves. This process built in momentum over the next six months. Its success was dependent solely on our WILLINGNESS to LET GO!!!

On *November 23, 1994*, Venus went direct and began Her forward movement into the new blueprint of the Divine Plan on Earth. The new, clearer energies created an atmosphere that allowed each of us to learn to *love through the acceptance of change and to allow change to transform our love nature.* This twofold activity enabled us to transcend obsolete patterns in our relationships that have resulted in compulsive, co-dependent, dysfunctional, obsessive patterns based in fear, rejection and abandonment issues. We are now able to soar into the Octaves of Divine Love where relationships are based on the highest momentum of self-worth, trust, integrity, honesty, respect, harmony, balance, tenderness, kindness, sharing, openness, caring and, above all, LOVE!!!

This Divine Activity of Light set the Earth on a new course of direction and brought Her to the gateway of the next step of Her evolution.

On *December 12, 1994*, Beloved Mother Earth and all

Her life Ascended into a frequency of energy, vibration and consciousness that allowed Humanity, Elementals and Angels to transcend the ramifications of the "fall of Humanity" and easily move into the Divine Octaves of LIMITLESS PHYSICAL PERFECTION.

There were many different interpretations of what was going to transpire on that *sacred day 12:12*, but the immensity of what actually took place far exceeded even the greatest expectations of Heaven. On that holy day, the **final sealing** of the Twelve Solar Strands of DNA was completed within ALL life on Earth. This allowed the circuitry between our God Presences and our four lower bodies to be permanently reconnected. The messages being received into our RNA/DNA genetic codes from our God Presences are now strong and clear instead of fragmented. This means that the atomic cellular structures of our lower bodies are now receiving the blueprint of our original Divine Intent which is *Limitless Physical Perfection.* As these messenger codes of perfection are activated within our genetic patterns, all frequencies of degeneration, aging, disease, dysfunction, imbalance and death will be transmuted into Light. It is *impossible* for discordant patterns to exist when the Twelve Solar Strands of DNA are given full dominion in our physical bodies. As this Solar Light is integrated into the cells of our bodies, they will be transfomed into expressions of eternal youth, vibrant health and radiant beauty. These perfection patterns will then begin to reflect into our sphere of influence, thus causing our physical realities to be transformed into *Limitless Physical Perfection.* This literally means that we will be changing every facet of our lives into the Heaven on Earth we have always KNOWN was our Divine Birthright.

Now, the important thing for us to understand is that we are creatures of habit, and we have the choice to stay stuck in our old patterns of limitation. We now also have the ABSOLUTE ability *not* to stay entrapped in the bonds of our human egos.

1995...A TIME OF NEW BEGINNINGS

1995 began on January 1st with a powerful New Moon that activated the Divine Plan for that holy year into the consciousness of all life on Earth. The august Presence enfolding the Planet that year was the Cosmic Angel of the New Dawn. S/He enveloped the entire Planet and breathed the Earth into the embrace of His/Her Twelve-fold Solar Heart Flame. This is where the Earth remained throughout the year as the Divine Plan unfolded step-by-step.

Surrounding the Cosmic Angel of the New Dawn were twelve glorious Stargates. These Stargates were portals into the Twelve Solar Aspects of Deity that radiate as the Causal Body of God. On *January 11, 1995*, to assist us during this magnificent, but sometimes difficult time, a Cosmic Dispensation was granted by our Father-Mother God to allow an amplified influx of the Solar Angels of Abounding Joy (see page 243) to pass through the Stargates into the atmosphere of Earth so that They could assist in alleviating Humanity's pain. This was a gift of mercy and compassion beyond our understanding.

Even in the midst of our greatest anguish, all we have to do is ask these selfless servants and exponents of Divine Love to assist us, and They will intervene in perfect alignment with our individual Divine Plans.

On *January 29 (= 11), 1995*, we experienced the *second New Moon* of the month. This is a rare occurrence and always brings amplified blessings. That New Moon (*Blue Moon*) activated an expansion of the Violet Flame of Limitless Transmutation through the Stargates of Aquarius. The Violet Flame built in momentum throughout that Sun Cycle. It entered the core of purity in every electron of precious life energy evolving on Earth and energized the awakening Divine Blueprint. This activity, though merciful in the extreme, caused a great deal of our negativity to surface in a way that seemed, with our limited perception, to be overwhelming. It exacerbated our daily challenges, and from outer appearances made things seem like they were getting worse. We were literally catapulted into a healing crisis.

It's easy to see now why we needed the added assistance of the Solar Angels of Abounding Joy. Imagine what it would have felt like without Their nurturing embrace.

All of that Divine Intervention moved us toward the shift that took place during the *Vernal Equinox, March 21, 1995*. That was a moment in time that had been predicted for hundreds of years by various groups of people. It was a time when we reached the critical mass for Limitless Physical Perfection. That means that the pre-encoded Divine Blueprint within the RNA/DNA genetic codes for all manifest form reached the point of activation that will assure the physical manifestation of Heaven on Earth. And NOTHING CAN STOP IT!!!

Now, we must remember that through the power of our attention, *WE ARE CREATING OUR OWN REALITY.*

If we focus on the loving, gentle, peaceful Ascension of this Earth into the Heavenly frequencies of Harmony and Balance, our rebirth into Heaven on Earth will be GLORIOUS and relatively pain free.

We don't have to experience cataclysmic destruction or major outer-world phenomena. We have the ability to create a gentle acceleration of the awakening and the opening of the Stargates of our Hearts that we are already experiencing. As usual, our experience of the event will be individual and unique to each of us. The more we allow our God Selves to take command of our thoughts, words, actions and feelings, the more we will receive the inner guidance and clarity of just how we can co-create a glorious, pain-free Ascension into the Light.

Moment-by-moment new opportunities are being given to us individually and collectively that will assist us in transforming our physical bodies and our physical realities into expressions of *Limitless Physical Perfection*. Our responsibility is to be *ever vigilant and ever observant* of the opportunities being presented to us daily and even hourly in our lives. Our physical transformation is unique. No two people have gone through the same experience to create the maladies reflecting in their bodies and their lives, and no two people will have the exact same process in transforming their bodies and lives into perfection. We each need to take advantage of the increased flow of Spiritual energies that will bathe the Planet during **Full Moons and New Moons, Solar and Lunar Eclipses, Solstices and Equinoxes, Spiritual Celebrations and other Global events that create a shift of consciousness toward the Divine Light of our Father-Mother God**. Listen carefully to your inner Heart Call, and RESPOND, according to your wisdom and understanding, to each and every opportunity.

Accepting Responsibility for Earth's Rebirth

1995 was dedicated by the entire Company of Heaven to freeing us from the belief and illusion of limitation. Now that we have finally Ascended onto our Spiral of Evolution, we are being given unprecedented assistance from On High to integrate the new patterns of perfection being transmitted through the Twelve Solar Strands of DNA into our atomic cellular structures.

For quite some time now, we have been talking about the fact that we are on the "Dawn of a New Age." That has triggered the initial impulse for a variety of changes in our lives, both personally and Globally. Sometimes we passed through the changes willingly and gratefully. Other times we were dragged through the changes kicking and screaming, but nevertheless, change we did.

Our environment reflects our consciousness, so in order to grasp the magnitude of our change of consciousness over the past several decades, all we have to do is observe the exponential advancement of our technology. Just fathom the fact that less than a century ago we were still in the horse and buggy stage, barely discovering the wonders of electricity. Now, we have space travel, computers, fax machines, satellite communication systems and medical advancements that are awesome to behold.

Unfortunately, our hearts and feeling natures didn't expand at the same rate our intellectual capacities did. Consequently, we also have an exponential growth in pollution, crime, governmental corruption, disease, poverty, dysfunctional families, war and general human suffering. The good news is that we are beginning to really understand the imbalance between our hearts and our minds, and we are now involved in a "Cosmic push" to reverse that trend.

Legions of people all over the World are saying, *"Wait a minute; enough is enough. We have to start accepting responsibility for our Earthly condition, and we have to do something to save this Planet and turn our lives around."* The fact that this awareness is awakening in the hearts and minds of the masses is not a coincidence. It is part of the colossal Divine Plan that is being orchestrated by the unified efforts of the God Selves of all Humanity and the entire Company of Heaven. Under the direction of our Father-Mother God, we are also receiving the assistance of Divine Sources from Galaxies beyond Galaxies and Suns beyond Suns. I know all of that sounds rather grandiose to our finite minds, but the Truth is that doesn't even begin to describe the immensity of the Divine Plan now in progress or the degree of assistance we are receiving from On High to fulfill that plan.

Up to this point, we have spasmodically participated in fulfilling our part of the Divine Plan. Whenever we were able to paddle fast enough to get our heads above the mud puddle of our Earthly experiences, we struggled to get a glimpse of the Light. Those brief moments of Enlightenment have been few and very far between. For all intents and purposes, the Divine Plan has actually slowly progressed *in spite of us, not because of us.* That may sound grim, but it is encouraging to know that the plan was able to progress *at all* with our fragmented and meager assistance. Even with all of the treachery, interference and resistance of our wayward human egos, which are strictly fear-based, *we made progress.* Even in the face of all of the adversity, anxiety and doubt that permeated our every moment, *we made progress.* Even in the immobilizing grip of poverty, disease, war, abandonment, rejection, low self-esteem, unworthiness and all of the other distorted beliefs we have clung to, *we made progress.* So instead of beating ourselves up with self-flagellation, *we should recognize the enormity of the power of our God Selves.* After all, we made progress with only a rare trickle of our Divine Light flowing through us into the Earth plane in sporadic, fragmented currents. Just imagine what can happen now since our God Selves are finally in a position to take full dominion of our four lower bodies and direct our thoughts, words, actions and feelings. The possibilities are limitless, and our potential is staggering.

GOOD NEWS!!!

You Are Doing Better Than You Think You Are!

I know that during this unique moment on Earth you are experiencing the gamut of trials and tribulations. I also know from what people are expressing to me and from my own personal experience, that your degree of success in handling your challenges probably, in your opinion, vacillates from fairly good to dismal failure.

We have all of this intellectual knowledge pulsating inside of us, and we *know* that we are creating our own realities. We also *know* we don't have to be victims, and yet we are still making choices that seem to continually sabotage our success. Nothing is more frustrating than knowing that we have the tools and the ability to change our lives into expressions of joy and abundance, while at the same time we seem to be doing everything we can to catapult ourselves into chaos and confusion.

We keep energizing the thoughtforms of lack and limitation. We keep acting out in the same dysfunctional behavior patterns that have wreaked havoc in our relationships. We keep abusing our physical bodies with all of the effluvia that we know causes degeneration and disease. We keep bombarding our psyche with self-flagellating thoughts and feelings of unworthiness. We keep empowering all of the negativity manifesting in our lives with fear and a sense of helplessness. We keep observing the atrocities happening all over the World and interpret them to be a sign of our impending doom. And, we keep misinterpreting all of the above to mean that we are miserable, worthless failures

After all, if we aren't able to *"walk our talk"* and DO what we KNOW will change our lives into *"Heaven on Earth,"* then that must mean we are horrible, terrible people, pitifully masquerading as Sons and Daughters of God. Right?

WRONG!!! WRONG!!! WRONG!!!

Please, once again open your heart, and ABSORB the following information. Bring it into the Flame of Illumined Truth blazing in your heart, and let the wisdom of this message resonate in the very core of your Being. It will be a source of strength to you, even in your darkest hours, if you will only *allow* it to be.

In Truth, you are a magnificent, multifaceted, multidimensional reflection of our Father-Mother God. You are a radiant Sun expressing ALL of the various frequencies of Divinity pulsating in the Causal Body of God. You are a God/Goddess, standing on the threshold of the

greatest leap in consciousness ever experienced in any System of Worlds. You are on the brink of co-creating a new Octave of Godhood, expanding, without measure, the infinite Body of God, thus lifting every particle of life ever breathed forth from the Core of Creation into the Dawn of a New Cosmic Day.

Every single thing that conflicts with the wonder and the TRUTH of your Divinity is an *illusion and a lie*.

Because of the urgency of the hour, there is rampant fear flooding through the lower strata of human consciousness that is exacerbating every thought, word, action or feeling we have ever had that denies our Godhood. This is not by chance. It is the result of the concentrated efforts of our lower human egos which are desperately striving to regain control so they can keep us trapped in the immobilizing grip of failure consciousness.

You see, this part of our lower personality doesn't understand that it is being given the opportunity to be transformed into Light. It thinks it is being destroyed, and it is determined to fight tooth and nail to prevent us from realizing our Divinity. This is happening because our lower human egos clearly know that once we remember that we are Sons and Daughters of God, they will have no power to manipulate us through our low self-esteem and feelings of failure. They will be disempowered, and the oppressive stranglehold this aspect of our lower personality is trying to re-establish will be PERMANENTLY burst asunder.

Through the tremendous shifts in energy, vibration and consciousness we have taken over the past several years, much of the power of our human egos has been dissipated, and they know it. The bonds of our human egos were broken through the activity of Light that took place on *April 1, 1994*. But, this wayward aspect of our personality does not give up easily, and it has worked incessantly to regain its grip on our four lower bodies. It has been mounting an all-out, last ditch effort to block our Ascension into the Light. That is truly *a mission based in futility*, but that doesn't mean that it hasn't caused us a lot of pain in the process.

Now, it is time for the struggle to be over. So all we have to do to shatter the chains of limitation is KNOW and ACCEPT the reality of who we are. That may seem like a monumental task in the face of our Earthly challenges, but it is nothing more than a slight adjustment in our awareness. Everything we need to shift our perception and adjust our awareness is in place.

In moments of inner peace, ask the Presence of God blazing in your heart to take full dominion of your thoughts, words, actions and feelings every moment of every day. Ask the Light of God to flood through you and increase in intensity with every breath you take. Ask, in moments of human frailty, for the Light of God to AUTOMATICALLY expand a thousand times a thousand fold through your Twelve Solar Meridians and transmute cause, core, effect, record and memory every electron of precious life energy you have misqualified.

Expect and ACCEPT that your invocation is answered instantaneously, and KNOW that it is increasing in power and momentum daily and hourly.

Where your attention is, there you are. Allow the focus of your attention to add *exclusively* to the joy of your life.

Contrary to ALL outer appearances, WE ARE SUCCEEDING. Keep focused on that inner knowing and the TRUTH that will set you FREE.

I want to sincerely thank you for all of the Light you are adding to the World, and I want you to know that "I Am" humbled and deeply honored to walk this Earth with you.

I Love You!!!

With the God Victorious success of all that had taken place during the final 15 years of our 500 year Period of Grace, **OUR ASCENSION IN THE LIGHT WAS ASSURED!!!**

Humanity had proved our willingness to once again accept responsibility as stewards of the Earth. And we had rededicated and consecrated our lives to the redemption of the Earth and all Her life.

The year 1995 ushered in the final stages of our redemption process and paved the way for the tangible physical manifestation of Heaven on Earth.

THE DIVINE FEMININE
ASSUMES HER RIGHTFUL AUTHORITY

Tragically, when Humanity fell into the quagmire of human miscreation, the Divine Blueprint was buried in the sludge of our effluvia, and we lost our direction. We forgot our Divine Heritage and our purpose and reason for being. Now, after millennia of struggle, we are awakening and beginning to remember that we are Sons and Daughters of God. We are learning to invoke the Light, and we are becoming *"the open door that no one can shut."* The Divine Love of our Father-Mother God is pouring through the cup of our consciousness and, at long last, we have reached the critical mass of Limitless Physical Perfection which was always the Divine Plan.

The *Divine Will of our Father God* has been the pre- dominant influence on Earth since our fall from grace. Sadly, our lower human egos distorted that Masculine Polar- ity of God into the gross mutation of what we have experi- enced for aeons of time as the abuse of power. This mutation of life manifested across the face of the Earth as an aggres- sive, dominating Patriarchal Society. The Feminine nature of God's Divine Love was suppressed, denied and smothered by the abusive Masculine nature of Humanity. Men and women acted out this tragic syndrome, and women became dishonored and oppressed. Men denied women equal rights and abused and brutalized them in a way that made men feel powerful and dominant. As this distorted scenario was acted out century after century, our abuse of power resulted in war, crime, corruption, disease, poverty, hatred and every other derivative of those maladies. Our myths reflected this situation as we continally witnessed the Knight in shining armor (the Divine Masculine) striving to slay the Dragon (the fallen human ego) in order to rescue the Damsel in distress (the Divine Feminine). For aeons we have tried to correct the problem with painfully little success. The masculine abuse of power has been the order of the day for far too long. But now, at last, through the unified efforts of Heaven and Earth, that difficult chapter is coming to a close. This is what we have all been waiting for, and the Cosmic Moment is NOW!

On *April 15, 1995*, we experienced a *Full Moon Lunar Eclipse*. The Full Moon of Aries is known as the Full Moon of Divine Love—the Christ. During that sacred time our Father-Mother God bathed all life on Earth in the essence of the Twelve-fold Aspect of Deity, thus preparing every electron of precious life energy to receive an intensified frequency of the Resurrection Flame.

April 16, 1995, was *Easter—Resurrection Morning*. As the first Rays of the Sun began to flood the Planet, our Father-Mother God projected an unparalleled Ray of the Resurrection Flame into the core of purity in every electron of energy on Earth. This sacred substance of Divine Light Resurrected the blueprint of the Divine Feminine in all life. The *Immaculate Heart* in each person was activated, and a higher frequency of the love nature of the Feminine Polarity of God was anchored in every heart. This caused the residue of our masculine abuse of power to be pushed to the surface for purification and transmutation. This, unfortunately, sometimes manifests in the world of effects.

On *April 19, 1995*, we witnessed in Oklahoma City the epitome of the masculine abuse of power. The explosion of the Federal Building reflected, symbolically, an attack on the *"heart"* of this nation. Even the news announcements were titled *"Terror in the Heartland."* The consciousness that is prompting people to actually believe that they will attain their freedom in this dawning Permanent Golden Age by harming **any other part of life** is directly associated with the most sinister aspect of the lower human ego, and people so inclined are being duped into being *pawns of the forces of imbalance.*

On *April 22, 1995*, Humanity celebrated the *25th anniversary of Earth Day.* As we turned our attention to Mother Earth, Humanity formed a Unified Cup through which the higher order of healing poured into the Planet and bathed the entire Elemental Kingdom in the Healing Unguent of our Father-Mother God.

On *April 23, 1995*, the *first anniversary of the opening of the Vortex of the Goddess in Los Angeles, California,* the Lords of Power from the Seventh Solar Aspect of Limitless Transmutation in the Great Central Sun traversed the psychic-astral realm and the physical realm of Earth. These selfless servants of God projected bolts of Violet Lightning in, through and around every man, woman and child. The Violet Lightning transmuted the misqualified energy from our past the maximum allowed by our Divine Plans. These magnificent Beings of Power and Protection have volunteered to remain in the atmosphere of Earth to assist us. All we have to do is ask for Their help, and They will instantly cut us free from the psychic-astral plane of human miscreation and chaos.

The purification by the Violet Lightning built in momentum daily and hourly until the *New Moon Solar Eclipse* on *April 29, 1995*. On this sacred day, all was in readiness for the transfer of authority from the Masculine Nature of God within us to the Love Nature of our Divine Feminine Selves.

A Divine Ceremony took place at inner and outer levels in which the Divine Masculine within each of us passed the staff of authority to the Divine Feminine—**thus empowering the Divine Love Nature within our hearts to take full command.** We (meaning all Humanity) were each invested with a gift of love from our Mother God that reflects into the world of form and bathes our everyday experiences on Earth with the Divine Love of the Twelve Solar Aspects of Deity. The Divine Feminine within us took Her rightful place in the Golden Throne Room of our Hearts.

May is considered the *"mystical month of May"* because so many Divine Activities take place in the Heavenly Realms during that Earthly time. On May 1st, the Temple of the Immaculate Heart of Beloved Mother Mary is opened each year in the Inner Realms, and all of the souls who will be conceived in the next 12-month cycle are drawn into that Focus of Light. Mother Mary assists in preparing them for their embodiment on Earth, and She accepts responsibility for holding the Divine Blueprint for the Immaculate Heart of each incarnating soul. In *1995*, Her service was expanded, and She was given authority by our Father-Mother God to prepare the *Divine Blueprint of the Immaculate Heart for the New Heaven and the New Earth*. On *May 7, 1995*, the Immaculate Heart for the New Heaven and the New Earth was anchored in the Sun of Even Pressure in the Center of the Earth. This paved the way for the greatest empowerment of the Divine Feminine the World has ever known.

May 8th is celebrated as the *Day of Ascension into Enlightened Consciousness*. On *May 8, 1995*, Humanity celebrated the 50th anniversary of the end of World War II. Symbolically, this represented the end of the atrocities of the Masculine abuse of power in the outer world of form. The World turned its attention to the celebration of the "end" of the abuse of power and focused on Freedom. Through the sacred geometry of the Pentecostal number of 50 (years) the essence of Holy Spirit—the Divine Mother—blessed the Earth.

This blessing of Divine Love built in momentum until the *Full Moon of Taurus, May 14, 1995*. This is the Full Moon of Enlightenment—the Buddha—the Wesak Festival—which fell that year (not by chance) on Mother's Day. On that special day when we all turned our attention to the Divine Feminine—Mother, the Earth and all Her life received a Baptism of the Divine Mother—Holy Spirit, which lifted us all a quantum leap into the frequencies of Divine Love. As this sacred gift from our Mother God bathed every fiber of our Beings, we were invested with the Divine Wisdom that will allow each and every one of us to eventually grasp the true significance of these wondrous times.

We are being given a unique opportunity to reclaim our Divine Heritage. **Like the Phoenix Ascending from the ashes, our Divine Feminine Self—the part of us that was always supposed to guide and direct our Holy Christ Self through Divine Love—is Ascending from the bondage of the human ego.** Never before have souls who have fallen so far from their original Divine Intent been given an opportunity to Ascend this quickly into the embrace of our Father-Mother God. This is an activity of unparalleled **GRACE.**

On *May 25, 1995, Ascension Thursday* (the day celebrated as Jesus' Ascension), Legions of the Ascension Flame from the electronic belt around the *Great Central Sun* entered the atmosphere of Earth and bathed every particle of life on Earth in the radiance of the Ascension Flame. This sacred substance prepared the physical plane of Earth at an atomic cellular level to move into the highest Octaves of Perfection we had been capable of experiencing since the "fall."

On *June 14, 1995*, the day celebrated in the outer world as *Pentecost—the day of the Baptism of the Holy Spirit*, our Mother God, held in the embrace of our Father God, *breathed this Earth and all Her life into the perfected frequencies of the Immaculate Heart of the Divine Feminine.* This is the collective Divine Feminine Presence Who is the resplendent manifestation of the unified Divine Feminine Selves of every man, woman and child evolving on Earth. This is the true Divine Love Nature of the collective Christ Presence of Humanity.

Embraced in the perfect balance of the Divine Masculine, this luminous, radiant Presence of the Divine Feminine assumed Her Divine Birthright.

The Divine Love of our Mother God reclaimed this Planet and will **NEVER AGAIN RECEDE FROM EARTH.**

Now, it is *our* responsibility to integrate the Divine Love of our Divine Feminine Selves into our everyday experiences. Remember, it is the frequency of Divine Love, which we release through our thoughts, words, feelings and actions, that is *the Key* to shifting the Earth into a compatible frequency so that we will complete our Ascension into the Light. Every moment is an opportunity for us to make a difference. That's why we are here.

Let's get busy!!!

CHAPTER
SIX

THE EARTH IS BECOMING A SUN!

How is that for a mind-boggling contemplation? As amazing as that seems, that is exactly what is happening. The Earth is not going to become exactly like our physical Sun, but as we Ascend into the next Spiral of Evolution, we are moving into a higher rate of vibration that will express itself on Earth as a Solar Reality. That is why we are now moving into the embrace of the Twelve *Solar* Aspects of Deity, our *Solar* Causal Bodies, our *Solar* Chakras and Meridians, our Twelve *Solar* Strands of DNA and our *Solar* Christ Presences.

Remember that during the last Cosmic Inbreath millions of years ago, all of the Planets and Suns that had volunteered to descend into the Third Dimensional experiment with the Earth Ascended back into the Fourth Dimension. Only the Earth remained in the Third Dimension, so that we could provide a Planetary Home for the six-billion fallen laggard souls who were going to be left behind from the other Planets. Our Light and Life Force have been sustained by our God Parents, Helios and Vesta, even though we are existing in a denser frequency of vibration. That was an act of extreme mercy and compassion.

Now, however, the Divine Fiat has been issued, and it is time for this prodigal, wayward Planet to return home to the embrace of our Father-Mother God. This particular Cosmic Moment was chosen by the Godhead because our God Parents knew we were going to need supernatural Divine Intervention in order for us to make the shift. You see, we are not only Ascending into the Fourth Dimension to catch up with the rest of the Planets in our Solar System, we are also Ascending with the rest of our Solar Sytem into the *Fifth Dimension,* which is a SOLAR REALITY.

Never has a Planet moved through TWO dimensional quantum leaps in energy, vibration and consciousness in the short time alloted the Earth. Our Father-Mother God chose this time frame so that we could take full advantage of all of the multifaceted assistance available from all levels of Creation.

One of the most powerful and fascinating *phenomenon* assisting us during our Ascension process is known as the PHOTON BELT.

THE PHOTON BELT

The Photon Belt is the forcefield of Light that the prophets of old foresaw when they described the Celestial event they called THE RAPTURE. As we move closer to this forcefield of Light, people all over the World are beginning to perceive this "Cosmic Cloud" of photon energy, and each person is interpreting what it is according to his/her wisdom and understanding. Depending on who is writing the article or discussing the Photon Belt, the information seems to inspire either elation or terror. Some people are saying that this forcefield of energy will flip the poles and destroy all life on Earth. Others are professing that it will instantaneously transform the Earth into a Planet of perpetual Light and Eternal Peace. The Truth, as usual, transcends all of the fear and confusion and brings a level of clarity that will allow us to utilize the Photon Belt to the highest advantage for all life on Earth.

First of all, we need to understand what the Photon Belt *really* is. In another part of this book on page 29, I described the 24,000 year orbit our Solar System is on that takes us counter-clockwise through the Heavens in what we call the "Precession of the Equinox." To further understand this orbit, I would like to elaborate a little bit.

The Pleiades is a well-known group of Stars in the constellation of Taurus, the Bull. These Stars are visible to the naked eye, and our astronomers agree that this is a System of Suns which revolve around ALCYONE, the largest and brightest Sun in the cluster. In the beginning, astrophysicists recognized that our own Sun is the outer Star, and Alcyone is at the center of our rotation. Modern astronomy also accepts that Alcyone is the center of a huge circulating system comprised of Stars and their Planets. There are more than six Suns whose movements this central Star controls, and our physical Sun occupies the seventh orbit.

Alcyone is surrounded by a huge RADIATION BELT COMPRISED OF PHOTON PARTICLES. THIS BELT IS IN THE FORM OF A DISC, and it is similar to the rings of Saturn. The PHOTON BELT around Alcyone extends hundreds of light years into space. Each planetary Sun will pass through this PHOTON DISC *twice* in completing one orbit around Alcyone. *Our Sun* passes through the Photon Belt every 10,000 years. Each time it takes approximately 2000 Solar years or 759,864 billion miles to actually pass through the Photon Disc.

This forcefield of Light contains disintegrated or split electrons. Photon Light particles are created when a collision takes place between an anti-electron (positron) and an electron. This nanosecond collision causes the two particles to destroy each other. The resulting mass of this collision is converted into photons or Light particles.

While passing through these Light particles, every molecule on Earth will be dramatically affected. The atoms contained within all manifest form will be accelerated to a higher frequency of vibration. This will incalculably enhance our Ascension process. It will allow us to easily move into our Light Bodies, thus making tremendous evolutionary strides forward at an atomic, cellular level. As awesome as this seems, this incredible acceleration of Light will also amplify the healing that is taking place as we reweave our Twelve Solar Strands of DNA and reconnect the circuitry that will enable us to communicate with all of the various Dimensions of Perfection. This process will gradually restore us to full consciousness and allow us to reawaken the

90 percent of our brains that fell into dormancy when we short- circuited our DNA Strands.

The Light Particles in the Photon Belt will also give us a major boost up the Spiral of Evolution and assist us into the frequencies of the Fifth Dimension.

The prophecies of old, including "Revelations," described this event in terminology that could be understood by the masses in ancient times. As usual, the most dire prophecies were given to motivate our lower human egos to change the course of history. Since our egos are fear based, they, unfortunately, use fear as their motivator.

It was never enough to just tell our egos to revere life and strive for harmony and balance through the path of Divine Love. They also had to be told the horror of what would happen if they didn't redeem themselves and repent. Only through that fear would our egos put forth the necessary effort to correct their recalcitrant behavior.

Even that approach didn't always work because our egos are so pessimistic and such fatalists that they often accepted the prophecies as *Law* instead of realizing that prophecies are ONLY A *POTENTIAL* OF WHAT COULD HAPPEN IF WE DON'T CHANGE OUR WAYS.

A FULFILLED NEGATIVE PROPHESY IS A FAILED PROPHESY!!!

If a negative prophesy is fulfilled, it means it *did not* accomplish its Divine Intent, which was to inspire Humanity to change our course of direction. For us to just sit around and wring our hands in despair waiting for ARMAGEDDON so Jesus will come and save the "good people" and destroy the "bad people" is a GROSS ERROR IN JUDGMENT.

The negativity surfacing on Earth *is* ARMAGEDDON. We are now moving into the Light, and OUR VICTORY IN THE LIGHT IS ASSURED.

But, this assurance comes *solely* because Humanity en

masse is awakening and recommitting our life energies to healing the distorted mutations our human egos have created and perpetuated.

Our Victory in the Light is assured because we have now reached the *critical mass,* and our **Solar Christ Presences are the predominant influences in our lives**. This is true in spite of the negativity that is being pushed to the surface to be purified and healed. This is true in spite of how far we may feel we are at the moment from expressing that Divine aspect of ourselves. And, this is true in spite of the fact that *a few people* are still doing deplorable things and acting out appalling and depraved behavior patterns. THE CRITICAL MASS OF HUMANITY IS *NOT*!!!

The critical mass of Humanity (51 percent or more) is genuinely and innately striving to reach our Divine Potentials; striving to BE Loving, Peace Commanding Presences on Earth; striving to heal our transgressions of the Laws of Harmony and Divine Love; striving to correct our course of direction and to help this Planet reclaim Her Divine Birthright of Heaven on Earth and striving to fulfill our Divine Plans as Sons and Daughters of God.

Even though the media is continually bombarding our consciousness with the negative things occurring on Earth so that we can invoke the Divine Light of Healing and Forgiveness into the situations at hand, the number of people perpetuating the negativity and chaos is a MINUSCULE FRACTION of the six-billion people evolving on Earth. This doesn't even include the additional four-billion souls between embodiments who are assisting us from the Inner Realms of Light. When we accept this Truth, we will recognize how very close we are to shifting the consciousness of the remaining souls on Earth. Then, we will truly believe and KNOW our Victory is assured.

The Photon Belt vs. the Prophecies of
Fire and Brimstone

Passing through the Photon Belt is a natural part of our Earthly experience that occurs every 10,000 years and lasts for approximately 2000 years. Some of the ancient legends of indigenous people in various lands told of 10,000 years of darkness and 2000 years of Light. As we tap greater levels of understanding in the Realms of Truth, we begin to see the potential of this phenomenon. The 10,000 years of darkness referred to the cycle we are now in when we experience the Light of our physical Sun for only a portion of our 24-hour day, and we are in darkness for the remainder of the 24-hour cycle. In other words, during the 10,000 years that we are not in the Photon Belt, we have both day and night.

During the 2000 years that we *are* in the Photon Belt, however, we experience a different phenomenon. The Photon Light particles affect the atoms and molecules on Earth in a way that causes them to emit their own Light. This is similar to the way cosmic radiation particles Light up the ionosphere producing the Northern Lights.

When we are fully in the embrace of the Photon Belt, this Light, which radiates no heat, will illuminate even the darkest caverns, and we will have perpetual illumination both day and night. This is the period the ancients referred to as the 2000 years of Light.

We are entering the fringes of the Photon Belt at this very moment, and we are experiencing the first frequencies of Light particles. This is causing a few challenges with our electromagnetic fields, and people all over the World are reporting unexplained electrical "blackouts" and frustrating things such as electrical appliances going awry or electrical systems in their cars functioning erratically and then working perfectly for no apparent reason. As we realize what is happening, we can invoke the Light to harmonize our electro-magnetic fields and accelerate the energy flowing through our electrical appliances and automobiles. This will elevate energies to a higher frequency, which will gradually bring all electrical fields into harmony so that they will be compatible with the Photon Belt.

In the past we didn't understand about electro-magnetic fields. Consequently, our consciousness after the fall was such that our experiences of the Photon Belt were always horrendous. That is why people are now tapping the past Etheric Records and prophesying the horror of the "end times" proclaiming that God will destroy the Earth with *"fire and brimstone."*

The Null Zone

The horror stories of the Photon Belt were perpetuated after the fall because the Earth's physical entry into this field of Light particles was very similar to the space shuttle's re-entry into the atmosphere of Earth. As you know, when the space shuttle first re-enters the atmosphere of Earth, there is intense friction and heat for two or three minutes as it passes through what we call the Null Zone. Then, once the shuttle completes re-entry, all of that dissipates and returns to normal.

The Null Zone surrounding the Photon Belt is a huge barrier of incredibly compressed energy. In this barrier the magnetic fields are so tightly woven together that it is impossible for any Third Dimensional electro-magnetic field to pass through it without being dramatically altered.

When the Earth fell into extreme frequencies of discord, our passage into the Photon Belt became a very traumatic jolt. As we passed through the Null Zone of the Photon Belt, which takes approximately 72 hours, the Earth experienced very tumultuous conditions. All of the extreme challenges the Earth has experienced can probably be traced back to our various re-entries into the Photon Belt: the flipping of the poles, instant ice ages, the disappearance of the dinosaurs, the timing of the sinking of Lemuria and Atlantis, falling off the Spiral of Evolution onto the Wheel of Karma, the disappearances of vast civilizations, etc.

The prophecies of old that describe these end times coincide as well with the phenomenon that occurred when we entered the Null Zone of the Photon Belt in the past.

When the **Sun** enters the Null Zone, we experience what appears to be a major Solar Eclipse for 72 hours. The prophecies say, *"For three days the Sun will turn blood red, and the Moon will not give forth Her Light."*

As the **Earth** enters the Null Zone, the Photon Light particles will Light up the ionosphere, and the atmosphere will appear as though it is on fire, but there will be no heat. The prophecies say, *"And fire and brimstone will fall from the sky,"* and *"Stars will fall from the sky."*

In the past, the trauma of passing through the Null Zone of the Photon Belt was catastrophic BECAUSE OF THE DISCORDANT FREQUENCIES OF THE EARTH'S VIBRATIONS. That is why ALL of the prophecies indicate that *if* Humanity will change our ways and return to a path of love and reverence for all life, THE CATASTROPHIES WILL BE AVERTED.

The concept of the *RAPTURE* indicates that if people are living lives of love, harmony and balance, they will be able to pass into the Photon Light particles unscathed, *"and they will be raised up into the air."* If there are those who are living lives of depravity and discord, they will not make it through the Null Zone and will perish as they move into the Photon Belt, *"and the remainder on Earth will be purged with fire and brimstone."* The prophecies continue to elaborate that after the *"purging,"* the Earth will be purified and transformed into Heaven on Earth, *"and change will come in the twinkling of an eye."* The souls who were *"raptured,"* in other words, those who made it through the Null Zone, will abide on Earth in a virtual Paradise of Splendor.

A CHANGE OF PLANS

The goal of our Father-Mother God and the entire Company of Heaven has *always* been for Humanity to awaken and regain our direction before we reached the Null Zone of the Photon Belt this time, so that *ALL* life on Earth could God Victoriously Ascend into the Fifth Dimension with the rest of our Solar System. Every single plan that has been implemented on Earth by the Godhead was designed to prod and prompt Humanity to return to the path of Divine Love that would permanently raise the Earth's vibration into a compatible frequency with the Photon Belt.

Every prophecy that has ever been given regarding these "end times" has clearly indicated that Humanity HAS A CHOICE.

Consistently, the prophecies of old stated over and over again that LOVE will make the difference. That may not sound very scientific, but actually it is.

Love is the cohesive power of the Universe, and there is no particle of life that can resist its call. Love is an unparalleled frequency of harmony. Love is a term and an experience that every single person on the Planet can understand. We don't have to comprehend the significance of the Cosmic Moment at hand. We don't have to grasp the science of energy, vibration and consciousness. We don't have to fathom the complexities of physics. We don't have to believe in a particular dogma or doctrine. We don't have to be adept in the Wisdom of the Ages. We don't have to be rocket scientists. We don't have to be any specific race, religion, nationality, creed, socio-economic status, gender, age or I.Q. in order to express the glory and wonder of love. Therefore, plans were set into motion time and again by the Powers On High to flood the consciousness of Humanity with the urgent need to bathe the Planet with the vibratory frequency of love. Every prophet, seer and Spiritual aspirant was infused with the burning desire to inform the multitudes of the need to release their wayward feelings of hate and embrace the love of all life.

Through the unified efforts of Heaven and Earth, the consciousness of Humanity began to shift, and we began to truly REMEMBER...the essence of Divine Love...pure, strong, gentle, complete and unconditional... is the vibration from which we were born out of the Heart of God and the vibration through which we must evolve and Ascend back to the Heart of God. This frequency of love has no bonds, no barriers, no conditions. Within the Infinite Power of Divine Love there is no pain or sorrow, no lack nor limitation. It contains within its essence our full potential to rise above all human conditions, all self-inflicted suffering, all manner of chaos, confusion, hopelessness and despair. Divine Love heals the illusion of separation. It rejuvenates, revitalizes and makes whole all it embraces. Divine Love is the single greatest source of forgiveness. It is the full-gathered momentum of our Eternal FREEDOM.

Through Divine Love, we will each be drawn up into the realization and acceptance of our own Divinity. Within the Wisdom of Divine Love is revealed the knowledge that each and every one of us holds a unique silken thread to the Tapestry of Life. Every single thread is necessary and critical to the perfect fulfillment of the Immaculate Concept of the Divine Plan for the Earth. As we tap the frequencies of Divine Love, we begin to experience gratitude for all of the blessings of God that contribute so generously to our Earthly pilgrimage. Within the flow of this mighty force, our faith in ourselves is renewed, and we once again perceive ourselves as valuable Human Beings. Never again will we say, *"What good could I possibly achieve? What value am I? What difference will one soul possibly make?"* We will recognize those thoughts to be a sacrilege before the Universe. We will know that we were created and sustained by God because God has chosen to express some beautiful manifestation through us. God has chosen us to fulfill a portion of the glorious Divine Plan, and asked that we release the unique perfume and music of our Beings to bless all life. The purity of our individual fragrance and tone is unlike any other ever released by the evolving souls on this sweet Earth. Something sacred is hidden in each of our souls that has never been known by another, some beautiful manifestation of life which God and our "I AM" Presences alone can externalize. It is time for all Humanity to accept this Truth and stand revealed as the Christ grown to full stature. Our Solar Christ Presences are waiting in our hearts today for the summons to burst the tomb of matter. As this occurs, the fullness of Their vital life will be released, transfiguring our flesh, revitalizing our Spirit and externalizing the Kingdom of Heaven to the periphery of our Spiritual influence.

There has been so much written about love it has almost become a platitude, but love in its purity is the mightiest force in the Universe. Love is a principle—a consciously maintained attitude of radiation. Love is the fulfillment of the Law, because there is no power that can deny it or fail to respond to its call. If we tap the heart of our God Selves and magnetize forth the peaceful radiation of impersonal Divine Love, all the good of the Universe will *flow* into our lives. THAT is the power of Divine Love As incredible as it seems—*that is the Law.*

As we truly experience the pure vibration of Divine Love, we recognize it as the most priceless element in all existence; we perceive it as a dynamic living force. Love is the vehicle upon which all Light is carried into form. It transcends time and space. It is Spiritual and all powerful.

As Divine Love is breathed into the world of form, it carries through the Heart Center of each soul the Christ Light that dispels all gloom and darkness. It banishes decay, misery and evil. It overcomes fear and separation. Negativity and discord cannot abide in the presence of Divine Love, for this sacred essence is a force of unlimited and unspeakable power. Divine Love is a creative force that is ALWAYS constructive and beneficial. It exalts and glorifies.

This gift of love from God is endowed with a deeper vision that peers beyond the scars and blemishes on the surface. Its healing tenderness penetrates all exteriors to behold the Truth of each soul, the reality of each experience. Divine Love pierces beyond the visible into the innermost depths of perfection and finds its resting place there.

Our purpose and reason for being is to be the bearers and transmitters of Divine Love. This sacred essence, which renews all to everlasting life, is the key to EVERY door.

Love is the cohesive power of the Universe binding into form all physical matter, every atom and particle of life. It holds families together—the World and the entire Universe. Without love all physical substance would disintegrate into unformed, primal energy. When we eliminate love from our lives, we, too, begin to disintegrate and fall apart. When we incorporate Divine Love into every aspect of our lives, we experience cohesiveness and success beyond the comprehension of our finite minds.

With the fully developed God-given faculty of love, we have the power to create whatever our Spiritual Vision of love beholds. As we command "LET THERE BE LIGHT," Eternity itself stands still in the wonder of that Presence. Through love, great Light is released, and through love, the Light fulfills Its glory, becoming the exalted essence of understanding, comprehension and knowledge. We, then, experience knowing the God within. It is through love alone that our Divine Selves can be contacted and developed.

As we develop our Divine Selves through love, we change and are transformed into new, vibrant Beings of radiant Light, expressing poise and power. We become increasingly attractive to our fellow Beings and we automatically begin to magnetize others into our lives. Those lifestreams in our spheres of influence will experience comfort and peace in our presence as our love pours forth from our hearts and fills the electro-magnetic energy field which surrounds us.

Our love amplifies the love in the people drawn to us, and they begin to experience the Glory of God as the Light expands within their hearts. This celestial Song of Love reverberating through every heart is the greatest gift from God available to us on Earth.

As love and Light are intermingled and brought forth through praise and gratitude, we begin to realize that nothing is impossible. We then *"Speak only with the voice of love, see only with the eyes of love and hear only with the ears of love."*

As we develop this perfect gift of Divine Love, our old stagnant beliefs and patterns begin to crumble, and Divine Ideas from the Mind of God fill our consciousness. Our whole Being assumes a new vitality, beauty, purpose and meaning. Compassion replaces condemnation; forgiveness replaces accusation; healing replaces disease; abundance replaces limitation and love replaces loneliness. As we are filled to overflowing with the essence of Divine Love, It begins to radiate out through every cell of our physical bodies, and we become vibrantly beautiful. Our hands, radiating forth love, bless all they touch; our eyes, seeing through love, perceive only perfection in all life; our ears, filled with love, hear the Music of the Spheres; and our nostrils, breathing love, inhale the fragrance of the Holy Spirit. Thus, we become renewed and Divine. In this exalted state of Divine Love we speak with wisdom, compassion, tenderness and understanding. Each loving word wings its way across the face of the Earth, blessing all life.

Then, we will know as never before: *"Though I speak with the tongues of men and of Angels and have not love, I am like a sounding brass or a clanging cymbal. And though I have the gift of prophecy and understand all mysteries and all knowledge and have all faith so I could remove mountains and have not love, I am nothing."*

Now, with great insight and a new level of awareness, we realize Divine Love is the highest attribute of the human soul. It is the most vital energy required for our Spiritual attainment, and the further we have advanced on the ladder of evolution, the more spontaneous and far-reaching will be our expression of love.

In our time of need, love is available to assist us as a positive, concentrated action. We receive it, according to our capacity to accept it, at the time of our call. Without love, the clearest vision remains but a cloudy vapor.

Through love we will have constancy in the most trying of circumstances, and we will be able to respond at the moment when it is needed most.

As we master this Divine Gift, we will continually pour forth our full-gathered momentum of love for the good of ALL. We will experience, through higher levels of awareness, our Oneness with all life. Then, the separation will be no more, and reverence for all life will be THE ORDER OF THE NEW COSMIC DAY.

In *1995,* we were finally in position to accelerate the Forcefield of Divine Love on the Planet into a frequency that would be compatible with the Photon Belt. Then, ALL LIFE ON EARTH WOULD BE ABLE TO PASS THROUGH THE NULL ZONE HARMONIOUSLY.

The Spiritual Hierarchy directed us to hold the Ninth Annual World Congress on Illumination in Colorado Springs, Colorado, during the anniversary of Harmonic Convergence *August 12-17, 1995*.

Colorado Springs was chosen for several reasons. Like Rio de Janiero, it represents the microcosm of the macrocosm on Earth. It reflects the dichotomy of what is transpiring on the Planet during these chaotic times. On one level, it displays the pristine beauty of Mother Earth through majestic mountains, crystalline waters, verdant landscapes and the Garden of the Gods in Colorado Springs. Yet, on another level, it conceals within a cloak of secrecy one of the largest military facilities in the World. This duality is symptomatic of the separation of the lower human ego from the God Presence, and it was imperative that this separation be healed in order to move into the frequency of harmony and balance that was necessary to accomplish our mission.

Another reason that Colorado Springs was chosen for this event is that aeons ago when Humanity was spiraling into oblivion after the initial impetus of our "fall," the indigenous people living in that region took a sacred vow and volunteered to hold within the Permanent Seed Atom of their hearts the Divine Blueprint for the Earth and all life evolving upon Her, as it was formed in the original Divine Intent of our Father-Mother God.

For millennia, these souls, under the direction of Lord Manitou, God of the Wind and Sacred Healing Waters, clung to the vision of the "New World." This was to be a World of God Conscious souls comprised of every race, nationality, religion and belief system, living together as one people under God, honoring and revering every part of life in harmony, mutual respect and love. This was to be the "I Am" Race.

The *"Garden of the Gods"* in Colorado Springs was declared sacred, and all of the Indian Tribes honored that sacred trust. It was the one place where councils could be held without fear of war. No person was allowed to take a weapon into the "Garden of the Gods." It was a meeting place for peace.

When Christopher Columbus responded to his inner heart call to find the "New World," the Divine Plan to reclaim the Earth from the oppressive grip of our human egos was set into motion. The Sacred Flame of Freedom was anchored in his heart and then carried to the indigenous people on the North American continent to form the matrix for the Immaculate Concept of the "New World." This was cradled in the vortex of the "Garden of the Gods."

Once the Flame was secured, the Clarion Call for Freedom reverberated through the ethers. Christopher Columbus returned to Europe, and the news spread like wildfire. Every oppressed person seeking Spiritual and physical freedom responded to his/her heart's call to go to the New World.

Unfortunately, our fear-based human egos got the upper hand, and the Divine Intent of the New World was virtually buried in the atrocities of human miscreation and the abuse of power. But, even in the face of this tragedy, Lord Manitou and the indigenous people in the area of Colorado Springs tenaciously held the Divine Blueprint, knowing that the time would one day come when Humanity would awaken and regain Her direction, reclaiming the "New World" as Her Divine Birthright.

THIS IS THAT TIME!!!

During the Cosmic Moment of the ninth celebration of Harmonic Covergence, a Divine Pageant unfolded.

At the opening ceremonies of the Ninth Annual World Congress On Illumination on *August 12, 1995*, seven Mighty Solar Angels of Divine Love from the electronic belt around the Great Great Central Sun in the Sixth Dimension, descended into the atmosphere of Earth bringing with Them the most intensified frequency of Divine Love the Earth has ever experienced. These exponents of God's Love took Their strategic positions around this Planet. Four of Them stood equal distances around the equator. One stood at the North Pole, one at the South Pole. The seventh Solar Angel stood within the Sun of Even Pressure in the center of the Earth.

The four Solar Angels positioned around the equator projected powerful shafts of Divine Love from the very Heart of our Father-Mother God through the equator into the center of the Earth.

The Solar Angels standing at the North and South Poles

projected powerful shafts of Divine Love through the axis of the Earth.

The Solar Angel positioned in the center of the Earth absorbed these unparalleled shafts of Divine Love and breathed this sacred essence through the Crystal Grid System of the Planet on the Holy Breath. This Earth and all Her life were enveloped in the invincible frequency of our Mother God's Love, and every particle of life was lifted on the wings of our Divine Mother's Love into a higher frequency of Light, preparing us for the moment at hand.

On *August 13, 1995*, several things occurred to further prepare us for our Ascent into Divinity. The collective God Presence of every Human Being, every Elemental and every Angel blended together to form a magnificent Chalice of Light that cradled this Earth and Her enfolding Heart of Divine Love. On the Holy Breath of God, this Chalice was lifted into a resplendent six-pointed star that was pulsating in the Fourth Dimensional frequencies of perfection. This star represented the Ascending Triangle of Humanity, Elementals and Angels blending and becoming one with the Descending Triangle of Divinity, the full expression of Godhood. Through this unification, the Oneness of God flooded into all of the Realms of Consciousness on Earth. Even the most depraved expressions of human miscreation and the most laggard souls were bathed in the **knowingness** of their innate Divinity. The spark within their hearts began to stir, and they began to remember.

The Transfer of the Laggard Souls

For several decades now the Spiritual Hierarchy has told us that through a merciful activity of Divine Grace, a Cosmic Dispensation had been granted whereby the souls who refused to move into the Light would one day be transferred to another System of Worlds. There they could progress at a slower pace. They will be born into approximately the caveman state of consciousness, which is a dramatic set-back, but it is infinitely better than going through the "Second Death."

It was determined by the Godhead that for us to move into the correct frequency of Divine Love, in order to be compatible with the Photon Belt, the laggard souls needed to be transferred to the other Planet. This process began as the first Rays of the *Summer Solstice* bathed the Earth on *June 21, 1995*. At that time, tens of thousands of the fallen laggard souls who had been manipulating, possessing and entrapping people on Earth from the psychic-astral plane, were removed from the Earth's atmosphere and taken to the inner schools of learning in preparation for their re-embodiment on the other Planet. That still left hundreds of thousands of laggard souls both in and out of embodiment who were going to be transferred very soon.

But, during that fateful day (*August 13, 1995*) when the Oneness of God bathed all realms of consciousness on Earth and stirred the Divinity within the hearts of all life evolving here, *the remaining laggard souls rededicated their life energies to the Light and made the conscious choice to move into the Octaves of Perfection with the rest of our Solar System.*

That was a Victory beyond the greatest expectations of Heaven, and the entire Universe rejoiced.

Additional assistance was given from Realms beyond Realms and Galaxies beyond Galaxies to assist these prodigal Children of God. During the remaining days of the World Congress On Illumination, the gifts from Heaven were unprecedented.

As the entire Universe stood in readiness, Beloved Elohae and Eloha, the Divine Representatives of our Father-Mother God from the Great Central Sun, summoned the Mighty Solar Archangels and Their Divine Complements, the Mighty Archaii, to come into the Heart of the Great Central Sun and stand before Their Luminous Presence to receive Their

Divine Investiture into a Higher Order of Service.

These glorious Archangels and Archaii, representing the Twelve Solar Aspects of Deity, responded in deep humility and gratitude as They presented Themselves before the resplendent Presence of Elohae and Eloha.

In a Sacred Ceremony of Light, each Archangel and Archaii was handed a staff of Power and Authority. This staff will allow Them to magnetize to Earth a frequency of the Twelve Solar Aspects of God beyond anything the Earth has ever experienced.

Once the Investiture into a Higher Order of Service was completed, the Solar Archangels and Archaii descended into the atmosphere of Earth and anchored the new frequencies of Divinity into the Twelve Solar Chakras and the Twelve Solar Meridians of all Humanity. This Divine Light was then projected into the Solar Chakras of Mother Earth, which pulsate along the axis of the Planet, and the new frequency of the Twelve Solar Aspects of Deity expanded through the Crystal Grid System into every electron of energy evolving on Earth.

On *August 14, 1995*, the Air Element and the Etheric Bodies of Human Beings, Elementals, Angels and Mother Earth were purified the maximum that Cosmic Law would allow.

The Spirit of the Resurrection Flame had entered the Great, Great Silence on *January 1, 1995*, in preparation for that Cosmic Moment. As the Keynote of the Resurrection Flame rang forth from the Heart and Mind of God, the Spirit of the Resurrection Flame descended to Earth from out of the Great, Great Silence and blazed and blazed and blazed the Resurrection Flame in, through and around every part of life on Earth. This Sacred Fire literally Resurrected the Etheric Bodies of Humanity, Elementals, Angels and Mother Earth Herself into the Divine Matrix of the Etheric Pattern for the New Heaven and the New Earth. This Divine Blueprint will now pulsate through all manifest form until It is physically and tangibly expressed on Earth.

On *August 15, 1995*, the day celebrated as Mother Mary's Ascension, the Water Element and the Emotional Bodies of Human Beings, Elementals, Angels and Mother Earth were purified the maximum that Cosmic Law would allow. This purification pierced deeply into the fear-based consciousness of our human egos, and this wayward aspect of our human personalities began to experience, for the first time in aeons, the Love Nature of our Solar Christ Presences.

The human ego of every man, woman and child, both in and out of embodiment, began to experience a level of comfort and peace as Mother Mary bathed each one in Her Motherly Love. A new level of trust was projected by each Solar Christ Presence into the Heart Flame of each person. As the trust expanded to envelop each human ego, this fragmented entity lifted up in consciousness enough to see the Solar Christ Presence and get a glimpse of the original Divine Intent of this Being of Light. The Solar Christ Presence of each person was able to integrate further into the four lower bodies.

This process will be accelerated as we affirm daily and hourly...

"I AM" MY SOLAR CHRIST PRESENCE
GROWN TO FULL STATURE,
NOW MADE MANIFEST AND SUSTAINED
BY HOLY GRACE!

On *August 16, 1995*, the Earth Element and the Physical Bodies of all Human Beings, Elementals, Angels and Mother Earth were purified the maximum that Cosmic Law would allow.

A Clarion Call from the heart of Beloved Mother Earth

rang out to the indigenous people who have been holding the Immaculate Concept for the New World for all of these many aeons of time.

The Directors of the Earth Element responded from Their Temple in the Sun of Even Pressure in the Center of the Earth. They sent a signal to all of the Beings of the Earth declaring that their Cosmic Opportunity was at hand.

Lord Manitou responded by sending forth His Clarion Call to all of the Gods of the Mountains; the Deva Rajas and the Devas; the Gnomes and Nature Spirits of the Earth.

These Beings of the Nature Kingdom heard the call, and every tree, plant, flower and blade of grass stood in readiness. Every rock and grain of sand began to pulsate with expectation. The animal kingdom responded to the call and entered a state of alert awareness. The Body Elementals of all Humanity prepared for the moment at hand.

The Spirit of the Resurrection accelerated the preparation by amplifying the Resurrection Flame through the core of purity within every electron in the substance of Earth.

Then, as one voice, one heartbeat, one breath, one energy, vibration and consciousness of pure Divine Love, the Beings of the Earth Element sang Their song of unity to the Heart of our Father-Mother God.

The Universe heard Their plea, and Beloved Helios and Vesta, the representatives of our Father-Mother God from our physical Sun, directed Their Legions of **God's First Cause of Perfection** into the atmosphere of Earth.

Beloved Alpha and Omega, the representatives of our Father-Mother God from the Central Sun, directed Their Legions of **God's Infinity Consciousness** into the atmosphere of Earth.

Beloved Elohae and Eloha, the representatives of our Father-Mother God from the Great Central Sun, directed Their Legions of the **Immaculate Concept for the New Heaven and the New Earth** into the atmosphere of Earth.

These Beings of Divine Cause traversed the Earth:

North, South, East and West. They descended into the physical substance of Earth and embraced every particle of the Earth Element in Their specific gifts from the Heart of God.

God's First Cause of Perfection was projected into the Divine Blueprint pulsating within the core of every electron of the Earth Element, and the First Cause of Perfection was permanently re-established on Earth.

The radiance of **Infinity Consciousness** was projected into the intelligence of every aspect of Earth. As this occurred, each part of the Earth Element, including the physical Bodies of Humanity, began to remember the Infinity of our multidimensional, multifaceted Being and *reclaimed* that Divine Birthright.

The **Immaculate Concept of the New Heaven and the New Earth**, in unparalleled frequencies from the Sun beyond the Sun beyond the Sun was projected into and permanently imprinted on the genetic codes of all manifest form, thus permanently establishing the Divine Matrix for the physical formation of Limitless Physical Perfection...the New Earth.

On *August 17, 1995*, the Fire Element and the Mental Bodies of all Human Beings, Elementals, Angels and Mother Earth were purified the maximum that Cosmic Law would allow. On this sacred day, the final preparation was made for Earth's Ascension into the embrace of Divine Love, the eternal frequency of supreme harmony that is compatible with the Photon Belt.

Through an unparalleled activity of the Violet Fire of Limitless Transmutation and Forgiveness, any frequency of vibration in the Physical, Etheric, Mental or Emotional strata of Earth that was not in harmony with the frequency of the Photon Belt was instantly transmuted.

At last, as the Universe stood in readiness, the Earth and all Her life Ascended on the Holy Breath of our Father-Mother God through the open Stargate of Di-

vine Love into a frequency that will allow Her to pass through the Null Zone of the Photon Belt in perfect harmony and Divine Order.

EFFECTS OF THE FRINGES OF
THE PHOTON BELT

As we begin to experience the fringes of the Photon Belt, our scientists are beginning to recognize that something very unusal is happening. They aren't calling it the Photon Belt yet, but the influx of articles proclaiming "new, previously unknown particles of energy" confirms their awareness of the fact that something astounding is going on.

The following is a sample of some information I have collected over the years.

1. In *1985,* a New York newspaper reported that the Earth is a target for unknown particles. It said that astrophysicists believe a Cosmic power source far out in space may be bombarding the Earth with subatomic particles different from any known to science.

Recordings taken deep in a mine at Soudan, Minn., an Ohio salt mine and beneath a World War II bunker at the University of Kiel in West Germany are believed to include scores of high-energy particles from the general direction of Cygnus X-3, a double-star system in the constellation Cygnus.

Scientists said that they were at a loss to explain the new data in terms of known forms

of radiation and stressed that the recordings
needed much more analysis.

But they said the data called into question
the suggestion made, on the basis of particles detected in a salt mine beneath Lake
Erie, that Cygnus X-3 may be a major source
of extremely high energy neutrinos.

Neutrinos are the most penetrating and
elusive of all known subatomic particles.
They can pass through the Earth or almost
any amount of detecting material without
producing any effect.

One member of the Ohio salt mine team
who have analyzed the observations there
said he is pretty well convinced that *some
new form of physics is involved in the
observed particles.*
(*Arizona Daily Star,* **March 21, 1995**)

2. In **1987,** the Associated Press reported
that billions of watts of new energy are
bombarding the Earth. The report stated
that electron showers were detected by
an instrument aboard a satellite. Each of
the showers dumps about a billion watts
of energy a second into the atmosphere
according to the Los Alamos National
Laboratory. The electrons tend to spiral
down the Planet's magnetic field lines.
The electron showers hit every 27 days
and last 2 and 1/2 days.

The report said that electrons are the elec-

trical charges whirling around the nucleus of atoms, which cause atoms to cluster in an energy field. So an "electron shower" would seem to indicate the appearance of a *new energy field* being stepped-down to the physical plane.
(*Associated Press,* **May 22, 1987**)

3. In another report appearing in a New York newspaper in **1987**, we were told a violent stellar explosion flared into view over the Southern Hemisphere on **February 23rd**, and it apparently spawned a mysterious twin, according to scientists. The observations show that the bright exploding star, or super-nova, is two points of Light, close together, one about 10 times brighter than its com-panion. Since neither was present before the explosion, astronomers assume that, mysteriously, both arose from the same blast.
(*New York Times Service,* **May 24, 1987**)

4. In **1988,** an Arizona newspaper reported that physicists were theorizing that a "beam" in space had new particles. It stated that a power-ful beam striking the Earth from a twin star system 14,000 light years away could herald a new type of particle that physicists said confounds the standard theories of physics.

The beam, carrying a million billion elec-tron volts of energy, comes from a neutron star, half of a binary star system named Hercules X-1 in the constellation Hercules.

The neutron star is nearly the size of Earth's moon, but is extremely dense with a mass nearly double the Sun's.

The other half of the star system, about 4 million miles from the neutron star, is a large, spinning magnet, generating massive electro-magnetic fields and giving off powerful radiation. The beam initially was believed to be electrical neutral gamma rays, which are *high energy Light waves or photons.*

The problem with that interpretation was that the beam hits way up in the atmosphere and produces a shower of particles.

Gamma rays are not supposed to do that. That is what was interesting and puzzling about the finding. The scientists said that there is the possible presence of a new particle that is coming out of the study of a powerful neutral beam. It isn't the power of the neutral beam; it's the particular interaction it has in the Earth's atmosphere.

The discovery should lead to new insights about sources of energy in the Universe and about the elementary structure of matter.

The scientists came up with several explanations for the strange beam, which also has been detected by observatories in Arizona and Hawaii. One explanation is that it is made of a *previously unknown particle.*
(Arizona Daily Star, October 11, 1988)

5. In *1990,* a California newspaper reported
that a mysterious gravity field was towing
Galaxies. Scientists said they had proved a
mysterious gravitational field is forcing our
Galaxy to streak toward a distant point in the
southern sky at nearly 400 miles per second.

The existence of the "Great Attractor" was
first postulated in *1987* by astronomers. The
controversial announcement immediately
plunged the scientists into debate with many
of their colleagues who doubted the Great
Attractor really existed. But, they returned to
the fray during a meeting of the American
Astronomical Society armed with evidence
that supported their contention that a giant
region of dense mass is pulling other Galaxies
toward it over a vast region of space.

In their observations, the scientists conclude
that more than a hundred Galaxies are being
influenced by the huge gravitational field. And
other teams of scientists have developed in-
dependent evidence that the Great Attractor
is even greater than had been thought.

The center of the Great Attractor is about 150
million light years away, the scientists reported.
And therein lies a mystery.

Scientists have long theorized that the Universe
is smooth and reasonably homogeneous, and
they see no reason why it should have giant
"lumps" of concentrated matter. And there is,
at this point, no clear understanding of just
what the material is that gives the Great At-

tractor its enormous mass.

The discovery was incompatible with the smoothness of the Universe's background radiation. Now we have found a very large lump, and that has sent theorists back to their computers.
*(Los Angeles Times, **January 13, 1990**)*

6. In *1990,* a "for your information" column answered the question: **Which is the most powerful force in the Universe—gravity or magnetism?**

Gravity is feeble compared to magnetism. At equal distances, if we give gravitation interaction a value of 4, we'd have to give electro-magnetic interaction a value of incredibly, (10 to the 37th power)
10,000,000,000,000,000,000,000,000,000,000,000,000
(Just think—you can overcome the force of the entire Earth's gravity with the little magnet that you stick on your refrigerator!)
*(Parade, **May, 1990**)*

7. In *1991,* a New York newspaper reported that astronomers were puzzled by a gigantic object that was discovered in space.

Astronomers reported that they had discovered a dark, mysterious and almost inconceivably massive object lurking within a shell of luminous gas that is circulating around two colliding galaxies at speeds of almost 2 million miles an hour.

If the object is a black hole, it is 10 to 100
times as massive as any black hole previously
known or even believed to be possible.

The object's enormous mass puts it in a class
astronomers have never encountered before,
according to the astronomers who found it.

Another possibility, the discoverers say, is that
the object is a dormant quasar of the kind from
which galaxies are believed to have been born
more than 10 billion years ago, when the Universe was young

But the scientists acknowledge that these and
several other possible explanations of the
peculiar object are difficult to reconcile with
established astrophysical theories.

The group found the object while studying a
bright galaxy named NGC 6240, which lies
300 million light-years from Earth. They say
that NGC 6240 consists of two whirling disks
of matter, which may be galaxies in collision.

In one disk, the rotation patterns of gases is
characteristic of all common galaxies, but
in the other the gases are rotating in patterns
and at speeds that can be explained only by
assuming that they are orbiting an extremely
massive object.

They stated that the object must be 100 billion
times as massive as the Sun—about the same
mass as Earth's galaxy, the Milky Way—but
occupying a space no more than one ten-

thousandth as great.

The scientists said the object might be a super-massive black hole. But if it is, it would be 100 million to a billion times as massive as the largest black hole astronomers believe to exist.

A black hole absorbs all Light or other radia-tion reaching it, and emits none of its own by which a distant observer could see it.

The astronomers said they were not certain at this point whether they were seeing one Galaxy tearing another Galaxy apart or whether one Galaxy is being disrupted by this super-massive object at the center of the other Galaxy. *(The New York Times, **April 11, 1991**)*

8. In *1991,* a London report claims that astronomers have spotted the brightest object ever discovered in the Universe, but it appeared so faint when seen from the Earth, being so remote in space and time, that they almost missed it. They don't know what it is.

The astronomers from the United States and Britain reported to a scientific journal that they had called the mysterious blob IRAS Faint Source 10214 + 4724.

They found it by accident on the 40th and last night of a trawl through the heavens looking for something else through a telescope in the Canary Islands.

It emits "enormous" luminosity, radiating
30,000 times the energy of the Milky Way,
if calculations are right.

It may be a quasar cocooned in a dusty
galaxy.

Some quasars (stars like heavenly objects)
are Galaxies with black holes devouring
matter in the middle of them. But they said
this discovery could be a protogalaxy—a massive Galaxy in the process of formation.

They said the distance of the object was about
12 billion light years, so that Light from it began its journey long before the Sun or the
Earth existed.
(The Phoenix Gazette, **June 27, 1991***)*

9. Another report in **1991,** said that experts
were surprised by satellite reports that were
finding gamma ray bursts throughout the sky.

An astronomy satellite detected short, powerful bursts of gamma rays in virtually every
corner of the sky, suggesting the signals may
originate from sources near the edge of the
Universe, scientists said.

The instrument detected gamma ray bursts
that were randomly scattered throughout
the sky. The scattered sources came as a sur-
prise because it was believed that gamma ray
bursts detected by earlier instruments were
all coming from the center of the Milky Way
Galaxy and were thought to be relatively rare.

Instead, the bursts are occurring about once a day and are coming from every point in the sky.

Gamma ray bursts have been observed for 25 years, but the source of these bright flashes in the sky remains a mystery. ***Determining the sources and their positions in the sky is one of the Holy Grails of astrophysics.***

Gamma rays are an invisible, high energy form of radiation. The gamma ray signals are thought to be produced from such events and objects as solar flares, black holes, quasars and supernovae. Previously, the gamma ray bursts were thought to come from neutron stars and would be seen to come from the center of the Milky Way Galaxy.

Since the bursts are randomly distributed, the scientists said that the source must be either small, exotic objects very near the Solar System or from ***monstrously powerful distant objects***. The sources could be in very distant corners of the Universe.

If they are beyond our galaxy, then the energy released in the brief one-second flash of gamma rays is many times the total energy released when a star explodes as a supernova.

There is no optical counterpart to the bursts. This means that astronomers have not found stars that radiate in visible Light that would explain the sources of the bursts.
(Star Ledger, Newark, NJ, ***September 26, 1991)***

10. In *1995,* physicists reported finding the
top quark.

Two research teams working independently at
the same laboratory declared they finally
found the elusive top quark—the last remaining
undiscovered member of the set of fundamental particles that make up all matter.

Definitive evidence of the top quark has been
eagerly sought because it was necessary to
validate the so-called "Standard Models" of
particle physics—the consensus view of how
matter and force behave in their most elementary forms.

In that view, all matter is made up of only two
kinds of particles: leptons (lightweight entities
such as the electron) and quarks.

Quarks were unknown and unimagined as recently as the *1960s*, and their discovery ranks
as one of the paramount accomplishments of
20th century science. They are the smallest
indivisible units of heavy matter. Each proton
or neutron in an atom's nucleus is composed
of three quarks bound together.

There is no remaining doubt about the existence
of the top quark.

QUARK FACTS

Q: What is a quark?

A: A quark is a tiny particle believed to be one of the building blocks of matter. Five quarks already have been discovered, and since they're believed to come in pairs, scientists theorized that a sixth, known as the "top" quark, must exist.

Q: How small is it?

A: The top quark is smaller than a trillionth of the thickness of a human hair and exists for only a trillionth of a trillionth of a second. Quarks make up an atom's protons and neutrons—formerly thought to be the smallest particles of matter.

Q: Why is it so important to find the top quark?

A: The Standard Model Theory—the widely accepted scientific explanation of what makes up the Universe—is tied to the concept of these tiny building blocks. If the top quark didn't exist, the theory could collapse, forcing scientists to rethink three decades of work. *(Washington Post, **March 3, 1995**)*

11. Another report in *1995* confirmed that a new type of lightning had been discovered above the clouds.

Bolts that shoot upward from thunderheads, long doubted by scientists, turn out to be the most bizarre and interesting kind of lightning.

Scientists have been studying lightning ever since Benjamin Franklin demonstrated its electrical nature some two centuries ago and have generally felt that its nuances were understood.

The bolts were white hot, spitting temperatures of 50,000 degrees Fahrenheit and strengths of several hundred million volts.

But it turns out that science missed the most bizarre and interesting bolts of all, which materialize above thunderheads and shoot upward, not downward, flickering across great distances. Such wonders were hidden from view until recently, when ground observers, aircraft and spacecraft managed to glimpse their ephemeral dance.

Hundreds of flashes, some pink or blood red, others dark blue, have now been photographed above electrical storms, the red ones soaring as high as 60 miles above the Earth, their wispy tendrils playing along the fringes of outer space, their lower parts turning bluish or purple before disappearing.

The flashes appear to produce strange emanations that are just starting to be measured and are far from being understood. Orbiting satellites have detected gamma ray bursts of extraordinary intensity coming from thunderheads, and the red flashes have been linked to powerful bursts of radio waves.

(Raleigh, North Carolina News and Observer,
  January 17, 1995)

12. In September *1995*, a report said that scientists had observed something that defies everything they know about the laws of physics. One scientist said, "It was like coming across an ice cube near the equator on a deserted island."

The research team observed, through optical cosmic ray detectors in Utah's west desert, something that left them "absolutely stunned."

Out of nowhere, the most powerful cosmic ray ever detected slammed into the atmosphere, made a brief flash and then rained down onto the Earth in a cascade of billions of microscopic particles. The energy of this ray was millions of electron volts higher than most accepted theories allowed. The scientists could not explain it, and they had no idea what caused it.

A similar ray was observed over Japan. The scientists said these are documented events, but there is no object that one can imagine anywhere in the Universe that has the capability of making such an acceleration.

The story goes back to the early part of the century. Cosmic rays—actually tiny particles such as protons or electrons that travel through space near the speed of light—were first discovered by pioneer researcher Victor Hess who detected them in high-altitude balloon trips in *1912*. Since that time, cosmic rays have led to the discovery of phenomena such as anti-matter and helped launch the first studies of particle physics. They are also constantly bombarding the Earth and are imperceptibly passing through us all every moment.

Lower energy rays are thought to be produced by the Sun or sometimes giant exploding Stars called supernovae. But no one knows what could have produced the powerful rays like those discovered over Utah and Japan.

Ever since cosmic background radiation was discovered in the early *1960s*, cosmic rays were thought to have an energy ceiling. Most cosmic rays encounter resistance from this magnetic force much as a runner feels wind resistance. This resistance causes cosmic rays to careen wildly across the galaxy, losing energy along the way. But the rays that hit above the Utah desert and Japan flew straight in, seemingly unimpeded by the massive uni-versal force.

(The Christian Science Monitor,
  September 26, 1995)

CHAPTER
SEVEN

REBIRTH
OF THE DIVINE MASCULINE PRINCIPLE

A Time for Healing and a Time for Forgiveness

As we progressed through our Earthly sojourn, alternating between masculine and feminine bodies in various lifetimes, we allowed our human egos to manipulate us into destructive situations, especially when we were in male bodies. When we are in a masculine body, our human ego is able to more effectively connect with the unbridled abuse of power through our Masculine Polarity. Then, it manipulates us into acting out aggressive behavior. *Ninety-eight percent* of all violent crimes are committed by men. *This means souls in masculine bodies.* As men, we participate in war; crime; governmental and political corruption; abuse of women; abuse of children; violent outer displays of prejudice and discrimination; terrorist acts; corruption at the corporate business level; abuse of the environment for the sake of greed, selfishness and power; abuse of authority; the suppression of women; dominance of women in the world religions and every other Global malady that reflects the abuse of power *ninety-eight percent more than women do.*

Now, that certainly does not mean that ALL men are participating in those destructive behavior patterns. It simply means that when we are acting out those negative patterns, we are usually in a male body.

When we are in a female body, we also abuse our power but in the opposite extreme. As women, our human egos manipulate us into rejecting our power. As a result of this malady, we *allow* ourselves to be victimized, abused, battered, suppressed, oppressed and negated. We play the role of second class citizens; we become weak, pitiful and pathetic, and we permit men to dominate us.

Once again, *this does not mean that ALL women are in*

this position, but when women do abuse their power, that is usually how it manifests.

We are in the process of transmuting all of the residue from the "fall," so that the Earth and all Her life can Ascend into the Octaves of Heaven on Earth. Needless to say, healing and forgiving all of the aspects of our abuse of power is crucial in the overall scheme of things. That is why major events reflecting the masculine abuse of power are surfacing at an accelerated pace. These things are appearing on the screen of life to draw our attention to them, so that we will invoke the Light of our Father-Mother God and transmute the cause, core, effect, record and memory of these atrocities back into Divine Harmony and Balance. They are *not* being drawn to our attention so that we will just wring our hands in despair and descend into a quagmire of hopelessness.

Throughout *1995* we witnessed very dramatic examples of how the masculine abuse of power is surfacing to be purged and transmuted. The most obvious example was the O.J. Simpson trial. For the entire year, America and the World were inundated with courtroom antics that could be attributed to no less than what I call "testosterone poisoning." Never has a trial of this nature transfixed the attention of Humanity so completely.

As I mentioned previously in this book (page 226), the Company of Heaven, in unison with awakened Lightworkers throughout the World devised a plan that would take full advantage of the collective focus of Humanity's consciousness on the tragic slayings of Nicole Brown Simpson and Ron Goldman. This focus of attention was utilized to assist in the process of healing the masculine abuse of power, the masculine abuse of women and the abuse of any aspect of the feminine nature of Humanity.

Throughout the entire ordeal, as the consciousness of Humanity was transfixed at various levels on this case, a Chalice of Healing was formed. This was a cup of collective consciousness through which the Light of God poured to transmute the atrocities men have perpetrated against women since the "fall." Once our attention is focused on something that has likewise drawn the attention of the masses of Humanity, our God Selves are able to utilize the focus of our attention for the *highest good*, even if we don't understand everything that is happening. All we have to do is *sincerely want Truth and Justice*, and our God Selves will do the rest, regardless of the deception and antics going on in the courtroom.

To accelerate this healing process, the Spiritual Hierarchy asked Lightworkers to gather in Monterrey, Mexico. At that gathering, which took place *September 30, 1995*, to *October 5, 1995*, perfection patterns for a newly-healed Humanity were encoded into our genetic patterns at an atomic cellular level.

The perfection patterns were imprinted with the Divinity of our God Selves and reflect...

Dignity, Humility, Patience, Reverence
and Courtesy...
the Qualities of the Arisen Christ
coming into daily life...
the New Humanity Ascended into Solar Being.

In order for that to be brought to fruition, the final healing and forgiveness of our fallen masculine nature had to be expressed by all Humanity.

On *October 2, 1995*, the jury in the O.J. Simpson trial reached a verdict, but Judge Ito decided not to announce it until Tuesday, *October 3, 1995,* at 1:00 p.m. EDT. This gave the entire World the opportunity to focus their attention on the event at the same time. Through the Unified Cup of Humanity's consciousness, an intensified activity of Divine Forgiveness and Healing poured into the Earth. The Divine Light of Healing through the Power of Limitless Transmutation and Forgiveness flooded this blessed Earth and bathed the masculine nature of all Humanity as it transmuted the maximum negativity associated with female abuse that Cosmic Law would allow. Through the unified Cup of Humanity's consciousness, all life on this Planet was lifted into a new level of Divine Harmony and Balance.

This event created a powerful forcefield through which much of the mass consciousness of the masculine abuse of the feminine was healed. This healing occurred in total perfection in the Realms of Cause and is now filtering into the world of effects as the process continues daily and hourly.

I know that the verdict conflicts with what we might perceive to be Divine Justice. But, it's difficult sometimes to see the greater plan.

In the eyes of most Americans and, in fact, most of the World, O.J. Simpson's acquittal was a gross miscarriage of justice and made a mockery of our entire judicial system. The resulting public outrage and indignation, however, actually shocked us out of our complacency. Even though his acquittal inspired a jaundiced, cynical flair in the media, it motivated legions of people into action in a way that his conviction never would have. Public involvement will now dramatically accelerate the healing of the human maladies of:

Domestic Violence
Abuse of Women
Racial Injustice
Police Corruption
Flaws in the Judicial System
Flaws in the Media
Abuse of Power
and much, much more.

O.J.Simpson will continally experience the ramifications of his actions, and his lifestyle will never be the same again.

Our greatest service to all life is for us to invoke the Violet Flame of Forgiveness and Transmutation into every facet of our abuse of power and heal the collective abuse of women, children and men everywhere. (Related information on page 388)

In addition to the remarkable healing that took place regarding our masculine abuse of the feminine, other facets of our masculine abuse of power were healed during the gathering in Monterrey, as well.

Taking place simultaneously in Geneva, Switzerland, was a Global Summit sponsored by the United Nations called *Telecom '95*. This event drew together an estimated 300,000 individuals and businesses from around the World to create a cooperative Global network of international communication.

Again, Humanity's attention being focused on this event created a cup through which the Divine Blueprint was activated for all facets of business throughout the World. This Divine Blueprint, which is pulsating with the God Qualities of *Cooperation, Reverence for all Life, Abundance, Integrity, Honesty, Trust and Mutual Respect* is now filtering into the consciousness of all Humanity. Anything that conflicts with this Divine Blueprint is being pushed to the surface for transmutation.

As we witness the negative energies surfacing, we must continually invoke the Violet Flame into the cause, core, effect, record and memory of every situation.

After that gathering, a building momentum of the Violet Transmuting Flame of Forgiveness and Healing blazed through *ALL* aspects of our masculine abuse of power. This created a purging of the negative effects of:

> Crime
> War
> Gangs
> Drug Dealers
> Corruption in Business

Corruption in Government
Corruption in the Justice System
Corruption in Religions
Corruption in Education
Corruption in Medicine
Corruption in the Media
Domestic Violence
Abuse of Women and Children
Terrorism
Racial Injustice
Abuse of Human Rights
Abuse of Animal Rights
Abuse of the Environment

and every other form of our masculine abuse of power.

This unprecedented cleansing was amplified on the *Full Moon Lunar Eclipse* that took place on *October 8, 1995*. With that amplification, every facet of our masculine abuse of power back to the "fall" was bathed with the Violet Flame of Limitless Transmutation.

On *October 16, 1995,* we witnessed the *Million Man March* in Washington, D.C. This was another event that reflected the awakening that is taking place as the masculine abuse of power is being healed and transmuted through the power of Divine Forgiveness. Once again, this event SYM-BOLICALLY represents the masculine side of Humanity acknowledging our abuse of power as we return to the source of power (symbolically represented as Washington, D.C.). In Washington, D.C., the men took a pledge to recommit their life energies to honoring and revering the women and children in their lives, and they promised the right use of power.

In spite of the negative press and bigoted verbiage of some of the organizers, what was most important was the Divine Intent in the hearts of that gathering of men. Many of the men who were interviewed clearly indicated that they were there to accept responsibility for their lives and to change the course of direction for men everywhere by committing to a new constructive way of life through their own self-empowerment. They were not there to "follow" anyone.

They openly promised to honor and revere their wives and children. They pledged to eliminate drugs, gangs and crime from their communities. They pledged to never use a knife or gun to harm another Human Being. And as one collective masculine force, they consecrated their lives to *prosperity, integrity, honesty, healing, forgiveness and to improving the quality of life for their families and fellow Human Beings.*

Another activity involving the shifting of consciousness in men is called *The Promise Keepers*. Some of their message gets a little bogged down in religious dogma, but the Divine Intent of this group is marvelous. Again, it is designed to create a positive vehicle through which men can rededicate their lives to fulfilling their highest potential by honoring women and children.

They renew their heart commitment to themselves and Humanity; they promise to fulfill their vows of marriage. They promise to interact in all of their relationships with integrity, harmony, gentleness and peace, and they promise to live the path of love that Jesus taught us to follow.

The success of these activities enhanced our forward progress, and the Light of our Father-Mother God built in momentum preparing all Humanity, and specifically the masculine polarity of Humanity, for the next wave of healing. That healing Light poured into the Planet through the unique *New Moon Solar Eclipse* that took place on *October 23, 1995.*

The Masculine Polarity of God enters the Earth in the area of the Himalaya Mountains near Tibet. On *October 23, 1995*, a *New Moon Solar Eclipse* passed directly over the anchorage point of the Masculine Polarity of God.   It embraced Tibet, northern India, Nepal, Iran and southern China. As this Celestial Event bathed the Earth in that area of the World...*Our Father-Mother God lifted the lower masculine nature in every man, woman and child into the Immaculate Concept of the Divine Masculine Principle.*

This means that our lower masculine nature has been reborn into its original Divine Intent.

On that sacred day, the United Nations celebrated its *50th* anniversary.   Leaders, representing their countries from around the World, gathered in New York City.   Once again, through the focus of our attention, our Father-Mother God blazed the Divine Blueprint for the New Heaven and the New Earth into the genetic codes and the Divine Mind of each world leader.   These patterns will now begin to filter into their conscious minds, accelerating immeasurably our Global transformation.

Through this Divine Intervention, our Divine Masculine Nature and our Divine Feminine Nature are expressing the balance and Oneness they were always supposed to reflect.

Now, for the very first time in the history of our Planet, Humanity's collective White Fire Being, which reflects the Divine Balance of both our Masculine and Feminine "I Am" Presences, has accepted the office of Planetary Logos, thus lifting this Earth into the initial impulse of Her new Solar Reality.

CHAPTER EIGHT

THE END OF ARMAGEDDON

Moving into the initial impulse of our new Solar Reality was the final phase of the Divine Plan that was needed in order to complete our *"need to suffer"* on Earth. As I shared with you on pages 2-11, now IS OUR TIME TO SOAR! As of the *Winter Solstice, December 21, 1995*, the part of the Divine Plan that required the Lightworkers to delve into the depths of human suffering was God Victoriously brought to fruition.

On *January 11, 1996*, with the first phase of our Divine Plans sealed in God's Victory, Uranus, the Planet of Divine Consciousness and Limitless Transmutation, moved into the forcefield of Aquarius, OFFICIALLY HERALDING THE NEW AGE OF SPIRITUAL FREEDOM AND ENLIGHTENMENT FOR THE SOLAR SYSTEM OF ALPHA AND OMEGA...THE AGE OF AQUARIUS!!!

With that Victory, the entire Company of Heaven dedicated Their life energies to assist Humanity in releasing and transmuting deeper levels of our baggage from the past. A special dispensation was granted by our Father-Mother God to allow the Spiritual Hierarchy to accelerate our transmuting process. This Divine Intervention allowed us to assimilate the frequencies of the initial impulse of our new Solar Reality in unprecedented ways.

Throughout *1996*, daily and hourly we received incredible assistance from On High to transmute the negativity from our past and love it FREE. *1996* was a 7 year (1+9+9+6=25 and 2+5=7). This aligns with the Seventh Solar Aspect of Deity, which projects into the physical plane of Earth the totality of the God qualities of Forgiveness, Mercy, Compassion, Limitless Transmutation, Freedom, Liberation, Divine Justice and Victory.

As Lightworkers invoked the Violet Flame of Limitless Transmutation into every facet of life on Earth, then focused the full power of their attention on the vision of the New Heaven and the New Earth, the floodgates of Heaven opened to assist us. The Company of Heaven said we would be astonished at the results of our humble efforts if we would just "keep on keeping on" throughout *1996*.

The opportunity was individual and collective. Remember, *"As 'I Am' lifted up, all life is lifted up with me." 1996* gave us an incredible opportunity to not only transmute our own remaining baggage, but to assist all Humanity to do the same.

That awesome year brought us opportunities and challenges that made each of us search our souls and redefine our belief systems. Sometimes we were shaken out of our comfort zones against our wills. Sometimes we were forced to listen to our inner knowing in spite of outer world phenomena and potential backlash. Sometimes we were asked to take a leap of faith in the face of tremendous resistance from our fear-based human egos, and sometimes we just held our breath and took a giant step forward into new uncharted waters. But, never have our humble efforts reaped more rewarding results. When *1996* was brought to fruition, we breathed a deep sigh of relief, and from the very core of our Beings said "Thank you, God!!!"

One day we will be able to step back and see the incredibly complex and synergistic symphony that has woven every facet of the marvelous Divine Plan for Earth's rebirth into one beautiful, God Victorious Accomplishment. When that day comes, we are going to be astounded at just how precise the timing was for this Cosmic Moment of Victory on Earth. We are going to clearly perceive that every single phase of the Divine Plan was calculated to the most minute detail, thus taking full advantage of ALL of the Spiritual currents of energy flowing forth from both Heaven and Earth.

On *January 11, 1996*, as Uranus moved into the forcefield of Aquarius, heralding the beginning of the New Age of Spiritual Freedom—the Age of Aquarius—we moved into new octaves of multidimensional, expanded consciousness.

In mid-January, the astronomical community was stunned by the discovery of other Planets in other Solar Systems. Our vision of the Universe suddenly expanded from our concept of ten billion Galaxies to probably fifty billion or more. This humbling experience quickly brought us to the realization of how very little we actually "know" or understand about our Universe. While we were still reeling from this awakening, a visitor came to bless our corner of the Heavens.

As the Sun entered 11 degrees of Aquarius, on *January 31, 1996*, an amateur astronomer from Japan named Yuji Hyakutake discovered a previously unknown comet. Astronomers believe now that Comet Hyakutake probably visited the Earth and the Sun 10,000 to 20,000 years ago. This was the brightest comet to pass the Earth since 1556, and it passed within nine million miles of our Planet. It had a solid nucleus about five miles in diameter and a huge vaporous tail that could be seen with the naked eye.

Comets herald change and have been considered the "Messengers of God," portending coming events on Earth. They represent new opportunities and potential Spiritual Awakening. Their "sudden," unexpected appearance indicates swift changes and new, rapidly occurring developments that have the ability to change the course of history. These changes can dramatically affect our personal lives as well as initiate profound Global transformation.

In ancient times, comets were considered to be foreboding omens from God, fortelling times of crisis and tribulation. That was due to the fact that in order for the Spiritual effects of the comet to manifest on Earth, the negativity had to be pushed to the surface to be cleared. This caused extreme imbalances. Humanity was so focused on the pain that we missed the glorious blessings that were being given to Earth by these Celestial events.

Fortunately, things have changed, and our ability to integrate Light has been totally transformed. Now we are able to experience the gifts and blessings that the Heavenly Bodies are projecting onto Earth without being overwhelmed by the healing process involved.

As Comet Hyakutake began blessing the Earth with its radiance, another Celestial event occurred. On *February 14, 1996*, when the Sun was in Aquarius, which is the sign of the Universal Love we need to embrace in order for the World to continue to exist, the Comet Chiron reached its perihelion.

Chiron has been called both a minor Planet and a comet. It was discovered on *November 1, 1977*. It is a small body that orbits the Sun *between* the orbits of Saturn and Uranus. It is perceived to open new doorways to Higher Consciousness, and it forms a bridge in consciousness between our human egos—physical consciousness (represented through Saturn) and our God Selves—Spiritual Consciousness (represented through Uranus).

Chiron takes about 49-51 years to complete one orbit, and in *1996*, it reached both its perihelion, its closest approach to the Sun, on *February 14, 1996*, and its perigee (or also called its "perihelion opposition"), its closest approach to the Earth, on *April 1, 1996*. A perihelion is when a Heavenly Body receives the most Light from the Sun and is the most "lit up." Chiron reached perihelion at 14 degrees Libra, the symbol of Liberty/ Liberation.

This comet has many Divine Momentums that flow through it to bless the Universe. It has been thought of as the archetypal fallen and risen child of Heaven and Earth as it bridges the divide between physical embodiment (Saturn) and limitless Divinity (Uranus). It is not by chance that Chiron's return coincided with the wondrous momentous changes that took place in *1996*.

As Chiron passed the Sun on *February 14, 1996*, our Father-Mother God amplified the unmanifest potential within that Celestial Body and greatly enhanced Chiron's ability to bless the Earth during Her moment of Liberation. As the Light of Chiron pulsated through the Universe, it penetrated deep into the physical, etheric, mental and emotional aspects of all life evolving on Earth, both in and out of embodiment. It affected every facet of life and actually paved the way for greater integration of our Solar Christ Presences through our four lower bodies. This profoundly changed the course of Human destiny.

On this incredibly powerful day, as we received the blessings from Chiron's perihelion and Humanity focused on love through the celebration of Valentine's Day, Archangel Michael called us to our greatest mission ever. He asked for our assistance in ridding the Universe of the force of "cosmic evil" for all Eternity.

During that Cosmic Moment, our Solar Christ Presences were empowered with the Light from Chiron and the influx of Divine Love effectively enough to rise to the occasion. They joyfully and humbly accepted this Divine Call to Service.

Never had our Light been more powerful, and never had our assistance been more profoundly needed in order to assist this Earth and all Her life through the final stages of Her birthing process.

Archangel Michael sent forth His Clarion Call invoking the assistance of every awakening Lightworker on Earth. *We were being called to the greatest Mission we had ever known.*

At that very *unique* time we were asked by the Spiritual Hierarchy in the Realms of Illumined Truth and Perfection if we would be willing to assist Them and move into a *Higher Order of Service*. This was for a very important and specific service that needed to be performed in order to FREE many of the Lightworkers from a deception that was designed to block them from fulfilling their Divine Missions on Earth.

Archangel Michael and His Legions of Power and Protection had been working ceaselessly to free us from the discord of human miscreation for aeons of time. Now, for that unique situation, They invoked our assistance. We were, at long last, vibrating at a frequency far above the forces of imbalance, and we had been trained at inner levels to help with that Divine Plan. Archangel Michael assured us that the information was being brought to the attention of whomever had been prepared to assist in that activity of Light.

As Archangel Michael revealed the plan to us, He asked us to remember that we are ONE WITH GOD AND THE ENTIRE COMPANY OF HEAVEN *observing* a situation that was vibrating at a frequency far below us. Consequently, it was unable to adversely affect us in any way, shape or form as we projected Divine Light into it from the Heart and Mind of God to transmute it back into the Light.

We were each being called to a Higher Order of Service, and it was critical *that we know that we know that we know* OUR VICTORY WAS ASSURED before we even began.

Archangel Michael said that as we prepared for our Solar Passage into the Eternal Realms of Light, there was one final attempt being made by the force of "cosmic evil" to block our Ascension up the Spiral of Evolution into the Fourth/Fifth Dimension. As usual, this negative energy had absolutely *no power over the Light*. Because of the incredible progress we had made since Harmonic Convergence and all of the wonderful healing activities that had taken place within all Humanity since that time, normally He would not even mention that negative force. But, a very unusual phenomenon was taking place on Earth, and even very discerning Lightworkers were reading the material of various entities and being mesmerized into thinking it was Truth. When asked specifically about the statements in the various books that are blatant and obviously the deception of the dark forces, the Lightworkers said, "I never saw that in the books." When the statements were shown to them, they were horrified that they could have missed such unmistakable trickery.

That confirmed that there was a new level of cunningness in this last-ditch effort, but *it was doomed to failure*. It was being exposed at that time because the Universal Law of that Cosmic Moment was *"all that is hidden must now be revealed."*

I will not empower the various entities associated with "cosmic evil" by naming them, but those of you who have read the material will know exactly who I am talking about. Those of you who have not come in contact with the information will now have additional knowledge to enhance your powers of discernment, if necessary, in the future.

"Cosmic evil" is the residue of fallen civilizations in Systems of Worlds that existed long before the creation of our Solar System. Since it has absolutely no power over the Light, *it could not reach Humanity unless we took very specific steps to lower our frequency to a level it could access.*

As I mentioned previously in this book, when we were at our lowest ebb, the force of "cosmic evil" seized the Earth and created a "magnetic grid" that held us trapped on the Wheel of Karma. This "magnetic grid" was actually in opposition to the Light of God, and for millions of years had very effectively blocked our Ascension process. This sinister force was only able to take Earth hostage after we "fell" into the depths of human miscreation, and the Life Force of God was withdrawn from the Crystal Grid System. At that time, we were considered "the dark star" in our Solar System, and we were extremely vulnerable.

The force of "cosmic evil" has been able to manipulate our fear-based human egos into doing its will for aeons of time. Consequently, the World religions professed that *"Satan rules the Earth."* To a great degree, that was actually true, due to our serious plight.

With the Crystal Grid activation that took place during Harmonic Convergence in *1987,* we shattered the "magnetic grid" of "cosmic evil" and began moving into a frequency of

Light beyond its reach. This destructive force knew that it was losing its control of Earth and implemented a plan to regain control.

It began communicating through various people in embodiment. These channels, through various modalities, enticed Lightworkers to invoke "implants." "Implants" are tools of manipulation and are *always designed to sever a person's connection with his/her God Presence, so the entity can use the person's body to fulfill its devious plan on Earth*. In this case, the plan was to rebuild its "magnetic grid."

Remember, in order for something to manifest on Earth, the energy for that particular manifestation must be drawn through the Divinity in the Heart Flame of someone abiding on Earth. Even God "needs a body."

Since we have Ascended into higher frequencies of Light, the forces of imbalance cannot easily take our bodies away from us anymore. Possession is extremely rare. So, now these entities of deception are tricking us into invoking "implants," which are tools to get us to *voluntarily* give up our bodies. *All implants* are tools of the forces of darkness, and *all implants*, regardless of what the entities claim, are designed to get us to give up our bodies. This is CLASSIC POSSESSION.

On *February 14, 1996*, Archangel Michael, Mother Mary and Archangel Gabriel implemented a plan to foil "cosmic evil's" attempt to regain control of the Earth. This plan would free the Universe of this negative force forever.

This activity of Light would fulfill the final phase of Armageddon and clear the way for Heaven to manifest on Earth.

The Divine Plan

Throughout Beloved Jesus' lifetime, Mother Mary held on tenaciously to the Immaculate Concept of His Divine

Plan. Even in the gravest moments of His worst temptations, She persevered. Even during the most excruciating hours of witnessing Her precious Son being reviled and crucified, She relentlessly clung to the vision of His God Victorious Resurrection.

As She walked down from the Hill of Golgotha after the "death" of Her Son, She said, "What I have done for You, my Beloved Son, I now do for all Humanity." In that Holy Breath, Her Divine Service was expanded to include every man, woman and child evolving on Earth—past, present and future.

Since that Cosmic Moment, Beloved Mother Mary has held the Immaculate Concept for each of our Divine Plans securely anchored in the Divinity of Her Heart. Even in our darkest hours, She perpetually held the Divine Vision before us that super-consciously prompted us to persist through our "dark night of the soul." She was not going to fail us now!!!

We had completed the phase of the Divine Plan that required us to walk through the pain of human suffering on Earth. Now, our ONLY JOB was to joyfully lift into the blissful Octaves of Heaven on Earth.

The sinister plan of "cosmic evil" to recreate the "magnetic grid" system and *reverse the polarity* of our Ascension in the Light was the *only* thing that was threatening to interfere with our glorious Ascension.

To understand the seriousness of the situation, let me explain that high on the Spiral of Evolution, in the frequencies of perfection that we are Ascending into, pulsates the Light Body of Mother Earth. There She has donned Her Seamless Garment of Light, and She is resplendent and scintillating. The Crystal Grid System in Her Light Body is activated, and it is aligned with the Crystal Grid System in the physical plane. The Crystal Grid System in the **Light Body** of Mother Earth is magnetizing the Crystal Grid System in the **physical body** of Mother Earth into the Realms of Perfection.

This is how we are Ascending physically and tangibly into

the frequencies of Heaven on Earth. ***Obviously, if the forces of imbalance could reverse this Ascension process by building a powerful enough "magnetic grid" system in opposition to the Light, our Ascension would cease.***

Due to the number of Lightworkers who were tricked into this devious plan, the Company of Heaven initiated a plan of Divine Intervention to reverse the adverse effects of this scheme. THIS IS WHERE OUR ASSISTANCE WAS NEEDED.

In order for the Spiritual Hierarchy to infuse the Crystal Grid System with the necessary Light to PERMANENTLY shatter the newly recreated "magnetic grid" AND **FOREVER** FREE THE EARTH FROM THE GRIP OF COSMIC EVIL, They needed Lightworkers in physical embodiment who would offer the Chalice of their consciousness as a HOLY GRAIL, through which the Divine Light from the Heart of our Father-Mother God could pour into the physical plane of Earth. This Light would open the flow into the Crystal Grid System and accelerate It into the frequencies of Limitless Physical Perfection.

Anyone who was willing to participate in that Divine Activity of Light was held in the eternal embrace of GRATITUDE by the Infinity Consciousness of our Father-Mother God.

It was *necessary* for Humanity to go through a process of preparation in order for the atomic, cellular substance of our bodies to be lifted into a frequency that would withstand the intensity of Light that was needed for the Victorious Accomplishment of this Divine Plan.

In cooperation with our Mighty "I Am" Presences, Beloved Mother Mary placed within the Twelve-fold Solar Flame blazing in every human heart a forcefield of Light. It was a Crystalline Lotus Blossom that had pulsating within Its stamen a glorious expression of the Flame of the Immaculate Concept. This Sacred Flame is Madonna Blue with the Crystalline White Radiance of the Ascension Flame.

Through that forcefield of Light, our Divine Plans were activated and pushed to the surface of our conscious minds with the Divine Intent of awakening us from the mesmerization of the forces of imbalance and preventing ANYONE from succumbing to the negative effects of the "implants."

Archangel Gabriel stationed a member of His Royal Court in each of our auras for the explicit purpose of enveloping every man, woman and child in an invincible forcefield of the Mother of Pearl Resurrection Flame. This Sacred Flame blazed through every electron of our four lower bodies and Resurrected us into the Light, daily and hourly.

The Cosmic Being LuElla from the Great Central Sun took Her strategic position above the portal of Healing through the Power of Limitless Transmutation in Tucson, Arizona, and She invoked Her Royal Court to take Their strategic positions within the core of purity in every chakra center, power point and sacred site along the Crystal Grid Meridians on Earth. These Divine Beings were given permission by our Great Central Sun to reverse the polarity of the "magnetic grid" system of the forces of imbalance temporarily until we could successfully perform that activity of Light for ourselves.

Finally, Legions of Light from the highest frequency of perfection the Earth could withstand, Who were specifically associated with the new Order of Healing through the Power of Limitless Transmutation, were given permission to descend into the atmosphere of Earth to assist LuElla and the Legions of Light associated with the Seventh Solar Aspect of God's Limitless Transmutation.

We were told that Activity of Light would build in power and momentum monthly until the Tenth Celebration of Harmonic Convergence, *August 17th, 1996*.

The Beings of Light asked us to organize the first annual World Congress On Illumination during Harmonic Convergence in *August 1987*. We were asked to hold the Congess at Diamond Head in Hawaii to create the Chalice for the anchoring of the Divine Light that would flow through the Crown Chakra of Mother Earth and create the initial impulse of the Activation of the Crystal Grid System.

In *1996,* we were directed, once again, to hold the World Congress On Illumination in Tucson, Arizona, within the permanent seed atom of the portal for the sacred Flame of Healing through the Power of Limitless Transmutation.

The first major Crystal Grid Activation took place during the *FIRST* Harmonic Convergence, *August 17, 1987.* It was not by chance that the *second major Activation of the Crystal Grid System* was to take place during the *TENTH* Celebration of Harmonic Convergence. Both resonate with a ONE vibration, which means rebirth, new beginnings, new cycles, initiative, leadership and oneness.

The Spiritual Hierarchy told us that the Divine Light that would initiate the SECOND ACTIVATION of the Earth's Crystal Grid System would be projected through the portal in Tucson, Arizona.

The Divine Plan was for the second activation to take place on *August 17, 1996.* At that time LuElla and Her Regal Court would expand the Light of God into the Crystal Grid System and increase the vibration of the Planet the maximum that we could safely tolerate. That Divine Activity of Light was to build in momentum, moment-to-moment until *August 22, 1996*, at which time the purification would be accomplished, and the Legions of Light would implement the *third activation* of the Crystal Grid System.

This third activation would restore the Crystal Grid System to its **original Divine intensity**. The Divine Plan was for this final activation to shatter, **for all Eternity**, the "magnetic grid" system and the "implants" of the forces of imbalance, thus freeing this Earth and all Her life **forever**.

Once this occurred, Beloved Archangel Michael and His Legions of Power and Protection would then envelop the force of "cosmic evil" in a RING-PASS-NOT OF GOD'S

FIRST CAUSE OF PERFECTION and command this dark force into Light where our Father-Mother God would love it eternally FREE.

This literally meant that the forces of darkness would be transformed by the Love of God and would NEVER AGAIN be able to cause pain or suffering to any part of life in the Universe.

Then, our Beloved Mother Earth would be free to Ascend to Her rightful place on the Spiral of Evolution and reclaim Her Divine birthright as Freedom's Holy Star!!!

As awesome as this Divine Plan seemed, Archangel Michael assured us that we had been preparing for thousands of years to accomplish this mission.

As we assimilated the influx of Light on *Februry 14, 1996*, and contemplated our part in the Divine Mission of Archangel Michael, Mother Mary and Archangel Gabriel, the Comet Hyakutake approached Earth.

During the *Spring/Vernal Equinox, March 21, 1996*, a sense of wonder filled the hearts of Lightworkers around the Globe. We felt a tremendous sense of expectation and experienced the inner knowing that something grandiose was about to happen. Lightworkers traveled to sacred sites all over the Planet, and in Ceremonies of Light, breathed the Divine Light from the Core of Creation into the Crystal Grid System to soothe and heal the battered Body of Mother Earth, preparing Her at an atomic cellular level to *receive* the Love of God.

Indigenous people around the World, the descendents of the ancient stewards of the Earth, have expected the return of the Comet Hyakutake for millenia. The Maya called this comet YAHK'YTAH, which means *"The Presence of the Love of God on Earth."*

The Hope prophesies say that when the huge comet comes, *"the Star people will return to Earth."*

The ancient Earth stewards know that *the cycles of darkness are over.* They are aware that Humanity can now move in consciousness into New Dimensions of Light and walk the boundaries between Worlds as we reach new levels of understanding and Cosmic Truth. Ancient Cosmic Wisdom is flooding the consciousness of all who care to perceive it.

During the *Vernal Equinox of 1996*, we reached a Global Renaissance of Spiritual Awakening. It was a uniquely pivotal transition of Global Rebirth. It was historically significant, and we will never be the same again. During that decisive moment, we each reached a critically defining point in our lives in which we were given a choice. We were given the opportunity to reconnect with the very Heart of our Father-Mother God and renew our own inner Spiritual connection with our Solar Christ Presences. This gave us an extraordinary opportunity to experience, at inner levels, what liberty and freedom from oppression really are, and it opened the door to limitless options.

With our positive, conscious choice to fully integrate with our Solar Christ Presences, we began a brand new cycle of tangible Divine Experience. The planetary seeds of a New Heaven and a New Earth were planted. This Spiritual seeding began to stir the Eternal Core of Creativity, and the unmanifest potential that has lain dormant within the infinite womb of Cosmic Potentiality breathed in the Holy Breath of God and reclaimed its Divine Right to burst upon the Screen of Life. This paved the way for the *final impulse of the Second Coming of the Christ through Humanity*.

On *March 24, 1996*, Archangel Gabriel's Feast Day, and on *March 25, 1996*, the day celebrated in the outer World as the day Archangel Gabriel announced to Mother Mary the coming birth of the Christ—the "Feast of the Annunciation," the Comet Hyakutake began its closest passage by the Earth. As the comet expanded the Presence of the Love of God on Earth, it magnetized into its Etheric Field any remaining discordant thought and feeling patterns that Humanity had released throughout the Ages that conflicted with Divine

Love. This allowed a healing to take place and a psychic cleansing throughout the astral plane. This created a new matrix to allow a paradigm shift into a new Divine Global structure that will transform the Earth politically, socially, economically, Spiritually, nationally, culturally and racially into the New Heaven and the New Earth as ordained by the Presence of Christ on Earth, **now made manifest through the Solar Christ Presences of all Humanity**.

After completing its Divine Healing mission, on *March 26, 1996*, Comet Hyakutake began its journey to the Sun.

After being blessed with the Presence of the Love of God, we were ready for the next phase of the Divine Plan. This part of the plan involved preparing Humanity, through all levels of consciousness, to transform our physical experiences and Karmic realities as represented through Saturn. On *April 1, 1996*, as Comet Hyakutake took the dross of Humanity away from the Earth, Comet Chiron reached its closest proximity to the Earth, its "perihelion opposition." Chiron brought with it, from the Heart of the Sun, the Divine Light of our Father-Mother God that would assist Humanity to release the resistance of our lower human egos and empower our Solar Christ Presences to take full dominion of our four lower bodies.

On *April 3, 1996*, we experienced a total *Full Moon Lunar Eclipse*. This was an opportunity we were given to change our perception of reality on Earth. Even though the mass consciousness of Humanity may not have consciously taken advantage of that Cosmic Moment and created a vision of Heaven on Earth for their personal lives, the Solar Christ Presence of every single person did. That aspect of our own Divinity literally pierced into the Heart and Mind of God and absorbed the Divine Wisdom recorded there that reflects the original Divine Intent of our Earthly sojourn. This information contains within its frequencies the Immaculate Concept of our individual Divine Plans and our purpose and reason for Being. This is knowledge that was suppressed and buried in darkness when we fell into the quagmire of human miscreation—knowledge that reflects the joy of the original plan on Earth, which was free of Karmic liabilities.

This activity also activated the Hall of Records on Earth and began preparing the Record Keeper Crystals that were destined to release their Sacred Knowledge of the original Divine Plan for Earth into the Crystal Grid System in the not-too-distant future.

That *Full Moon Lunar Eclipse* was on Wednesday and began the traditional acknowledgment of Passover. Passover and the Seder were Thursday, *April 4, 1996*. Thursday was also the day Passover was celebrated when Jesus had the "last supper." In *1996*, the holy days leading up to Easter were the same days that the actual pageantry of Jesus took place. This gave added impetus to the Divine Momentum of the Resurrection of the Christ that had been building for 2000 years.

On *April 7, 1996*, *Resurrection morning*, as the first rays of the Sun began to bathe the Earth, Saturn moved into the forcefield of Aries. Since the "fall" of Humanity, Saturn has been a Planet of extreme duality. It was originally supposed to bring opportunities to us that accelerated our self-mastery and our learning experiences in a Third Dimensional reality. These were to be experiences that would lead to Godhood and complete our lessons of co-creation. When we fell into the depths of human degradation, Saturn became the bringer of Karmic liabilities. As a result of this glitch in the Divine Plan, Saturn has been associated with pain and suffering—even war and destruction. It is a Planet that has been feared and dreaded.

This time it was different because our reality on Earth was in the process of transformation. This time, as Saturn entered Aries in the full momentum of the Resurrection Flame and the unfolding return of Humanity's Solar Christ Presences, the original Divine Intent of Saturn's mission was restored. This is a Divine Plan that we have been orchestrating for millenia in cooperation with the entire Company of Heaven.

As Saturn entered Aries on *Easter morning, April 7, 1996*, the combined Divine Qualities of Saturn and Aries were expanded through every part of life on Earth. Those qualities included:

> *Fulfilling our Divine Plans and learning our lessons on Earth through joy instead of pain and suffering.*
>
> *Life's Eternal Victory over death—New Life, not sacrificial death.*
>
> *Humanity's ability to be Courageous, Inspiritional, Daring, Idealistic, Energetic, Competent Leaders.*
>
> *New Beginnings.*
>
> *Healing dualistic consciousness, separation and the schism between heart and mind.*
>
> *Return to the Divine Plan.*
>
> *Healing the maladies of human miscreation and the human ego.*
>
> *Oneness, Unity, Acceptance, Tolerance, Cooperation, Inclusivity and the Integration between extremes.*
>
> *An extraordinarily powerful promise of rebirth.*
>
> *Sincere and consistent application of our Highest Ideals and Principles.*

Self-Healing and Self-Realization.

Spiritually Revolutionary.

Increasing desire for Peace.

Structural Transfiguration, Bridging to New Dimensions, Quantum leaps in consciousness.

Humanity's Epiphany.

These Divine Qualities built in momentum for one year, until the ***Vernal Equinox and Easter***, the Celebration of the Resurrection, in the ***Spring of 1997***.

On ***May 1, 1996***, the day celebrated as the day of Ascension into Freedom, the Comet Hyakutake passed closest to the Sun and released Humanity's misqualified energy into the Sun to be repolarized and transmuted into Light. As this occurred, the comet amplified the Presence of the Love of God through all dimensions and levels of consciousness in the Universe. This greatly increased our Solar Christ Presences' ability to integrate into our four lower bodies. This allowed us to collectively move a quantum leap forward into Christ Consciousness.

Then, we God Victoriously passed through several accelerations of Light on the Planet:

> ***May 3, 1996***, was the ***Full Moon of Taurus*** and the celebration of the Wesak Festival which floods the Earth with the consciousness of Enlightenment
>
> ***June 1, 1996***, was the ***Full Moon of Gemini*** and the celebration of the Good Will of Humanity.

June 20, 1996, was the *Summer Solstice*, the
greatest expansion of Light (the longest day
in the Northern Hemisphere).

July 4, 1996, was the celebration of Freedom
and Liberty in America—"I AM" RACE.

July 7, 1996=7-7-7, was a day that the Legions
of Light associated with the Seventh Solar Aspect of Deity infinitely expanded the Violet
Flame of Limitless Transmutation throughout
all Creation. On that rare and glorious day,
the Violet Fire blazed through the Planet and
struck the final blow to "cosmic evil's" attempt
to thwart Archangel Michael's plan to free the
Universe from its paralyzing grip.

As the information regarding the Divine Plan that was
unfolding spread throughout the World, the force of "cosmic
evil" attempted to create a battle that would separate the
Lightworkers. It tried to manipulate its pawns to create
dissension and to take "sides," but its efforts were in vain.

The power of the Violet Flame lifted all Humanity into a
new level of understanding and Divine Wisdom. Through our
Higher Consciousness, we KNEW that the Divine Mission
we had all embarked upon which was calling to the Divinity
blazing in our hearts, was about LOVE!!! This was *not* a
battle. This was *not* Light against darkness or good against
evil. This *was* the fulfillment of a Divine Plan each of us had
been in training for since we first became aware of the plight
of the Earth aeons ago.

This was the moment our Father-Mother God and the
entire Company of Heaven had been waiting for; this was the
time when, finally, there were enough awakened souls in
embodiment on Earth to create a forcefield of Divine Love
that was so powerful "cosmic evil" could not escape it. This

forcefield of Divine Love would embrace "cosmic evil" as a Mother holds an injured child, flooding it with compassion and mercy. Held in the arms of Divine Love, "cosmic evil" would gradually calm itself to the point of desiring, on its own, to rejoin the Kingdom of Heaven. Then, it would once again find its proper place in the Universe. In perfect Divine Order, "cosmic evil" would be *Loved Eternally Free*.

It was only through the outer personality of our fear-based human egos that there appeared to be a separation among Lightworkers in this Divine Plan. In Truth, we were each fulfilling our right and perfect roles. Whether we perceived this force as "cosmic evil" and volunteered to consciously create the forcefield of Divine Love that would free this energy into the Light, or whether we perceived this force had been unjustly "attacked" and chose to love and defend it, was immaterial. Both perceptions were based in love and would build the forcefield of Divine Love that was needed for God's Plan to be accomplished *Victoriously*.

I am always amazed at how the Realms of Cause filter into the world of effects. When this occurs, people in the world of form pick up the various thoughtforms and often make them available for all to see. It is not by chance that the movie *DragonHeart* was released at that incredible time. It is really a wonderful METAPHOR that reflected the Divine Plan that was unfolding.

The force of "cosmic evil" has always been depicted as a beast that was to be battled and slain. Our fear-based human egos have been the "dragon slayers" doing battle with that force of evil throughout history. The legends of old have reiterated this theme time and time again, but *DragonHeart* was different. This time the "evil" dragon was *befriended* by the dragon slayer and held in the embrace of friendship and love until it chose to regain its path and was Loved Eternally Free into the Light. That was done, of course, in typical Hollywood fashion, but the message was profound.

As the *Summer of 1996* progressed, daily and hourly our

preparation continued. Every moment we were held in the loving embrace of our Father-Mother God, and the frequency of vibration of our four lower bodies was raised the maximum we could withstand. We were brought to the brink of our "comfort zones," and as a result, we experienced feelings of pressure in our awakening brain centers—our pituitary, hypothalamus and pineal glands and the ganglionic centers at the base of our brains. We also experienced slight discomfort in other areas of our bodies, even flu-like symptoms. Mother Mary said that if we would invoke the peach colored radiance of the Eleventh Solar Aspect of Deity and bathe our bodies in the Light of Divine Purpose, Comfort, Enthusiasm and Joy, which are the God Qualities associated with that Aspect of Deity, our discomfort would be dissipated.

Mother Mary also said that within the Etheric Temples of John the Beloved, known as the Holy Cities of Healing and Music, which pulsate in the Etheric Realms over Arizona in the United States of America, She has a specific focus of Healing through the Flame of the Immaculate Concept. She drew each of us into Her Healing Focus in our finer bodies as we slept at night. There we experienced the Healing Activity described below. She asked that we consciously focus on that healing process during the day and said it would empower our preparation.

This is a visualization that will greatly accelerate our physical transformation into limitless physical perfection, eternal youth, vibrant health and radiant beauty.

Transforming our Lower Vehicles

A GIFT FROM MOTHER MARY

With this exercise you will begin to experience, first hand, the assistance being given to Humanity from On High. This activity is dedicated to re-establishing the Divine Pattern and Plan...the Immaculate Concept...within our physical, etheric, mental and emotional vehicles.

Through this exercise we energize the perfect blueprint within each vehicle until it is a pulsating force of Divine Reality. This regenerates health and order physically, etherically, mentally and emotionally in all of our bodies.

To begin...sit comfortably in a chair with your arms and legs uncrossed and your spine as straight as possible. Breathe in deeply, and as you exhale, completely relax and gently close your eyes. Feel yourself enveloped in an invincible Forcefield of Protection, which prevents anything that is not of the Light from interfering with this Sacred Activity. This is a journey in consciousness that will physically manifest through the power of your true God Reality "I AM".

Visualize yourself Ascending into the Realms of Light. You are now standing before a magnificent Crystalline Temple of Healing. You gracefully ascend the steps and pass through the massive golden doors. You are guided by a beautiful Angelic Presence into the central chamber, and you notice that there are four surrounding chambers at the cardinal points. Pulsating in the center of the central chamber is a radiant Crystal Lotus Blossom, and blazing within the center of the Lotus Blossom is a Madonna Blue Flame with a Crystalline White aura. It is the Flame of the Immaculate Concept.

An Angelic Being beckons you, and you enter the Crystalline Lotus Blossom and stand within the scintillating essence of the Flame of the Immaculate Concept. You begin to experience the vibratory rate of your four lower bodies being accelerated. Your consciousness is rising, and you perceive, more clearly than ever before, the Divine Blueprint for each of your bodies.

Pouring forth now from the very Heart of God is a tremendous Ray of Light that is pulsating with the God Qualities of Restoration, Transformation, Healing, Eter-

nal Youth and Radiant Beauty. This shaft of Light enters the Flame of the Immaculate Concept and then expands out to the outer chambers at the cardinal points, which are each dedicated specifically to one of the four lower vehicles of your life expression.

You now consciously project your Emotional Body and all of your feelings into the chamber at the cardinal point to the East. God's Holy Light begins blazing in, through and around this vehicle, transmuting every trace of imbalance. Your God Presence now projects the Divine Blueprint for your Emotional Body through this vehicle, and it begins pulsating as a Light Pattern, transforming your Emotional Body instantly into the Immaculate Concept of your Divine Plan.

You now consciously project your Mental Body and all of your thoughts into the chamber at the cardinal point to the West. God's Holy Light begins blazing in, through and around this vehicle, transmuting every trace of imbalance. Your God Presence now projects the Divine Blueprint for your Mental Body through this vehicle, and it begins pulsating as a Light Pattern, transforming your Mental Body instantly into the Immaculate Concept of your Divine Plan.

You now consciously project your Etheric Body and all of your memories and records of the past into the chamber at the cardinal point to the North. God's Holy Light begins blazing in, through and around this vehicle, transmuting every trace of imbalance. Your God Presence now projects the Divine Blueprint for your Etheric Body through this vehicle, and it begins pulsating as a Light Pattern, transforming your Etheric Body instantly into the Immaculate Concept of your Divine Plan.

You now consciously project your Physical Body: every cell, atom, gland, muscle, organ and function into the chamber at the cardinal point to the South. God's Holy Light begins blazing in, through and around this vehicle, transmuting every trace of imbalance. Your God Presence now projects the Divine Blueprint for your Physical Body through this vehicle, and it begins pulsating as a Light Pattern, transforming your Physical Body instantly into the Immaculate Concept of your Divine Plan.

Now, one by one, you magnetize these purified balanced vehicles back into the Flame of the Immaculate Concept where they are brought into perfect alignment: first the Physical, then the Etheric, then the Mental, then the Emotional.

The entire Activity of Light is sealed through the following Affirmation:

> **Through the Flaming Presence of God...
> anchored in my heart, I ask that this Trans-
> forming, Healing Activity of Light be main-
> tained, eternally self-sustained, daily and
> hourly increased moment-by-moment until
> each of my four lower vehicles is outpic-
> turing the perfection ordained for me, and
> "I AM" wholly Ascended and Free.**

> ### *It Is Done!!! And So It Is!!!*

Gently return your consciousness to the room. Experience the buoyancy and the harmony of your purified vehicles and maintain this thoughtform of perfection.

Beloved Mother Mary asked if, after purifying our four lower bodies through the Healing Activity, we would be willing to assist in empowering the Crystal Grid System by saying the "Rosary of the New Age" that She has given to us.

By repeating the Rosary twelve times, once for each of the Twelve Solar Aspects of Deity and visualizing this Divine Light as It flows through our Heart Flames into the Crystal Grid System, we will help all life evolving on Earth in the glorious Ascension process unfolding.

As each "Hail Mother..." is stated, visualize the color and qualities of the corresponding Ray entering your heart and flooding through you to bathe the Crystal Grid System.

"THE ROSARY OF THE NEW AGE"

Hail Mother, full of Grace, the Lord is with Thee. Blessed art Thou amongst women, and Blessed is the fruit of Thy womb "I AM".

Hold for us NOW the Immaculate Concept of our true God Reality from this moment unto our Eternal Ascension in the Light.

"I AM" that "I AM".

Focusing on a different Ray each time, repeat from the * twelve times. Recite **"HAIL MOTHER"**...

	RAY	COLOR	QUALITIES
1st Time	1st Ray	Blue	God's Will
2nd Time	2nd Ray	Yellow	Enlightenment
3rd Time	3rd Ray	Pink	Divine Love
4th Time	4th Ray	White	Purity & Ascension
5th Time	5th Ray	Green	Truth & Healing
6th Time	6th Ray	Ruby	Divine Grace
7th Time	7th Ray	Violet	Freedom & Forgiveness
8th Time	8th Ray	Aqua	Clarity
9th Time	9th Ray	Magenta	Harmony & Balance
10th Time	10th Ray	Gold	Eternal Peace & Prosperity
11th Time	11th Ray	Peach	Divine Purpose, Enthusiasm & Joy
12th Time	12th Ray	Opal	Transformation

After reciting the "Hail Mother..." twelve times, focusing on a different Ray each time, repeat the following affirmation three times:

> *"I AM" the Immaculate Concept of my true*
> *God Reality and the God Reality of*
> *Mother Earth NOW made manifest and*
> *sustained by Holy Grace! (3X)*

At the conclusion of the entire series, the energy is sealed and permanently sustained by decreeing:

IT IS DONE!!! AND SO IT IS!!! "I AM"

Mother Mary said if we will repeat these exercises daily, their power and effectiveness will build in momentum, lifting us to the highest frequency of vibration we have ever experienced. This will prepare us beyond measure to be the physical conduits through which the Divine Light of God will pour, greatly assisting this blessed Earth and all life evolving upon Her into the perfection of Heaven on Earth.

Keynote Visualization

The following visualization has been given to us by the Spiritual Hierarchy. It is designed to help us further prepare all aspects of ourselves in order to be all we are capable of being in our glorious Divine Mission of loving all life on Earth Eternally FREE.

Becoming All "I Am"

Breathing rhythmically and deeply, I greet this sacred day from within the peace of my liberated God Presence on Earth. Centered here, I feel one with all life, and I now realize that "I Am" all Humanity standing forth as the Arisen Solar

Christ. I feel an upward rushing force of the Ascension of Humanity's *Free Will* back to the Christ. All *Free Will* is Ascending into the Realm of Limitless Physical Perfection for this Star of Freedom. In this meditation, I now stretch into and accept the Infinity of my own God Consciousness, all of which I claim here in the physical vehicle. But "I Am" also all of Humanity, and I feel Her Infinity Consciousness as the Stargate of Her Heart opens Globally. I dwell in the peace of my personal and Global God expression, and I know "All things are in Divine Order."

Standing forth within my Solar Twelve-fold Flame, I begin to profoundly experience God Power on all planes. I experience my Divine Integrity, knowing my Presence on Earth is just one aspect of my Infinity Consciousness. In this awakening, "I Am" now **a Universal Instrument on Earth**.

As I inbreathe and absorb the Flaming Presence of Light streaming into my heart, I know myself on many levels. "I Am" the Celestial Christ Self in the Perfected Realms of Planet Earth, performing my Cosmic Service of loving free all lesser energies. I find my gentle rhythm in this Aspect of my Divinity, and "I Am" that "I Am". Then, my awareness increases into the Mighty "I Am" Presence in the Electronic Realms around the Sun. Here I experience myself as a Cosmic Flame with Light Rays radiating out in all directions of the Universe. I know myself as God in Action...here, there and everywhere present. As the rhythm of this Aspect of my Divinity anchors into the core of my physical Being, I again know "I Am" that "I Am". Then, I further Ascend along my Solar Silver Cord into the Galactic Presence of my White Fire Being within the Great Central Sun. Here "I Am" whole, my full Masculine and Feminine God Self as one glorious Being of Light. Here I see, feel and become part of the service of our glorious Central Sun, Alpha and Omega. Here I also begin to experience the Great Central Sun of Elohae and Eloha. I experience the endless Ocean of Light and the great Infinity of Suns beyond Suns beyond Suns...and I know

"I Am" that "I Am". Here I rest in Eternity.

Yet, on the very same breath, in this moment of timelessness, I also experience this Ocean of Infinity *within the Solar Atoms composing my physical vehicle*. I live within the very Eternity that I seek. I now experience my entire physical presence as a Solar Atom. I see and feel my Twelvefold Flame as the nucleus. The periphery of my atom is my Electronic Aura. All the energies of my four lower vehicles now exist in the Divine Fifth Dimensional space within the atom which "I Am". I have now become collectively what each of my atoms expresses individually. I see and feel each of these atoms and my entire physical presence as **Divine Instruments of Endless Light** in service here on Earth. In this one breath, I have realized that "I Am" simultaneously every aspect of Divine Life along the Silver Cord, from the Highest Electronic Realms within the Great Central Sun through to the atoms expressing here in the physical plane, and I accept now all that "I Am" *here in my physical body*.

I now experience the Celestial Aura of my entire Infinity Consciousness...my **Causal Body**. It envelops all that "I Am" in a great multicolored, multidimensional sea of dazzling Light. These Spheres of Glory around me are all the Divine Blessings which I have ever generated—every good and perfect thought, feeling and action I have ever created in my service to God on **any plane of existence**. All that "I Am" as a White Fire Being, as an "I Am" Presence, as a Solar Christ Self now envelops me as a great Celestial Aura of the many Dimensions and Solar Aspects of God. This Causal Body enfolds every Aspect of my Being, including every physical atom. I pause now and feel this deeply within my body.

My Causal Body is really the Limitless Realms of *my own Universe unfolding*, for "I Am" a potential Sun God or Goddess, someday possibly to parent my own Universe of Divine Life. This Solar Causal Body is *"my treasures stored in Heaven,"* and I now assimilate all of this into my physical life on Earth, for "I Am" that "I Am", here and now! And with

344 What On Earth

every breath, I flood the World with the countless Spheres of Perfection that "I Am".

Connecting all of these Aspects of my Divine Being is a great River of Cosmic Light, my Solar Silver Cord. As I breathe slowly and deeply, I gently become just this River of Divine Light flowing from Infinity to Infinity. It may express Itself as the various Aspects of my Divine Self, but I may also choose to know myself *only as this Celestial River of endless Light*, and "I Am" that "I Am". "I Am" the River of Light. "I Am" the Ocean of Infinity *from* which It flows, and "I Am" the Ocean of Infinity *into* which It flows. This River of Light is made up of perfection particles and perfection Light Waves, all of which constitute my Divine Creation flowing through the Universe...my Cosmic Thread in the Celestial Tapestry of the Great Solar Day. "I Am" Creation's endless expansion.

In becoming this Celestial River of Light, I now understand my Infinity Consciousness and claim every Aspect of my Divine Being along Its "banks" into my *physical* Spiritual Freedom, for this Cosmic River of Light may now flow unimpeded through my Christed physical Body of Light. "I Am" now releasing into the Light all thoughts, feelings and memories less than this Immaculate Concept of myself. "I Am" embodied on Earth to express my *Free Will choice* to function as a Divine Instrument of Service and to experience the joy of physical perfection but, all that "I Am", all the God Perfection that flows along my Solar Silver Cord is here with me now, and I let it **blaze forth into the physical realm**. "I Am" at peace in the physical realm.

Resting now in the Supreme God Confidence of Infinity Consciousness manifesting on Earth, I feel the opening of the Stargate of my Heart. I immediately see the Truth of life all around me. Once again I see all imbalanced energies as they were to be seen in the expanded Divine Plan...innocent primordial Light entering my awareness to be redeemed. I now greet all imbalanced energies as would the God Parents from within the Flame of Peace, Detachment, God Confidence and Supreme Authority. I take this energy into my Being, holding it in my arms of Light as I would an injured child. I do not let it overwhelm me or control me, nor do I need to fear it or shun it. I simply hold it and love it...until it has calmed, desiring on its own part to rejoin the Kingdom of Heaven, *which is within me*! As this energy releases itself into the Light, it experiences the Infinity Consciousness which "I Am", and it again finds its proper place in the Universe. It shall now be Eternally Free, with all things in Divine Order. I affirm to all life everywhere:

> *"Come unto me and be raised up into the Father-Mother God."*

> *"Come unto me and be raised up into the Father-Mother God."*

> *"Come unto me and be raised up into the Father-Mother God."*

As this practice grows more rhythmic and established in my day-to-day life, I realize "I Am" in Holy Communion...the constant Communion of my Father God and my Mother God within me expressing now as the Christ "I Am". I experience the Holy Communion of all of my energies around my Flame...all of my will becoming God's Will...all of my love becoming God's Love...all of my Being becoming God's Being. I experience my full Solar Integrity, my full Solar Ancestry, as the **Harmony of my True Being**!...the Communion of all my energies within my Flame, on every level of my Infinite Being. This Communion includes all of what "I Am" in the Electronic Realms of the White Fire Being, in the Ascended Master Realms as the "I Am" Presence, in the Fifth Dimensional Realms as the Solar Christ Awakening on Earth *and all the unascended energies of my physical* *embodiment.* All of what "I Am"—Ascended and unascended—is now dancing around my Heart Flame, assimilated into my physical Being with every breath, every heartbeat, every action that I take. I now take every aspect, every atom of my life's energies with me along the Great Cosmic Inbreath into Eternity.

As the Harmony of my True Being sustains my Ultimate Protection, I know that I can safely accept unascended energies into myself as an Instrument of Transformation. Rather than feeling rejected and thus lingering as patterns of disease and distress, these energies will, instead, feel accepted, held in love and revered as the innate God Energy they are. They will then voluntarily release themselves into the Light, into all the great forcefields and momentums of Light "I Am", for "I Am" the full power of the Mother God in Action doing this. The Father God is my ability to stretch into Infinity, and the Mother God is my ability to be with this energy until it chooses freedom. My Holy Communion is the unity of all my Ascended Forcefields and Momentums with all my own unascended energies and all impersonal laggard energies I have volunteered to redeem on this Planet. All of this is now taking place within my physical presence on Earth as a great *Dance of Transformation* within me. I both participate in this dance and observe it in the detached peace of the Great "I Am". The present Cosmic Moment on Earth is taking place right inside my embodied vehicles...and I know the Light of God is always Victorious.

I remain in harmony within the Father God's Confidence, Protection and God Authority and the Mother God's Love and Divine Compassion as They Commune together in Their Sacred Dance within me...out of which comes the Resurrection and Ascension of my full Christ Being, physically expressing on Earth. I rejoice in my service of allowing my White Fire Being, my Mighty "I Am" Presence and my Solar Christ Presence Their Sacred Service on Earth through these vehicles, and I rejoice that unascended energy will now find its way Home through me. I release myself into the peace of knowing:

> *"My Perfection is handling ALL imperfection Perfectly."*

> *"My Perfection is handling ALL imperfection Perfectly."*

> *"My Perfection is handling ALL imperfection Perfectly."*

(Through Group Avatar)

With those tools of Light blazing through Humanity's Solar Christ Consciousness, we progressed to the next phase of the Divine Plan.

The Victory of the Summer Olympic Games
July 19, 1996—August 4, 1996

The Olympic Games have always been an incredibly powerful time of increased Light on the Planet. It is a time when the nations of the World put aside their differences and join together to reach the highest level of excellence as we "push the envelope" of human potential to new octaves of accomplishment. In *1996*, 197 nations participated in this glorious event.

The Olympic Games grasp the attention of the entire World, inspiring approximately four billion people daily for 17 days, creating a focal point of Humanity's attention that is unrivaled in any ongoing World event. The collective focus of Humanity's attention, pulsating with the Divine Qualities of Hope, Expectancy, Promise, Commitment, Determination, Discipline, Courage, Strength, Joy, Elation and Victory reaches into the depths of our souls and taps the unmanifest potential awaiting in dormancy there. It awakens within us a glimmer of the Divinity blazing in our hearts, and through the multidimensional facets of our God Selves, it opens a door into the Heart and Mind of God that no one can shut.

The collective focus of Humanity's consciousness, which occurs during the Olympic Games, also creates a tremendous Chalice of Light through which our Father-Mother God and the entire Company of Heaven can pour the Healing Unguent of Divine Light that soothes Humanity's wounded hearts and bathes our battered souls. Never had that comforting Light been more urgently needed.

The moment was at hand when Archangel Michael and the entire Company of Heaven, in unison with the God Selves of all Humanity abiding on Earth, were destined to create a powerful enough forcefield of Divine Love that the ancient fallen force known as "cosmic evil" would be encompassed and held in the...RING-PASS-NOT OF GOD'S FIRST CAUSE OF PERFECTION until it chose on its own to release itself into the Light. That was to be the fulfillment of the prophecy that clearly stated, *"In the latter days Satan will be bound and cast from the Earth."* As awesome and unbelievable as that seemed to the outer consciousness of our lower human egos, we had each been preparing for thousands of years to fulfill our individual parts in that wondrous Divine Plan, and we were ready. We each had everything we needed within us to accomplish, God Victoriously, what we had volunteered to do.

Sooner or later, that moment had to come. We knew in the very core of our Beings that one day the forces of imbalance would *be no more*, and Humanity would be eternally freed from their oppressive grip and interference. We just never dared to dream that it would be in our lifetime. But, lo and behold, there we were, standing on the threshold of our Eternal Freedom in the Light.

It was not by chance that the Summer Olympic Games were held in Atlanta, Georgia, just days before the Crystal

Grid Activation that would permanently free the Earth from the "magnetic grid" of "cosmic evil."

Prior to Harmonic Convergence, *August 15-17, 1987*, there were two attempts made to free the Earth from the "magnetic grid" of "cosmic evil." The initial impulse of the fall of Humanity began on the continent of Lemuria after the coming of the laggards, and Lemuria was the place where the first attempt was made to reactivate the Crystal Grid System.

At that time, there were illumined souls who were hopeful that they had developed sufficient skills to reactivate the Crystal Grid System and break the Earth free from the grip of "cosmic evil." Unfortunately, they underestimated the strength of that sinister force, and as they increased the Light through the Crystal Grid System, the force of "cosmic evil" amplified the "magnetic grid" and caused the Light to implode through the Crystals in a way that intensified Humanity's pain and suffering immeasurably.

When our Father-Mother God realized the agony this was causing Their Sons and Daughters, They invoked the Mighty Builders of Form and issued a Divine Fiat to submerge Lemuria below the healing waters of the Pacific Ocean as a merciful act of compassion.

Prior to the sinking of Lemuria, our Father-Mother God asked the Beings of Light serving the Earth to transfer the Record Keeper Crystals into the Heart Center of a tremendous monolith for safekeeping. These Record Keeper Crystals contained within their genetic codings all of the unmanifest potential that the Earth was encoded with when She was first breathed forth from the Core of Creation. They contained the Immaculate Concept of all manifest form and the Divine Plan for all Lifeforms assigned to evolve on Earth.

When the cataclysms occurred which broke Lemuria apart and sank the majority of that continent beneath the waters of the Pacific, the portion of land containing the monolith with the Record Keeper Crystals was pushed deep into the Southern Hemisphere. It is the continent we now call Australia, and the monolith is Ayers Rock.

The Record Keeper Crystals contained in Ayers Rock pulsate with all of the unmanifest potential the Earth would have experienced if we had never fallen from Grace, but since it was not part of the original Divine Plan for us to fall into the depths of human degradation, there was no blueprint or plan in the original Record Keeper Crystals to salvage the Earth and no plan of how we would regain our direction after the fall.

To remedy that problem, a contingency plan was set into motion by the Company of Heaven and our God Parents to imprint new Record Keeper Crystals with an alternate plan. This plan contained the Divine Blueprint of just how this sweet Earth would regain Her path of Divinity and how Humanity, Elementals and Angels would work together to restore the Earth and all life evolving upon Her into the Immaculate Concept of Limitless Physical Perfection.

The new Record Keeper Crystals were placed strategically within the Crystal Grid System on the continent of Atlantis and were sustained by the embodied Lightworkers there. At one point in time, the Lightworkers hoped they could reactivate the Crystal Grid System and finally free the Earth from the "magnetic grid" of "cosmic evil." Alas, once again their numbers were too few, and the force of "cosmic evil" was able to invert their efforts and implode the Light through the Crystals into the Earth. The resulting amplification of pain and suffering caused our God Parents to issue another Fiat to submerge Atlantis beneath the healing waters of the Atlantic Ocean. This time, our Father-Mother God directed the Beings of Light to transfer the Record Keeper Crystals containing the new contingency plan to a huge monolith on the North American Continent. For 12,000 years those Crystals have been held in dormancy within the Heart Center of Stone Mountain in Atlanta, Georgia.

The hope was that one day Humanity would heal our self-inflicted separation from God and our schism with the Elemental and Angelic Kingdoms sufficiently to allow the Crystal Grid System to be reactivated to its original potential and power which would permanently shatter the "magnetic grid" of "cosmic evil." The Divine Knowledge contained within both sets of Record Keeper Crystals, those in Ayers Rock and those in Stone Mountain, could then be released into the Crystal Grid System, and the Divine Plan would be restored on Earth.

After millenia of preparation, the first successful Crystal Grid Activation took place during *Harmonic Convergence on August 17, 1987*. That activation built in momentum for several years and lifted Humanity up in energy, vibration and consciousness enough for us to perceive the urgent need to regain our Divine Position as stewards of the Earth. We clearly saw the importance of healing our rift with the Elemental Kingdom in order to save the Earth from total destruction.

The *1996 Summer Olympics* signaled the Cosmic Moment when the Divine Knowledge and the genetic codings of Limitless   Physical Perfection for the Earth contained within the Record Keeper Crystals in Ayers Rock and Stone Mountain could be released into the Crystal Grid System. For that reason, the Summer Olympics in 1996 were held in Atlanta, Georgia, and the Summer Olympics in the year 2000 will be held in Australia.

During the *1996 Summer Olympics*, the entire World focused on Atlanta and was told about the next Olympics to be held in Australia. As that information bathed the consciousness of four-billion people for 17 days, a tremendous open Portal formed between Heaven and Earth. Through the Cup of Humanity's consciousness and the focus of our unified attention, the Record Keeper Crystals in Stone Mountain and Ayers Rock were activated, and ALL of the Divine Knowledge, Wisdom, Truth and Perfection Patterns contained within those Crystals was RELEASED INTO THE

CRYSTAL GRID SYSTEM. This was the final preparation necessary to assure the God Victorious activations of the Crystal Grid System that were to take place *August 17, 1996*, and *August 22, 1996*, during the Tenth Annual World Congress On Illumination.

Tremendous shafts of Light had been anchored through the four cardinal points on the Planet to strengthen and reinforce the faults, cracks, fissures and tectonic plates throughout the body of Mother Earth.

We were asked by the Company of Heaven to offer our first four free seminars for *1996* in the largest cities in the nation. We scheduled our free seminars over a year in advance and responded to that inner Heart Call without fully understanding the magnitude of the plan.

Later we were shown what actually occurred during those gatherings of Lightworkers. Our first free seminar in *1996* was held in *Los Angeles, California,* on *January 21st*. During that seminar, a tremendous shaft of Light was anchored at the western cardinal point through the Equator into the center of the Earth. This is a gift of the entire Company of Heaven that is being sustained by the collective consciousness of all of the races, nationalities, creeds and cultures represented in Los Angeles.

Our second free seminar in *1996* was held in *Houston, Texas,* on *March 17th*. During that seminar, a tremendous shaft of Light was anchored at the southern cardinal point through the South Pole into the center of the Earth. Again, this Divine Light is a gift from the entire Company of Heaven, and it is being sustained by the collective consciousness of all of the races, nationalities, creeds and cultures represented in Houston.

Amazingly, there were people at the Houston seminar who were originally from Bolivia, Brazil, Chili, Venezuela, Columbia, Guatamala, Mexico, South Africa, England, Asia and the usual wonderful melding pot of nationalities we are blessed to experience in America, including a native American Indian.

Our third free seminar in *1996* was held in *New York City*, on *May 5th*. During that seminar, a tremendous shaft of Light was anchored at the eastern cardinal point through the Equator into the center of the Earth, and sustained through the collective consciousness of all of the lifestreams represented in New York.

Our fourth free seminar in *1996* was held in *Chicago, Illinois*, on *June 9th*. During that gathering of Lightworkers, a tremendous shaft of Light was anchored at the northern cardinal point through the North Pole into the center of the Earth, and it is sustained by all of the lifestreams represented in Chicago.

Through these four Pillars of Light—North, South, East and West—our Beloved Spiritual Hierarchy projected the Harmony and Balance of our Father-Mother God to *brace* the Body of Mother Earth and *reinforce* ALL of the faults, cracks, fissures and tectonic plates on the Planet. This would allow the two Crystal Grid Activations that were going to be done in August to be accomplished without any serious cataclysmic backlash. This time, the Divine Light would flow through the Crystal Grid System and ONLY bless life as we Ascended a quantum leap in energy, vibration and consciousness. There would be no cataclysmic backlash because this time the number of awakened Lightworkers on the Planet was legion, and *nothing could stop our forward progress into the Light*.

Another preparation for the incredible Activity of Light in August took place at our fifth free seminar in *1996*. That seminar was held in *Tucson, Arizona,* within the permanent seed atom of the portal of Healing through the Power of Limitless Transmutation.

That seminar was held on *June 23rd* following the monumental influx of Light that poured into the Planet during the *Summer Solstice,* which occurred on *June 20, 1996*.

During that gathering of Lightworkers, Beloved Archangel Michael and the entire Company of Heaven utilized the increased Light on the Planet to create an invincible Forcefield of Protection in, through and around the Portal of Healing through the Power of Limitless Transmutation. This Forcefield prevented anything that was not of the Light from interfering with the *unprecedented Divine Plan to free the Earth and the Universe from the influence of "cosmic evil" FOR ALL ETERNITY!!!*

Unfortunately, the force of "cosmic evil" functioned at a level of fear and ignorance that prevented it from recognizing the wonderful opportunity it was being given to move into the Light. Therefore, it was striving to do whatever it could to block the Divine Plan from being fulfilled. We witnessed its heinous act when TWA Flight 800 exploded and fell from the sky, killing all 230 people aboard. This sinister act was specifically designed to mock the Summer Olympics and, through fear, distract Humanity's attention away from the Divine Intent of the Olymic Games. So that there would be no question about that evil intent, the force of "cosmic evil" manipulated the crash of a plane that was coming from Athens, the original home of the Olympics and the location where the Olympic Games were reintroduced to the World 100 years ago. The plane was traveling to the United States, the location of the current centennial celebration of the Olympics, on its way to Paris, the homeland of Baron Pierre de Coubertin, the man who inspired the World to begin the Olympics again after a hiatus of 1500 years. The two official languages for the Olympics were English and French. A group of English-speaking students, traveling with their French club, were going to France to practice the language.

That was one of the final ranting and flailings of that force of imbalance. It reflected, once again, the time that was foretold in the Bible when St. John said, *"In the latter days Satan will be loosed on the Earth."*

The force of "cosmic evil" could only work through our

natural propensities. Therefore, during that time, it was critical that we stay focused in the Light and not allow our lower human egos to manipulate us into thoughts, words, actions or feelings that this rampaging force could latch onto and amplify. During that unprecedented Cosmic Moment, it was imperative that we not play the game with that force of negativity. Instead, we needed to realize that this was a glorious opportunity to clear our pasts and be the Hands of God on Earth.

The Spiritual Hierarchy and our God Selves truly work in awesome ways. During the Olympic Games, Kerri Strug from Tucson, Arizona, in a heroic performance, successfully did her final vault on an injured ankle to win the Gold Medal for the women's gymnastic team competition. This is the first Gold Medal the United States of America ever won in that particular event, so, needless to say, elation was abounding. We are multidimensional Beings, however, and winning the Gold Medal was just one facet of the Divine Purpose involved in her Victory.

Kerri's dramatic accomplishment elevated her to the focal point of the Olympics, and for several days, four-billion people witnessed her courage and were consistently told that she was from Tucson, Arizona. As that information played through the consciousness of four-billion people day after day, the full-gathered momentum of the Olympics was projected into the Forcefield in Tucson, Arizona, through which the force of "cosmic evil" was to be PERMANENTLY REMOVED FROM THE PLANET.

In order to draw that kind of attention, Kerri's performance had to be dramatic and unique, and that it certainly was. As people focused on her heroic Victory, their thoughts and feelings were filled with compassion, inspiration, joy, amazement, admiration, determination and hope. They were also consumed with thoughts and feelings of Victory, strength, confidence, healing and, above all, courage. Remember, COURAGE is not about doing something when we feel strong, powerful, self-assured and confident. COURAGE is about doing something when we are scared to death, and we decide to go ahead and do it anyway.

As people throughout the World focused on Kerri with those incredibly powerful thoughts and feelings, tremendous highways of Light were projected into Tucson and amplified the invincible Forcefield of Light that was building in momentum.

Amy Van Dyken is also from Tucson, Arizona, and as she Victoriously won FOUR Gold Medals in swimming, she, too, succeeded in turning Global attention to the building Forcefield of Light in Tucson.

July 30, 1996, was the *Full Moon in Aquarius*. This full moon amplified the winds of change through all of our belief systems, both conscious and unconscious, clearing the way for the New Age of Spiritual Freedom.

During the closing Ceremonies on *August 4, 1996*, the Divine Light from the Olympic Games was permanently sealed in the core of purity in every electron of precious life energy evolving on Earth. The indigenous people of Australia, the Aborigines, have known throughout time that there would be a moment when the keynote of Beloved Mother Earth would sound and the healing of the Crystal Grid System would occur. For millenia, they have focused on this keynote and energized it through the ancient 40,000-year-old wind instrument, the Didjeridu.

During the closing ceremonies of the *1996 Summer Olympic Games*, the Didjeridu was played, and as over four-billion people around the World watched and listened, they were brought into alignment with the keynote of Mother Earth.

This Holy Light built in power and momentum for eleven days until the *Anniversary of Mother Mary's Ascension, August 15, 1996*. At that time, the Divine Love of our Mother God/Holy Spirit poured into the Planet and Baptized every particle of life on Earth in the essence of Divine Love.

This Baptism of the Holy Spirit built in intensity until the third day, *August 17, 1996*, the tenth celebration of Harmonic Convergence.

"SATAN IS BOUND AND CAST FROM THE EARTH"

Lightworkers from all over the World responded to their inner heart call and came to Tucson to participate in the Tenth Annual World Congress On Illumination and to be the Hands of God in the World of form. They came from:

Argentina	Canada	South Africa
Aruba	Croatia	Switzerland
Australia	England	Venezuela
Belgium	France	
Bolivia	New Zealand	

and from the United States of America:

Arizona	Nevada
Arkansas	New Jersey
California	New Mexico
Connecticut	New York
Florida	North Carolina
Georgia	Ohio
Hawaii	Oregon
Idaho	Pennsylvania
Illinois	South Carolina
Maryland	Texas
Massachusetts	Washington
Michigan	Wisconsin
Minnesota	Wyoming
Missouri	Puerto Rico
Montana	

In addition to those who physically attended, Lightworkers from all over the World joined with us in consciousness. Many held group meetings in their own localities that coincided with our activities of Light. In addition to those tuning in, in consciousness from a distance, there were the God Selves of every man, woman and child belonging to or serving the Earth at this time (both in and out of embodiment), the entire Elemental Kingdom and the entire Angelic Kingdom who joined with us at inner levels and wove their magnificent energies into this unprecedented Cosmic Moment.

Truly, every particle of life on Earth contributed to the fulfillment of this Divine Plan, whether they were consciously aware of it or not, and every single Human Being, Elemental and Angel was critical to the God Victorious success of this Divine Mission. No one's part was any more significant than another. We are ALL ONE, and without our collective force of Light we would not have succeeded...**BUT succeed we did!!!** And words cannot begin to express the gratitude pouring forth from the Heavenly Realms in appreciation for the Light YOU have added to the World.

August 17, 1996

August 17, 1996, began with a Global Activity of Light that was called:

INVOKING THE REALITY
OF LOVE ON EARTH

The organizers of this event invited Humanity to synergistically join together at 12:00 NOON GREENWICH MEAN TIME to express our gratitude for the transformations that have taken place since the momentous event of Harmonic Convergence on *August 17, 1987*, nine years earlier. We were asked to make a powerful commitment to leap individually and collectively into a dynamic **New Reality where Peace, Love and Abundance for all prevails on Earth.**

We were invited to celebrate through Prayer, Meditation, Song and Dance our Unification as One Mind, One Heart, One Soul, One Breath eternally united with Divine Inspiration, the Ascended Realms of Light, Mother Earth and each other.

We were asked to co-create a Planetary Union of Hearts that initiated an unprecedented expansion of love in all planes and in all dimensions of life. And we were asked to open the Stargates of our Hearts like magnificent Roses, initiating a Reign of Divine Love on Earth.

This Global influx of Divine Love created the perfect forcefield on Earth to usher in the Opening Ceremonies of the Tenth Annual World Congress On Illumination.

The Opening Ceremonies commenced with over 500 people physically in attendance. Through our multidimensional, multifaceted God Selves, we joined in consciousness with all Humanity, Angels and Elementals evolving on Beloved Mother Earth. We also joined in consciousness with all of the Beings of Light from Suns beyond Suns and Galaxies beyond Galaxies and the collective expressions of Divinity throughout all of Creation back to the Heart of our Father-Mother God. All of the Legions of Light throughout Infinity joined in and watched, in breathless awe, the miracle taking place on Earth.

Divine Love from the Heart of our Father-Mother God expanded through our Heart Centers as tremendous Starbursts of Light. This Divine Love formed a glorious Chalice that engulfed the entire Planet Earth. Every man, woman and child, every Elemental and every Angel evolving on Earth was held in the embrace of our Chalice of Divine Love, and together we Ascended in consciousness into a new octave of awareness, where we were clearly shown the Divine Mission we were being called to fulfill.

Our forcefield of Divine Love grew in strength and power, and when it reached its maximum intensity, our Father-Mother God issued a Divine Fiat and commanded the forces of "cosmic evil" throughout the Universe to enter our forcefield of love.

From every conceivable corner of the Universe these wayward, fallen souls came. From North, South, East and West, in lines as far as the eye could see, they marched into our expanded forcefield of Divine Love. Every fallen soul that we have ever referred to throughout recorded history was there: Lucifer and all of his legions of fallen angels; all of the energies associated with Satan and the Satanic forces of evil; the force referred to as the Devil and the sinister forces of the psychic-astral plane; all of the expressions of "cosmic evil" that were deceiving Humanity with various names and games of deception; entities representing all of the overlords of darkness throughout history: Baal, Beelzebub and various other Princes of Darkness that are less well-known but, nonetheless, committed to evil. Every force entrapping Humanity in darkness was drawn into our invincible forcefield and held in the all-powerful embrace of Divine Love!

As this collective force of "cosmic evil" was bathed in love, ever so slowly it began to soften and began to realize that its moment was at hand, and its reign of terror was over. Our Father-Mother God issued a command for this sinister force to be silent and listen to our collective voice of love.

As we spoke the Truth of Oneness and Love with one breath, one heartbeat, one voice, one consciousness of Divine Love, the Heart Flames within these fallen souls began to stir, and as our Father-Mother God breathed on the Flame of Divinity in each Heart Center, "cosmic evil" began to surrender into our forcefield of Divine Love, and it began to glimpse its original God Reality. As we spoke, these fallen souls heard and perceived the Truth of their own Divinity for the first time in billions of years. As this force, that fell long before our Solar System was even created, listened in the silence of their Heart Flames, they began to remember that they were Sons and Daughters of God who had lost their way aeons ago. They listened to our collective voice as we spoke to them as loving sisters and brothers in the Light.

The collective force of "cosmic evil" absorbed this Truth and began to lift up in consciousness as it further surrendered into our embrace of Divine Love. As this occurred, the collective God Presence of all Humanity invoked additional assistance from the very Heart of God.

In response to our plea, a Higher Order of Galactic Solar Angels entered the atmosphere of Earth and traversed the Planet. These exponents of God's Love were from a dimension of Light beyond anything the Earth had ever been able to experience. As They entered the auras of every man, woman and child, They embraced each person in a higher frequency of Divine Love than Humanity had ever been able to endure.

These magnificent Solar Angels bathed our battered bodies and our wounded hearts in Their comforting Flames of Divine Love and prepared us at a cellular level for the Crystal Grid Activation that would permanently shatter the "magnetic grid" of "cosmic evil."

During the Opening Ceremonies of the World Congress On Illumination, the Didjeridu was played, and the body of Mother Earth was prepared for the Crystal Grid Activation that would permanently free Her and all Her life from the oppressive grip of "cosmic evil."

As the Didjeridu sounded the keynote of Mother Earth throughout the Universe, the Directors of the Elements took Their strategic positions around this Planet to reinforce the Body of Mother Earth in Their invincible forcefields of comfort and protection.

The Directors of the Air Element stood at the cardinal point to the North, the Directors of the Water Element stood at the cardinal point to the East, the Directors of the Earth

Element stood at the cardinal point to the South and the Directors of the Fire Element stood at the cardinal point to the West. These resplendent Beings of Light projected the Divine Essence of Comfort and Protection through the elemental vehicles of all Humanity and through every Being associated with the elements: the Sylphs of the Air, the Undines of the Water, the Gnomes and Nature Spirits of the Earth and the Salamanders of the Fire Element.

When every part of life was secure, Mother Earth signaled our Father-Mother God, and the Twelve Solar Aspects of Deity began to flow from the Heart of God into the open portal in Tucson, the portal of Healing through the Power of Limitless Transmutation. Beloved LuElla, the Solar Being from the Great Central Sun, absorbed this Divine Light and breathed It into the center of the Earth. As It merged with the Divine Momentum blazing there, It began to expand out through the Crystal Grid System. LuElla's Regal Court, which was stationed at every Chakra Center, Power Point and Sacred Site along the Meridians of the Crystal Grid System, absorbed this Healing Unguent and expanded It without limit through every electron of precious life energy on Earth.

On the Holy Breath of the collective God Presence of ALL Humanity, this sweet Earth was lifted higher and higher in frequency and vibration as the Light expanded through the Crystal Grid System. As we Ascended in energy, vibration and consciousness, the "magnetic grid" of "cosmic evil" lost its grip and began to fall away from the Crystals of Earth. Our collective God Presence accelerated the influx of Light on the Holy Breath, and we were lifted higher and even higher until the oppressive tar-like substance that the force of "cosmic evil" had cloaked over every electron on Earth shattered into minuscule particles of debris and was instantly transmuted back into Light through the Power of the Flame of Healing through Limitless Transmutation.

In Australia, the etheric records were frozen, resulting in snow falling in areas where it never snows. The etheric records of the first impetus of the fall were frozen in order to allow the Divine Blueprint for the New Heaven and the New Earth to be activated into the physical substance of Earth, unimpeded by previous human miscreation.

As the Earth burst asunder the "magnetic grid" of "cosmic evil," the ancient shamans accepted the Divine Blueprint for the New Heaven and the New Earth into their Heart Flames and telepathically transmitted it to the other sacred stewards of the Earth: first the Aboriginal Shamans, then the Native American Shamans and Holy Ones in North America. Next, the Divine Blueprint was transmitted to the Indigenous Shamans and Holy Ones in South America, including the Incas and Mayans; then it flowed into the Heart Flames of the Inuits of Alaska. From this point the transmission was projected into Russia and Europe, then Africa and the Orient. It was then transmitted to the Middle East, Asia and every other part of Earth. Instantaneously, the consciousness of the New Heaven and the New Earth expanded to all life on Earth, and at inner levels, the God Selves of all Humanity consecrated and rededicated the energies of the lower human egos to healing the Earth and expressing the Universal Laws of Divine Love and Harmony.

A new covenant was established between our God Selves and our lower human egos, and a new atmosphere of Divine Cooperation and Healing is now interpenetrating all levels of consciousness on Earth.

With the God Victorious Accomplishment of that activity of Light, **the force of "cosmic evil," embraced in the arms of Divine Love, was taken into the Inner Sanctuary of Divine Grace that pulsates in the Golden Throne Room of the Holy Cities of John the Beloved.** This complex of etheric Temples expands over Arizona in the United States of America. The Hierarch of this complex of etheric Temples is John the Beloved, the disciple to whom Jesus gave the Revelations of these latter days.

It is not by chance that John the Beloved is taking such an

active role in bringing to fruition the final stages of the Revelations he was given.

Throughout the Etheric Realms of Illumined Truth there are myriad Temples of Light and glorious Beings of the Spiritual Hierarchy associated with each Temple Who are working ceaselessly to assist Humanity and Mother Earth in our Ascension in the Light. All of Them are equally important and critical to the success of our unified Divine Mission.

At this time, John the Beloved is being brought to the forefront of our consciousness for a very specific reason. He was given "St. John's Revelations" to inform Humanity what would occur during these "end times" according to our course of direction 2000 years ago. But, remember, a fulfilled negative prophecy is a *failed* prophecy. The ONLY reason details of possible catastrophic events are revealed through Divine Inspiration is so that Humanity will recognize the error of our ways and change our course of direction.

From the moment John the Beloved was given Revelations on the Isle of Patmos in Greece, 2000 years ago, he has worked ceaselessly to raise the consciousness of Humanity so that we would avert the cataclysmic destruction described in Revelations.

In our finer bodies, as we slept at night, Humanity has been drawn into the Holy Cities over Arizona and clearly shown what must occur in order to move onto the Path of Divine Love and off of the path of self-destruction. This Sacred Wisdom and Knowledge has been filtering into our awakened consciousness and has been a major factor in the Global Spiritual Awakening taking place on Earth.

John the Beloved's plan has been God Victorious. Through his selfless efforts and the assistance he received from the entire Company of Heaven, as well as the cooperation of awakened Lightworkers in embodiment, the holocaust, cataclysmic destruction of the Earth and Humanity as foretold in St. John's Revelations HAS BEEN AVERTED.

Now, through the God Victorious Accomplishment of the Divine Mission which Archangel Michael, Mother Mary and Archangel Gabriel called us to do, ST. JOHN'S REVELATION WAS FULFILLED. The final stage of the plan, *"casting Satan from the Earth,"* freed us to Ascend into the Permanent Golden Age of Enlightenment and Eternal Peace.

August 18, 1996

On that sacred day, John the Beloved and the entire Company of Heaven amplified the Flame of Divine Grace blazing on the altar in the Inner Sanctuary of the Holy Cities over Arizona. As this occurred, the collective force of "cosmic evil," held in our embrace of Divine Love, was bathed in the Grace of God and lifted into the timeless, spaceless Eternal Moment of Now. In an act of unprecedented Divine Grace, this incredibly destructive negative force which had been wreaking havoc throughout the whole of Creation for literally billions of years was given the opportunity to transmute ALL of its past transgressions of the Laws of Harmony and Love in *"the twinkling of an eye."*

As this force of "cosmic evil" basked in the mercy of Divine Grace, millions of lifetimes of negativity passed before its mind's eye and, through the Grace of God, the Law of Forgiveness transmuted every electron of misqualified energy back into its original Divine Intent.

As this merciful activity of Light progressed at inner levels, in the outer world of form, Humanity was equally blessed with the Grace of God. After being entrapped in the grip of "cosmic evil" and buried in the tar-like substance that oozed into the very fiber of our Beings, we were sorely in need of healing. After the removal of "cosmic evil," the atomic and sub-atomic substance on Earth that comprises every cell and organ of our bodies and the body of Mother Earth was like a raw, open wound. Our Father-Mother God granted a Cosmic Dispensation, and through Divine Grace we, too, were given an unprecedented opportunity to heal. The Lords of Power associated with the Flame of Healing through the Power of Limitless Transmutation received permission from our God Parents to amplify the Emerald Green Flame with Its Amethyst Radiance through every part of life on Earth and *instantly,* in "the twinkling of an eye," our tormented, battered cells were bathed in the Light of God and lifted into the embrace of the Holy Comforter.

For 48 hours this healing process continued.

August 19, 1996

On that special day, the Light of God flowed through the bodies of Humanity into the wounded, battered cells, molecules, atoms, electrons, sub-atomic particles, down to the most minute expression of life in the body of Mother Earth.

Our pain and suffering was gently released into the Flame of Healing through the Power of Limitless Transmutation, and all of the residue of the negative effects of "cosmic evil" was transmuted into the Light.

After the healing was complete in the Realms of Cause, all life on Earth was bathed in the Light of the Twelve Solar Aspects of Deity of our Father-Mother God. This prepared each soul for a unique gift of healing that had never been attempted before.

"Implants" are the most destructive tools used by "cosmic evil" to keep Humanity entrapped in negativity and accessible to its manipulation. The Beings of Light from the Realms of Truth have reiterated to us time and time again that NO BEING OF LIGHT WOULD EVER ENTICE A PERSON INTO RECEIVING AN IMPLANT OF ANY KIND. Implants are *always* designed to manipulate and control and do not have the ability to heal or accelerate our Spiritual growth. They are a trick, and the information given to us that indicates they can benefit us in any way is ALWAYS A LIE.

In order to free Humanity from these tools of deception and manipulation, our God Parents invoked our God Presences and gave each of our God Presences the opportunity to use the accelerated influx of Healing Light to short-circuit *all* of the implants that "cosmic evil" had placed in our four Earthly bodies from any time frame or dimension.

The God Presence of every man, woman and child gave permission for this Divine Intervention, and as a result EVERY IMPLANT, EVERY CORD, EVERY INSTRUMENT OF MANIPULATION in every Human Being and the body of Mother Earth, as well, was short-circuited, removed and transmuted into Light. The wounds from these un-Godly implants were bathed in the Light of Healing and Comfort. **Then, our God Presences were once again able to gain dominion over our physical, etheric, mental and emotional bodies.**

August 20, 1996

With our God Presences once again restored to Their rightful authority over our four lower bodies, this day was dedicated to the Violet Flame of Limitless Transmutation. The God Presences of ALL Humanity invoked the Violet Flame in, through and around the cause, core, effect, record and memory of every thought, word, action or feeling ever released that did not express the Divine Intent of Heaven on Earth. The Violet Flame transmuted Humanity's negativity the maximum that Cosmic Law would allow and prepared us for our Ascension into the Fourth Dimension.

August 21, 1996

On this momentous day, our Father-Mother God breathed this Earth and all Her life into a higher consciousness of Divine Grace than we had ever been able to bear. This healing essence bathed every particle of life on Earth in its merciful essence. Then, through arisen Humanity, God's Divine Grace was projected in, through and around the consciousness of every aspect of "cosmic evil" and prepared these fallen souls for the final stages of their redemption process.

Our Father-Mother God invoked Cosmic Solar Angels of Limitless Forgiveness, Transmutation, Mercy, Compassion, Divine Justice, Liberty and Victory into the atmosphere of Earth. These exponents of the Violet Flame encircled the collective force of "cosmic evil" gathered in the Golden Throne Room in the Holy Cities of John the Beloved and stood shoulder-to-shoulder around these fallen lifestreams. They blazed the Violet Flame into the last vestiges of "cosmic evil's" misqualified thoughts, words, actions and feelings.

As this merciful activity of Divine Grace accelerated, "cosmic evil" realized through all levels of consciousness that its days of perpetuating mischief, pain and suffering were over. With that inner knowing of the Truth, *every* fallen soul associated with the force of "cosmic evil" surrendered to the Divine Will of God and released every remaining thought pattern of miscreation it had ever formed into the Violet Flame of Limitless Transmutation.

As "cosmic evil" released the negative thought patterns, the Violet Flame fulfilled Its Divine Intent, and every remaining misqualified thought, word, action or feeling that these wayward souls had ever expressed, known or unknown, throughout infinity, was instantly transmuted into Light.

After this activity of Limitless Transmutation, our Father-Mother God breathed higher frequencies of the Grace of God into the force of "cosmic evil," and these fallen souls were lifted into a new Octave of Illumined Truth. In this new state of awareness, "cosmic evil" began to perceive the Truth of its own God Reality.

Each fallen soul saw the radiant splendor of its Solar Christ Presence, and it remembered, *"I Am" a child of God.* In humble awe and wonder, every fallen soul surrendered to its own Divinity.

As one breath, one heartbeat, one voice and one consciousness, the redeemed force of "cosmic evil" affirmed:

> *"I AM" a Child of God on the return journey in consciousness to the House of my Father-Mother God. I do believe and accept my inevitable, instantaneous, miraculous and complete transformation into Solar Christ Consciousness.*
>
> *As I reach this Cosmic Moment in my life, "I AM" PURIFYING, PURIFYING, PURIFYING my fallen consciousness with Sacred Fire through every thought, feeling, word, action and reaction in my life.*
>
> *"I AM" now building a life in Christ Consciousness.*

As this Truth resonated in the Heart Flame of each fallen soul, the redemption process continued, and "cosmic evil" Ascended into the Truth of its original Divine Intent and accepted and knew:

> *" I AM" a Being of Light...an emanation of my Father-Mother God.*
>
> *The Light "I AM" is the Consciousness of God in action...and as it is in every other realm, so it is now through me.   "I AM" that "I AM".*

After "cosmic evil" accepted the realization of its own Divinity, all was in readiness for the next step of the Divine Plan.

Under the direction of Archangel Michael, the Galactic Solar Beings of the **Ring-Pass-Not of God's First Cause of Perfection** descended from out of the Great, Great Silence and entered the Golden Throne Room of Divine

Grace in the Temple of John the Beloved where the re-deemed souls of "cosmic evil" were gathered.

In one Mighty Stroke, These exponents of the *Ring-Pass-Not of God's First Cause of Perfection* projected an invincible forcefield of this Divine Light around the re-deemed force of "cosmic evil" and encapsulated all of these souls in the invincible Light of God, thus offering them safe but *secured* passage into the Temple of the First Initiation. This forcefield of Light prevented a single fallen soul from changing its mind and allowed each and every single expression of "cosmic evil" to be safely escorted into its next learning experience.

One Forcefield of the Temple of the First Initiation, which is the Initiation into the Reverence for All Life, pulsates above a sacred mountain near Tucson, Arizona. The mountain is called Mt. Lemmon. Another focus of the Temple of Reverence for All Life pulsates above the Focus of the Grand Teton Mountain Range near Jackson Hole, Wyoming.

On *August 21, 1996*, the redeemed force of "cosmic evil" was escorted in the Ring-Pass-Not of God's First Cause of Perfection into the Temple of the First Initiation of Reverence for All Life above Mt. Lemmon. There, this redeemed force was taught to revere *every* particle of life.

When Cosmic Events begin to filter through the ethers, Humanity perceives the moment at hand at various levels of awareness. If we will be observant, we will see outer world confirmation of the Truth of the moment.

The booklet *Daily Word* is distributed by Unity to mil-lions of people throughout the World. On *August 21, 1996*, "cosmic evil" surrendered into the Light and accepted the Truth of its own Divinity.

The sharing in the *Daily Word* for *August 21, 1996*, was:

TODAY, I BREAK THE BONDS OF NEGATIVITY
AND CLEAR THE WAY FOR HARMONY!

THE EARTH ASCENDS
INTO THE FOURTH DIMENSION

August 22, 1996

After the redeemed force of "cosmic evil" was bound in the Ring-Pass-Not of God's First Cause of Perfection and transferred to the Temple of the First Initiation by Archangel Michael and His Legions of Angels, we were ready to fulfill the FINAL WORDS OF ST. JOHN'S REVELATIONS. We were ready to complete our Ascension process into the Fourth Dimension. We were ready to begin our unified preparation for our Solar Passage into the Fifth Dimension. As overwhelmingly awesome as that sounds, that is exactly what transpired on *August 22, 1996*.

The difference between what St. John's Revelation prophesied would happen and what actually occurred is that through the Grace of God, Divine Intervention and the unified efforts of awakened Lightworkers embodied on Earth, *every man, woman and child, every Elemental and every Angel belonging to or serving the Earth at this time, was granted a cosmic dispensation of Divine Grace by our Father-Mother God and given permission to Ascend onto our next Spiral of Evolution*—the Fourth Dimension. **Divine Grace** is an activity of the Godhead that FORGIVES and REDEEMS far beyond what we deserve. It is only through the incredible mercy of **Divine Grace** that this miracle could have occurred. But, occur it did, and on that sacred and holy day, this sweet Earth and all Her life Ascended into the Fourth Dimension.

With the final Crystal Grid activation on *August 22, 1996*, the Earth and all life evolving upon Her accelerated in energy, vibration and consciousness. Then, as the Light of Polaris blazed through the North Pole and the Light of Magnus blazed through the South Pole into the axis of Mother Earth, all Humanity and the entire Company of

Heaven serving the Earth joined hearts, heads and hands with the Builders of Form—the Mighty Elohim; the Directors of the Five Elements: earth, air, water, fire and ether; ALL Solar Angels, Galactic and Cosmic Beings throughout Infinity; and the omniscient, omnipresent, omnipotent Presence of God.

Through this collective Body of Divinity, as one heartbeat, one breath, one energy, vibration and consciousness of Divine Love, we breathed forth, from the very Core of Creation, the most intensified activity of the Ascension Flame ever manifested in the history of time. As this Sacred Flame poured into the core of purity pulsating in the center of every electron of life energy on Earth, this precious Planet Ascended back into the embrace of the rest of our Solar System and completed her Ascension into the Fourth Dimension.

This was the quantum leap we were hoping to complete by the year *2012*. This was the **Ascension**, the **Rapture** that we have always known would bring us into alignment for our Solar Passage into the Fifth Dimension where we will permanently and tangibly transform this Planet into Her Divine Solar Birthright and Her original Divine Intent, which is Heaven on Earth.

The Earth has made Her long-awaited orbital shift into the parallel Universe of the Fourth Dimension. In one final quantum leap, She completed Her Ascension onto Her next Spiral of Evolution. She has donned Her Seamless Garment of Light, and She now stands in readiness for the final stages of preparation that will allow Her Solar Passage into the pure land of boundless splendor and infinite Light—the Fifth Dimension.

The sharing in the Daily Word for *August 22, 1996*, was:

I TOUCH THE LIFE OF GOD,
AND I SOAR TO NEW HEIGHTS!

HEALING THE RESIDUE
OF WAR AND HUMAN CONFLICT

The next phase of the Divine Plan involved healing the etheric records and the wounds of the consciousness of war and human conflict on Earth. Once "cosmic evil" was removed and the Earth was vibrating at Fourth Dimensional frequencies, it was infinitely easier to clear the etheric records of the atrocities Humanity has perpetrated on each other throughout history.

Because all frequencies of hate and war are interrelated and since World War II represented, through the atom bomb, Humanity's greatest abuse of power, the archetype of World War II was used by the Company of Heaven and the Lightworkers on Earth to dissipate and transmute ALL archetypes of war.

We were asked by the Company of Heaven to hold our sixth free seminar for *1996* near the forcefield of Muir Woods in Northern California.

Fifty is the Pentacostal number that represents the Baptism of the Holy Spirit. The Holy Spirit is the Divine Mother Principle, our Mother God, Who reflects the Love of God on Earth.

The Comet Chiron returns to Earth approximately every *50 years* and is the healer of wounds, pain and hurts in the human psyche. The healing it brings allows our wounded human self to move into our healed Divine Self.

The Comet Hyakutake brings the "Presence of the Love of God to Earth" (Holy Spirit). Comet Hyakutake was discovered by an amateur astronomer from JAPAN—the location where our greatest abuse of power (the atom bomb) was used *50 years* ago during World War II.

On *September 6, 1996=22*, (the number 22 is a master number carrying the momentum of Power on ALL Planes), Lightworkers were drawn into Muir Woods in Northern California. Muir Woods is the location where the United

Nations was formed *50 years* ago.

On *May 19, 1945*, world leaders from all over the Globe gathered amidst the 600-year-old Redwood Trees—and within nature's resplendent "Cathedral of Peace," consecrated their life energies to healing the Earth and the Family of Humanity. Because "cosmic evil" still had the Earth in its paralyzing grip at that time, the Divine Intent of the United Nations was not fulfilled.

On *September 6, 1996*, the healing effects of the Comets Chiron and Hyakutake still pulsated through the Earth, and our Liberation from the force of "cosmic evil" was expanding. Our Father-Mother God breathed the Breath of Life through the Heart Flames of Lightworkers gathered in Muir Woods into the archetype of war and all of the atrocities associated with war and human conflict of any kind. This activity of Light dissipated the consciousness of war and human conflict the maximum that Cosmic Law would allow. The Etheric Records of all human conflicts were transmuted through the Law of Divine Grace and returned to the Light of God.

Then, our Father-Mother God breathed the Breath of Life into the matrix of the United Nations. Through the God Selves of all world leaders associated with the United Nations, our Father-Mother God projected the consciousness of Reverence for ALL Life and the Divine Intent of the United Nations. This new level of Enlightened Consciousness will gradually filter into the world leaders' minds and hearts and transform their consciousness of war and human conflict into the consciousness of Eternal Peace.

As Lightworkers, we have the responsiblity not to empower, with fear or the power of our attention, the antics of the rebellious human egos of world leaders that may result in skirmishes in various pockets of past confusion on the Planet. Instead, we need to consistently invoke the Light of Eternal Peace and Enlightenment into the consciousness of every world leader, and blaze, daily and hourly, the Violet

Flame of Limitless Transmutation through all thoughts, words, actions and feelings of human conflict anywhere on Earth.

ARCHANGEL MICHAEL RETURNS "COSMIC EVIL" TO THE HEART OF GOD

September 22, 1996

On *September 22, 1996=11*, (11 is a master number that reflects the transformation of physical life into a Spiritual Reality). Every soul that has ever been associated with "cosmic evil" was transferred from the Temple of the First Initiation over Mount Lemmon in Tucson, Arizona, to the Temple of Reverence for All Life over the Grand Tetons in Wyoming. That is the open portal between Heaven and Earth through which Archangel Michael descended, escorting the first inhabitants to Earth, the first Root Race, billions of years ago. It was quite fitting for Archangel Michael to escort "cosmic evil" back to the Heart of our Father-Mother God through that same portal.

To prepare our Chalice in the Tetons, we needed to focus our attention on this marvelous forcefield of Light. It was not by chance that for ten days leading up to *August 21, 1996*, President Clinton vacationed at the Grand Tetons, and the media bathed the consciousness of the World with beautiful images of the Grand Teton Mountains.

Wy-OM-ing

The word WyOMing is a Native American Indian word with links to the Inca and Mayan civilizations. The Native Americans named geographic locations with tonal frequencies that expressed unique energetic qualities. The sound WyOMing translates to, **"Land Where the Mother Goddess Is Loved."** The qualities contained in the ancient sound reflect receptivity, spaciousness, creativity, inclusivity and generosity.

The metaphysical dimensions of WyOMing extend from the core of the Earth to the center of the Galaxy. WyOMing pulsates with a tangible closeness to the Sun of Even Pressure in the center of the Earth and opens an unobstructed portal to the Celestial Center of the Galaxy.

The *Autumn Equinox* is the moment when the Sun conjuncts the super Galactic Center and the Universe breathes out the Breath of Life to the Cosmos. On the *Autumn Equinox that year, September 22, 1996=11, at 11:11 am..* Wyoming time (MDT), an event took place that will be recorded in the annals of history for our Universe for all Eternity.

On that sacred and holy day as the Universe breathed out the Breath of Life to the Cosmos, our Father-Mother God breathed in to the very Core of Creation in the super Galactic Center, the collective redeemed force formerly known as "cosmic evil." These redeemed souls, held in the embrace of the Ring-Pass-Not of God's First Cause of Perfection and escorted by Beloved Archangel Michael, returned to the very Heart of God to be repolarized and reinstated to their original Divine Intent as Sons and Daughters of God.

This merciful activity of Divine Grace brought to God Victorious Fruition the Revelation of St. John in which he proclaimed, *"In the latter days, Satan will be bound and cast from the Earth."*

Through this activity of Light "cosmic evil" was LOVED ETERNALLY FREE, never again to adversely affect any part of the Universe.

OUR FATHER-MOTHER GOD
FORGIVE THE SINS OF THE WORLD!!!

In the Piscean Age now ending, it was stated that *"Jesus died for our sins and forgave the sins of the World."* As we reach into the Realms of Illumined Truth, the true meaning of that statement and the Truth of Jesus' mission are being revealed.

Of course, Jesus didn't **"die"** for our sins. The whole purpose of His crucifixion and Resurrection was to prove to all the World that there is no amount of betrayal or treachery that Humanity's human egos can inflict on a soul that will destroy the Divinity of the Christ within. Jesus did not die. In fact, His Holy Christ Self Resurrected His physical body into His immortal Light Body to demonstrate that the Christ is Eternal.

In order to get the attention of the World and leave a lasting impression, His demonstration had to be dramatic. If Jesus had "died" in His bedroom of a heart attack and Resurrected His body, He would have gotten very little public attention. But, when He was reviled and crucified for all the World to see and then Resurrected His body, He created the spectacle that was needed to demonstrate the immortality of the Christ to the World.

Nevertheless, Beloved Jesus **did** forgive the sins of the World. A very important facet of His Divine Mission was that He brought to the Earth in the Piscean Age the *Law of Forgiveness*. Prior to the Law of Forgiveness, the Earth functioned under the Universal Law of Cause and Effect, literally, *"An eye for an eye, a tooth for a tooth."*

With the coming of the Age of Pisces, a dispensation was granted by our Father-Mother God to allow Humanity to *"ask to be forgiven, and so it is."* In addition to this merciful act of Divine Grace, Jesus was given permission to forgive the sins of the World.

As Jesus hung on the cross invoking forgiveness for all Humanity, *"Forgive them, Father, for they know not what they do,"* the Centurion came with a sword and pierced Jesus' side to accelerate His "death" and end His suffering. When Jesus' blood poured onto the Earth, the LIFE FORCE OF THE CHRIST flowed through the Etheric Body of the

Earth and transmuted, through the Law of Forgiveness, every electron of precious life energy that had ever been misqualified by Humanity through the misuse of our creative faculties of thought and feeling.

Every negative thought, word, action or feeling from **that moment** back to the initial impulse of the "fall" was forgiven and transmuted into Light. Needless to say, that was an incredible gift of love. Unfortunately, its effects were fairly short-lived. Our rebellious, recalcitrant human egos and the overwhelming ability "cosmic evil" had to manipulate our egos to do its will caused us to begin immediately rebuilding the sea of negativity around the Earth.

All we have to do is observe the atrocities Humanity has perpetrated on each other and the Earth over the past 2,000 years to see that the psychic-astral realm of human miscreation has been recreated and is thriving. Our negative thoughts and feelings have been wreaking havoc in our lives. Now, if we will just imagine that the force of "cosmic evil" was amplifying our negativity probably a thousand times a thousand fold, it becomes very clear why we have been in such a mess. But IT IS OVER!!!

On the *Autumn Equinox, September 22, 1996*, once the force of "cosmic evil" was returned to the Heart of God, a Divine Fiat was issued by our Father-Mother God.

Through the collective Solar Christ Presence of ALL Humanity, the life force of our Father-Mother God poured onto Earth and transmuted every remaining electron of precious life energy Humanity has recreated since Jesus forgave the sins of the World!

At **12:12** p.m. (MDT), the Light of God flowed through the collective Solar Christ Presence of ALL Humanity and forgave the sins of the World!

Every remaining electron of precious life energy that had ever been misqualified by any man, woman or child evolving on Earth was forgiven and transmuted into Light through the Law of Divine GRACE.

That activity of Light shifted our reality on Earth into a KARMA-FREE REALITY!

This literally means that EACH AND EVERY ONE OF US, AT THIS VERY MOMENT, IS **KARMA FREE!!!**

We still have Free Will. We still have our human egos, and we still have the ability to misqualify our thoughts, words, actions and feelings to recreate chaos in our lives. But, if we choose not to, if we choose to revere our gift of life and use our creative faculties to add to the Light of the World, we can transform our lives into expressions of joy, love, abundance, happiness and every other *manifestation* of Divinity we desire.

Without the interference of "cosmic evil," it is going to be **infinitely** easier to control our egos and command that wayward, dysfunctional aspect of our personalities into the Light.

Since "cosmic evil" was taken into the forcefield of Divine Grace on *August 21st*, I have witnessed an unusual phenomenon that I would like to share with you as a word of encouragement. "Cosmic evil" was the strength and power behind our human egos that gave our egos the confidence to fight us so tenaciously. Now that back-up support system is not there to empower our human egos, and they are terrified. Consequently, they are raging out of control to try and make us believe that they are still powerful and still the masters of our lives. I'm sure each one of you could tell me of an instance since *August 21st, 1996*, in which your ego went amuck.

If we will just look at this with patience, we will see that our egos are behaving exactly like the Wizard of Oz. They are acting out just like the little, befuddled man behind the curtain trying to manipulate things to project a big, menacing image on the screen of life so that they can intimidate us into doing their will and believing that they are still in control. It is vital that we now know and accept the Truth that OUR EGOS HAVE NEVER BEEN LESS POWERFUL!!!

If you will just think of your ego in that Light and flood it with love as you command it into the Light, it will stop resisting and release itself into the arms of your Solar Christ Presence.

A KARMA-FREE NEW BEGINNING

12:12

12:12 is a number that reflects the sacred Geometry of this Solar System. 12 x 12=144. It also reflects the frequency of our Ascension into Solar Reality. At *12:12 p.m.* on *September 22, 1996*, Lightworkers gathered at the summit of Signal Mountain in the Grand Tetons to form a Chalice through which the Light of God could pour to forgive the sins of the World. That paved the way for our Solar Passage into the Fifth Dimension. The summit of Signal Mountain is 7,593 feet, 7+5 and 9+3=12:12. Interestingly, we celebrated the Jewish New Year, Rosh Hashanah, on *September 14, 1996*. It is the year 5757 on the Jewish Calendar; 5+7 and 5+7=12:12.

Goddess of Liberty

On the *Autumn Equinox, September 22, 1996*, which is the first impulse of the Forcefield of Liberty to the Earth each year (Libra), the Goddess of Liberty projected Her luminous Presence to envelope the entire Planet Earth. The Earth is now resting within Her Heart Flame, and She is Liberating every part of life from the memory of the old Karmic patterns and genetic codes that our egos are trying to recreate out of fear. The Violet Flame of Liberty is also flooding the Planet and transmuting the negative thoughts, words, actions and feelings being recreated each day by

Humanity.

We have a new level of accountability now, and we must be eternally vigilant in monitoring, every moment, just how we are using our gift of life. If we are not expressing our highest Divine Intent, we must invoke the Flame of Liberty through the misqualified energy and transmute it back into its original perfection.

It's difficult to grasp the full magnitude of just what occurred on *September 22, 1996*, but we are now singing the Song of Creation, and our visions of the New Heaven and the New Earth are manifesting in tangible form.

September 26, 1996

On *September 26, 1996*, we experienced a very rare, total *Full Moon Lunar Eclipse*. All of the Divine Light that entered the Earth during the *Full Moon Lunar Eclipse* on *April 3, 1996*, reached a crescendo during the *September 26th Full Moon Lunar Eclipse*. At that time, the visions that our Solar Christ Presences absorbed from the Divine Heart and Mind of God on *April 3rd*, were projected through all levels of our new Karma-Free Realities and anchored through all levels of our consciousness.

Saturn, the Planet of physical experience, was held in the embrace of the Lunar Eclipse, and through the forcefield of Aries, it infinitely expanded its Divine Qualities through every facet of our Earthly experience for the first time since the "fall," unimpeded by past Karmic liabilities. This allowed a whole new octave of unmanifest potential to flood the Earth from the Core of Creation.

This increased the Goddess of Liberty's (Libra's) ability to Liberate Humanity from the cause, core, effect, record and memory of the residue of old Karmic patterns and genetic codes. This Liberation freed us to soar to new heights. Our Solar Christ Presences tapped new Octaves of Spiritual Knowledge in the Heart and Mind of God. We each

Ascended into new levels of understanding at inner levels and reached into higher frequencies of unmanifest Divine Potential.

Through the Realms of Cause, new ideas for our Karma-Free Reality are now filtering into our conscious minds. During the *Lunar Eclipse of September 26, 1996*, the building process for new Octaves of Divinity began. The sacred New Earth and the sacred New Humanity were born. The visionaries and those who are reaching into the Divine Mind of God to bring to Humanity the Divine Ideas for Planetary Transformation are moving to the forefront.

During this critical moment on Earth, Lightworkers are being raised into positions of influence in order to focus Humanity's attention on sustainable, viable changes through practical, orthodox means. The Earth Summit brought to the forefront many leaders committed to healing the Earth. During the Earth Summit, I had the opportunity to be involved in an event that had Vice President Al Gore as a keynote speaker. He has written a book on the environment, and he is determined to reverse Humanity's destruction of the Earth. During his speech to a large group that included many children and men as well as women, he said that in order to change the direction we are headed, more women must get involved in every facet of the political, economic and social arenas. He said he believes much of the masculine consciousness has not aligned with the love and nurturing feminine qualities necessary to turn things around on the Planet.

I believe he was speaking both literally and metaphorically. His words reflected our abuse of masculine power and the suppression of the Divine Feminine in each of us, individually and collectively. The reason I mention Al Gore is so that we can all experience the wonderful synchronicity of the Divine Plan now unfolding.

Since the healing that took place at the Earth Summit, we have been catapulted forward by leaps and bounds to the present moment of TRANSFIGURATION.

We are now creating a new paradigm in a Karma-Free Reality. With the *New Covenant* between Humanity and the Elemental Kingdom that took place at the Earth Summit in *1992*, and the removal of "cosmic evil" and the forgiveness of our past Karmic liabilities that took place in *1996*, everything was in place for the next phase of the Divine Plan. We were ready, through an activity of Divine Alchemy, to integrate and merge, *at a cellular level*, with our Solar Light Bodies.

To fully understand the magnitude of just what that means, we must realize that our Solar Light Bodies vibrate at a frequency of Limitless Physical Perfection. They pulsate at a vibrational frequency above *any* octave of discord. That literally means the maladies of aging, degeneration, disease and death cannot exist in these Bodies.

We have always known that after Armageddon, when Heaven manifests on Earth, disease, aging, death and dying as we know it, will no longer exist. We just didn't know exactly how that would occur. We have always held onto the belief that we are so incredibly worthless and incapable we can't possibly assist in the process of our own Transformation. But, the Realms of Illumined Truth are revealing the natural process to us. And, guess what? Our personal physical TRANSFIGURATION into our Solar Light Bodies will be a JOINT EFFORT between Heaven and Earth. We *must* consciously participate in this process in order to succeed and, as always, *we are receiving miraculous assistance from On High.*

We arranged to have our Sixth Free Seminar for *1996* in Atlanta, Georgia, on *December 8, 1996.*

December 8th is celebrated in the outer world as the day of Mother Mary's *Immaculate Conception*. This honors the day Mother Mary was conceived without original sin. In our modern terminology we would say that She was conceived without Karma or Karma-Free. Her birthday is celebrated nine months later on September 8th.

The SYMBOLOGY of Her conception reflects the Truth that the Christ will be conceived within pure, Karma-Free vehicles.

When Mother Mary conceived Jesus, it was called the *Miraculous Conception*, which SYMBOLICALLY reflects the Truth that the Christ will be conceived through the perfect balance of the Divine Feminine and the Divine Masculine within each soul's Karma-Free vehicles.

On *December 6, 1996*, Vice President Al Gore came to Tucson, Arizona, for an event that was being held at Ventana Canyon Resort. This resort pulsates within the permanent seed atom of the Flame of Healing through the Power of Limitless Transmutation. This Emerald Green Flame with a Violet radiance is the most powerful frequency of Healing on Earth. The sacred essence of that Flame was anchored within Al Gore's Heart Flame and the Heart Flames of the people in his entourage by their God Presences. After his speech in Tucson, they all went directly to Bolivia, magnetizing with them the Flame of Healing through the Power of Limitless Transmutation.

Bolivia is the location where the Feminine Polarity of God enters the Earth as a tremendous shaft of Divine Love. (The Masculine Polarity of God enters the Earth in the Himalaya Mountains near Tibet.) At the same time that Al Gore and his entourage were traveling to Bolivia, several of us from Tucson went from the Forcefield of the Flame of Healing through the Power of Limitless Transmutation to the focus of the Record Keeper Crystals at Stone Mountain in Atlanta, Georgia, to prepare for our Free Seminar that was going to be held on *December 8th*. There it was revealed to us that due to the wondrous Victories of *1996*, Humanity was finally ready for the *Immaculate Conception of our Solar*

Christ Presences in Their Solar Light Bodies. These Bodies will be our Earthly Vehicles in the new Solar Reality.

During the seminar in Atlanta on December 8th, the Flame of Healing through the Power of Limitless Transmutation blazed through the Forcefield of the Divine Feminine in Bolivia into the center of the Earth. The Healing Unguent expanded through the Sun of Even Pressure in the center of the Earth into the Crystal Grid System and prepared the physical, etheric, mental and emotional strata of the Earth for the Immaculate Conception of our Solar Vehicles.

As this preparation occurred, the Record Keeper Crystals in Stone Mountain released the Divine Blueprint for the TRANSFIGURATION of our four lower bodies into our Solar Light Bodies. This Divine Blueprint blazed through all levels of consciousness and interpenetrated every electron of precious life energy on Earth. As this occurred, the genetic codes in Humanity's physical, etheric, mental and emotional bodies were imprinted with the Solar DNA of our Solar Light Bodies.

This activity of Light was very complex, but in simple terms it means that our actual genetic codes at a cellular level were imprinted with the Divine Blueprint of our Solar Light Bodies.

Through a process of Divine Alchemy, our Solar Christ Presences then began the process of transforming our actual cells from base physical elemental substance into a frequency of Light that will be able to withstand the higher vibrations of our Solar Christ Presences.

The Divine Alchemy built in momentum for four days, reflecting through one of our four lower bodies each day, first the physical, then the etheric, then the mental, then the emotional.

On ***December 12, 1996=12:12***, all was in readiness for the final step of preparation. On that sacred and holy day, through Divine Ceremonies that took place at both inner and outer levels, the Sacred Heart of every man, woman and child was prepared for the *Immaculate Conception of our Solar Christ Presences in their Solar Light Bodies*. **December 12th** is the day that is dedicated to the Virgin of Guadalupe and carries the full expression of the Divine Feminine that expands from Bolivia throughout South America and Mexico. It is a holy day that expresses the Love Nature of the Divine Mother as well as the numerical fiat (*12:12*) which contains the Sacred Geometry for our Solar Passage into the Fifth Dimension.

The Divine Ceremonies performed that day actually by-passed all blocks and resistance to our new Solar Light Bodies at a heart level and prepared the Sacred Heart blazing in every Human Being to birth the Solar Christ within. The gestation period took nine days. Then, **AS THE LIGHT OF THE WINTER SOLSTICE BLESSED THE EARTH ON *DECEMBER 21, 1996*, THE EMBRYONIC SOLAR CHRIST PRESENCE IN ITS SOLAR LIGHT BODIES WAS BORN IN THE SACRED HEART OF EVERY HUMAN BEING EVOLVING ON EARTH.**

This is the very first time since we volunteered to descend into a Third Dimensional physical reality that our Solar Christ Presences in Their Solar Light Bodies have been able to connect with our four Earthly vehicles at a physical level through our Sacred Hearts. Previously, this aspect of our God Presence was only able to reach our hearts through muted, stepped-down frequencies. Those frequencies became grossly distorted in the physical plane of Earth after the fall. The birth of our Solar Christ Presences within our Sacred Hearts was a *vitally* important step in preparation for our Solar Passage into the Fifth Dimension. It was accomplished God Victoriously!!!

Now, we will have a plethora of opportunities to expand our Sacred Hearts so that our embryonic Solar Christ Presences can grow in leaps and bounds.

The most important thing we need to do is surrender our lower human egos to the perfection of our Solar Christ

Presences. Daily and hourly this simple affirmation will accelerate the Divine Alchemy of our Ascension into our Solar Light Bodies.

"I AM" surrendering all aspects of my human ego into
the loving embrace and full dominion of my
Solar Christ Presence.

Every single day our Solar Christ Presences will magnetize into our experiences the lessons and opportunities that are right and perfect. Each lesson and opportunity will be designed to accelerate our individual preparation for our Victorious Ascension into our Solar Reality in the Fifth Dimension.

Be alert and observant!
Be in the moment!
Pay attention!
Listen to your heart!
Respond! Respond! Respond!
Be God in Action!

Cosmic Moments come and Cosmic Moments go!

Grasp this Cosmic Moment. It is an opportunity unprecedented in the history of all Creation.

As we moved into *1997*, we were blessed with several Celestial gifts from the Heavenly Bodies that surround the Earth. In January we began to feel the rumblings of the massive changes that were coming in *1997* to literally and tangibly change the course of history. It was a uniquely powerful time for new beginnings and personal, as well as Global transformation. We are experiencing the Enlightenment of the Planet. We are being brought into alignment with Divine Will, and we have new opportunities to bring an awakened level of leadership to all levels of our communities and our governments at national, state and local levels. This awakened leadership is ready to burst upon the screen of life in every facet of our Earthly existence. In *1997*, we will see both grassroots and Global changes as we birth a Spiritually-motivated Planetary Consciousness which will create extraordinary potentials for growth, self-realization and evolution.

The quality of information will improve as we experience an expanded dissemination of Sacred Knowledge.

We are now integrating physical and Spiritual Realms which allow us to evolve and mature, both Spiritually and genetically. We are physically able to integrate more Light, and we are experiencing our own metamorphosis.

The foundations of responsible inner work are being laid as we revolutionize our Spiritual and personal freedoms.

Our commitment to Truth is changing the order of the Planet as we let go of our outmoded habits and beliefs.

The Divine is breathing the winds of change through the very fiber of our Beings, and we are learning how to honor all life and all living things. We must now put into practice all we know about Compassion, Tolerance and Divine Love.

After the acceleration of energy, vibration and consciousness that took place on a Global scale in January, we were in a position to permanently anchor the Chalice of Healing that had been building in momentum for almost three years.

In *February 1997*, we brought to fruition the Final Victory of our Chalice of Healing that was created through the tragic deaths of Nicole Brown Simpson and Ron Goldman.

The O.J. Simpson saga seemed endless, but at long last...It is done! And, So It Is!

Throughout *1996*, and the initial impulse of *1997*, we experienced the final phase of the Divine Plan for our Collective Chalice of Healing that has been building in momentum for almost three years. That was the phase in which the Divine Healing Light to heal the imbalance between our masculine and feminine selves reached a crescendo and was sealed in the core of purity in every electron of precious life energy on Earth, establishing once and for all a PERMANENT BALANCE between our DIVINE FEMININE and our DIVINE MASCULINE SELVES.

This phase of the Divine Plan also contained within its frequencies the blueprint for healing the old archetypes that reflect our masculine abuse of power. And it contained the new archetypes that will allow us to shift into a whole new paradigm of REVERENCE FOR ALL LIFE.

Once again, in order to Victoriously accomplish that goal, the collective focus of Humanity's attention was critical. It was not enough, however, for us to just focus our attention on O.J. Simpson's civil suit and the impending outcome. We also needed to focus our attention on new options and alternative plans that reflect Oneness and Reverence for ALL Life.

A Divine Plan was set into motion in cooperation with the entire Company of Heaven and the Solar Christ Presences of all Humanity. On *February 4, 1997*, the jury for the civil suit which was brought against O.J. Simpson by the families of Nicole Brown Simpson and Ron Goldman reached a verdict.

This was, *not coincidentally*, the same day that was scheduled for President Clinton's State of the Union Address. The media announced in the afternoon that the verdict had been reached, and it would be read in the early evening.

The President's speech was scheduled to begin at 6:00 p.m. California time. The fervor over the impending announcement of the O.J. Simpson verdict drew the attention of millions of Americans and people around the World who would probably never have even considered tuning in for President Clinton's State of the Union Address.

In Divine Order, the announcement of the verdict did not come prior to President Clinton's speech. Consequently, there was a tremendous "captive" audience that heard the words describing the blueprint for the new paradigm of Oneness and Reverence for ALL Life.

It is very important for us to understand that the Divine Plans pouring forth from the Heart and Mind of God are always designed to work toward the highest good for all concerned. It is only our lower human egos which distort and contaminate the Divine Intent of the plans with separation, greed and lack of understanding.

I will repeat the principles discussed in the State of the Union Address. As we focus on the concept of each phase of the plan, we need to set aside our personal agendas and opinions of how to accomplish each step of the plan. Set aside partisan affiliations, and KNOW that when we come together, genuinely striving for the highest good for all concerned, we will reach into the Divine Heart and Mind of God and tap viable, sustainable solutions for all of Earth's maladies.

If we will each lift above our personal opinions, our likes and dislikes, and focus on the message that was given, we will see the **Divine Intervention** involved in the words that bathed the consciousness of all Humanity and brought to fruition the final phase of our *Chalice of Healing.*

President Clinton read a passage from the Bible that reflects this Cosmic Moment and the Divine Intent of the Chalice of Healing.

ISAIAH 58:12

And some of you shall build the old waste places;
you shall raise up the foundations of many generations,
and you shall be called the repairer of the breaches,
the restorer of paths to dwell in.

As you read the principles stated in President Clinton's State of the Union Address, think of this blueprint on a GLOBAL scale.

Key Points in the State of the Union Address:

• The state of our Union is strong.
• Our greatest strength and our greatest asset is our DIVERSITY.
• This is the decisive moment when we must rise to the occasion and make our nation and our World better than any we have ever known.
• We face no imminent threat, but we do have an enemy. The enemy of our time is *inaction*.
• The greatest step of all, the highest threshold to the future we must now cross, is to ensure that our children have the best education in the World.
• We must raise our standards and lift our children up.
• We must all get involved. Every state should assist in turning welfare checks into private sector paychecks. Every religious congregation, every community, non-profit organization and every business should hire someone off of welfare.
• The economy is strong.
• Crime and welfare rolls are declining.
• The Cold War is receding.
• The United States is helping to win peace and prosperity

around the World.
- We must be the shapers of events, not observers.
- The budget can be balanced, and people can be *protected* and *honored* simultaneously.
- Together, we can create viable methods to balance the budget while protecting families and the environment, Medicare, Medicaid, education and Social Security.
- Ethics and integrity will be the cornerstone for electing all political figures.
- Science and advanced computer technology will be available to all Americans [and Humanity] to speed research into health, genetic research, cancer, AIDS, strokes, etc.
- More money will be spent to develop solutions to prevent crime, increase protection and improve judicial systems.
- Tolerance: We must eliminate bigotry and intolerance in our country *and* in our hearts.
- We must work toward Global unification economically, while bringing peace and Humanitarian principles to every land.
- Toxic-waste dumps and our waterways must be cleaned up, and the pristine beauty of the Earth must be protected.

At the conclusion of President Clinton's speech, Congressman J.C. Watts from Oklahoma, the only African-American Republican in Congress, gave his words of support.

J.C.Watts said, "President Clinton was right on target tonight. He said the people want bipartisanship. They do. They want the kind of bipartisanship that results in progress."
Congressman Watts supported the theme of families and family values where mothers and fathers can be the guiding force in their children's lives. He eloquently expressed the need for Americans to love, honor and respect each other as

we work together to heal our separation and our country under God's guiding Hand.

It was *not by chance* that J.C.Watts was chosen for the Republican's comments on the State of the Union Address. Being African-American, he served as a gentle, loving, Spiritual, Peace-Commanding Presence in the face of the possible backlash brewing in Los Angeles. He was a focus of harmony and lifted the entire atmosphere of the moment into one of cooperation and mutual respect.

At the conclusion of the speeches, the unanimous guilty verdict was read, and the Goldman family was awarded compensatory damages of 8.5 million dollars.

Aquarius New Moon

On *February 7, 1997*, we experienced a powerful New Moon in Aquarius. Venus, Uranus and Jupiter were also conjunct each other in Aquarius during the New Moon, which greatly amplified its effect. This unique New Moon brought with it the hope for a future World where unconditional love, harmony, tolerance, balance, cooperation and responsibility prevails. It created an atmosphere that expanded, without limit, the Light of our Healing Chalice and began Humanity's forward movement toward harmonizing ourselves with each other and the Earth.

On *February 10, 1997=11* (symbolizing physical transformation into Spiritual reality), the final step of the O.J. Simpson civil suit was completed, and the jury decided the punitive damages for Nicole Brown Simpson's and Ron Goldman's families.

Even though money can never replace their loss, the money *symbolized* the Victory of the healing that took place through the Chalice of Healing.

8.5 million dollars compensatory damages to the Goldmans. **8** is the symbol for "As above, so below." 1997=**8.**

12.5 punitive damages to the Browns.

12.5 punitive damages to the Goldmans.

12:12 is the Sacred Geometry of our Solar Passage into the Fifth Dimension, which began during the Vernal Equinox in 1997.

_____

33.5 Total moneys assessed. **33** is the Master Number that reflects our Ascension into Christ Consciousness.

The saga has ended, and as always, the Light of God is Eternally Victorious.

Our Chalice of Healing has been anchored in the center of the Earth, and Its Healing Unguent will bless all life until this sweet Earth is wholly Ascended and Free!

It Is Done! And, So It Is!!!

(Related information on pages 226 and 307)

After the Chalice of Healing was anchored in the Center of the Earth, the Light of our Father-Mother God expanded each of us beyond where we had previously been and lovingly pushed us away from old, familiar patterns that no longer served our highest good. They inspired us to move forward toward our true Selves and our true Divine Missions on Earth as They implored us to open up to new, personal paths of excellence.

Changes that we have been needing to make for a lifetime were pushed to the surface of our conscious minds. The only choice we had was to let go and fly or stagnate and perish in the throes of anxiety and fear.

In the outer World another Divine Plan that has been in motion for quite some time was brought to its next level of healing. I will reiterate a little of the background of that Activity of Light so that, once again, we will recognize the magnitude of the opportunity at hand.

Remember, when Humanity fell into the depths of human miscreation, we closed down our Heart Centers so that we would not feel so much pain. This, tragically, blocked the flow of Divine Love from our Mother God. When this occurred, our right brain hemispheres became almost dormant, which caused our brain centers to atrophy. As our pituitary, pineal and hypothalamus glands and the ganglionic centers at the base of our brains began to degenerate and malfunction, it caused our Crown Chakras to close and recede into dormancy. This horrific situation created an imbalance that caused Humanity to begin using our Masculine Polarity—left brains and the Power Centers in our throats—without the balance of our Feminine Polarity—right brains and the Love Centers in our hearts.

Since all life is interrelated, this identical imbalance began to reflect in the body of Mother Earth, as well.

The Feminine Polarity of God enters the Earth as a tremendous shaft of Light in the area of Lake Titicaca in Bolivia, South America, and the Masculine Polarity of God enters the Earth as a tremendous shaft of Light in the area of the Himalayan Mountains near Tibet. When the Feminine Polarity of God—the Divine Love of our Mother God—began to recede on Earth, the portal in South America began to close. Then, for the first time, Humanity began using the Masculine Polarity of God's Power without the balance of Divine Love and Reverence for ALL Life. This created the devastating abuse of our Masculine Polarity of Power by our human egos. That is actually the basis for all of the maladies existing on Earth today. Needless to say, correcting this imbalance is the number one priority in our Ascension Process.

For literally aeons of time, the Company of Heaven, in cooperation with illumined souls on Earth, has implemented one plan after another to try to balance and heal our masculine abuse of power. Very illumined souls embodied in the area of the Himalayan Mountains in Tibet, and tremendous foci of Light were created which expanded throughout the entire Orient.

When the force of "cosmic evil" witnessed the Light building in the Orient, it knew that it needed to block that Light in order to maintain control of the Earth. Consequently, it began manipulating human egos in the area to be its pawns. These fallen souls, empowered by the back-up force of "cosmic evil," created a system of dominance and oppression through the guise of communism. This oppressive system forced Spiritual aspirants into exile and extinguished every attempt made to free the souls living in the area.

In *1989*, the Flame of Freedom was anchored in China through the Heart Flames of the students in Tiananmen Square (see related information on page 137). Even though that activity ended tragically, the Flame of Freedom has been building in momentum daily and hourly in China.

After the first successful Crystal Grid Activation in *August 1987*, awakened Lightworkers and the Company of

Heaven redoubled Their efforts to free the Portal of the Divine Masculine in the area of Tibet and return the Orient to its original Divine Intent as an open Portal for our Father-Mother God.

In the *Summer of 1995*, a Global conference called *The United Nations World Conference on Women* was held in Beijing, China. Tens of thousands of the World's most powerful, influential, caring women were drawn into the Forcefield of the Masculine Polarity of God. Through their collective God Presences, the Light of the Divine Feminine—our Mother God—was anchored through the Cup of their Consciousness into the very core of every electron of precious life energy evolving there. This created a nurturing Forcefield of Divine Love that is building in momentum daily and hourly. This Feminine Forcefield of Divine Love created a catalyst for Healing that no one will be able to stop.

In *October of 1995*, the Light bathed the Earth through our Chalice of Healing at the conclusion of the O.J. Simpson criminal trial. Then, we experienced the *Full Moon Lunar Eclipse* that took place on *October 8, 1995*. With that amplification, every facet of our masculine abuse of power back to the "fall" was bathed with the Violet Flame of Limitless Transmutation.

Next, on *October 16, 1995*, we witnessed the *Million Man March* in Washington, D.C. The success of that activity enhanced our forward progress, and the Light of our Father-Mother God built in momentum preparing all Humanity, and specifically the Masculine Polarity of Humanity, for the next wave of healing. That healing Light poured into the Planet through the unique *New Moon Solar Eclipse* that took place on *October 23, 1995*.

On that Holy Day, the *New Moon Solar Eclipse* passed directly over the anchorage point of the Masculine Polarity of God. It embraced Tibet, northern India, Nepal, Iran and southern China. As this Celestial event bathed the Earth in that area of the World...*Our Father-Mother God lifted the lower masculine nature in every man, woman and child into the Immaculate Concept of the Divine Masculine Principle.*

With that activity of Light, our lower masculine nature was *reborn into its original Divine Intent.*

On that sacred day, the United Nations also celebrated its *50th* anniversary. Leaders representing their countries from around the World gathered in New York City. Once again, through the focus of our attention, our Father-Mother God blazed the Divine Blueprint for the New Heaven and the New Earth into the genetic codes and the Divine Mind of each world leader. These patterns will now begin to filter into their conscious minds, accelerating immeasurably our Global transformation.

On *February 10, 1997*, our Chalice of Healing was anchored in the center of the Earth. That Divine Light built in momentum for nine days. Then, the next phase of Healing was set into motion.

On *February 19, 1997*, Chinese leader Deng Xiaoping left the physical plane of Earth. His reign in China SYMBOLICALLY reflected the epitome of the masculine abuse of power. Even his open door policies and economic advancements were always for personal power and gain at the expense of Human Rights and Freedom. His death symbolizes the end of the old menacing guard and the residue of the influence of "cosmic evil."

"Cosmic evil" no longer exists, and we have Ascended into a new Karma-Free Reality. It is our responsibility now to transmute the oppressive consciousness remaining in China and invoke the Light of Illumination, Wisdom, Enlightenment and Understanding into that area and all life on Earth.

As usual, we are receiving unprecedented Divine Intervention in this incredibly synchronistic Divine Plan.

Immediately following Deng Xiaoping's death, Madeleine Albright, the first woman to ever hold the office of Secretary of State for the United States of America, went to Beijing, China. She attended a summit meeting that was scheduled long before anyone knew that Deng Xiaoping was going to make his transition. Her feminine presence created a Global focal point of attention that allowed the billions of people in the Orient to identify, not only with a woman in a position of power, but with a woman guiding Global Affairs in regard to the military—a woman representing the country that is perceived to be the most powerful Peacemaker in the World.

That dramatic shift of consciousness opened a portal between Heaven and Earth into China that created a new level of Divine Balance through the Masculine Polarity of God which is anchored there.

On *March 8, 1997*, we experienced a *Total Solar Eclipse* that specifically bathed the Masculine Polarity of God in Northern Asia: China, Mongolia, Siberia and even the North Pole. That Celestial event took place during the New Moon, and it was expanded without limit by the Ascension Flame being brought to Earth in the embrace of the Comet Hale-Bopp.

Amazingly, *but not concidentally, March 8th* is the day celebrated in the outer World as *International Women's Day*. As the power of the Ascension Flame lifted up all of the remaining misqualified energies associated with the masculine abuse of power, the World gave homage to women and all that women have done to bring a balance of love, nurturing and Reverence for ALL Life to every evolving Being on Earth.

That monumental New Moon Solar Eclipse prepared every electron of precious life energy on Earth to receive the maximum benefit of the Comet Hale-Bopp.

THE COMET HALE-BOPP

The Comet Hale-Bopp was discovered on *July 23, 1995*, by Alan Hale and Thomas Bopp, two amateur astronomers in

Arizona and New Mexico.* When the amateur astronomers simultaneously discovered this comet, the Sun was almost exactly 0 degrees Leo, which is one of the most powerful points on the Zodiac.

On *July 22, 1995*, just 30 to 36 hours before the comet was discovered, there was a "Star of David" or Grand Hexagram Planetary pattern in the sky. The Star of David has always been the sacred symbol that reflects the Oneness of God and Humanity. The descending triangle symbolizes God reaching down to Humanity, and the Ascending triangle symbolizes Humanity reaching up to God. The Star of David symbolizes the unification of the two when Humanity becomes One with God.

July 22nd is also the day celebrated as Mary Magdalene's Feast Day. Even though Mary Magdalene was a real person, her mission in the Christian Dispensation was more symbolic than literal. SYMBOLICALLY, she represented, at one point, the depths to which the Divine Feminine fell in the throes of the masculine abuse of power. Then, she represented the heights that the Divine Feminine soared to by following the path of Divine Love and surrendering through Divine Service to the Christ within.

Healing the Divine Feminine, the Love of God within each of our hearts, and becoming One with God again as we integrate our Solar Christ Presences, are two of the most vital aspects of our planetary transformation. The fact that these two facets of our healing process were being amplified by the Sun just prior to the moment the Comet Hale-Bopp appeared on the Screen of Life is profound indeed.

On a personal note, this is the day my Beloved Father-in-law made his transition into the Light from his home in Tucson, Arizona. I told my husband that the comet was probably just his Dad shooting through the sky on his journey Home.

It is truly awesome to witness the precision of the Divine Plan that is now unfolding on Earth. Every minute detail has been taken into consideration by our Father-Mother God so that we will have the full assistance of all of the Celestial Currents of Spiritual Energy to enhance our humble efforts.

THE DIVINE PLAN

The *initial impulse* of our Ascension onto our next Spiral of Evolution—the Spiral of the Fifth Dimension—was a process that took 72 hours. That event occurred through the combined efforts of both Heaven and Earth. It involved the collective cooperation of the Solar Christ Presences of ALL Humanity and the entire Company of Heaven throughout Infinity. It involved a unique Divine Alchemy in which base physical matter was accelerated at an atomic cellular level into Solar frequencies of Limitless Physical Perfection. That occurred God Victoriously, through the Realms of Cause, and it was anchored physically through our Solar Christ Presences Who have been born within our Sacred Hearts.

Our Ascension onto the Spiral of the Fifth Dimension began at *12:00 a.m. March 20, 1997*, local time. It built to fruition and was God Victoriously Accomplished at *11:59 p.m. March 22, 1997*, local time.

At the exact moment of the *Spring/Vernal Equinox* in each location on the Planet, our Solar Christ Presences breathed in the Divine Alchemy of the Ascension Flame being brought to Earth by the Comet Hale-Bopp. The Sacred Substance of the Ascension Flame, which blazes with the Divine Qualities of Ascension, Resurrection, Transfiguration and Transformation, was projected by our Solar Christ Presences into the core of purity pulsating within every electron of precious life energy on Earth. That created a tremendously amplified activity of Light that blazed around the Globe in an ever-increasing wave of God's Glory.

On *March 22, 1997* (which equals *33*, the master number that reflects Christ Consciousness), the Comet Hale-Bopp began its closest passage to the Earth. The full momentum of Celestial Blessings brought to Earth by this "messenger of God" lifted the Earth and all Her life in the Divine frequencies of the Fifth Dimension.

On *March 23, 1997*, Comet Hale-Bopp continued approaching the Earth, and at that time, its Celestial Gifts activated within the core of purity in every electron of precious life energy—every electron of manifest form on Earth—*the Immaculate Concept of our New Karma-Free Solar Reality*. This Divine Blueprint contains the genetic codings of the full, unmanifest potential of the NEW HEAVEN AND THE NEW EARTH.

On *March 23, 1997*, we were also embraced in the Celestial event of a *Full Moon Lunar Eclipse*. That Lunar Eclipse was centered in South America within the Forcefield of the Feminine Polarity of God and infinitely expanded the Love of our Mother God throughout the Planet.

That incredible gift of Divine Love permanently sealed all life on Earth in the frequencies of the Fifth Dimension. We were given several days to assimilate and integrate the activation of the Divine Blueprint. As that occurred, the Divine Ideas from the Heart and Mind of God flowed through all levels of consciousness in preparation for the next phase of the Divine Plan.

On *Easter Morning, March 30, 1997*, as the Resurrection Flame expanded the radiance of our Solar Christ Presences through our Heart Flames, *Divine Revelations* for our New Karma-Free Solar Reality poured into Earth from the Heart and Mind of God.

Greece is the focus on the Planet that gave birth to the paradigms for modern civilization. The existing archetypes for ART, MUSIC, DANCE, SCIENCE, MEDICINE, ATHLETIC EXCELLENCE, PHILOSOPHY, RELIGION, ARCHITECTURE AND POLITICAL SYSTEMS were born in Greece.

It is not by chance that St. John The Beloved was given Revelations on the Isle of Patmos in Greece. It was the models of modern civilization formed in Greece that "cosmic evil" had manipulated our human egos to burst asunder and destroy through fear and greed. It was those very systems that were threatening to be the ruination of the Earth and all life evolving upon Her.

Beloved Jesus gave St. John the Revelations within that forcefield in Greece to wake up Humanity so that we would stop our self-destructive descent into oblivion. St. John was given the prophecies of the potential destruction that would occur during these "end times" while he was within the forcefield of Greece to try and shatter "cosmic evil's" grip on the social, political, scientific, religious, philisophical, economic and artistic systems of the World. The goal was to restore the original Divine Intent of those social structures.

Since that time, St. John has worked ceaselessly to avert the destruction prophesied in Revelations and to inspire Humanity to change the course of Human destiny. Fortunately, his selfless efforts have been God Victorious! Together we have succeeded in averting the cataclysmic destructions of the Earth and the loss of the majority of life evolving here.

Now, we are ready to receive the Divine Revelations that will help us implement the glory of our new Solar Reality. On *Resurrection Morning, March 30, 1997*, through the open portal that pulsates between Heaven and Earth on the Isle of Patmos in Greece, the Sacred Knowledge that contains *the new paradigms for all of the systems in our New Solar Reality poured into the Cup of Humanity's Consciousness.* This occurred through the open door of Humanity's collective God Presences.

This time, Divine Revelation is different in that we will not have to depend on one person to interpret the Revelations to us. Instead, the Revelations that contain the archetypes for the social, political, economic, scientific, medical, artistic, athletic, philosophical and religious systems of our New Solar Reality of Limitless Perfection were anchored through the Solar Christ Presences of ALL Humanity into our Heart Flames.

Then, on *April 1, 1997*, as the Comet Hale-Bopp reached its closest passage to the Sun, its perihelion, a tremendous explosion of Light occurred that infinitely expanded those patterns of Limitless Physical Perfection through all levels of consciousness.

Humanity will now hold this Sacred Trust in our Heart Flames and await the approaching Cosmic Moment when those Divine Ideas will flow into our conscious minds for implementation in the world of form.

NOW IS THE TIME FOR THE FUN TO BEGIN!

We have been aware of the plight of the Earth for millions of years. We have watched empathetically from distant Star Systems; we have assisted from Inner Realms, and we have embodied on Earth thousands of times. We have soared into the Divine Heart and Mind of God and co-created the myriad Divine Plans to intervene and salvage this fallen Planet. We have taken vows in the Heart of God to love all life on Earth FREE! Sometimes we were able to succeed in taking tiny baby steps, however our progress has been painfully slow, sometimes non-existent.

In some lifetimes we were part of the solution, but more often than we would care to know, we became part of the problem. Our struggles have been arduous and, at times, overwhelming, but we kept coming back and volunteering over and over again to try and free the Earth from Her desperate situation.

Now, in the Light of what has occurred, we can clearly see that our struggles were infinitely worth it. We have God Victoriously succeeded!

OUR HUMBLE EFFORTS TRANSCENDED THE PROPHECIES OF OLD AND CHANGED THE COURSE OF HUMAN HISTORY.

Every prophecy, both ancient and modern, had such dire prospects of Humanity's ability to correct our course of direction that even the most optimistic prophecies had a mere fraction of Humanity making the shift into the Fourth Dimension. They also predicted that tremendous land masses would be lost under the seas in the process. Some predictions said only ten percent of the human population would survive Armageddon; others professed that only 144,000 would make it.

Those woeful predictions were made under the assumption that only the souls who had truly transformed the fallen aspects of their lower human egos and given full dominion of their four lower bodies over to the authority of their Holy Christ Selves would make the cut. In Truth, that *was* the original Divine Plan, and if that requirement were still mandatory, only a fraction of Humanity *would* have survived the shift into the Fourth Dimension. But, because of the immense love the awakening Lightworkers have for their sisters and brothers in all of the Kingdoms evolving on Earth—Human, Elemental and Angelic, and because of the Lightworkers' selfless commitment to the Light of God and their willingness to persevere until all life on Earth is Ascended and FREE, a contingency plan has been set into motion by the GRACE OF GOD.

This contingency plan reflects the mercy and compassion of our Father-Mother God, and through it we can glimpse the magnitude of Their Love for us and this blessed Planet.

The Contingency Plan

The contingency plan has to do with a concept that is part of the vernacular of modern physics: the "critical mass."

The critical mass is a point that is reached when the changing energy, vibration and consciousness of a particular "thing" accumulates enough momentum to shift the remaining energy, vibration and consciousness of the "thing" into a whole new form. That is exactly what has taken place on Earth.

Due to the tremendous number of illumined souls who have embodied on Earth in the last 100 years and the incredible success the increased influx of Light from our Father-Mother God has had in awakening Humanity, we have reached the critical mass of Christ Consciousness on Earth. That literally means that 51 percent OR MORE of the accumulated thoughts, words, actions and feelings of Humanity is vibrating at a frequency of love and harmony that is compatible with Christ Consciousness.

It is *vitally* important for us to really grasp this Truth because we become who we believe we are. We are so used to beating ourselves down into the *"worthless worm in the dust"* consciousness that most of Humanity may feel it is even blasphemous to think we could ever reach Christ Consciousness. To ease that resistance, we need to let go of the belief that to have Christ Consciousness means we're saying that we are like Jesus. That is far too great a leap for most people to comprehend. Christ Consciousness is a state of Being that reflects Love, Harmony, Hope, Forgiveness, Compassion, Caring, Peace, Contentment, Joy and Happiness.

People are BASICALLY GOOD AND LOVING. Whenever there is a disaster of any kind, the initial instinct of people is to listen to their heart's call and help their fellow Human Beings. Every now and then we hear about a crowd of people that stood around and watched when someone needed help, but the reason it makes the news is because it is so abhorrent to our natural tendencies that we are shocked and dismayed.

We are bombarded by the media with negative things people are doing all over the World, so we mistakenly think things are getting worse. There are six-billion people evolving on Earth. The ones we hear about on the news are a **minuscule fraction** of Humanity.

These are challenging times, and people are going through a lot, but even in the face of all of your adversity, what would your answers be if I asked you the following questions?

> Do you love and care about people?
> Do you try to make a positive difference whenever you can?
> Do you reach out to help people if you can?
> Do you love animals and the nature kingdom?
> If you knew how to heal the Earth and eliminate pollution, would you?
> Do you long for peace and harmony for all Humanity?
> If you had abundance, would you share your wealth?
> If you could be a significant factor in manifesting Heaven on Earth, would you be willing to do what it takes to fulfill your part of the Divine Plan?

Now, ask yourself, do I know **anyone** who would say "no" to these questions? If you do know someone who would say "no," would it be to all of the questions or just one or two? Of all of the people you know, what percentage would say "yes" to these questions compared to the percentage who would say "no?"

Hopefully, now, you are beginning to understand what 51

percent Christ Consciousness really means. It is not the few times that our lower human egos manipulate us through our human frailties that determines who we are. It is the pre-dominant all-encompassing feelings that resonate at the very core of our Beings.

At this very moment, beyond a shadow of a doubt, in spite of our Earthly challenges, 51 percent OR MORE of Humanity's energy is expressing Christ Consciousness. For every depraved human ego that is acting out negatively 24 hours a day, there are hundreds, probably thousands, of Human Beings who are consciously and deliberately striving to be a positive, loving force on Earth. That is precisely why a Cosmic Dispensation was granted by our Father-Mother God to allow **every** part of life evolving on Earth to Ascend into the Fourth Dimension.

Because all life is interrelated, the *Universal Law* is *"As 'I Am' lifted up, all life is lifted up with me."* When we reached the "critical mass" of Christ Consciousness on Earth, our Father-Mother God knew that *we,* you and I and every other awakening soul on Earth, had the heart's desire, commitment, strength, courage, skill and willingness to persevere in our service to the Light until the remaining 49 percent OR LESS of Humanity is expressing the perfection of Christ Consciousness.

Because of our heartfelt pleas on behalf of unawakened Humanity, our God Parents agreed to allow us to be our brothers' and sisters' keepers. They agreed to allow every part of life evolving on Earth to Ascend into the Fourth Dimension, *knowing full well* that we would be willing to "keep on keeping on" until every single person on Earth awakens and returns to Christ Consciousness.

That is what we have been hoping for; that is exactly why we were willing to delve into the depths of human suffering and pain, lifetime after lifetime.

WE SUCCEEDED! WE WON!
VICTORY IS OURS!

All life on Earth has gotten a *reprieve*, and now we have the opportunity to continue lifting this sweet Earth and all Her life into the Octaves of Harmony and Balance as we Ascend into the Fifth Dimension.

Now, our responsibility is to continue the process of rebirth and transformation to our fullest capacity. The difference is THE HARD PART IS OVER. We don't have to be in misery anymore. The negativity of our pasts has been forgiven and transmuted into the Light. Now, we are beginning to experience the more rarified frequencies of the Fifth Dimension where our thoughts and feelings will manifest at a greatly accelerated pace. In addition to that, the oppressive force of "cosmic evil" has been removed from the Earth and returned to the Heart of God.

"SATAN" *NO LONGER* RULES THE EARTH!

WE ARE FREE!!!

So what does all of this mean, practically and tangibly, for Humanity?

It means that we have the opportunity and the *ability* as never before to transform our lives into expressions of Joy, Love and Fulfillment. It means that by holding the vision of Heaven on Earth and living out of that vision, we can manifest that perfection in physical form **here and now**.

The wonderful part of our Ascension is that we don't have to fully *understand* what being in the Fifth Dimension really means. We don't have to truly *know* that "cosmic evil" has been removed from the Earth. We don't have to *accept fully* that our time of suffering is over. We don't even have to *believe* that all of that is true. All we have to do is *allow it to be a possibility in our lives and act out of that **unmanifest*** *potential.*

Our thoughts and feelings are creative. We are on Earth to learn how to use those creative faculties to co-create Heaven on Earth with our Father-Mother God. Never have we been at a more perfect time and space continuum to succeed in our efforts. All we have to do is JUST DO IT!!!

MANIFESTING HEAVEN ON EARTH

Manifesting Heaven on Earth is far easier than it sounds. It just takes determination and consistency. First of all, we need to create the vision. What would Heaven on Earth be like for you?

Ask your God Presence, *"If I could create Heaven on Earth in every facet of my life right now, what would my life be like?"* Then, write down your vision in detail.

> What are my relationships like?
> What is my job like?
> What is my health like?
> What is my Spiritual life like?
> What is my social life like?
> What am I doing to fulfill my Divine Plan,
> my Hopes, my Dreams?
> How am I adding to the Light of the World?

Now, *accept* that your vision is a viable reality for you right here and right now, and ask your God Presence to transmute any blocks or resistance that may interfere with bringing your vision into manifest form. Go over your vision every day. Ask that your vision manifest in alignment with THE HIGHEST GOOD FOR ALL CONCERNED. Affirm that your vision is already blazing in the ethers in every detail and will manifest in the Eternal Moment of NOW, possibly with the next breath you take!

If there is any facet of your vision that indicates you want something at the expense of another person or if any aspect of your vision is harmful to any part of life on Earth, then KNOW that it is coming from your human ego and NOT your God Presence. Your God Presence will only give you ideas that add to the joy of your life and enhance the joy for all life on Earth.

If any part of your vision is not reflecting the highest good for all concerned, then release that part into the Light and ask your God Presence to flood your consciousness with new ideas that will create fulfillment and happiness in your life and bless every particle of life on Earth. Dare to dream. Reach into the Octaves of Wonder and Awe for your vision. The possibilities are limitless, and no matter how magnificent your vision is, you are going to barely be scratching the surface of your Divine Potential.

In your mind's eye, see yourself living your vision. Feel the joy and happiness living your vision brings you.

Handle any challenges that come up as a detached observer. Know that these challenges are just residue of your old reality that are coming up for you to release, so that your vision can manifest.

> ***Know*** *in your heart that the time for suffering is over.*
> ***Know*** *that it is time for Heaven to manifest on Earth.*
> ***Know*** *that the old paradigm of "cosmic evil" does not exist anymore, and you are FREE.*
> ***Know*** *that you are in a new energy, vibration and consciousness where your vision can manifest in the "twinkling of an eye."*
> ***Know*** *that manifesting the glory of Heaven on Earth is the most important job you have to do right now.*
> ***Know*** *that you are blazing a path into the Realms of Perfection that will assist all Humanity to do*

the same.

We are the microcosm of the macrocosm, and as we transform our personal lives into Heaven on Earth, we have the ability to assist the rest of Humanity to do the same. We have volunteered to *"be our brothers' and sisters' keepers,"* so those of us who recognize that "cosmic evil" does not exist anymore have an added obligation to transmute the thoughtforms and fears of people who are still empowering the "devil" and other obsolete belief patterns.

We have the obligation to invoke illumination and enlightenment into the hearts and minds of people who are still clinging to the empty shells of entities in the psychic-astral plane and still trying to entice people into taking "implants" and other tools of manipulation.   Without the force of "cosmic evil" to empower these empty shells and thoughtforms, the energy behind these destructive activities will be dissipated if we just keep blazing the Violet Flame through them. We have the responsibility to invoke the Law of Forgiveness and the Violet Transmuting Flame into all patterns of deceit, fraud, manipulation, corruption, fear, limitation and every other malady that people may be trying to perpetuate.

The more vigilant we are in holding and energizing our vision of the New Heaven and the New Earth, the sooner that reality will manifest for all life evolving here.

As we empower our visions, this sacred process will build in momentum daily and hourly.

We have begun the initial ascent onto our next Spiral of Evolution. This is the beginning of our Ascension into the Fifth Dimension. This is the initial impulse of our Solar Passage into the Pure Land of Boundless Splendor and Infinite Light.

How long it takes us to complete this Ascension process into the Realms of Limitless Physical Perfection will be up to YOU and me. But, in all of the past activities of Light I have described to you in this book, whether you participated consciously or super-consciously through your God Self, you succeeded beyond the greatest expectations of Heaven. And, as a result of *your* Light, we are far ahead of schedule. Don't ever underestimate the potential of your God Self to work through the limited consciousness of your human ego.

You are magnificent beyond your most extravagant dreams. All you have to do to KNOW the Truth of that statement is to...

REMEMBER WHO YOU ARE!

The Beginning!

EPILOGUE

A TIME FOR CLARITY AND UNDERSTANDING

SEPARATING THE WHEAT FROM THE CHAFF

A TIME FOR CLARITY AND UNDERSTANDING

This is the moment for which we have all been preparing for thousands of years...the moment when this sweet Earth and all Her life will transcend the ramifications of the fall of Humanity and Ascend into Her rightful place in the Universe, accepting Her Divine Birthright as Freedom's Holy Star.

Through wondrous, multifaceted, multidimensional activities of Light that took place in 1996, we God Victoriously moved through the final phases of Armageddon and brought to fruition the fulfillment of St. John's Revelations.*

This Victory was accomplished through the Realms of Cause, and now, through our concentrated efforts, will be drawn tangibly into the world of effects—the physical plane of Earth.

The physical plane is the VERY *LAST* DIMENSION TO REFLECT CHANGE, but once something has been accomplished in the Realms of Cause, ***nothing*** can prevent its eventual physical manifestation in the world of effects.

In 1996 the oppressive force of "cosmic evil" was bound by Archangel Michael in the Ring-Pass-Not of God's First Cause of Perfection. Through an act of unparalleled Divine Grace and Divine Love, this sinister force was returned to the very Heart of our Father-Mother God to be transformed and loved eternally FREE into its original Divine Intent. It will never again be able to adversely affect any particle of life.

Now, it is our responsibility as Lightworkers to clean up the ***residue*** left behind by this incredible force of imbalance.

Even though "cosmic evil" no longer exists on Earth, we still have our wayward human egos and the recalcitrant souls from the human evolutions that are presently choosing to remain stuck in the psychic-astral plane. "Cosmic evil" was the power behind our human egos and the fallen souls on Earth. It was that outside force that gave our egos and the fallen souls the strength to fight so tenaciously to keep us stuck in fear and limitation. Now that "cosmic evil" no longer exists, these fallen aspects of Humanity don't have a back-up

---

Information regarding the glorious activities of Light that took place in 1996 to accomplish the fulfillment of St. John's Revelations is available on two cassette tapes titled "It's Time For Us To Soar" by Patricia Diane Cota-Robles. There is an order form on page 445 for your convenience if you are interested in ordering these tapes.

system to support them. They can't wreak the havoc and terror that they used to be able to inflict on Humanity *unless we choose to re-empower them with our belief systems*. Remember, we are on Earth to learn how to use our creative faculties of thought and feeling so that we can become co-creators with our Father-Mother God. If we choose to empower negative or distorted thoughtforms and belief systems with our thoughts, words, actions and feelings, we can re-create all of the limitations and negativity our hearts desire. But, if we choose to lift into the Realms of Illumined Truth and tap the perfection patterns for Earth contained within the Divine Mind and Heart of God—*Heaven on Earth can be our reality*.

I will collectively refer to the fallen souls from the evolutions on Earth who are still abiding in the psychic-astral plane and the wayward human egos who are still resisting their transformation into Light as the forces of imbalance. These forces are very aware that they no longer have the power of "cosmic evil" behind them. They also know that their ability to control and manipulate us into doing their will has been greatly dissipated. Therefore, they are desperately trying to fill the empty shells and thoughtforms left behind by "cosmic evil" so that they can perpetuate the misinformation, disinformation and activities of deception that were deliberately created by "cosmic evil" to *distract* us from our Divine Plans and the Truth.

In order to prevent them from succeeding in their plot, we are being asked by our Father-Mother God and the entire Company of Heaven to lift up in consciousness into the Realms of Illumined Truth. We are being asked to perceive the Higher Truth now pouring forth from the Heart and Mind of God. With *new eyes* to see and *new ears* to hear, we can fine-tune our belief systems and reach into new Octaves of Clarity and Understanding.

It is never the Divine Intent of our Father-Mother God for us to do battle with any other part of life. *Their intent is always for us to embrace every part of life in the full-gathered momentum of Reverence for All Life so that it can be Loved Eternally FREE.* It is important that every single person who comes in contact with this information knows, through every fiber of their Being, that this information is being revealed to us at this critical time so that we can evaluate our **own** belief systems and separate the wheat from the chaff.

We are not, under any circumstances, to use this information to judge, criticize or condemn ourselves or any other person, organization or activity on Earth. As you read these words, ask the Divinity blazing in your heart to envelop you in a forcefield of Discernment and Illumined Truth. Ask that every trace of human consciousness drop away, so that you can clearly perceive any aspect of this information that will, in any way, enhance your ability to fulfill your Divine Plan and improve your ability to be an effective force of Light on Earth. See yourself as a detached observer, efficiently sifting and sorting through your information and beliefs, carefully selecting only the Pearls of Divine Knowledge that will accelerate your Ascension into the New Heaven and the New Earth.

In order to prevent the forces of imbalance from succeeding in re-creating negativity on Earth, we do not have to do battle with them. *We merely have to withdraw our attention from their activities of deception, and focus on the Truth.* Without our energy to sustain them, their activities will simply dissipate and cease to exist.

If we will invoke the Violet Flame of Limitless Transmutation to transmute the cause, core, effect, record and memory of any person, place, condition or thing involved in any negative belief system or activity, it will help immeasurably. Then, if we will invoke the God Presence of every man, woman and child involved in perpetuating negativity of any kind on Earth, and ask that each person be filled with Enlightenment, Illumined Truth, Clarity and Understanding, our humble efforts will be expanded without limit.

The law is "As 'I Am' lifted up, all life is lifted up with me." As we fine-tune our *own* belief systems and separate the wheat from the chaff, we will create an upward rushing momentum of Truth that will assist all life into the new reality of Heaven on Earth.

AFFIRMATION

Through the Power of God pulsating in my heart...I invoke my Mighty God Presence "I Am"...the Omniscient, Omnipresent and Omnipotent Presence of God and the entire Company of Divinity throughout all Creation.

Forces of Light! COME FORTH NOW!!!

Blessed Ones, I offer myself as a Cup, a Holy Grail, through which the Light of God that is Eternally Victorious will pour to lift all life evolving on Earth into the Realms of Illumined Truth.

I invoke the most intensified activity of the Violet Flame of Limitless Transmutation ever manifested in the history of time. Sacred Violet Fire, blaze through me into the cause, core, effect, record and memory of every person, place, condition or thing that is, in any way, perpetuating negative belief systems or activities on Earth.

Powers of Light, lift every single Human Being who is involved in perpetuating negativity of any kind into the loving embrace of his/her "I Am" Presence. Empower each person's God Presence to take full dominion of their thoughts, words, actions and feelings.

Fill every soul with Enlightenment, Illumined Truth, Clarity and Understanding. Let each one be filled with Divine Discerning Intelligence, Divine Sense and Reason.

Give each person the skill and wisdom to separate the wheat from the chaff without judgment, criticism or condemnation.

Instill every man, woman and child with the courage and commitment to stand in their newfound Truth, even in the face of all adversity.

I accept that this call has been Victoriously Accomplished through the Power of God "I Am".

IT IS DONE!!! AND SO IT IS!!!

SEPARATING THE WHEAT FROM THE CHAFF

For each and every one of us, this process is going to be extremely complex and often challenging. We have been through a multitude of experiences during our Earthly sojourns, and we are always a sum total of everything we have ever experienced. Our belief systems were developed through Divine Wisdom, inner knowing, intuition, inspiration, believing what other people we trusted taught us, our own experiences and wading through the mud puddles of trial and error. We have all, at one time or another, made mistakes, believed things that were inaccurate and been deceived by the forces of imbalance.

At the present time, we are all involved with various Spiritual groups, friends and loved ones, fellow Lightworkers, activities, etc., that we have felt aligned with and trusted. Some of this information may challenge what we have believed to be true, and we each have the free will to accept or reject this information.

What is most important about this information is that we focus strictly on the facet of the belief system that the Spiritual Hierarchy is trying to correct. We must NOT focus on the person, organization or activity that is giving us the inaccurate information.

In most instances, the people involved are very loving, sincere people who genuinely believe they are teaching Truth. This is a time, however, when *we must not confuse sincerity with Truth*.

The force of "cosmic evil" knew that we were not stupid, so it did not say, "I am the sinister force, and I have come to ruin your life." It said, "I am god; follow me." This is the time Jesus forewarned us about when he said, "You will hear, 'Lo, I am here, and lo, I am there,' but by their works alone shall they be known."

"Cosmic evil's" most effective method of deception was to infiltrate the Truth with misinformation and disinformation. This enabled that malevolent force to counteract the effectiveness of the Divine Plan and neutralize our efforts.

The information that is being revealed to us now from On High is designed to gently inform us as to how the forces of imbalance have distorted the Truth in order to distract us from our real missions.

Remember, as you are reading this information, *focus on the aspect of the Truth that has been contaminated*— NOT the people involved. If you find yourself forming an opinion about the people involved that is critical or judgmental, then KNOW you are becoming part of the problem instead of part of the solution.

Begin by reading and absorbing the following principles through your open, loving heart.

Code of Conduct of a Disciple of the Holy Spirit

1. Be ever conscious that you aspire to the full expression of God, and devote all your Being and service to that end, as expressed so ably in the First Commandment.

2. Learn the lesson of harmlessness; neither by word nor thought or feeling inflict evil upon any part of life. Know that action and physical violence are but the lesser part of the sin of harmful expression.

3. Stir not another's sea of emotion, thoughtlessly or deliberately. Know that the storm in which you place their Spirit will sooner or later flow upon the banks of your own Lifestream. Rather, bring tranquility to life, and be, as the Psalmist so ably puts it, "oil on troubled waters."

4. Disassociate yourself from personal delusion. Let self-justification never reveal that you love the self more than the harmony of the Universe. If you are right, there is no need to acclaim it; if you are wrong, pray for forgiveness. Watching the self, you will find the rising tides of indignation among the more subtle shadows on the path of right, called "Self Righteousness."

*5. Walk gently through the Universe, knowing that the body is a temple in which dwells the Holy Spirit that brings Peace, Truth and Illumination to life everywhere. Keep your temple always in a respectful and cleanly manner as befitting the habitation of the **Spirit of Truth**. Respect and honor, in gentle dignity, all other temples, knowing that oft times within a crude exterior burns a* *great Light.*

6. In the presence of Nature, absorb the beauties and gifts of Her Kingdom in gentle gratitude. Do not desecrate Her by vile thoughts or emotions or by physical acts that despoil Her virgin beauty.

7. Do not form nor offer opinions unless invited to do so, and then only after prayer and silent invocation for guidance.

8. Speak when God chooses to say something through you. At other times, remain peacefully silent.

9. Make the ritual of your living the observance of God's rules so unobtrusive that no one shall know that you aspire to Godliness, lest the force of their outer will be pitted against you or lest your service become impinged with pride.

10. Let your heart be a song of Gratitude, that God has given unto your keeping the Spirit of Life, which through you chooses to widen the borders of God's Kingdom.

11. Be alert always to use your faculties and the gifts loaned to you by the Father-Mother God of all Life in a manner to extend God's Kingdom.

12. Claim nothing for yourself, neither powers nor principalities, any more than you claim the air you breathe or the Sun. Use them freely, knowing the God ownership of all.

13. In speech and action be gentle, but with the dignity that always accompanies the Presence of the Living God that is within your temple.

14. Constantly place all the faculties of your Being, and all the inner unfoldment of your nature, at the Feet of the God Power, especially when endeavoring to manifest perfection through one in distress.

15. Let your watchwords be Gentleness, Humility and Loving Service, but do not allow the impression of humility to be mistaken for lethargy. The servant of God, like the Sun in the Heavens, is eternally vigilant and constantly outpouring the gifts which are in his/her particular keeping.

Cosmic Holy Spirit

THE VIOLET FLAME
AND THE ASCENDED MASTERS

Because of our lower human ego's propensity for drama/trauma, it was very easy for the forces of "cosmic evil" to manipulate and distract us into focusing on things that actually prevented us from doing what we came to Earth to do. This negative force was very adept at infiltrating the Truth with nefarious plans. It would calculate deliberate distractions and then manipulate human egos to implement its will. One of its greatest coups involved contaminating the Truth of the Ascended Masters and the Violet Transmuting Flame.

The most powerful tool of the dawning Aquarian Age is the gift of the Seventh Solar Aspect of Deity—The Violet

Flame of Limitless Transmutation. This Solar Aspect of our Father-Mother God flows through the forcefield of Aquarius and will bathe the Earth for the next 2000 years. It is the Divine Balance of our Father God—the Sapphire Blue Ray of Divine Power, which activates our left brain hemisphere and the Power Center in our throat...and our Mother God—the Crystalline Pink Ray of Divine Love, which activates our right brain hemisphere and the Love Center in our heart.

When the Light of our Father-Mother God is balanced within our brain structure, it creates the Violet Flame (Blue + Pink = Violet). This Sacred Alchemy of our Father-Mother God activates our pituitary, pineal and hypothalamus glands and the ganglionic centers at the base of our brain. When this occurs, it awakens the Center of Enlightenment at the crown of our head known as our Crown Chakra and lifts us into a state of Enlightenment called Christ Consciousness. This is a vital step in our personal and planetary transformation process. The Violet Flame is a fundamental part of our Ascension in the Light, and our Victory cannot be accomplished without it.

Beloved Saint Germain, Jesus The Christ, Mother Mary and all of the Ascended Masters, Archangels, Angels and Cosmic Beings of Light have been teaching us about the Violet Flame since the late 1800s. The Immaculate Concept for expanding the Sacred Knowledge of the Violet Flame was amplified through all levels of consciousness from the most powerful focus of Reverence for ALL Life on the Planet, the Grand Teton Mountains.

For decades the Sacred Truth of the Violet Flame has gently bathed the consciousness of all life on Earth preparing for the current Cosmic Moment of Awakening. As the forces of "cosmic evil" witnessed the preparation for Humanity's mass awakening, they realized that they needed to do something to block this activity of Light and interfere with its effectiveness.

The force of "cosmic evil" knew that the only way to stop the process was to contaminate the Truth of the Violet Flame and discredit the Ascended Masters. They magnetized an activity into the Forcefield of Reverence For ALL Life in the area of the Grand Teton Mountains, and through a decreeing process that induced a form of mesmerization and mind control, they manipulated the group to generate a consciousness of fear and war. The information sent forth from the group expounded that they were being guided by the Ascended Masters and the Violet Flame. They built bomb shelters, stockpiled weapons and sent literature around the World encouraging Lightworkers to do the same. This drew the attention of the mass media who reported this activity on national television to all the World.

We are all One. The Divine Fiat of this New Age of Spiritual Freedom is REVERENCE FOR *ALL* LIFE! When awakening Lightworkers began to hear about the activity taking place in the area of the Grand Tetons and realized that it was supposedly associated with the Ascended Masters and the Violet Flame, they didn't want any part of it. They consciously chose not to use the Violet Flame and began to believe that the Ascended Masters were not of the Light. This, of course, is exactly what the forces of "cosmic evil" wanted to accomplish.

Now that "cosmic evil" is gone, we need to embrace the Truth of the Violet Flame and the Ascended Masters and transcend the damage that was done by the activity in Montana. We can do this by using the Violet Flame to transmute **all** consciousness of fear and war on Earth and **all** misinformation and disinformation regarding the Violet Flame and the Ascended Masters.

EARTH CHANGES

For literally millenia seers and prophets have been foretelling devastating Earth changes and cataclysmic events that would occur during these "end times" *if* Humanity did not change our course of direction. Once again, because of our fear-based human ego's proclivity for drama/trauma, this area was fertile ground into which "cosmic evil" could sow its seeds of deception.

"Cosmic evil" manipulated channels around the World for several decades to predict one devastating Earth change after another. As it cunningly wove its plan of deception through the consciousness of various channels, it claimed to be Mother Mary, various Beings of Light, commanders of various space confederations, entities from other dimensions, inspired visions of future events and a multitude of other deceptive ploys. As the timeframe for one predicted cataclysm came and went, another dire prediction would be made. Their intent was to keep us distracted from our Divine Missions and empower negative thoughtforms of mass destruction that could actually be brought into manifestation.

They worked incessantly to entice Lightworkers to flee the troubled areas and move to "safe ground." They had people distribute maps and visual images of predicted Earth changes to empower their efforts and increase our fear. All of this activity, of course, was diametrically opposed to the Divine Plan.

It is true that if Humanity had not healed the atrocities that were inflicted on Mother Earth and changed our course of direction, the potential for a cataclysmic purging, as predicted in ancient times, was possible. But, A FULFILLED NEGATIVE PROPHESY IS A FAILED PROPHESY!

The only reason Divine Inspiration reveals possible negative events is so that we will heed the warning, correct our behavior patterns and AVERT the negative prediction.

We have all been preparing for thousands of years to be in embodiment at this critical moment on Earth for the specific purpose of invoking the Light through our Heart Flames effectively enough to AVERT THE DEVASTATING EARTH CHANGES.

The Earth is a living, breathing organism, and She is going to move and breathe. With the cooperation of the Elemental Kingdom and the embrace of Humanity's love and Light, however, She can cleanse Herself in far less destructive ways without destroying millions of lives.

God needs a body, and in order for something to manifest in the physical plane of Earth, the Light to create that manifestation must be drawn through the Divine Heart Flame of someone abiding on Earth. For that very reason, legions of Lightworkers have volunteered to embody in, or move to, various areas where potential earthquakes and cataclysms could occur. They are there to anchor the Light through the faults, cracks and fissures. They are there to make peace with the Elemental Kingdom involved and heal Humanity's abuse of Mother Earth.

If "cosmic evil" had been able to terrify and coerce enough Lightworkers into fleeing to "safe ground," thus leaving the vulnerable areas unprotected, it could indeed have created its destruction. Fortunately, its sinister plan was foiled.

The First Earth Summit held in Rio de Janeiro, Brazil, in 1992, was the outer world demonstration the Elemental Kingdom needed to be assured that Humanity had recognized the error of our ways and that we were consciously choosing to once again accept our mission as stewards of the Earth. Through this activity of Light, a New Covenant was established between the Human Kingdom and the Elemental Kingdom. This New Covenant created an atmosphere of cooperation in which the body of Mother Earth will be purged and cleansed with the least loss of Human life. THE DEVASTATING EARTH CHANGES HAVE BEEN AVERTED.

Instead of the immense loss of land masses and life, we will experience what appears to be unusual weather conditions. Earthquakes will occur in obscure places, or if they occur in populated areas, there will be a minimal loss of life. We will also experience built-up pressure being released through volcanoes and tumultuous water conditions, but still, with little loss of Human life.

Our responsibility now is to withdraw our attention and our support from thoughtforms and activities that are still striving to perpetuate a consciousness of mass destruction. We must invoke the Violet Flame to transmute the thoughts, words, actions and feelings empowering these negative predictions. We must also invoke the God Presences of everyone involved to fill each person with Illumination, Understanding, Enlightenment, Wisdom and Truth.

WAVES OF ASCENSION AND MASS LANDINGS

For aeons of time "cosmic evil" kept us entrapped and oppressed in the worthless, "worm-in-the-dust" state of consciousness. This deception was specifically designed to prevent us from recognizing our own Divinity. This nefarious force knew that if we remembered who we are—Divine Sons and Daughters of God—it would not be able to control our human egos or manipulate us into doing its will.

Our belief that we are inept and worthless gave "cosmic evil" another very effective avenue through which it could distract us from our Divine Plans. It instilled within our belief systems the *lie* that we cannot possibly save ourselves and that there would be some "superior" outside force that would have to come and rescue us. Because of our feelings of worthlessness and inadequacy, that thought seemed very logical and very comfortable. The problem with that belief system, of course, is that it is completely untrue and causes us to give our power away to others instead of restoring us to our Divine Reality as empowered Children of God.

Once again there were a variety of methods "cosmic evil" used to deceive us and keep us stuck. It infiltrated messages from channels all over the World and professed to be members of a space confederation who had come to save us. To give the space confederation credibility, the commanders claimed that members of the Spiritual Hierarchy were riding around on their space ships. They claimed that these Beings of Light were performing Their various duties from spacecraft.

Because we have been immersed in a time and space continuum in this physical reality, at some level, that belief seemed logical.

In Truth, the Ascended and Cosmic Beings from the Realms of Illumined Truth abide in the timeless, spaceless Realms of Perfection. They are radiant forcefields of scintillating Light, and They can project Their luminous Presence anywhere in the Universe with a single thought.

They can stand within the auras of every man, woman and child on Earth simultaneously, or they can expand Their luminous Presence to envelop the entire Planet and cradle the Earth in Their Heart Flames.

It is true that these Beings of Light are assisting us at this time the maximum that Cosmic Law will allow, but THEY CANNOT DO IT FOR US. We are in the midst of a unique experiment that has never been attempted in any System of Worlds. And, we truly have drawn the attention of the entire Universe.

Never has a Planet that has fallen to this depth of negativity been given an opportunity to move into the Light. In every previous instance, a Planet emulating this level of degradation had the Lifeforce withdrawn by our Father-Mother God and experienced what is known as the Second Death.

We are experiencing an unprecedented activity of Divine Grace, but the rules for our Ascension are very clear. In order for us to Ascend into our next Spiral of Evolution and attain our Solar Reality, *souls in embodiment on Earth must invoke the Light of God and project It through their own Heart Flames into the physical plane of Earth effectively enough to transmute the patterns of negativity and human miscreation. No outside force can do this for us. We must accomplish this Divine Fiat while abiding on Earth in physical embodiment.*

The entire Universe knows these rules, and every Solar System is bound to comply by Cosmic Law. Therefore, we are not going to be lifted off in "waves of mass Ascension" or rescued by mass landings. These ideas were designed by "cosmic evil" to distract us from our true missions.

Instead of striving with every fiber of our Beings to transmute the negativity on Earth and lift into our fully empowered God Selves, we have been waiting for some outside phenomenon to happen and for someone to rescue us.

We are **not** going to be "lifted off" in waves of Ascension or lifted into spaceships and rescued.

We are **not** going to be salvaged by mass landings.

We are **not** going to saved by a single Avatar, either in or out of embodiment.

We are **not** going to be magically transformed by the Photon Belt.

The wonderful news is, however, that, as is always the case, the Divine Plan is infinitely more glorious and wondrous than any diversion the forces of imbalance can envision.

Since we are always the sum total of everything we have ever experienced and since never in the history of all Creation has a Planet that has fallen to this depth been given the opportunity to Ascend into a Solar Reality, WE ARE ACTUALLY CREATING A NEW LEVEL OF GODHOOD!!!

Through the collective efforts of embodied Humanity, we must transmute the negativity on Earth and invoke the Light that will transform our physical reality into Heaven on Earth. We are receiving the maximum assistance that Cosmic Law will allow from every Octave of Perfection and every Galaxy

in the Universe, but They cannot interfere with the experi-
ment. *Those of us who are physically embodied on Earth
have the ultimate responsibility for transforming this
Planet into Heaven on Earth and regaining our Divine
Birthright as empowered co-creators with our Father-
Mother God—Sons and Daughters of God.*

PHOTON BELT

Some of the information regarding the Photon Belt has
also been infiltrated by the forces of imbalance to distract us
and create confusion. It has been stated that when we move
into the Photon Belt all electrical equipment will cease to
operate. Then, supposedly, there will be mass landings and
Beings from other Solar Systems who will teach us about a
new technology that will rescue us.

Well, as you know, every physical object on Earth is
comprised of atoms, molecules, electrons, neutrons, protons
and various other sub-atomic particles. This includes our
physical bodies as well as the bodies of the animals and
plants. It is **electrical impulses** that flow through our bodies
and activate our brains and beat our hearts. If, instantly, all
electrical impulses on Earth cease to function, we will die. So
will the animals and plants.

I know that the information states that somehow we will
be magically transformed, but if the electrons in our physical
bodies can be transformed, so can the electrons in our
electrical equipment. That, in fact, is exactly what is happening now through a gradual acceleration process.

Through the concentrated efforts of both Humanity and
the Company of Heaven, the frequency, vibration and consciousness of every particle of life on Earth was accelerated
into a compatible frequency with the Photon Belt during the
Ninth Celebration of Harmonic Convergence in **August 1995**.
We have since entered the fringes of the Photon Belt. We are
experiencing some effects such as electrical blackouts and the
erratic failure of appliances and automobiles as they fail to
work one day and curiously work the next day without
intervention. Our physical bodies are also reflecting some
stress as our God Presence accelerates our vibratory frequency the maximum we can withstand every 24 hours.
People are experiencing flu-like symptoms, water retention,

painful joints, head pressure and pain and various other physical maladies.

But, since the physical plane of Earth is the *very last* dimension to reflect change, there is an overwhelming probability that we will harmoniously move through the null zone into the full embrace of the Photon Belt with very little, if any, outer world phenomena.

The effects of this incredible acceleration, however, will greatly assist our Ascension and move us forward by leaps and bounds in our transformation process.

We need to remove our attention from distractions such as mass landings and electrical failure. Instead, we need to focus on raising our vibrations up, and we need to listen to the inner voice of our God Presence for guidance as to how each of us can most effectively assist the Earth during this glorious moment of Her rebirth and Ascension into the Light.

It is time for us to become the most powerful and effective force of God Light we are capable of being.

It is time for us to focus on the missions we came to Earth to do.

CALCULATED DISTRACTIONS

One of the most important things awakening Lightworkers need to do in order to effectively reach the sleeping multitudes is to be NORMAL. We have volunteered to integrate into mainstream Humanity. We have agreed to work in mainstream professions and jobs. We have promised to live conventional lives and shift the consciousness of Humanity by our *example*, not by expounding verbiage that we fail to live up to.

We have taken vows to "walk our talk," and we know that the most significant contribution we can possibly make at this time is to *empower everyone* who comes into our sphere of influence to realize their **own** Divinity as a Child of God.

Even though we have come from various Star Systems and various Dimensions of Light, our effectiveness in reaching the greatest number of evolving Human Beings is DEPENDENT ON OUR ANONYMITY. It is critical that there be no separation and that Humanity be empowered by realizing that *what one soul can accomplish, ALL evolving souls can accomplish.*

The evolutions of Earth must not give their power away to outside sources. They must be consistently directed to go within to the Divinity in their own hearts to tap the Truth of their own Beings.

"Cosmic evil" was very aware of the need for our oneness and the unification of the Family of Humanity in order for the Divine Plan on Earth to be fulfilled. Consequently, it mounted an all-out counter attack to divide and conquer. It implemented its plan by appealing to our lower human egos. It whispered sweet nothings in our ears and stroked our egos and our pride. It inspired us to feel "holier than thou" and amplified the insidious influence of spiritual pride through our consciousness. Then, it manipulated us into doing things that created separation and caused us to appear to the outer world as oddities instead of normal Human Beings. We can see the residue of this malevolent plan scattered throughout the New Age community.

Lightworkers were encouraged by "cosmic evil" to use their inner Spiritual names in the outer world in a way that caused separation and confusion. People were told to openly communicate about their origins. Lightworkers began declaring to the public that they were walk-ins, members of the space confederation, Ascended Masters, Angels, Galactic Beings, Ancient Masters, Pleiadians, Sirians and Masters from other Star Systems. They professed having unique skills that no one else has or can have. They claimed that they alone are capable in one way or another to perform specific things that Humanity needs in order to be saved. Lightworkers were deceived by the forces of imbalance into believing that this information must be shouted from the roof tops in order for them to reach the masses. They were told that they would receive notoriety and abundance by making this information known. But, in fact, that was a trick.

The information being revealed to us about who we are, where we are from, what our sacred skills are and what our mission is on Earth IS A SACRED TRUST THAT MUST BE HELD IN THE SILENCE OF OUR HEARTS.

By professing this information to all the World, we render ourselves ineffective. People perceive us as oddities, which discredits our work and makes people want to disassociate themselves from us. This causes separation and resistance, and it builds walls that prevents us from reaching Humanity.

That, of course, was exactly what "cosmic evil" was trying to accomplish.

It is not too late to get back on track, however. We just need to recognize where our human egos went amuck and correct our course of direction.

Our God Selves are anxiously awaiting the opportunity to guide us forward to our highest level of unmanifest potential. All we have to do is ask for our God Selves to take full dominion of our four lower bodies and command our recalcitrant human egos into the Light.

JESUS THE CHRIST

Someday we will be able to review this unique moment on Earth, and when we do, we will be utterly astounded at the complexity and synchronicity of the Divine Plan that is now unfolding. Every minute detail has been taken into account, and the success of the Divine Plan is dependent on every facet being fulfilled.

The Sacred Science of Numbers and Symbols—Sacred Geometry—plays into every aspect of the Divine Plan and is a critical part of our transformational process.

Eleven (11) is a Master Number that symbolizes our Ascension from a physical reality into a Spiritual Reality. On **January 11, 1992**, we Ascended through the Doorway of the 11:11. This was the *initial impulse* of our Ascension from a Third Dimensional Spiral of Evolution onto a Fourth Dimensional Spiral of Evolution. The number 11:11 also represents our personal Ascension from our physical bodies into our Light Bodies and from our human egos into our Holy Christ Presences.

Beloved Jesus came to Earth at the inception of the Piscean Age, which is now coming to a close, for the explicit purpose of demonstrating to Humanity the path of Divine Love. This, of course, is the path into Christ Consciousness. Through His selfless service to the Light He created an archetype and a matrix through which every man, woman and child evolving on Earth will eventually Ascend into Christ Consciousness...thus fulfilling the Second Coming of the Christ.

During this monumental moment on Earth, every person

evolving here is being held in Jesus' matrix and encoded with the archetype of Christ Consciousness. Through the Sacred Geometry of 11:11 we are Ascending from our physical bodies into our Light Bodies and from our human egos into our Holy Christ Presences.

Jesus The Christ has expanded His luminous Presence to envelop the entire Planet Earth, and He is radiating the full-gathered momentum of the Cosmic Christ through all levels of existence.

As you can see, His mission is prodigious, and it is essential in order for us to regain our path of Christ Consciousness.

The name Jesus The Christ is encoded with the numerical vibration of 11:11. Jesus = 11 and The Christ = 11. Every time we use Jesus' name, it empowers the process of transformation into Christ Consciousness that is now unfolding for all Humanity.

"Cosmic evil" was very aware of that fact, and it infiltrated the consciousness of channels throughout the World to use other names for Jesus The Christ. Some of the names caught on and became very popular; others were used spasmodically here and there. The intent of the various names was *always* to distract us from our Ascension into Christ Consciousness and to dissipate the archetype and matrix that Jesus is holding to assist all Humanity into the perfection of our Light Bodies and our Holy Christ Selves.

Various entities anxiously filled the empty shells that were left behind when "cosmic evil" was removed from the Earth. Consequently, channels are still receiving information from entities in the psychic-astral realm who claim to be Jesus The Christ, but who are asking to be called by other names.

Fortunately, the Light of God is ALWAYS Victorious, and all we need to do is withdraw our attention from other names and focus on the Truth of Jesus The Christ and His Divine Mission. Then, we must invoke the Violet Flame and transmute the cause, core, effect, record and memory of "cosmic evil's" plan of deception.

TIMELESSNESS

We completed our Ascension into the Fourth Dimension on **August 22, 1996**. Now, we are hurtling at warp speed toward the *initial impulse* of our Ascension onto the Fifth Dimensional Spiral of Evolution.

The Third and Fourth Dimensions are the only dimensions that have been stepped down into the constraints of a time and space continuum. All of the higher dimensions of evolution function in a timeless, spaceless existence.

We have been living in the boundaries of time and space for so long that the concept of timelessness or spacelessness is mind-boggling. But, when we complete our Solar Passage into the Fifth Dimension, we will experience firsthand the octaves of timelessness.

For several years we have been going through a gradual collapsing of time. Everything is being accelerated, and we are experiencing time in a new frequency as it seems to just fly by.

Throughout civilization we have used various calendars to measure our Earthly existence. We have used calendars that reflect both **Lunar** and **Solar** Cycles. Once again the Sacred Science of Numbers and Symbols—Sacred Geometry—is involved in our preparation for Solar Passage into timelessness.

Even though various cultures and religions use a variety of calendars and mark time in different ways, the collective Global use of the Solar Calendar is used to unify all outer world activities. We have been prompted to do this by our Father-Mother God for a very important reason.

As we prepare to Ascend into our Solar Reality, it is imperative that we be able to easily assimilate and integrate the Twelve Solar Aspects of Deity that are radiating forth from the Heart of our Father-Mother God in the Great Central Sun. These Divine Qualities of God bathe the Planet each day as the Earth revolves on Her axis every 24 hours and each year as the Earth revolves around the Sun. Every year each of the Twelve Constellations in the natural zodiac that surrounds the Earth reflects one of the Twelve Solar Aspects of Deity to the Earth during the time that our Planet is held in its embrace. This is called a Sun Cycle.

January ... Capricorn
8th Solar Aspect—Aquamarine—Clarity

February...Aquarius
7th Solar Aspect—Violet—Freedom

March ... Pisces
6th Solar Aspect—Ruby—Divine Grace

April...Aries
5th Solar Aspect—Emerald Green—Truth

May... Taurus
4th Solar Aspect—Crystalline White—Purity

June...Gemini
3rd Solar Aspect—Crystalline Pink—Divine Love

July...Cancer
2nd Solar Aspect—Sunshine Yellow—Enlightenment

August...Leo
1st Solar Aspect—Sapphire Blue—Divine Will

September...Virgo
12th Solar Aspect—Opal—Transformation and
                    Transfiguration

October...Libra
11th Solar Aspect—Peach—Divine Purpose

November...Scorpio
10th Solar Aspect—Gold—Eternal Peace and
                    Abundance

December...Sagittarius
9th Solar Aspect—Magenta—Harmony and Balance

During each Sun Cycle (28-31 days), our God Presence accepts the opportunity to lift us into the energy, vibration and consciousness of the particular Solar Aspect of Deity the Earth is being bathed in.

In addition to this activity of Light, our daily cycle of 24 hours allows us the opportunity to experience the inbreath and the outbreath (the magnetization and radiation) of the Twelve Solar Aspects of Deity.

The outbreath (radiation) of the Twelve Solar Aspects of Deity begins at 12:00 a.m. and builds in momentum for 12 hours. Each hour a different Solar Aspect is accentuated and enhanced by our Father-Mother God beginning with the First Solar Aspect and ending with the Twelfth.

The inbreath (magnetization) of the Twelve Solar Aspects of Deity begins at 12:00 p.m. and also builds in momentum for 12 hours. Once again a different Solar Aspect is amplified each hour, beginning with the First and ending with the Twelfth.

This activity of Light reflects the Sacred Number of our Solar Passage—12:12.

As 11:11 represents the Ascension of our physical bodies into our Light Bodies and our human egos into our Holy Christ Presences, the Divine Alchemy of 12:12 reflects the Solar Passage of our Light Bodies into our **Solar** Light Bodies and our Holy Christ Presences into our **Solar** Christ Presences.

This is the next step of our Ascension process, and it is a vital facet of our transfiguration into Solar Beings.

The force of "cosmic evil" was aware of this activity and, as usual, created a plan to contaminate the Truth and infiltrate our work on Earth in a way that would create separation and confusion.

As the Divine Feminine—our Mother God—is being brought into balance through all levels of consciousness, Humanity's attention is being drawn into South America. This is the continent in which the Feminine Polarity of God enters the Earth. The actual anchorage point is in the area of Lake Titicaca in Bolivia.

The Mayan civilization and the Mayan calendar are being brought to the forefront. The knowledge of the Divine Feminine and Her *Lunar* expressions are filtering into Lightworkers' consciousness all over the World. This is bringing balance by blending the awareness of the cycles of both the Divine Mother—*Lunar* and the Divine Father—*Solar*. This is an important part of our healing, and we should be focusing on **both** Lunar *and* Solar Cycles.

The forces of imbalance, however, took this a step further and manipulated people into *rejecting* the Solar Calendar and demanded that we change to the thirteen-cycle Mayan Lunar calendar for outer world use. This plan was designed to confuse and separate the Lightworkers and to, once again, make us appear as oddities to mainstream Humanity.

The Truth is that we are Ascending at warp speed into the timeless, spaceless dimensions of our Solar Reality. It is a distraction, at this time, for us to be changing from the limited constraints of one measurement of time into the limited constraints of another measurement of time.

Even if some Lightworkers choose to make the change, the masses never will, so it will just cause more separation. The World has been trying to get the United States of America to change to the metric system for 40 years, and we won't even do that. By the time we consider changing to a whole different measurement of time—time won't exist.

Again, all we have to do is withdraw our attention from the misinformation and focus on the Truth. Then, use the Violet Flame to transmute the residue of confusion and separation.

CHANNELING

"Cosmic evil" effectively deceived many channels into believing that it was a trustworthy source of information. This cunning force always gave us enough Truth to trick us into believing it was a reliable teacher. It could say it was anybody, and it did. It claimed to be Jesus, Mother Mary, Saint Germain, Archangel Michael and a multitude of other Beings. It also gave us names of various entities that we had never heard of before or knew anything about.

Through an incredible Gift of Divine Grace, the malevolent force of "cosmic evil" was removed from the Planet and returned to the Heart of God. Now, even though "cosmic evil" no longer exists, there are still wayward souls stuck in the psychic-astral plane who are choosing to fill the empty shells and thoughtforms left behind by that sinister force. Consequently, channels believe the deceptive entities they were channeling still exist. The wayward souls are having a field day striving to carry on "cosmic evil's" mischief by continuing to spread misinformation and disinformation through the various channels.

Fortunately, the power of these wayward souls is minuscule compared to the power of "cosmic evil." If we will all use Divine Discerning Intelligence and remove our attention and support from any activity that is not aligned in Truth, the energy to sustain the empty shells and thoughtforms of "cosmic evil" will be dissipated, and the deceptive activities will just simply cease to exist.

Every time we receive *any* information from *any* source, we need to sift and sort through every word to see if it resonates as Truth in our hearts. We must separate the wheat from the chaff and accept only the Sacred Knowledge and the Truth that will set us FREE!

We must perpetually invoke Illumined Truth and Enlightenment into the consciousness of all channels and all Humanity.

GOVERNMENT AND TAXES

The original Divine Plan for the Earth was for us to co-create the perfection of Heaven in the time and space continuum of a physical reality, thus fulfilling the Universal Law of "As Above, So Below."

In the Heavenly Realms there is a structure of Divine Government that is based on Divine Service through Divine Wisdom, Knowledge, Understanding and Reverence for ALL Life. Our governments in the outer world were supposed to reflect those archetypal patterns. Needless to say, with the fall of Humanity we fell into the depths of degradation and corruption. Now, we are in the process of transmuting the maladies on Earth and restoring **all** aspects of our Earthly existence back into their original Divine Intent.

We are functioning within the Universal Law of—As I Am lifted up, ALL life is lifted up with me. For this to occur, *we have to be an integral part of the person, place, condition, system or thing we are lifting up*.

In order for Heaven to manifest on Earth, it is imperative that the governments of the World be transformed into their original Divine Intent of Divine Service and Reverence for

ALL Life. The *only* way this can happen is for Lightworkers to be integrated into the system to instigate change and motivate a shift of consciousness into Oneness. Shifting the consciousness of governments throughout the World is an ***urgent need of the hour***.

"Cosmic evil" knew that and did everything it could to deceive Lightworkers into removing themselves from a position of effectiveness.

No one will argue that our tax system is extremely flawed, but for us to refuse to pay taxes at this point creates a situation that blocks us from implementing sustainable change.

We may get away with not paying our personal taxes, but in order to do so, we must become invisible. We must give up our social security numbers, bank accounts, driver's licenses, credit cards and any other traceable form of identification. If we don't do that, we could end up in litigation with the Internal Revenue Service for the rest of our lives (which would be a horrendous distraction) or find ourselves sitting in jail, which also has a tendency to interfere with our Divine Plans. All of those situations prevent us from being effective in tangibly changing the system.

Any information that is perpetuating the mentality of ***"us against them"*** is part of the residue of "cosmic evil." If we will just reflect on that *simple Truth*, we will clearly recognize the activities from which we should withdraw our attention and support.

Any information or activity that is drawing our attention to negativity in a way that incites anger and/or separation and inspires us to do battle with it instead of effectively changing it, is a remnant of "cosmic evil."

For example:

The anti-government militia and all anti-government groups.

Gangs, drug dealers, organized crime.

White supremacist groups and all groups promoting conflict of any kind involving our ethnic backgrounds—our race, culture, nationality, religion, socio-economic status, gender or age.

People perpetuating greed and selfishness, such as the activity of corporate downsizing where CEO's are drawing salaries of tens of millions of dollars while they simultaneously lay off tens of thousands of people, casting families into situations of poverty, fear and incredible anxiety.

Individuals and organizations who are destroying the environment for the sake of their own personal gain.

Doctors and health care workers who are refusing to cooperate with each other to promote the most effective healing modalities for Humanity.

Judicial systems that are not working toward the highest Truth and the highest good for all concerned.

Facets of the movie, media and music industries that perpetuate visions and thoughtforms of violence, abuse, perversion and all manner of human degradation.

and on and on, ad infinitum.

Blaze the Violet Flame of Limitless Transmutation through every electron of precious life energy that is not reflecting the Divine Intent of Heaven on Earth. Then know...

WHERE MY ATTENTION IS, THERE "I AM". WHATEVER I PUT MY THOUGHTS, WORDS, ACTIONS AND FEELINGS INTO, I WILL BRING INTO FORM!!!

Focus on your vision of the New Heaven and the New Earth. Observe, as a detached, objective observer, the things that are not all right in your personal life and in the World. Then ask yourself, "What do I want instead of that?" and set about bringing the alternative into manifestation.

There are literally thousands of powerful Lightworkers, activities, groups and organizations throughout the World that are aligned with the Truth. They selflessly work in cooperation with the Beings of Light in the Realms of Illumined Truth, and they joyously weave their unique gifts and talents into the glorious Divine Plan that is now unfolding on Earth. SEEK THEM OUT in your area. Give them your support, and add your Divine Momentum and the gift of your Light to their work. Create a loving support system for yourself; make new friends and enhance your ability to be an effective force of Divine Light.

As we withdraw our attention from the patterns of deception and the residue of distorted belief systems left behind by "cosmic evil," new doors of opportunity will open up for us. Our God Presences are anxiously waiting to guide us to our next level of Divine Service. Ask for guidance, discernment and clarity. Be receptive. Trust your heart. Listen.

All is in Divine Order, and our Victory is assured!

We have been in training for thousands of years for this very opportunity!

Grasp the moment, and together, we will SOAR TO NEW HEIGHTS!

TAKE CHARGE OF YOUR LIFE

This newsletter is a timely, monthly publication that shares information on the unprecedented activities of Light now taking place on Earth. These activities involve the unfolding Divine Plan that is now ushering in the reality of Heaven on Earth.

Take Charge of Your Life includes information that is pouring forth from the Realms of Illumined Truth and guidance from the Spiritual Hierarchy that will assist all Humanity during these wondrous, but challenging, times. It contains words of encouragement that will lift you up and fill your heart with hope and joy.

The subscription rate is $36.00 per year for USA. For Canada and Mexico, the rate is $42.00 per year. For all other foreign countries, the rate is $46.00.

ORDER COUPON

____ Yes, I would like to subscribe to the monthly newsletter *Take Charge Of Your Life*. I am enclosing my check or money order for $_____.

NAME_____

ADDRESS_____

CITY_____STATE_____ZIP_____

COUNTRY_____PHONE_____

If paying by credit card, please fill out the information below.

VISA   MASTERCARD   Amount_____

Card Number_____Exp. Date____

Name on Card_____

Signature_____

Please mail to *The New Age Study of Humanity's Purpose*
PO Box 41883, Tucson AZ 85717

ADDITIONAL OPPORTUNITIES

_____ If you are not on our mailing list and would like to be, please check here.

_____ Information on available tapes and books from The New Age Study of Humanity's Purpose.

_____ Sample newsletter Take Charge Of Your Life.

_____ Information on The World Congress On Illumination.

_____ Information on the Free Seminars.

_____ All of the above.

NAME_____

ADDRESS_____

CITY_____

STATE_____ZIP_____PHONE_____

COUNTRY_____

Please mail to:
   The New Age Study Of Humanity's Purpose
   PO Box 41883, Tucson AZ 85717
   or FAX to 520-751-3835

TWO NEW TAPES

By Patricia Diane Cota-Robles

IT IS TIME FOR US TO SOAR

1996 brought to God Victorious fruition
St. John's Revelations!

Armageddon is OVER!

Satan has been bound and cast from the Earth!

The Earth and all life evolving upon Her
have been RAPTURED!

A detailed description of the incredible acts of Divine Grace that took place in 1996 to fulfill St. John's Revelations is available on two cassette tapes that are now being offered at a reduced rate. Each set is $15.00 plus postage and handling.

ORDER COUPON

I would like to order ___ set(s) of the tapes *It Is Time For Us To Soar.* Please make check or money order payable to The New Age Study of Humanity's Purpose. Send to PO Box 41883, Tucson, AZ 85717

NAME_____

ADDRESS_____

CITY_____STATE_____ZIP_____

COUNTRY_____PHONE_____

If paying by credit card, please fill out the information below.

NAME ON
CARD_____

CARD#_____EXP. DATE_____

TYPE OF CARD: VISA — MASTERCARD — AMOUNT_____

SIGNATURE_____

POSTAGE AND HANDLING

Up to $20.00........................$5.00	For all Canada & Mexico orders, *please add an additional 6% of the subtotal.* For all other foreign countries, *please add an additional 8% of the subtotal.*
$20.01-$36.00......................$6.00	
$36.01-$50.00......................$7.00	
$50.01-$75..00....................$9.00	
$75.01-$90.00....................$10.00	
$90.01 and over................$11.00	

TWO NEW TAPES

By Patricia Diane Cota-Robles

LIFTING THE VEIL

*1997 is a year that will go down
in the annals of history for our Universe.*

*1997 will be eternally celebrated
as the year the Planet Earth and all Her life began the return
journey back to the Heart of God.*

*It will be heralded as the year the Earth began Her ascent
into a Solar Reality.*

These two audio cassette tapes share some of the monumental events that will occur to accomplish that glorious feat. They sell for $15.00 per set plus postage and handling.

ORDER COUPON

I would like to order ___ set(s) of the tapes *Lifting The Veil.*.
Please make check or money order payable to The New Age Study
of Humanity's Purpose. Send to PO Box 41883, Tucson, AZ 85717

NAME_____

ADDRESS_____

CITY_____STATE_____ZIP_____

COUNTRY_____PHONE_____

If paying by credit card, please fill out the information below.

NAME ON
CARD_____

CARD#_____EXP. DATE_____

TYPE OF CARD: VISA ___ MASTERCARD ___ AMOUNT_____

SIGNATURE_____

POSTAGE AND HANDLING

Up to $20.00........................$5.00	For all Canada & Mexico orders,
$20.01-$36.00.......................$6.00	*please add an additional 6% of the*
$36.01-$50.00.......................$7.00	*subtotal*. For all other foreign countries,
$50.01-$75..00......................$9.00	*please add an additional 8% of the*
$75.01-$90.00.....................$10.00	*subtotal.*
$90.01 and over.................$11.00